THE CENTURY OF SCIENCE: THE GLOBAL TRIUMPH OF THE RESEARCH UNIVERSITY

INTERNATIONAL PERSPECTIVES ON EDUCATION AND SOCIETY

Series Editor: Alexander W. Wiseman

Recent Volumes:

Series Editor from Volume 11: Alexander W. Wiseman

Volume 20: Annual Review of Comparative and International Education 2013

Volume 21: The Development of Higher Education in Africa: Prospects and Challenges

Volume 22: Out of the Shadows: The Global Intensification of Supplementary Education

Volume 23: International Educational Innovation and Public Sector Entrepreneurship

Volume 24: Education for a Knowledge Society in Arabian Gulf Countries

Volume 25: Annual Review of Comparative and International Education 2014

Volume 26: Comparative Sciences: Interdisciplinary Approaches

Volume 27: Promoting and Sustaining a Quality Teacher Workforce

Volume 28: Annual Review of Comparative and International Education 2015

Volume 29: Post-Education-for-All and Sustainable Development Paradigm: Structural Changes with Diversifying Actors and Norms

Volume 30: Annual Review of Comparative and International Education 2016

Volume 31: The Impact of the OECD on Education Worldwide

Volume 32: Work-Integrated Learning in the 21st Century: Global Perspectives on the Future

INTERNATIONAL PERSPECTIVES ON EDUCATION AND
SOCIETY   VOLUME 33

THE CENTURY OF SCIENCE: THE GLOBAL TRIUMPH OF THE RESEARCH UNIVERSITY

EDITED BY

JUSTIN J. W. POWELL
University of Luxembourg, Esch-sur-Alzette, Luxembourg

DAVID P. BAKER
The Pennsylvania State University, University Park, PA, USA

FRANK FERNANDEZ
The University of Houston, TX, USA

United Kingdom – North America – Japan
India – Malaysia – China

Emerald Publishing Limited
Howard House, Wagon Lane, Bingley BD16 1WA, UK

First edition 2017

Copyright © 2017 Emerald Publishing Limited

Reprints and permissions service
Contact: permissions@emeraldinsight.com

No part of this book may be reproduced, stored in a retrieval system, transmitted in any form or by any means electronic, mechanical, photocopying, recording or otherwise without either the prior written permission of the publisher or a licence permitting restricted copying issued in the UK by The Copyright Licensing Agency and in the USA by The Copyright Clearance Center. Any opinions expressed in the chapters are those of the authors. Whilst Emerald makes every effort to ensure the quality and accuracy of its content, Emerald makes no representation implied or otherwise, as to the chapters' suitability and application and disclaims any warranties, express or implied, to their use.

British Library Cataloguing in Publication Data
A catalogue record for this book is available from the British Library

ISBN: 978-1-78714-470-5 (Print)
ISBN: 978-1-78714-469-9 (Online)
ISBN: 978-1-78714-938-0 (Epub)
ISBN: 978-1-83867-932-3 (Paperback)

ISSN: 1479-3679 (Series)

INVESTOR IN PEOPLE

CONTENTS

LIST OF CONTRIBUTORS	vii
ACKNOWLEDGMENTS	ix
PREFACE	xi
FOREWORD *Roger L. Geiger*	xiii
INTRODUCTION: THE WORLDWIDE TRIUMPH OF THE RESEARCH UNIVERSITY AND GLOBALIZING SCIENCE *Justin J. W. Powell, Frank Fernandez, John T. Crist, Jennifer Dusdal, Liang Zhang and David P. Baker*	1
HIGHER EDUCATION EXPANSION AND THE GROWTH OF SCIENCE: THE INSTITUTIONALIZATION OF HIGHER EDUCATION SYSTEMS IN SEVEN COUNTRIES, 1945–2015 *Mike Zapp*	37
THE EUROPEAN CENTER OF SCIENCE PRODUCTIVITY: RESEARCH UNIVERSITIES AND INSTITUTES IN FRANCE, GERMANY, AND THE UNITED KINGDOM *Justin J. W. Powell and Jennifer Dusdal*	55
SCIENCE PRODUCTION IN THE UNITED STATES: AN UNEXPECTED SYNERGY BETWEEN MASS HIGHER EDUCATION AND THE SUPER RESEARCH UNIVERSITY *Frank Fernandez and David P. Baker*	85

CHANGING SCIENCE PRODUCTION IN JAPAN: THE
EXPANSION OF COMPETITIVE FUNDS, REDUCTION
OF BLOCK GRANTS, AND UNSUNG HEROES
  Kazunori Shima   *113*

THE RISE OF HIGHER EDUCATION AND SCIENCE IN
CHINA
  Liang Zhang, Liang Sun and Wei Bao   *141*

SCIENCE PRODUCTION IN TAIWANESE UNIVERSITIES,
1980–2011
  Yuan Chih Fu   *173*

THE GROWTH OF HIGHER EDUCATION AND SCIENCE
PRODUCTION IN SOUTH KOREA SINCE 1945
  Hyerim Kim and Junghee Choi   *205*

"A FEVER OF RESEARCH": SCIENTIFIC JOURNAL
ARTICLE PRODUCTION AND THE EMERGENCE OF A
NATIONAL RESEARCH SYSTEM IN QATAR, 1980–2011
  John T. Crist   *227*

STEM+ PRODUCTIVITY, DEVELOPMENT, AND
WEALTH, 1900–2012
  Iris A. Mihai and Robert D. Reisz   *249*

ABOUT THE AUTHORS   *277*

INDEX   *281*

LIST OF CONTRIBUTORS

David P. Baker	The Pennsylvania State University, University Park, PA, USA
Wei Bao	Peking University, Beijing, China
Junghee Choi	The Pennsylvania State University, University Park, PA, USA
John T. Crist	George Mason University, Incheon, Korea
Jennifer Dusdal	University of Luxembourg, Esch-sur-Alzette, Luxembourg
Frank Fernandez	University of Houston, Houston, TX, USA
Yuan Chih Fu	The Pennsylvania State University, University Park, PA, USA
Hyerim Kim	The Pennsylvania State University, University Park, PA, USA
Iris A. Mihai	West University of Timisoara, Timisoara, Romania
Justin J. W. Powell	University of Luxembourg, Esch-sur-Alzette, Luxembourg
Robert D. Reisz	West University of Timisoara, Timisoara, Romania
Kazunori Shima	Tohoku University, Sendai, Japan
Liang Sun	The Pennsylvania State University, University Park, PA, USA
Mike Zapp	University of Luxembourg, Esch-sur-Alzette, Luxembourg
Liang Zhang	New York University, New York, NY, USA

ACKNOWLEDGMENTS

The editors and authors gratefully acknowledge the Qatar National Research Fund, a member of Qatar Foundation, for supporting the Science Productivity, Higher Education, Research and Development, and the Knowledge Society (SPHERE) project (NPRP Grant #5-1021-5-159). The findings herein are solely the responsibility of the authors: David P. Baker, Wei Bao, Junghee Choi, John T. Crist, Jennifer Dusdal, Frank Fernandez, Yuan Chih Fu, Hyerim Kim, Iris A. Mihai, Justin J. W. Powell, Robert D. Reisz, Kazunori Shima, Liang Sun, Mike Zapp, and Liang Zhang. Coordinated by John T. Crist at Georgetown University School of Foreign Service in Qatar, the SPHERE project organized an international team of researchers who established and coded the global database and conducted the case studies in this volume. At the Institute for Higher Education Research (HoF) of the Martin Luther University Halle-Wittenberg, our team member Manfred Stock hosted several important project meetings to discuss theory and data, continuing formative conversations we had had with Gero Lenhardt over the years, especially during original project conceptualization discussions at the WZB Social Science Center Berlin, Germany. HoF researcher Isabell Maue contributed coding of the organizational data for Germany, as did Pauline Siebert in Halle and Leipzig, and Gudrun Calow was unfailingly supportive in administration at HoF Wittenberg. The entire team gratefully acknowledges the assistance in Qatar throughout the project provided by project manager Roshi Moeini. We also thank Georgetown student research assistants Tamim Alnuweiri, Emad Hassan, Hisham Hassan, Atul Menon, and Leena Nady-Mohamed. At the University of Luxembourg, Haythem Kamel assisted in organizing literature and translating Arabic texts. We also appreciate many colleagues in the Comparative and International Education Society who attended our conference presentations and commented on our findings over the years. Special appreciation goes to Roger L. Geiger at Penn State for many helpful conversations throughout the SPHERE project and for writing a compelling foreword. We thank Alexander W. Wiseman, the editor of *International Perspectives on Education and Society* for including this book in the series. Alex carefully selects volumes that improve the field of comparative and international education and we appreciate that our project findings appear here. Finally, we are grateful to the editorial staff at Emerald Publishing, especially Kerry Laundon, Kimberley Chadwick, and Rachel Ward for shepherding the project through to publication.

PREFACE

In this volume of *International Perspectives on Education and Society*, a multicultural team of authors examines the global rise of scholarly research in science, technology, engineering, mathematics, and health (STEM+) fields. Case studies of selected countries in Europe, North America, East Asia, and the Middle East illustrate recurring themes: the institutionalization and differentiation of higher education systems, the proliferation of university-based scientific research, and government research policies that support the continued expansion of higher education and scientific production that fosters the knowledge society. Throughout the world, people increasingly seek to attain higher education, resulting not only in postsecondary education becoming ever more central to contemporary societies, but also vastly increasing these countries' capacity for science. Governments and firms increasingly rely on university-based researchers to create new knowledge, certified by the peer-review process that guides publication of cutting-edge research in thousands of scientific journals, now mainly in the English language. Expanding worldwide with public and private funding, research universities appear to be the most legitimate sites devoted to knowledge production.

Few countries, such as Germany, France, the United Kingdom, the United States, and Japan, began the 20th century with the prerequisites in place for the emerging paradigm of university-based research. Each of these countries had strong research communities, but their increasing research capacity developed according to different models and in a variety of organizational forms. In the United States, higher education was mostly unregulated and grew quickly throughout the century in thousands of private and public colleges and universities. In Europe and Japan, governments more tightly controlled the growth of universities, nearly all publicly funded, and have remained top science producers. Leading European countries also sought and developed alternatives to universities, in the form of research institutes or government agencies, as the global center of scientific production moved first toward the United States and then toward Asia, with Europe continuously crucial in global production. Countries in East Asia, including China, South Korea, and Taiwan, experienced contrasting historical legacies and conflicts in education. If these countries generally did not expand the size and scope of their university systems until later in the 20th century, when they did, explosive growth followed. These Asian case studies offer unique blends of private and public sector universities, diverse policy initiatives, and extraordinary rates of growth in publishing scientific findings. And in the Middle East, Qatar recently embarked on an ambitious government-driven effort to develop a world-class university sector and cultivate academic STEM+ research from scratch. Such recent entrants to the global scientific enterprise pose the question whether it is possible to leapfrog across decades, or even centuries, of building university systems, to compete globally. Yet, more than ever, leading science implies collaboration across cultural and political borders as scientific production is fully globalized.

The Century of Science: The Global Triumph of the Research University provides sociological and historical understandings of the ways that higher education has become an institution that, more than ever before, shapes science and society. The case studies offer new insights into how countries develop the university-based knowledge thought fundamental to meeting social needs and economic demands. In addition to publishing scientific work in STEM+ fields, universities train highly skilled workers, advance basic research that serves as the foundation for new technologies, support firm-based research and development, and build capacity to improve healthcare and other social support systems. Despite repeated warnings that universities would lose in relevance to other organizational forms in the production of knowledge, the chapters in this volume demonstrate incontrovertibly that universities have become more – not less – important actors in the world of knowledge. The past 100 years have seen the global triumph of the research university.

Justin J. W. Powell
David P. Baker
Frank Fernandez
Editors

FOREWORD

The university role of creating and disseminating objectively verifiable knowledge is the subject of *The Century of Science*. The university's effectiveness as the home of science is largely, if indirectly, responsible for the cultural authority it has come to exercise. It also underpins the isomorphism that has seen the university replicate itself around the world, effectively superseding alternative organizations for research and advanced education. Universities are the central institution of the modern global knowledge society. As such, universities fulfill a multitude of roles. Foremost, they confer legitimacy and authority to knowledge and thus occupy a privileged position in the constitution of the knowledge society. This dominion unites the knowledge of things with culturally based knowledge. In fact, the greatest impact of universities on society derives from their cultural authority. Culturally contingent, yet authoritative, university knowledge lies at the foundation of global commitments to human rights, environment and economic policies, and a value system anchored in human agency. University training connects the occupational structure of societies to universalized cultural knowledge. Even professional education, which once was provided for teachers, engineers, doctors, and lawyers in specialized settings, has since associated itself with the cultural authority of universities. Thus, John Meyer, Francisco Ramirez, David Frank, and Evan Schofer (2007) can write "the myth of the 'knowledge society' is very much at the heart of the university's centrality in the postnational and increasingly global world," serving to both empower actors and to provide a basis for coordination among them.

The chapters in this volume are based on bibliometrics – the analysis of patterns of publications in science, technology, engineering, mathematics, and medicine – STEM+. Scientific papers represent the unit contributions to scientific knowledge. While such contributions are partial and sometimes fallible, their cumulative effect advances understanding in a very particular way. Academic knowledge – that produced in universities – is at once objective and universal. Objective, in that it exists outside the observer and is based upon stated evidence. Universal, in that it pertains to a general class of phenomena. These essential criteria are largely embodied in paradigms – constructs of theories and exemplars that unify understanding of phenomena. Paradigms are the building blocks of academic disciplines, and as such their nature varies greatly across spheres of knowledge. Literary paradigms are founded upon aesthetic assumptions; social science paradigms tend to be perpetually contested, in whole or in part; but paradigms in the natural sciences represent the state of knowledge verified with empirical evidence. Even in science, the certainty of paradigms can vary: proof of findings in medicine can be difficult to replicate, but an infinitesimal aberration in a painstakingly constructed laser was proof enough for physicists of the existence of gravitational waves. Whether strong or weak paradigms, science provides universal knowledge, and scientists across the globe participate in the same endeavor.

Scientific papers are intended to be contributions to the paradigms that constitute the knowledge base of scientific disciplines. The papers analyzed in this volume have already passed one significant test: they have been reviewed by peers prior to publication. Collectively, they represent the quantity of scientific activity at an acceptable level of quality in a given place and time. Thus, by identifying the origins of these papers, the analyses in this volume reveal patterns in the evolution of scientific activity within countries, across countries, and over the past century. In recent decades, especially, significant shifts have occurred in the geography of these activities. Underlying these dynamics is the relationship between science and universities.

In conceptualizing this relationship, science emerges as the fundamental actor, universities as social receptacles. The essential feature of science is its cumulative nature. Existing understandings are displaced, sooner or later, by better knowledge, and this cumulative process – not just addition but replacement – makes science a self-organizing activity. At the heart of science, this process depends on the exchange of knowledge, so that scientists can learn of and assimilate superior findings or new discoveries. The Royal Society is credited with launching modern cumulative science in the 17th century through the formal presentation and publication of learned papers. This process has favored whatever kinds of functional arrangements could improve scientific communication. In the 19th century, disciplinary associations proved to be more functional than scientific societies. These associations brought together scientists who shared esoteric knowledge for face-to-face exchange in annual meetings. They also instituted formal exchange of papers through scientific journals, the forerunners of the journals analyzed in this volume. Hence, social organizations are a key variable in the facilitation of scientific exchange.

Universities have proved to be an effective locus for scientific activity by supporting full-time researchers to hone their expertise and pass it on to the next generation. German universities were the first to institutionalize these arrangements by furnishing proven scientists with institutes to further their research and train followers. Enormously successful in the 19th century, longer term these arrangements concentrated too much authority for too long in a limited number of *Ordinarien*. American universities after 1900 developed a more flexible and functional departmental structure that allowed larger numbers of scientists to advance their learning and careers. The dependence of American departments on teaching could also be constraining, but after World War II the widespread incorporation of externally supported centers and institutes permitted research to develop autonomously (Geiger, 2004). Structures evolve slowly but scientific activity tends to expand most readily where institutional arrangements are most congenial – most functional – within countries or across national systems.

Science has become virtually homogeneous across the globe. An organic chemistry lab will be similar in Berkeley, Berlin, or Beijing. University systems and research organizations, however, vary from country to country. They are shaped historically by national educational systems, government funding of research, and terms of faculty employment. The efflorescence of American research universities after 1945 has induced a high degree of isomorphism. In the last two decades, as research universities have been linked with economic development, at least in the minds of policymakers, governments have adopted concerted efforts to develop "world-class universities." But organizations are not easily transposed from one national setting to another. American universities failed to imitate German models, but succeeded in emulating their dedication to academic research. Isomorphism requires innovations to be compatible with national institutional structures, which often precludes certain aspects of the desired model. Most resistant to change are the civil service status of professors, the division of labor among different kinds of institutions, and modes of research funding. But countries have still found ways to emulate successful features of American research universities and to develop effective and efficient indigenous ways to organize scientific work. Given propitious conditions, scientists know how to do the rest, resulting in higher degrees of scientific productivity.

Hence, the compilation of scientific papers in this volume is not a competition for bragging rights: it is a telling indicator of the effectiveness of the organization of science in each respective country. A great strength of this volume is presenting the dynamics of scientific productivity in a rich national context for nine countries. This provides material for any number of comparative observations or further inquiry. Concentrating science production in top universities at the expense of mid-level ones seems to have enhanced science outputs in Great Britain, but retarded them in Japan. Separating research funding from higher education appropriations has allowed private universities to become significant participants in the science matrix in Korea and the United States.

This volume addresses the most intriguing comparative issue: why have universities exhibited a growing dominance over the production of science? The organization of science is in fact complex in every country. In the United States, universities have performed roughly 50% of basic research consistently over time, with national labs, federal agencies, nonprofit research institutes, and industry all performing specialized roles in the division of a scientific work. But Fernandez and Baker (*infra.*) report that university-based scientists authored or coauthored 75% of American scientific papers, which once again underlines their centrality. In a knowledge society, the best, or most advanced, scientific knowledge is the most valuable for advancing or utilizing knowledge. As the editors emphasize (Introduction), the greater the distributed scientific activity in society, the *more* important the contribution of universities become. The leading American universities concentrate the most productive scientists in the most fundamental fields and provide them with optimal conditions for advancing their research. They also train the next generation of scientists who will seed both academic and non-academic laboratories. And university scientists collaborate with their peers, wherever they may be found. Indeed, one of the key findings of the **SPHERE** project is the large and rising extent of international collaboration on scientific papers. *The Global Triumph of the Research University* is one of the most significant developments of contemporary global society (Baker, 2014), and this volume is an indispensable contribution to its understanding.

Roger L. Geiger
The Pennsylvania State University, USA

REFERENCES

Baker, D. P. (2014). *The schooled society: The educational transformation of global culture.* Stanford, CA: Stanford University Press.

Geiger, R. L. (2004). *Research and relevant knowledge: American research universities since World War II.* New Brunswick, NJ: Transaction Publishers [1993].

Meyer, J. W., Ramirez, F. O., Frank, D. J., & Schofer, E. (2007). Higher education as an institution. In P. J. Gumport (Ed.), *The sociology of higher education: Contributions and their contexts* (pp. 187–221). Baltimore, MD: Johns Hopkins University Press.

INTRODUCTION: THE WORLDWIDE TRIUMPH OF THE RESEARCH UNIVERSITY AND GLOBALIZING SCIENCE

Justin J. W. Powell, Frank Fernandez, John T. Crist, Jennifer Dusdal, Liang Zhang and David P. Baker

ABSTRACT

Purpose — *This chapter provides an overview of the findings and chapters of a thematic volume in the* International Perspectives on Education and Society *(IPES) series. It describes the common dataset and methods used by an international research team.*

Design/methodology/approach — *The chapter synthesizes the results of a series of country-level case studies and cross-national and regional comparisons on the growth of scientific research from 1900 until 2011. Additionally, the chapter provides a quantitative analysis of global trends in scientific, peer-reviewed publishing over the same period.*

Findings — *The introduction identifies common themes that emerged across the case studies examined in-depth during the multi-year research project* Science Productivity, Higher Education, Research and Development and the Knowledge Society (SPHERE). *First, universities have long been and are increasingly the primary organizations in science production around the globe. Second, the chapters describe in-country and cross-country patterns of competition and collaboration in scientific publications. Third, the chapters describe the national policy environments and institutionalized organizational forms that foster scientific research.*

Originality/value — *The introduction reviews selected findings and limitations of previous bibliometric studies and explains that the chapters in the volume address these limitations by applying neo-institutional theoretical frameworks to analyze bibliometric data over an extensive period.*

Keywords: Science production; research policy; research university; sociology of science; bibliometrics; Science Citation Index Expanded (SCIE)

SETTING THE GLOBAL STAGE

This volume of *International Perspectives on Education and Society* presents results of a multi-year, cross-national investigation of the influence of higher education development, specifically the research university, and science capacity-building on scientific knowledge production. Although there have been important descriptive reports of recent cross-national differences in scientific productivity, this study uniquely includes systematic analysis across an extensive historical scope, from 1900 to 2011. It analyzes countries of different size and histories of university institutionalization and scientific production. The global comparative project called "Science Productivity, Higher Education, Research and Development and the Knowledge Society" (SPHERE) produced a comprehensive longitudinal and worldwide dataset of scientific journal publications on science, technology, engineering, and mathematics, plus health (hereafter STEM+) cataloged in the Science Citation Index Expanded (SCIE), customized and acquired especially for this project from Thomson Reuters' (now Clarivate Analytics) Web of Science (formerly ISI Web of Knowledge).

Comparing dynamics in the oldest and largest research environments with trends in fast-developing knowledge economies, the SPHERE project contrasts institutionalization pathways and scientific productivity in selected countries in Europe, North America, East Asia, and the Middle East. While non-university research institutes continue to generate new science, the project shows that over the past century it has been research universities, plus a growing number of less research-intensive universities, leading the way in the expansion of science. So much so that worldwide annual scientific publications authored by at least one university-based scientist grew exponentially from about one half in the 1960s to currently 85% of all STEM+ papers. The project's overall results demonstrate that, despite numerous wars, regime changes, and global economic crises, there has been no lasting decline or slowing of the growth of scientific research – up to today. In fact, "big science" was itself transformed by unprecedented heightened production, beginning just after mid-century. At the same time, the project's institutional analyses show interesting similarities and differences in national models, of varying global influence, that facilitated the ongoing development of research universities and non-university institutes in contrasting systems – some more reliant on universities and others with research capacity distributed across multiple institutional sources of science and organizational forms. Our case studies include China, France, Germany, Japan, Qatar, South Korea, Taiwan, the United Kingdom, and the United States. These analyses have been conducted and written by scholars either working in the countries analyzed or heralding from those cultures, facilitating explanation of long-term cross-national trajectories in scientific productivity across the world centers of higher education expansion and scientific production.

The chapters assembled here respond to mid- and late-20th century scholars, many of whom predicted the decline of "big science," with which World War II was won (Kleinman, 1995), and later scholars who claimed that universities would not keep pace with private industry in producing new scientific knowledge. Scientometricians were among the first to mark the advent of "big science" in the 1960s, yet they also predicted that over the next few decades, the pure exponential growth of science publications would slow down significantly due to saturation, reducing the global rise in science production (de Solla Price, 1963). Yet, they failed to anticipate a crucial rising trend, and what supported it. Starting in the 1960s, the world's capacity to generate new scientific knowledge went to a new level – "mega-science" (Elzinga, 2012). As shown in Fig. 1, STEM+ publications grew at an exponential annual rate of 3.5%, so that now well over one million new research articles are published every year in a plethora of peer-reviewed scientific journals. At the same time, what was once mostly done by scientists in European and North American universities has become a global undertaking. The United States' past predominance of science is increasingly shared with other countries. For example, although in 2011 the United States produced almost 282,000 publications (26% of total STEM+ publications had at least one U.S.-based author) compared to China's 152,000 publications (14%). The world's center of gravity of science production is moving away from North America, returning toward Europe, with its very strong science-producing countries, also due to the rise of Asian production (Zhang, Powell, & Baker, 2015). And, as noted above and detailed in the following chapters, increasingly the world's new science is rooted in the exceptional expansion of higher education and the on-going development of research universities.

The SPHERE project coded and analyzed over 20 million records from the SCIE dataset to show that the number of STEM+ papers published in scientific journals over the 20th century grew extraordinarily rapidly (Zhang et al., 2015). Starting from slightly above 9,500 in 1900, the annual number of new publications grew to about 50,000 in 1960, nearly doubling again by 1965. This early

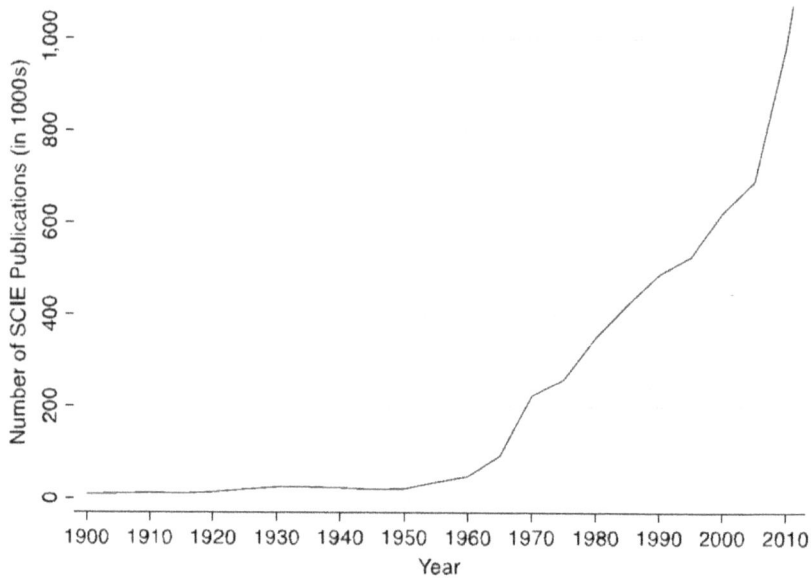

Fig. 1. Exponential Growth in STEM+ Articles Published Worldwide, 1900–2011.
Source: SPHERE project database of SCIE publications
(Thomson Reuters' Web of Science).

trend, often referred to as "big science," was then transformed into what we will refer here to as "global mega-science": pure exponential growth reflecting extraordinary and continued growth in peer-reviewed publications between 1980 and 2010, leading to over half a million SCIE publications in 1995 and doubling again by the year 2011 (Fig. 1).

Next to the massive rise in the absolute number of published STEM+ papers, especially since 1960, another important phenomenon was the globalization of science. The numbers of countries contributing to this extraordinary total output also grew impressively. While in 1900 only around two dozen countries and territories participated in the production of STEM+ papers, by 1950 this number increased to three dozen. By 1980, this number more than quadrupled again, and by the turn of the century around 200 countries and territories had produced science (Mihai & Reisz, 2017). The average number of papers produced by a country has also increased since 1900, from 416 to 1,189 in 1950, and 3,779 in 2000. By 2010, within just one decade, the average number, 6,262, had risen again by 65%. These illustrate the growth, but mask an accompanying global bimodal process. Early in the century, scientists in a small number of countries produced most STEM+ papers, then by expanding their capacity are annually publishing thousands by the end of the century. But also over the century, scientists working in ever more countries begin to produce significant amounts of papers, and by the end of the century even smaller, and in some ways unlikely, countries such as Luxembourg (Powell & Dusdal, 2016) and Qatar (Crist, 2017), are participating in global mega-science.

It is generally recognized that recent and unprecedented science production derives from the prior expansion of every level of education, and the resulting greater production of those capable and willing to conduct advanced research. It also results from the long-term evolution of publication outlets, with some journals publishing the most significant scientific results for decades, and the rising number of journals and the ongoing specialization of science. There has been a significant rise in the volume of SCIE publications from scientists in a growing number of nations – in other words, the globalization of science (The Royal Society, 2011). The 10 countries that produced the most SCIE publications (in 1,000s) in 2011 were the United States (282,000), China (153,000), Germany (80,000), the United Kingdom (74,000), Japan (69,000), France (57,000), Canada (46,000), Italy (46,000), India (43,000), and Spain (41,000). Thus, currently, Europe is the region with the most countries contributing largely to global scientific production, based on ancient universities embedded in high-capacity, publically funded science systems.

Thus, not only were early arguments about the decline of the research university wrong, but again in the 1990s leading scholars in science studies argued incorrectly that other organizational forms would become central. Although research universities have, for decades and indeed centuries, been key sites of knowledge production (Geiger, 1986; Rüegg, 2004, 2011), many contemporary scholars questioned the role of universities in knowledge production and innovation – or even began to predict that the locus of scientific research would shift away from largely state-funded higher education to a variety of other organizational forms (see Hessels & van Lente, 2008; van Rooij, 2014 for reviews). Indeed, the era since the Great Recession has challenged the public funding of higher education and research, again leading to questions about the economic and social contributions of universities in many countries. Whereas the two dominant Anglophone science-producing countries of the United States and the United Kingdom have seen retrenchment in public investments in higher education, state funding remains central in most other countries analyzed in this volume, with the exception of South Korea.

Today, higher education, particularly research universities, and science systems continue to experience transformation. Not least this is due to active governance or retrenchment, the definition of strategic goals and elaborate research evaluation systems, and performance-based funding of university researchers (Hicks, 2012). The orientation to scientific "excellence" or "quality" and "relevance" or "impact" worldwide has led to innumerable initiatives to advance these often competing, yet sometimes complementary goals. While numerous approaches try to explain how these changes have developed, scholars continue to contest their sources. Private enterprises play different roles in various types of scientific production, often emphasizing industrial applications and patents to secure commercialization of scientific discoveries. Yet increasingly inter-sectoral collaboration, academic engagement, and career mobility as well as hybrid organizational forms that tie universities and industry together facilitate diverse forms of scientific communication and output (Dietz & Bozeman, 2005; Perkmann et al., 2013).

Instead of examining patents as a measurable form of scientific productivity or output deriving from R&D investments (Griliches, 1984), the SPHERE project focuses on fundamental or "basic" research as measured in peer-reviewed articles in leading journals, considered the "gold standard" in the academic world. Here, we pay more attention to the absolute and relative growth of academic research and multidisciplinary and international collaborations than to the citations accruing to any single article. Unlike much of the existing literature on the topic of scientific production, this volume of *International Perspectives on Education and Society* reports on new systematic estimates of the number of worldwide STEM+ science publications from 1900 to 2011, combined with in-depth historical case studies of research university and research institute development as well as higher education and research policy.

This remarkable productivity reflects two contrasting and simultaneous phenomena — rising competition across nations and universities at the macro and meso levels and globe-spanning collaboration among universities, research groups, and individual scientists at the meso and micro levels. These developments must be understood in the context of the global knowledge society, itself precipitated by three trends. First, the institutionalization of schooling and education at all levels and throughout the world (Baker, 2014; Drori & Krücken, 2009; Meyer, 1977). Second, the massive and continuing expansion of university enrollments around the world that has transformed science into an everyday activity everywhere (Meyer, Ramirez, Frank, & Schofer, 2008; Schofer & Meyer, 2005). And third, as new universities were founded around the world, and tertiary education became increasingly accessible as well as institutionally embedded, the *research university* became a global model for higher education and knowledge production and this strengthened research capacity worldwide (Baker, 2014). Higher education expansion led to new forms of knowledge and policymakers have increasingly identified and actively managed education and science as key sources of economic growth (Drori, 2000). We find increased scientization in global culture (Drori, Meyer, Ramirez, & Schofer, 2003), including especially information technologies, educational exchange and scientific mobility, and supranational governance also evident in the ongoing regional standardization of higher education systems (Powell, Bernhard, & Graf, 2012).

SPHERE was the first project of its kind to analyze factors behind cross-national trajectories of scientific knowledge across the entire last century, building on a neo-institutional theoretical approach and a comprehensive dataset, and to pair this with systematic historical quantitative cross-national comparisons to examine shifting national contributions to global science. Theoretically, we focus on the increased legitimacy of the university and other scientific organizations in pursuing educational and scientific activities and the institutional models that gained influence globally as diverse organizational forms grew within complex organizational fields. We compare different institutionalization pathways of complex higher education and science systems. Our cross-cultural project team, based in eight countries, created and analyzed a new, huge global dataset on research articles in "mainline" scientific journals – science, technology, engineering, mathematics, health and medical fields (STEM+) between 1900 and 2011. The resulting cross-national database provides indicators to assess the influence of higher education development and science capacity-building on scientific knowledge production. Conducting a series of case studies to examine how systems of higher education developed and nations' capacity for scientific research grew, the team relied on the knowledge of the assembled experts to assess the impact of the research university and expanding higher education on postindustrial societies in Europe, North America, East Asia, and the Middle East.

This volume's chapters contribute to this scientific aim as well as they may inform national and supranational policymakers seeking to enhance contributions to the global enterprise of higher education and science, especially as countries diverge in the relative contributions of public and private sources invested in these systems. The findings may support policy recommendations to meet the challenges of the global knowledge society. This introduction first connects the SPHERE project to existing literatures, then discusses in-depth the methodological approach and choices made in preparing the data for analysis, examines global trends longitudinally and comparatively across the selected countries, and introduces the country and comparative studies included in this volume.

EMBEDDING SPHERE IN SCIENTIFIC LITERATURE

As mentioned above, a key strand of literature relating to higher education and science discusses the different organizational forms that contribute to scientific production. Old and new institutionalists emphasize organizational forms and fields that structure complex institutional environments (Scott, 2015). From research universities and institutes to government agencies and military to industry as well as scientific academies, laboratories, and museums (among others), diverse organizational forms regularly utilize, produce, and distribute what, at that time, is considered scientific knowledge (on Germany, see Dusdal, 2017). The contributions, in their intellectual and physical forms, and their modes of distribution vary considerably over time, but for centuries, the university has been a key environment facilitating the construction, transmission, and advancement of knowledge, in the *lingua franca* of each era – more than ever in formalized written forms, such as the research monograph and article.

The Organization of Science Production: Research Universities at the Center

If tremendous diversity exists in the organizations producing science today, our analyses show that the very center of scientific productivity has become — and remains — the research university. University-affiliated research complements science production in the private and governmental sectors in several ways. Government research was often developed for military purposes, but the military gradually declined as a research-producing institution, while universities took on ever more central roles in society (Etzkowitz & Leydesdorff, 2000). University researchers have tended to be more focused on long-term knowledge production that has led to the rise of new, multi- or interdisciplinary fields, such as molecular biology and biotechnology (Etzkowitz, Webster, Gebhardt, & Terra, 2000). Similarly, because universities are often involved in knowledge production in emerging areas of scientific inquiry, those research projects were often problematic or risky (Hall, Link, & Scott, 2003, p. 485): Although those projects "experience[d] more difficulty and delay," the involvement of university partners meant that the studies were less likely "to be aborted prematurely." In part, these sorts of findings have been attributed to academic freedom as a central tenet of the research university and faculty members' prerogative to pursue research on new topics without corporate constraints (Aghion, Dewatripont, & Stein, 2008), relating to the need to make profits in the foreseeable future. Furthermore, the unique combination of elements of university missions, including intergenerational knowledge transfer and the certification of new knowledge via the granting of doctoral degrees, ensures continuous renewal and innovation. For example, in both France and Germany, despite crucial extra-university institutions that produce the most cutting-edge science, the universities retain centrality via their authority to train each new generation of scientists (Powell & Dusdal, 2017).

Although research universities have historically been the key sites of knowledge production (Riddle, 1989; Schofer, 2004), many scholars began to predict that the main locus of scientific research would shift away from higher education. In *The New Production of Knowledge*, Gibbons and colleagues postulated that there would be a shift from "Mode-1" to "Mode-2" production of knowledge, in which "universities, in particular, will comprise only a part, perhaps only a small part, of the knowledge producing sector" (Gibbons et al., 1994, p. 85; Nowotny, Scott, & Gibbons, 2001; see also Godin & Gingras, 2000). This work spawned a lively debate about the state of scientific research and the role of the research university in contemporary society — in fact, it became the most widely cited work on the topic (Hessels & van Lente, 2008). In contemporary science and society, the challenge remains to operationalize the principles of Mode-2 science for particular disciplines (but see Kropp & Blok, 2011 on sociology; Zapp & Powell, 2017 on education).

Scholars from various fields introduced competing models of the university's multidimensional role in science production, from "academic capitalism" (Slaughter & Leslie, 1997; Slaughter & Rhoades, 2009) to the "triple helix" of university/industry/government relationships (Leydesdorff & Etzkowitz, 1998; Leydesdorff & Meyer, 2006) and "post-academic science" (Ziman, 2000), to the "emerging global model" of the "Super Research University" (Baker, 2014; Mohrman, Ma, & Baker, 2008). Depicting various causes and consequences of such shifting constellations, such models all acknowledge that universities and science are embedded in a multidimensional space without one complete source of governance or funding. They identify changes in the ways in which universities produce knowledge in an increasingly interconnected, collaborative, globalized, and, despite policy rhetoric touting support for universities, resource-constrained world. As Delanty (2001) emphasizes, the contemporary transformation in communication fundamentally alters the modes of constructing and disseminating knowledge. However, some of these theories, in questioning the adaptability of the university as a highly institutionalized organizational form, have lacked empirical bases, leading to diverse normative judgments and contrasting implications for policymakers.

If policymakers think that universities contribute declining shares of science production, they will not only suffer fundamental misunderstandings of how knowledge is produced in most countries today, but also they may misallocate resources that support scientific research that is the basis for innovation and development. By contrast, our analyses in the selected country case studies of China, France, Germany, Japan, Qatar, South Korea, Taiwan, the United States, and the United Kingdom show that the university has in fact increased its output, related to its internationalization and rising collaborations across borders, be they geographic, political, cultural, or organizational. Indeed, Adams (2013) finds that internationally collaborative work from the United States and the United Kingdom is more likely to be cited than purely domestic research, with the scientific cutting edge now driven by collaborations among leading research groups working in multiple cultural contexts, albeit usually within the *lingua franca* of English.

Limited Empirical Studies on Science Production

Until now, our understanding of the long-term development of global science production has been limited by available data. Empirical studies and bibliometric analyses have examined scientific publications as early as the 1970s (Schofer, 2004), but most have focused on the decades since 1980 (Adams, 2009; Adams, Black, Clemmons, & Stephan, 2005; Bornmann & Mutz, 2015; Godin & Gingras, 2000) or the era since 1990 (Bornmann, Wagner, & Leydesdorff, 2015). Moreover, comparative studies have considered the number of universities in each country, but have not focused on the different institutional models that shaped the development of the higher education sector, and ultimately, universities' capacity for scientific research (Meo, Al Masri, Usmani, Memon, & Zaidi, 2013; Meo, Usmani, Vohra, & Bukhari, 2013; Teodorescu, 2000). This limited perspective has severely reduced the potential of comparative and historical case studies that directly examine how different institutional models evolved in historical context − and the consequences for research capacity at national and organizational levels. Yet this is necessary if we are to understand the long-term developmental factors that determine regional and national capacity-building. If we hope to make meaningful comparisons across countries, an understanding of the development within the cases is necessary; this volume collects diverse case studies in this vein.

A Brief History of Bibliometric Analysis

Bibliometric databases are used to collect information about publications of a single researcher, a research group, or an entire organization (Havemann, 2009). Increasingly, with the advent of supercomputers, the outputs of even entire research associations, types of organizations, and countries can be aggregated, which the contributions in this volume do. These databases are used as a tool to gain insights into scientific publication output in general, the integration of scientific communities and their expanding networks, and internationally visible research results (Ball & Tunger, 2005). Bibliometrics as an independent field of research deals with the statistical analysis of bibliographic information, especially with study of authors, publications, and organizations. The French term *bibliométrie* was introduced by Paul Otlet in 1934, gaining worldwide fame decades later in 1969 when Alan Pritchard defined the English term *bibliometrics* as "the application of mathematical and statistical methods to books and other media of communication" (Pritchard, 1969, p. 348), providing an alternative to the earlier common term "statistical bibliography." Other researchers define bibliometrics as a discipline more narrowly as the quantitative study of works reflected in bibliographies (White & McCain, 1989) or as "the application of those quantitative methods which are dealing with the analysis of science viewed as an information process" (Glänzel, 2003, p. 6). Or, more broadly, bibliometric research is considered to include all aspects and models of science communication, storage, distribution, and publication (Glänzel & Schöpflin, 1994).

Publishing and citing references as fundamental scientific activities have been done for thousands of years, even if not in the elaborate form of scientific references of today (Jovanovic, 2012). Outstanding early bibliometric analysis have been conducted by such scientists as Alfred J. Lotka (1926), Samuel C. Bradford (1934), and George K. Zipf (1949). Further milestones in the history

Introduction 11

of bibliometrics in the 1960s and 1970s include the first publication of the Science Citation Index (SCI) that Eugene Garfield developed in 1963 (Garfield, 1964), and publication of the foundational works of Derek J. de Solla Price (1961, 1963). These works, among others, popularized bibliometrics worldwide and helped to establish it as an independent research field (Glänzel, 2003). The tremendous increase of computing power and the invention and tremendous (and ongoing) expansion of citation indices has made it much easier for researchers to analyze global publication and citation patterns.

Comparison of Web of Science (Thomson Reuters) and Scopus (Elsevier)

Today, two major providers dominate the world market of scientific data, mainly in the form of journal publication data gathered in citation indices: Thomson Reuters (TR) (now: Clarivate Analytics) with its Web of Science and Elsevier with its Scopus database. These document the valorization of certain scientific products as valuable via the selection of journals, calculating "impact factors" (a measure that reflects the yearly average number of citations to recent articles published in that same journal), and collecting citations and cross-references. More inclusive than ever before, Scopus and the Web of Science reach across the world to gather scientific metadata in all fields and in many different languages, even if the most leading journals – especially in the STEM+ fields analyzed in this volume—publish in English.

The two main databases for abstracts and citations of peer-reviewed literature, the TR's Web of Science (WoS) and Elsevier's Scopus, were compared to discover differences in coverage and selectivity.[1] The results show that the two databases exhibit similar trends in coverage (becoming more inclusive via the gradual, continuous addition of journals) and in overall rising production. We compare whole counts from each database for 10 countries – China, France, Germany, Great Britain, Japan, Russia (USSR), Qatar, South Korea, Taiwan, and the United States. The recoded TR data from 1900 to 1970 in the SPHERE database consist of the randomly selected, coded, and weighted data; thereafter, we use the regular WoS database. The correlation coefficient for each of these countries between the WoS and Scopus data follows: China (0.993), France (0.958), Germany (0.956), Great Britain (0.970), South Korea (0.998), Japan (0.979), Russia (USSR) (0.545), Qatar (0.983), Taiwan (0.998), and the United States (0.959). In most countries, the aggregate publication volume in Scopus surpasses that recorded in WoS, and we find more publications in Scopus than WoS for each country through 2011; however, this coverage in Scopus is related to more different types of publications and non-STEM+. Similar trends, whether increasing or decreasing coverage for each country, were found for both datasets. The slope indicating increasing or decreasing trends from each dataset roughly matched, except in the case of

Russia (USSR), which showed noticeable differences in the representation of journals in the two databases (on Russian and Chinese university-based science, see Oleksiyenko, 2014). Thus, despite challenging questions of representativity in the overall coverage of the major databases, they are quite similar, which is crucial for comparing the results presented here with analyses on the basis of Elseviers' Scopus. Other frequently used databases, such as Google Scholar or academic social networking platforms like Academia.edu or ResearchGate.net, as user-driven and user-dependent sources of bibliographic data, are even more selective than WoS or Scopus and provide unreliable representations of scientific sources.

Today, the Web of Science indexes 12,000 journals, roughly equal to a quarter of the regularly published research serials globally and representing those leading journals that attract more than 95% of the citations (cross-references) among scholarly articles (Adams, 2011, p. 6). Thus, while highly selective, the indices do represent those journals that review, collect, and present the research with the greatest (potential for) scientific impact.

Due to the transformation and global spread of the scientific landscape, bibliometric analyses are applied as an evaluation instrument of national and organizational scientific capacity (Ball & Tunger, 2005). As part of research evaluation systems (Whitley & Gläser, 2007) or performance-based research funding systems (Hicks, 2012; Roberts, 2006), these measures of science have become regular instruments of scientific management and science policy, as they transform the governance of research and patterns of scientific production around the world. Target groups of this particular form of quantitative analysis are bibliometricians (for basic research), scientific disciplines (with wide-ranging interests), and science policy and research management organizations (Glänzel & Schöpflin, 1994). More than ever, policymakers (attempt) to use big data to monitor the performance of universities and other science-producing organizations; however, the most visible focus in key media has been on ranking the world's top higher education organizations, usually based upon a few quantitative indicators and reputational estimates instead of systemic and comprehensive comparisons (Espelund & Sauder, 2007, 2016; Hazelkorn, 2011). In many countries analyzed here, we show that, in fact, the research university contribution to scientific output has increased proportionally to other organizations in the context of pure exponential growth and the broadened inclusivity of the key databases gathering and cataloging scientific information.

METHODOLOGY AND DATA

The SPHERE project's centerpiece involved the creation of a huge dataset representing all scientific journal articles published in peer-reviewed journals within Thomson Reuters' SCIE collection of STEM+ journals between 1900 and 2011. The following section describes how this dataset was created through years of archival research and (re)coding.[2]

Data Source, Sampling, and Coding

The chapters in this book are based on analyses of Web of Science publication data (SCIE) compiled and sold by Thomson Reuters (TR) and its precursor organizations covering the years from 1900 to 2012 and obtained by the research team in Fall 2012. Data included every five years from 1900 to 1980 and every year from 1980 to 2012. Since data for 2012 was not completed at the time of delivery from TR, 2011 was the final year analyzed. We focus here only on research articles (of varying length), not on other types of publication in the database, such as reviews or letters.

For SCIE data from 1900 to 1970, we found that the majority of research articles[3] were missing information on organizational affiliation and/or address and country information. The proportion of country information from 1900 to 1940 missing ranged from 56% to 90% annually. The proportion from 1945 to 1970 missing was even greater, from 98.6% to 99.8%; thus, analysis of global trends by country prior to 1975 would have been impossible for some years and highly unreliable for others. Given this situation, we randomly sampled and coded journal articles for each of the relevant data years by directly consulting the scientific journals – in archives, libraries as well as Internet databases – to make reliable population estimates.

In sampling, we proceeded as follows. First, we selected journals[4] through a stratified sampling procedure. We extracted a list of all the journals for each year from TR data and then we grouped those journals into four categories: S (Science), T (Technology), H (Health), and O (Other). Second, we randomly selected 5% of all the journal titles reflecting the composition rate of those four categories in each year. If 5% of journals amounted to less than 30 titles, we randomly selected more journals in order to make the number of our sampled journals equal 30 for all categories combined in that year. For example, there were 226 journals in 1940, and 35% of them were categorized into "Science," 10% into "Technology," 55% into "Health," and 0 into "Other." This resulted in 11 journals in category "S," 3 in "T," and 16 in "H" for 1940. Following this procedure, 30 journals were randomly selected every five years from 1900 to 1960. Sixty-four journals were selected for 1965 and 108 for 1970. Journals in the "Other" category were included only for the years 1940, 1945, 1965, and 1970. In 1970, two out of five selected journals in this category were not coded because they were sociology journals (non-STEM).

In order to estimate the time it would take to code each article, we experimented with selected journals from 1950 to 1960 (8 journals in 1950; 7 in 1955; 1 in 1960). Based on this sample, and with the advice of statisticians collaborating in the project, we randomly selected 30 articles from each annual journal volume when there were 35 or more articles in that journal, while all articles were coded if there were less than 35 articles. Coders sometimes found that selected articles did not qualify as research articles. (This reflected coding errors in the original SCIE data purchased from TR.) Similarly, in a small percentage of cases, coders could not find articles selected from SCIE data in the print or electronic versions of the journal. In both cases, replacement articles were selected to maintain a minimum of 30 articles for each journal. If all the listed articles were already coded, then the problematic article identification number ("Accession Number" in the WoS system) was dropped and the total number of articles for that journal decreased accordingly.

We established three additional replacement rules for the journals. First, if the missing rate of country information for authors in one journal was greater than 20%, that journal was dropped and another journal was randomly selected. This rule was applied to coding from 1940 to 1970, and all journals with a missing rate greater than 20% were replaced. The only exceptions were for one journal in 1950 and two in 1970. Those three journals were kept in our coded data despite exceeding the 20% missing rate because any coded results were deemed preferable to journals with completely missing country information.

For the period 1900–1935, finding journals with 20% or fewer articles with missing country affiliation was difficult because journals were less likely to note authors' institutional affiliations in articles. This necessitated an additional coding procedure in order to locate author affiliations. For those journals with over 20% missing rate between 1900 and 1935, coders searched the Internet to identify the author names and affiliations. If an author's name was not identifiable through Internet research, the WoS website was used to infer the author's country information based on his or her affiliation in other publications around the same time. This coding strategy was used only for country information, not for organization information. If neither searching the WoS online portal nor searching other databases was successful, that case was coded as missing.

Another situation required us to replace a few journals after the first round of randomized selection. The total number of articles based on our TR data in some selected journals did not match the total number of articles of the same journals on the WoS website. For example, in the Journal "*Physical Review A*" in 1970, there were 429 articles based on the search result on the WoS website, but the TR data contained only 293 articles. Such journals were not coded, but replaced with new randomly selected journals. Finally, a few selected journals did not include any research articles. They featured only reviews, editorial essays, and comments. These journals were also dropped and replaced by further random selection.

It is a common critique of the WoS data that journals written in English are more likely to be included in its database than those with contributions in other languages. During the coding process, we found that the replacement journals

Introduction

for the journals that were not published in English were likely to be journals that were published in English. Thus, if we dropped non-English language journals due to the 20% missing rule, non-English language journals were even less likely to be included in our sampling procedure. So as not to exacerbate this bias, two French journals (in 1940 and 1945) and three Russian ones (in 1970), even though they firstly violated the 20% missing rule, were included after successful Internet searches for author information.

The data purchased from TR also included a small proportion of journals not traditionally considered to be in STEM+ fields. TR indicated that some journals are indexed in both the Science Citation Index Expanded (SCIE) and the Social Sciences Citation Index (SSCI) due to their cross-disciplinary nature. We did not exclude these multi disciplinary journals in our analysis, especially for the years from 1980 to 2011, due to their inclusion in SCIE and their relevance to STEM+ researchers.

How SPHERE Counted Collaboratively Written Research Articles

Especially multiple authorships and cross-national comparisons and collaborations give rise to technical problems in counting publications (Gauffriau, Larsen, Maye, Roulin-Perriard, & von Ins, 2007, 2008). When counting total publications worldwide, we used the number of unique research articles regardless of the organizational affiliation and address(es) of each article. That is, for global totals, any single-authored or collaboratively written paper is counted as one, regardless of the number of authors and countries involved. In other words, we do not double (or multiple) count collaborative publications for world totals.

When counting publications in multiple regions or across countries, things necessarily become more complicated. Consider a publication with the following co-authors: 2 from the United States, 1 from Germany, and 1 from France. There are three typical options available in the bibliometric literature. The first option is whole counting, in which one credit is conferred to each country contributing to a publication regardless of the number of authors. For the above article, each of the three countries (i.e., the United States, Germany, and France) gets 1 credit. One problem of whole counting is that the numbers are not additive, that is, the sum of country numbers exceeds world total due to international collaborations (that have been increasing considerably in recent decades). This is especially important to consider when counting publications by regions. That is, if one is interested in comparing regional production (e.g., North America and Europe), then the above identified paper should be counted as 1 for North America (United States), and 1 for Europe (Germany, France).

A second option is called fractional counting, in which 1 credit is divided equally among the countries contributing to a publication. For the above publication, each of the three countries (i.e., the United States, Germany, and

France) would receive ⅓ credit. Alternatively, the number of authors working in a country can be taken into account. For the above publication, the United States receives ½, Germany receives ¼, and France receives ¼. Of course, given the global flows of scientists, this does not indicate the nationality of the researcher(s). Furthermore, researchers increasingly have multiple affiliations, collaborations are rising exponentially, and the number of authors in total and on each paper is growing. Having researched the organizational addresses that reflect where the research was conducted, we assign the credit on that basis. We selected the whole counting method for the country comparisons shown in this volume.

Transformative Regime Change: The Dissolution or Unification of Countries

Because of the significance of an author's country affiliation — not their actual citizenship status, but rather the host country of the research organization with which they are affiliated — for our analyses, the dissolution or unification of countries required careful attention (e.g., the former Soviet Union breaking up into many countries or Germany after unification). Because of the lag time between research completion, article submission, and article publication date, a decision rule was adopted that allowed an article to be attributed to the former country up to three years after the date of transformative political regime change. For example, the USSR was divided into 15 nations on December 26, 1991. Based on the 3-year rule, USSR in TR data was coded as such through the end of 1994.

If an article attributed to an author from a research organization in the USSR appeared in 1995 and afterwards, the country affiliation was recoded into the correct current country name by cross-checking the organization or city as necessary. Similarly, if countries such as Russia, Azerbaijan, and other states of the former Soviet Union were identified in the TR data before 1991, they were recoded as USSR. A contrary case is unification of multiple states. When occupied Germany was divided into the Federal Republic of Germany (West Germany) and the German Democratic Republic (East Germany), articles were thus coded. During the period prior to 1949, all articles published by scientists in research organizations in the territories belonging to Germany were counted under "Germany." After reunification in 1990, articles from authors in both parts of the country were again attributed to "Germany." Further, precise coding rules are available upon request from the authors.

COMPARING RESULTS

We now turn to selected comparisons of the case study countries, beginning with an historical charting of the evolution of worldwide STEM+ publications from 1900 and continuing until 2011, driven largely by the countries analyzed in-depth in this volume. This overarching analysis discusses key trends in the century of science for the whole world before we turn to the chapters devoted to single or comparative case studies of the institutionalization of higher education and science systems and research policy.

The country cases studied in-depth over the duration of the project included Belgium, China, France, Germany, Japan, Luxembourg, Qatar, South Korea, Taiwan, the United Kingdom, and the United States, not all of which can be presented in this volume (for Belgium and Luxembourg compared to France and Germany, see Powell & Dusdal, 2016). We also emphasized the mapping of global growth, regional competition, and collaboration across borders that have led to the surge in scientific productivity worldwide. The evolution of SCIE publications across the 20th century up to the current decade shows major shifts in the regional development of universities and science — and the particularly strong recent growth in China and other East Asian countries (see also Shin, Postiglione, & Huang, 2015). Regarding the United States, the largest science producer for decades, its world-leading capacity is built upon an unusual combination of mass and elite, academic and practical, education in one complex, highly differentiated higher education system, growing especially strongly since the World War II (Labaree, 2017). In Europe, our comparisons of higher education and extra-university research institutes show that these different organizational forms have contrasting contributions in the traditionally top science producers of France, Germany, and the United Kingdom. Despite the different relative significance of these organizational forms in these contexts, both are crucial to overall scientific productivity in many countries. Further, science productivity in Japan has been shown to depend not only on the elite universities, but also on the range of national and regional universities throughout the country. Our research on South Korea shows the significant contribution of private universities and investments to the extraordinarily fast growth of that country's higher education and research systems. Qatar, one of the most rapidly growing countries anywhere in the world has, within 15 years, developed a comprehensive national research system, albeit on a small scale befitting its size. All of these country cases examined thus far, most discussed in the following chapters, show how higher education and research, as key pillars of the knowledge society, have expanded dramatically since 1900, yet beginning in different eras.

Global Mega-Science

Long historical trends in scientific discovery led mid-20th century scientometricians to mark the advent of "big science" — extensive science production (de Solla Price, 1961, 1963). They also predicted that over the next few decades, pure exponential growth would slow down, resulting in lower rates of increase in production at the upper limit of a logistic curve. Yet they were mistaken. The findings presented here show that, in fact, "big science" was itself transformed by unprecedented production, with exponential growth continuing through to the contemporary era. This remarkable growth reflects two contrasting and simultaneous trends – rising competition across nations and international collaboration among scientists.

Global mega-science has been powered by strong European science systems that pioneered discoveries over the centuries and were rebuilt after World War II. Another pillar is North American investment in science capacity rising over the 20th century, with the United States and Canada among the most prolific countries globally. The third dominant region with expanded science capacity is East Asia, especially Japan (since the 1970s), China, Taiwan, and South Korea (all since the 1980s). Most recently, strong investments by countries in the Arabian Gulf countries have established infrastructure and provide global sites for research, especially in dozens of international branch campuses, although their overall contribution to global production of journal articles is small (Crist, 2017; Wiseman, Alromi, & Alshumrani, 2014). For example, as Crist demonstrates, 75% of Qatar's entire research output between 1980 and 2011 involves collaboration between a locally based author and an author based outside of Qatar. Countries in other regions also participate in this globe-spanning expansion of collaboration within a diversity of forms of university structures, including university networks and international branch campuses.

Global Differentiation and Competition

If in 1900 the top 10 countries in the world published 87% of all papers, in 1950 their proportion increased slightly to 90%, but by 2000 this had dropped to around two-thirds (69%) and by 2010 to only three-fifths (63%). Thus, the share of production that smaller contributors make to world science has witnessed major development: The number of countries producing more than 0.1% of STEM+ papers in the world has increased from 18 in 1900, to 24 in 1950, and later to 38 in 1980 to 45 in 1990, 51 in 2000 and 55 in 2010 (see Mihai & Reisz, 2017). In fact, the huge increase in the numbers of countries involved in the production of science has occurred at the low end of the spectrum. In other words, most countries now contribute at least some STEM+ science published in citation index journals. The case studies analyzed in-depth in the volume focus on top producing countries, such as the United States and China, strong mid-sized producers in Europe and East Asia, and a small, but growing producer, Qatar, in the Middle East.

The global center of gravity of SCIE publications shifted over the century, as measured by calculating the annual weighted geographic centroid of each country by the number of SCIE publications produced in that country (Zhang et al., 2015). By 1900, the global center of SCIE production had already moved significantly west of the founding European centers of modern scientific inquiry. Early in the 20th century, France, Germany, the United Kingdom, and the United States largely dominated scientific production, with the last in marked ascendancy (Fernandez & Baker, 2017; Powell & Dusdal, 2017). Over the next 40 years, U.S. universities, emulating the model of the German research university preeminent in the early 20th century, became increasingly productive (Baker, 2014; Geiger, 1986). But despite the victory of World War II and massive investments in higher education and science (Kleinman, 1995; Labaree, 2017), American dominance waned due to the renewal of Europe's diverse higher education and science systems.

Like the trajectory of the world's center of economic gravity (Dobbs et al., 2012), a new world pattern emerged in the middle of the century as the scientific center of gravity turned back east, beginning the trajectory it has charted for the ensuing 60 years, toward Europe and, in most recent decades, East Asia. What the SPHERE results show, insufficiently recognized earlier, is that these trends of global diffusion and regional differentiation began much earlier in the 20th century than commonly understood. This volume contributes to the literature presenting case studies that analyze data – painstakingly recoded in years of archival and Internet-based research – over a much longer period of time than previous studies, which have tended to study scientific production over shorter time spans; typically a few recent decades (see subsection "Limited Empirical Studies on Science Production").

Today's global competition for scientific impact is no longer solely taking place in the Atlantic world. Rather, it is one that encompasses the entire Northern Hemisphere, with the scientific superpowers – the United States and China – competing with each other, along with the many less populous European countries with their well-established and highly productive science systems. Although growth in SCIE publications decreased in Japan during the 1990s, the rise of other Asian countries – in particular China and South Korea (which ranked 11th in 2011, with annual growth of over 20 percent since 1980) – pulled the center of gravity further eastward across the North Atlantic during the past two decades, at a pace of about 0.90 degree per annum, passing the prime meridian in 2000 (Kim & Choi, 2017; Shima, 2017; Zhang et al., 2015; Zhang, Sun, & Bao, 2017). This dramatic change in direction is a function of both fast growth in East Asian countries and slowing growth (in fact: *relative* decline) in scientific production in the United States, which has posted an average annual growth one full percentage point lower than the world average since 1980s. Yet simultaneously with broadened competition between countries, organizations, and research groups, another global pattern is also remarkable for its strength, namely the inexorable rise in collaborations between scholars and scientists across cultural and political borders.

International Collaboration: Boundary-spanning Dynamics

There has been substantial and growing international collaboration, particularly from 1980 onward. Concurrent with the development of much science policy aimed at advancing national capacity to compete globally, collaboration by teams of scientists based in multiple nations not only increased after mid-century but entered an uninterrupted period of pure exponential growth from 1980. One-third of all research papers worldwide result from international collaboration and less than 26 percent are the product of one author alone. Indeed, the number of coauthored papers has more than doubled since 1990 and over a third have authors conducting research in multiple countries. Obviously, the scientific landscape exhibits myriad linkages, as the search for new knowledge has always crossed borders. If growth is common to all countries, established economies collaborate more than rapidly growing scientific nations, such as China, India, or Brazil; furthermore, the largest countries, including the United States and China, do not collaborate as much as do European scientists (Adams, 2013). Europe with centuries of experience in navigating multicultural and multilingual communication in scientific debates, the smaller size of many of these higher education and science systems, and considerable mobility across the Continent facilitates cross-cultural collaboration. In no small measure, the programs of the European Union support the communication and exchange at the heart of this dynamic development. For example, the Erasmus Programme facilitated 3.3 million student exchanges and 470,000 staff exchanges in just a quarter-century. The European Research Council (ERC) finances "frontier" research throughout the Continent and creates new supranational scientific elites (Flink, 2016; Hoenig, 2017; König, 2016). And the Framework Programme of EU Research Funding explicitly supports cross-border collaborative research projects to establish sustainable research networks and coordinated research agendas (European Commission, 2015; Zapp, Marques, & Powell, forthcoming).

The well-documented rise of China and the less well-known renewed scientific ambitions in the Middle East, millennia after the previous peak of Islamic science (on contemporary publication patterns in the Islamic world, see Sarwar & Hassan, 2015), provide new opportunities for the production of science and for international collaboration. As investments in international branch campuses and knowledge hubs in the Arabian Gulf countries attest (Crist, 2017; Miller-Idriss & Hanauer, 2011; Wiseman et al., 2014), more than ever higher education and science are becoming global enterprises in which collaboration across borders are key sources of innovation. If competition is never far from the rhetoric of policymakers and science administrators, individual research teams and scientists seem motivated by the belief that collaborating on the cutting-edge problems in their fields provides a successful strategy to accomplish more and to make their results more visible beyond their own cultural context.

The unprecedented, exponential growth in article production reflects the increased importance of higher education and science in countries worldwide. The shifting center of gravity away from the United States emphasizes its relative decline as especially Asian and European countries heavily invest in their national higher education and research capacity. Simultaneously, the pursuit of cutting-edge knowledge production relies on successful intercultural communication and the building of international bridges between scholars. Thus, research and development requires investment not only in individuals within organizations, but also in the networks, connections, and exchanges that facilitate discoveries (Kosmützky & Putty, 2016).

Connections between Science Production and Economic Prosperity

The concurrent shift and eastward movement of the centers of science production and economic prosperity (Dobbs et al., 2012) since 1950s are not surprising. The relationship is likely mutualistic. In "the schooled society" (Baker, 2014), growth in all levels of education have not only transformed learning across the life course and knowledge production, but also whole professions and occupational groups, with considerable impact on economy and society. And as education-driven economic development provides resources necessary for research and scientific production, this in turn spurs further economic growth. Although no simple model of causality can be inferred from this concerted change, decades of economic research have convincingly shown that education, science, and technology have all played crucial roles in economic growth (Goldin & Katz, 2009; Romer, 1986; Solow, 1957). Recently, studies have addressed this issue for OECD countries, asking in which direction causality flows, and finding unidirectional causality from research output, measured in articles published, to economic growth for the United States, Finland, Hungary, and Mexico, but the opposite – from economic growth to research articles published – in Canada, France, Italy, New Zealand, the United Kingdom, Austria, Israel, and Poland; furthermore, none for the other countries (Ntuli, Inglesi-Lotz, Chang, & Pouris, 2015; see also Mihai & Reisz, 2017).

Investments in science and education are obvious explanations for the determination of scientific productivity. Indeed, the most productive countries in the world of STEM+ are countries with high values of per capita GDP and high investments in education and science. Yet while scientific giants like the United States or China account for a high proportion of absolute global scientific journal article production, the most productive countries on a per capita basis are a few smaller ones (e.g., Israel, Scandinavian countries, and Switzerland) (May, 1997; Mihai & Reisz, 2017). Highly internationalized, these smaller research systems contribute importantly to scientific output and invest substantially in higher education and R&D. When adjusting for the size of population and the economy, the proportion of GDP spent on R&D, or the number of researchers, some smaller European countries are more productive than mid-sized or even large ones (e.g., Belgium, see Powell & Dusdal, 2016). Thus, global scientific capacity-building is not only the province of large countries. The wealth of countries, measured by per capita GDP or other similar indicators, has an essential impact on scientific productivity, but wealth alone does not explain the considerable differences in scientific output.

Indeed, across the countries examined in-depth in the volume, we find historical and cross-national variation in the "research intensity" or the gross expenditure on R&D as a proportion of GDP (Fig. 2). If South Korea leads today, this reflects tremendous growth over just a few decades. Japan, still investing a similar proportion as the United States and Germany in the 1980s, has risen over recent decades. Taiwan has also increased its research intensity, but at a lower level than the other East Asian countries. Neck-and-neck, Germany dipped below the United States in the period following reunification, but has since risen to around 3%, the 2020 target set by the European Union, and is above the United States. Just below the OECD average (2.4%), France shows a research intensity of 2.3%, followed by China, which has also followed the trend of its East Asian neighbors, but at lower level (2%). The United Kingdom, equal to the OECD average and France in the mid-1980s, has

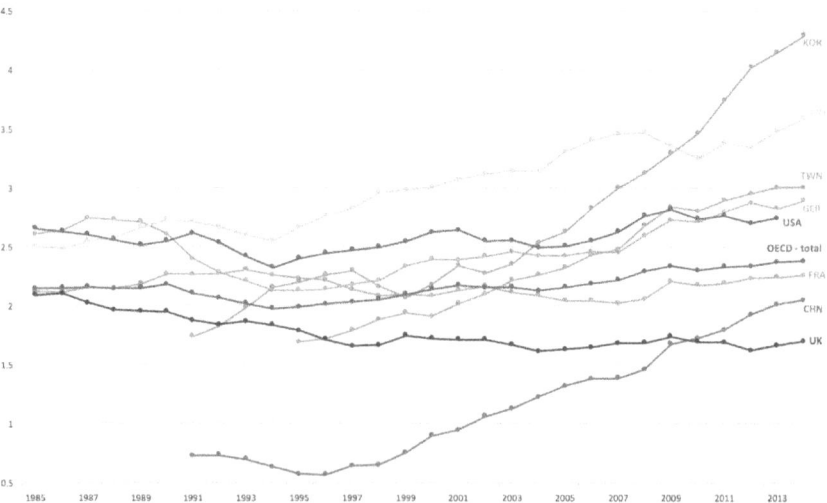

Fig. 2. Research Intensity in Select Case Study Countries and OECD Average (GERD as a Proportion of GDP), 1985–2014. *Source*: OECD.Stat (2017): Main Science and Technology Indicators. Accessed on October 1, 2017.

dropped off to only 1.7%, exhibiting by far the lowest research intensity in this group of high-producing science countries.

The research intensity indicator is widely used to gauge the volume of investments in R&D, yet these countries' economies have different scales. Turning from the input measure to outputs – namely volume of published STEM+ papers in the SCIE – we standardize on the basis of overall population and, in a more proximal measure, the number of researchers in full-time equivalents (although here distinctions cannot be made by discipline, circumscribing the specificity of this indicator). Comparing the volume of papers produced across a subset of countries analyzed in the SPHERE project reveals quite a different picture than that of the input side. Here, the United Kingdom, the country with the lowest research intensity, has the most publications per million inhabitants, clearly reflecting its highly internationalized and very productive universities as well as the enormous advantage of the English language and the large number of journals edited and published there. Generally, universities seem to provide the most prolific climate for research, more so than extra-university research institutes (May, 1997), despite the fact that both Germany and France invest considerably in such institutes. Quite a bit lower, Germany, the United States, and France have similar results, again with varying expenditure levels. Japan exhibits a relatively similar trend to those countries, but with flat productivity since 2000. In distinct contrast, South Korea manifests a similar extraordinary growth curve in its publications as in its R&D investments, nearly quadrupling in less than two decades. China, with its vast population, has nevertheless risen to around 100 such publications per million inhabitants annually. The range between these top science-producing countries remains stark; more than a factor of six between China and the United Kingdom (Fig. 3).

Turning now to the development of the ratio of publications to 100 researchers (full-time equivalents, FTE) also shows considerable spread across these countries in different regions and contrasting institutionalization pathways of higher education and science (Fig. 4). Indeed, confirming the analysis by Adams (2013), the United Kingdom stands out as much more productive per researcher than the other countries for the entire period, with 27 published papers in 2010 (albeit with a stark drop in 2005), reflecting that country's multiple advantages, including hosting among the world's strongest and internationalized universities, operating naturally in the English language, benefiting from being a center of scientific publishing, and perhaps also resulting from an elaborate research evaluation system developed over decades that has pressured academics to produce more research articles than other forms of scientific output (Marques, Powell, Zapp, & Biesta, in press). Germany (23 published papers), France (22), and the United States (22) now cluster when measuring their papers per 100 researchers (FTE), with Germany catching up on this measure. Taiwan is the most productive of the four East Asian comparator countries, with 17 published papers in the SPHERE database per 100 FTE

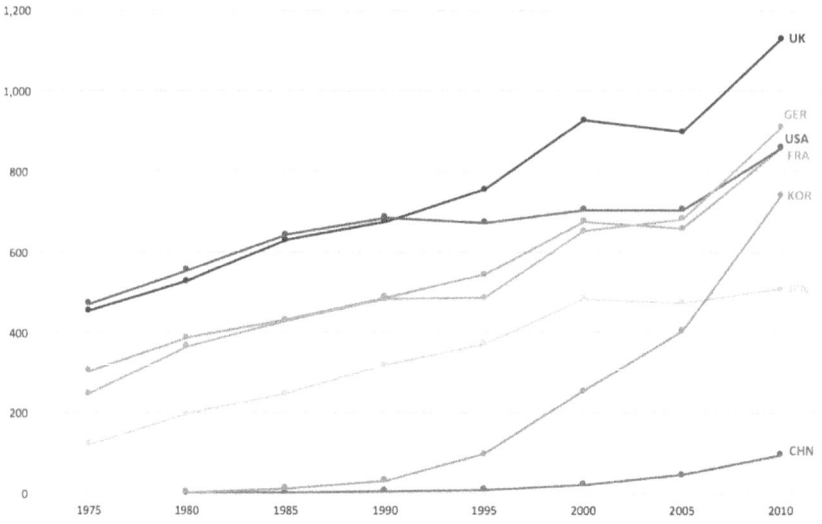

Fig. 3. Publications (SCIE) per Million Inhabitants, 1975–2010. *Source*: OECD. Stat (2017): Main Science and Technology Indicators. Accessed on October 1, 2017; SPHERE project database of SCIE publications (Thomson Reuters' Web of Science).

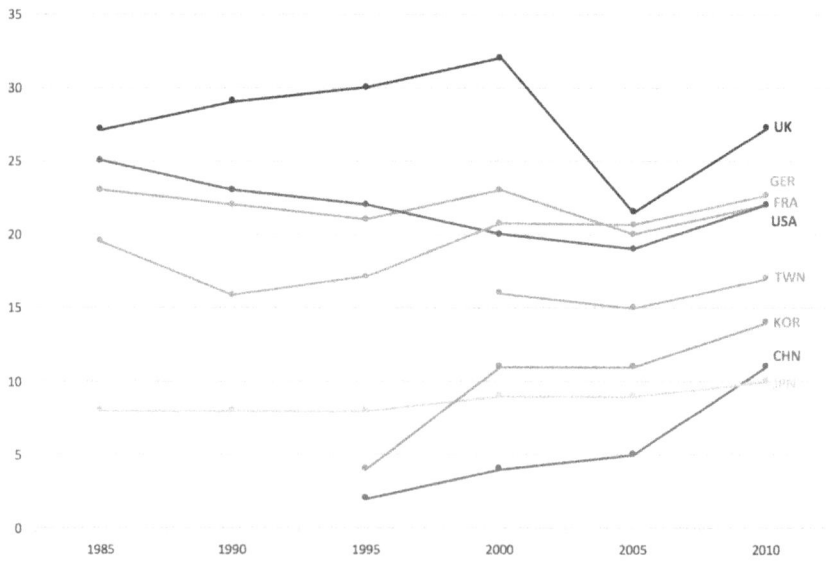

Fig. 4. Publications (SCIE) per 100 FTE Researchers, 1985–2010. *Source*: OECD. Stat (2017): Main Science and Technology Indicators. Accessed on October 1, 2017; SPHERE project database of SCIE publications (Thomson Reuters' Web of Science).

researchers. South Korea (14) and China (11), with their recent extraordinary rise is absolute production, have most recently overtaken Japan (10), which exhibits stability over the period with a recent uptick in this publication to researcher ratio.

Such historical and spatial variance in key indicators of research and development, measuring both inputs and outputs, demands further investigation, to which we turn in the following chapters.

CHAPTER OVERVIEW

In his *cross-country comparative chapter*, Mike Zapp examines global higher education expansion and the growth of science. He charts the institutionalization of higher education systems in seven countries from 1945 to 2015, exploring various trajectories of higher education expansion and its political and social conditions in China, Germany, Japan, Qatar, South Korea, Taiwan, and the United States. The analysis relies on longitudinal and cross-sectional data gleaned from the World Higher Education Database, UNESCO, and the OECD. All these countries have seen remarkable higher education expansion in the 20th century in terms of enrollments and the foundings of universities, with particularly strong growth over the immediate post-World War II period and since 1990. For the particular case of STEM+ fields examined here, the author shows that in those higher education systems in which growth took off relatively late, universities oriented toward the STEM+ fields are more dominant than in those with a longer history, reflecting the humanities and professions orientation of early universities. Countries with more recently institutionalized higher education systems stress technological development more than those that look back on multiple centuries of higher education expansion with their canonical legacies. Comparing these highly dissimilar countries nevertheless reveals important common patterns, and the variable paces of growth can be explained by national social and political factors driving the institutionalization of higher education and research.

Focusing on the three key science-producing countries in *Europe*, Justin J. W. Powell and Jennifer Dusdal compare growth in scientific productivity and institutional symbiosis between research universities and extra-university research institutes in France, Germany, and the United Kingdom. The authors chart significant growth in universities and in scientific productivity over the 20th century. The analysis presents the development and current state of universities and research institutes that bolster Europe's leading position in global science. Ongoing internationalization and Europeanization of higher education and science has been accompanied by increasing competition as well as collaboration. Despite the political goals to foster innovation and further expand research capacity in all three countries, in cross-national and historical comparison shifting research policies (and the resultant level of R&D investments) do not fully account for the differential growth of scientific productivity. Based on a comprehensive historical database, this analysis uncovers both stable and dynamic patterns of productivity from 1975 to 2010 in France, Germany, and the United Kingdom – the three major European science producers. Measured in peer-reviewed research articles collected in Thomson Reuters' SCIE, we also identify individual organizations leading in research output. These results show the varying contributions of different organizational forms, especially research universities and research institutes, with universities' contribution nearly half but rising in France; ultrastable in Germany at four-fifths, and growing and around two-thirds in the United Kingdom. Contrasting institutionalization pathways created the conditions necessary for continuous, but varying growth in scientific productivity in the European center of global science.

Crossing the Atlantic, Frank Fernandez and David P. Baker examine science production in the *United States* throughout an era of massified higher education and the "super research university." The authors argue that U.S. scientific production resulted from an unexpected synergy between the rise of research universities, particularly public ones, and the comparatively rapid development of mass schooling, leading to mass access to higher education. From humble beginnings, U.S. universities organized faculty into modern academic fields, and their members established national scientific societies. Across the country, expanding primary enrollments gave way to the creation of the comprehensive high school, and near-universal secondary school enrollments led to mass higher education. Universities not only offered access to broad segments of the public, they also added to the U.S. – and global – stock of scientific researchers by training large numbers of new PhDs in STEM+ fields. Toward the end of the 20th century, some observers sought to characterize universities as weak organizations; they speculated that universities' share of scientific publications would decline and that universities would be outpaced by private companies. Yet academic researchers continue to not only produce a majority of U.S. scientific publications, they also collaborate with non-university partners to author more than three-quarters of all STEM+ scholarly works. The research university and the inclusive educational practices originating from public institutions over the last century serve as the backbone of American scientific production.

Turning next to Asia, Kazunori Shima evaluates science productivity in *Japan* by focusing on the so-called unsung heroes of the Japanese university system, which – as in the other countries mentioned thus far – forms the core of knowledge production. Other producers, including business enterprises, make up the second largest group, but the number of articles they published has fluctuated. Top national universities (former imperial university & pre-World War II universities) have been the main scientific producers, but the second-tier national universities (post-World War II universities) sustained Japan's world ranking of scientific productivity into the 2000s. Yet Japan was the only major country that did not increase the number of STEM+ articles it produced between 2005 and 2010, and as a result, Japan went from being the second-largest knowledge producing country in 1990 to the fifth in 2010 worldwide. Unsurprisingly, as funding from basic government block grants and expanding competitive funds decreased, article production at second-tier universities also decreased or stagnated. These findings call into question the widespread belief among education and scientific policymakers in Japan that competition is inherently beneficial for scientific productivity and emphasize the importance of in-depth analyses of different organizational forms and research capacity within the university sector.

Examining *China*, the main competitor nation to the U.S. in overall, absolute publications, Liang Zhang, Liang Sun, and Wei Bao show the transformation of higher education and research and development policies since 1949. Providing a thorough historical overview of policies that have governed and guided scientific research in China, the authors divide this historical period into four stages, each with distinct R&D policies: a period of socialist transformation (1949–1955), a phase of struggle for higher education and research development in a rapidly changing political environment (1956–1965), the lost decade of the Cultural Revolution (1966–1976); and, since 1976, a phase when major national policies have significantly promoted scientific research throughout China. Using data from SPHERE and a set of Chinese research universities, the authors demonstrate changes in scientific publication rates concurrent with these policy reforms and programs. This analysis suggests that there is a tight connection between national policy and scientific research productivity in higher education in China.

Taking a similar perspective, Hyerim Kim and Junghee Choi examine the significant contribution of private universities to higher education and research in *South Korea*. Higher education has been a key foundation for South Korea's rapid economic development. However, unlike many other countries, the growth of Korean higher education was heavily dependent upon private institutions or investments – rather than state funding so crucial elsewhere. Research is a relatively new mission for Korean universities, as through the 1980s, the Korean government saw colleges and universities as primarily providing human resources for national industries, less as the organizations responsible for generating scientific research. In order to investigate how especially private universities have contributed to the growth of Korean higher education and research, this chapter compares student enrollments and science production by university-based researchers over time. In Korea, the proportion of publications by private universities has exceeded that of national and public universities since 1998, which challenges the conventional wisdom that public universities are per se better suited to pursue basic (and perhaps less immediately profitable) scientific research because of their orientation to the public interest.

In the chapter on *Taiwan*, Yuan Chih Fu elaborates the development of higher education there, also comparing the relative contributions to scientific productivity of different types of organizations, including higher education and the Academy of Sciences (Sinica). To fully appreciate the development of technological innovation in Taiwan, it is crucial to understand the rise of Taiwanese universities. Taiwan has one of the most intensely schooled populations in the world, thus even though its scale is comparatively small, its research power is considerable. Historically, the development of higher education and science capacity-building focused on cultivating a centralized, publicly funded system. The massification of Taiwanese higher education allowed universities to expand student enrollments and accommodate more researchers. In addition to the expansion of higher education, internal changes within the university sector also spurred scientific production. Several strategies for competition were adopted by the leading universities and eventually became common practice nationally – such as choosing cutting-edge research topics, organizing researchers into clusters, crafting international research teams, inviting distinguish scholars as project leaders, and recruiting PhD holders from top global universities as faculty. Through internal and external policy changes, Taiwan changed the way its university-based researchers conduct and publish research.

Turning to the Middle East in a final case study chapter, John T. Crist analyzes the rapid development of a national research system in *Qatar*. This small desert nation, a peninsula in the Arabian Gulf, is at the forefront of a contemporary renaissance in science across the Arab and Islamic world. This is a remarkable achievement because Qatar has only recently developed its higher education sector and is among the latest entrants in the global competition of science production. The first and only national university was established in 1978, shortly after formal independence from Britain; 20 years later, Qatar franchised the development of higher education via international branch campuses to leading Western universities. The development of the higher education sector in this novel fashion was tied to a national development plan that envisions a transformation of the economy away from dependence on hydrocarbon resources toward a "knowledge economy" by 2030. The principal finding about growth in scientific journal productivity in Qatar is that it unfolded almost entirely in partnership with global, non-Qatar-based research institutions; indeed, the country profits from highest degrees of international collaboration. A significantly more difficult and long-term goal than building a research infrastructure to attract global science to the Gulf is the nurturing of indigenous capacity. Given Qatar's dependence on foreign scientific labor, high rates of international collaboration will persist even as the regional hub develops.

Exploring the complex relationship, noted above, between *economic and scientific development*, Iris A. Mihai and Robert D. Reisz examine productivity in relation to economic development. Throughout the 20th century, the overall development of world science as seen in the numbers of STEM+ publications was exponential. Alongside the massive rise in the number of scientific publications, another important phenomenon was the globalization of science. The

Introduction

wealth of countries, measured by per capita GDP, has an essential impact on scientific capacity, but wealth alone does not explain the differences in scientific output. While scientific giants such as the United States and China are naturally the largest contributors to absolute article production across the globe, the relatively most productive countries are in fact much smaller ones. Mihai and Reisz discuss how the institutional settings in which research is conducted affects countries' scientific productivity, concluding that the relationship between economic wealth and knowledge production is mutualistic, with the scientific advance of earlier times facilitating economic development, which in turn provides resources necessary for further scientific study, which in turn spurs further economic growth. To disentangle the complex institutional factors responsible for contrasting higher education and science systems and the diversity in scientific productivity, however measured, requires in-depth analysis of country contexts, provided in this volume, including the different institutional environments and organizational forms that provide the resources within which scientists conduct their research.

DISCUSSION AND OUTLOOK

In addition to the global, long-term historical analysis of SCIE data, we examined the relationship between university development and scientific productivity in key cases from around the world. These case studies employed a neo-institutional framework to explore and explain how the tremendous expansion of higher education and science across the world was revealed in particular countries. The authors adopted a mixed methods approach to analyze institutional models of higher education development, research policy, and science capacity-building over time and the consequences thereof for scientific production measured in longitudinal quantitative analyses of peer-reviewed papers published in leading (indexed) journals. The contributions focus in particular on the two organizational forms responsible for the vast majority of state-funded research, namely research universities and non-university research institutes of various sizes and operating in diverse associations. Read together, the chapters demonstrate the considerable differences across time and space in the institutional settings, organizational forms, and organizations that produced the most cutting-edge research across the 20th century and up to 2011.

The analyses illustrate how differences in national models in developing research universities and institutes explain long-term cross-national trajectories in system development and scientific productivity. Regarding the United States, the largest science producer for decades, we find that its world-leading capacity is built upon American mass higher education, especially since the World War II. In Europe, our comparisons of higher education and research institutes show that these different organizational forms have contrasting contributions in France, Germany, and the United Kingdom — traditionally top science producers. Despite the different relative significance of these organizational forms in these Western European countries, research universities are most crucial to overall scientific productivity. Our research on South Korea shows the significant contribution of private universities and investments to the fast growth of that country's higher education and research system. Qatar, one of the most rapidly growing countries anywhere in the world, developed a comprehensive national research system within just 15 years, further evidence of the capacity of certain smaller, well-resourced states to out-perform the traditionally (quantitatively) dominant states when scientific productivity is standardized.

Among the potential beneficiaries of the project research results presented in this volume are the scientific community of science researchers, the universities and research institutes and other organizations devoted to peer-reviewed science, and policymakers not only in the partner countries, but indeed in all countries as they invest in higher education and R&D. Analyses and discussion of the presented trends and patterns in productivity — depending on the structures and investments in R&D — will also profit scientists themselves as they reflect on their own contexts and conditions for scientific work and publication constraints and opportunities. In terms of research communities, scientists involved in bibliometrics, science studies, and neo-institutionalists who chart the massive expansion of science production and collaboration across the globe may engage with these results. The rise of evaluation and audit as tools to steer innovation relies on processes of comparison and peer review that are explicitly linked in the SPHERE project to illuminate issues of quantity and quality in publishing scientific discoveries.

Higher education, and in particular research universities, is key to the future development of science capacity in all countries examined. Science policy should be conceived, planned, and implemented in conjunction with (higher) education policy. Research should not focus solely on the United States. Even among the other top global producers of STEM+ research — including China, Germany, Japan, France, Canada, Italy, India, and Spain — there is limited longitudinal, multi-level or explicitly comparative research. Furthermore, many other countries that are developing their research capacity and these patterns should be the subject of future research, for example the case of Qatar. Especially given the rise of international collaborations, alongside competition, empirical studies should be — indeed must be — comparative to capture the cooperative ventures and exchange of ideas necessary for innovative research.

While the SPHERE project members invested tremendous efforts to recode especially the historical data (1900–1975) through considerable archival and Internet-based research, limits of time and access to archived journals circumscribed the geographic and linguistic scope of these historical analyses. To ensure the reliability of the analyses, we conducted preliminary comparisons of the TR SCIE and Elsevier Scopus databases, yet these comparisons should continue to be done systematically to ensure reliable trend analysis – and the selectivity of these mainly Anglophone, Western databases acknowledged. Future research should extend horizontally beyond SCIE to include all the disciplines and fields of scientific inquiry and vertically within specific disciplines (and journals) to better understand in-depth publication patterns and trends. The wide-ranging effects and often unintended consequences of research evaluation systems, rankings and ratings, and other forms of competitive comparison must be analyzed for disciplines, fields, organizations, departments, and scientists, with future research not focused solely on STEM+. Such work should utilize new data collection methods to improve measurement of science produced in diverse languages and with different formats (Internet-based, books, patents, etc.). Network analysis of international collaborations promises to illuminate the processes that lead to scientific discovery and publication.

To conclude, we have shown that "big science" has been transformed by unprecedented production worldwide since the 1950s. We can now speak of "global mega-science." Pure exponential growth in article production reflects the increased importance of higher education and science worldwide, for economy and society. Despite major wars and global economic crises since 1900, there has been no lasting decline or even saturation of exponential growth in science production up to today.

Competition for scientific impact is global. All regions, in particular the dominant scientific regions (North America, Europe, East Asia), examined in this volume, are in direct competition. Yet simultaneously with this rising competition, we find vastly increased collaboration across national, linguistic, and organizational boundaries. Information technology and accessible international travel (that has given rise to vast conference participation and educational and scientific exchange) have extended the global reach and relevance of individual scholars and facilitated global research projects in diverse organization forms and across the disciplines.

Still dominant in absolute figures, the United States suffers from relative decline in scientific productivity, as especially Asian and European countries invest heavily in their national higher education and research capacity. Newer competitors such as Qatar attempt via massive investment in university and R&D structures to play relevant roles in global science. Wealthy and internationalized smaller states with strategic investments contribute disproportionately to overall productivity. Reducing concentration among a few top producers, more and more countries have joined the enterprise of science, producing cutting-edge papers in the STEM+ fields. Such a worldwide scientific enterprise requires the sites of research capacity-building to fit into global production flows and demands infrastructures that facilitate collaboration, which has also grown exponentially over the past several decades. Indeed, alongside competition for scientific impact, the pursuit of cutting-edge knowledge production relies on building international and intercultural scholarly networks (and at all levels, not simply established members of scientific academies). Research and development requires investment not only in cutting-edge campus facilities or laboratories, but also in the networks, connections, and exchanges that facilitate discoveries — and have, whatever the difficult-to-ascertain value of any individual article — led to such expansion in the publication of scientific results in peer-reviewed journals.

NOTES

1. We are grateful to Kazunori Shima for his efforts in comparing systematically the coverage of these two key databases.
2. The authors would like to especially thank Jennifer Dusdal, Yuan Chih Fu, and Seung Wan Nam for their dedication in coding and data analysis for the duration of the project, from 2012 to 2015, coordinated and hosted at Georgetown University School of Foreign Service in Qatar.
3. Web of Science has its own categorization of writings in their database such as research article, review, editorial, and letter, which we also keep in our working process. In other words, an "article" or "research article" in this report means that it is classified by TR as a research article (k_code = @).
4. A journal title was counted only once, no matter how many volumes or issues in each year were published.

REFERENCES

Adams, J. (2011). Thomson Reuters Global Research Report: United Kingdom. Leeds: Evidence.
Adams, J. (2013). Collaborations: The fourth age of research. *Nature*, *497*, 557–560.
Adams, J. D. (2009). *Is the U.S. losing its preeminence in higher education?* NBER Working Paper No. 15233. Retrieved from http:www.nber.org/papers/w15233
Adams, J. D., Black, G. C., Clemmons, J. R., & Stephan, P. E. (2005). Scientific teams and institutional collaborations: Evidence from US universities, 1981–1999. *Research Policy*, *34*(3), 259–285.
Aghion, P., Dewatripont, M., & Stein, J. C. (2008). Academic freedom, private-sector focus, and the process of innovation. *The RAND Journal of Economics*, *39*(3), 617–635.
Baker, D. P. (2014). *The schooled society: The educational transformation of global culture*. Stanford, CA: Stanford University Press.
Ball, R., & Tunger, D. (2005). Bibliometrische Analysen — Daten, Fakten und Methoden. Grundwissen Bibliometrie für Wissenschaftler, Wissenschaftsmanager, Forschungseinrichtungen und Hochschulen. Schriften des Forschungszentrums Jülich. Band 12. Jülich: Forschungszentrum Jülich.
Bornmann, L., & Mutz, R. (2015). Growth rates of modern science: A bibliometric analysis based on the number of publications and cited references. *Journal of the Association for Information Science and Technology*, *66*(11), 2215–2222.
Bornmann, L., Wagner, C., & Leydesdorff, L. (2015). BRICS countries and scientific excellence: A bibliometric analysis of most frequently cited papers. *Journal of the Association for Information Science and Technology*, *66*(7), 1507–1513.
Bradford, S. C. (1934). Sources of information on specific subjects. *Engineering: An Illustrated Weekly Journal*, *137*(3550), 85–86.

Crist, J. T. (2017). "A fever of research": Scientific journal article production and the emergence of a national research system in Qatar, 1980–2011. In J. J. W. Powell, D. P. Baker, & F. Fernandez (Eds.), *The century of science: The global triumph of the research university* (Vol. 33). International Perspectives on Education and Society. Bingley: Emerald Publishing Limited.

de Solla Price, D. J. (1961). *Science since Babylon*. New Haven, CT: Yale University Press.

de Solla Price, D. J. (1963). *Little science, big science, and beyond*. New York, NY: Columbia University Press.

Delanty, G. (2001). *Challenging knowledge: The university in the knowledge society*. Buckingham: Open University Press.

Dietz, J. S., & Bozeman, B. (2005). Academic careers, patents, and productivity: Industry experience, as scientific and technical human capital. *Research Policy, 34*, 349–367.

Dobbs, R., Remes, J., Manyika, J., Roxburgh, C., Smit, S., & Schaer, F. (2012). *Urban world: Cities and the rise of the consuming class*. McKinsey Global Institute. Retrieved from http://www.mckinsey.com/insights/urbanization/urban_world_cities_and_the_rise_of_the_consuming_class

Drori, G. (2000). Science education and economic development: Trends, relationships, and research agenda. *Studies in Science Education, 35*, 27–57.

Drori, G. S., & Krücken, G. (2009). World society: A theory and a research program in context. In G. Krücken & G. S. Drori (Eds.), *World society: The writings of John W. Meyer* (pp. 3–35). New York, NY: Oxford University Press.

Drori, G. S., Meyer, J. W., Ramirez, F. O., & Schofer, E. (Eds.). (2003). *Science in the modern world polity: Institutionalization and globalization*. Stanford, CA: Stanford University Press.

Elzinga, A. (2012). Features of the current science, policy regime: Viewed in historical, perspective. *Science and Public Policy, 39*, 416–428.

Espeland, W. N., & Sauder, M. (2007). Rankings and reactivity: How public measures recreate social worlds. *American Journal of Sociology, 113*(1), 1–40.

Espelund, W. N., & Sauder, M. (2016). *Engines of anxiety: Academic rankings, reputation, and accountability*. New York, NY: Russell Sage Foundation.

Etzkowitz, H., & Leydesdorff, L. (2000). The dynamics of innovation: From national systems and "Mode 2" to a Triple Helix of university–industry–government relations. *Research Policy, 29*(2), 109–123.

Etzkowitz, H., Webster, A., Gebhardt, C., & Terra, B. R. C. (2000). The future of the university and the university of the future: Evolution of ivory tower to entrepreneurial paradigm. *Research Policy, 29*(2), 313–330.

European Commission. (2015). *Seventh FP7 Monitoring Report: Monitoring Report 2013*. Luxembourg: Publications Office of the European Union.

Fernandez, F., & Baker, D. P. (2017). Science production in the United States: An unexpected synergy between mass higher education and the super research university. In J. J. W. Powell, D. P. Baker, & F. Fernandez (Eds.), *The century of science: The global triumph of the research university* (Vol. 33). International Perspectives on Education and Society. Bingley: Emerald Publishing Limited.

Flink, T. (2016). *Die Entstehung des Europäischen Forschungsrates*. Weilerswist: Velbrück Wissenschaft.

Garfield, E. (1964). Science Citation Index: A new dimension in indexing. *Science, 144*(3619), 649–654.

Gauffriau, M., Larsen, P. O., Maye, I., Roulin-Perriard, A., & von Ins, M. (2007). Publication, cooperation and productivity measures in scientific research. *Scientometrics, 73*(2), 175–214.

Gauffriau, M., Larsen, P. O., Maye, I., Roulin-Perriard, A., & von Ins, M. (2008). Comparisons of results of publication counting using different methods. *Scientometrics, 77*(1), 147–176.

Geiger, R. L. (1986). *To advance knowledge: The growth of American research universities, 1900–1940*. New York, NY: Oxford University Press.

Gibbons, M., Limoges, C., Nowotny, H., Schwartzman, S., Scott, P., & Trow, M. (1994). *The new production of knowledge: The dynamics of science and research in contemporary societies.* Thousand Oaks, CA: Sage.

Glänzel, W. (2003). *Bibliometrics as a research field: A course on theory and application of bibliometric indicators* (Course Handout). Retrieved from http://citeseerx.ist.psu.edu/viewdoc/download?doi=10.1.1.97.5311&rep=rep1&type=pdf

Glänzel, W., & Schöpflin, U. (1994). Little scientometrics, big scientometrics−and beyond? *Scientometrics, 30*(2−3), 375−384.

Godin, B., & Gingras, Y. (2000). The place of universities in the system of knowledge production. *Research Policy, 29*(2), 273−278.

Goldin, C. D., & Katz, L. F. (2009). *The race between education and technology.* Cambridge, MA: Harvard University Press.

Griliches, Z. (Ed.) (1984). *R&D, patents, and productivity.* Chicago, IL: University of Chicago Press.

Hall, B. H., Link, A. N., & Scott, J. T. (2003). Universities as research partners. *Review of Economics and Statistics, 85*(2), 485−491.

Havemann, F. (2009). *Einführung in die Bibliometrie.* Berlin: Gesellschaft für Wissenschaftsforschung.

Hazelkorn, E. (2011). *Rankings and the reshaping of higher education.* Basingstoke: Palgrave Macmillan.

Hessels, L. K., & van Lente, H. (2008). Re-thinking new knowledge production: A literature review and a research agenda. *Research Policy, 37*(4), 740−760.

Hicks, D. (2012). Performance-based university research funding systems. *Research Policy, 41*(2), 251−261.

Hoenig, B. (2017). *Europe's new scientific elite: Social mechanisms of science in the European research area.* Abingdon: Routledge.

Jovanovic, M. (2012). Eine kleine frühgeschichte der bibliometrie. *Information, Wissenschaft & Praxis, 63*(2), 71−80.

Kim, H., & Choi, J. (2017). The growth of higher education and science production in South Korea since 1945. In J. J. W. Powell, D. P. Baker, & F. Fernandez (Eds.), *The century of science: The Global Triumph of the Research University* (Vol. 33). International Perspectives on Education and Society. Bingley: Emerald Publishing Limited.

Kleinman, D. L. (1995). *Politics on the endless frontier: Postwar research policy in the United States.* Durham, NC: Duke University Press.

König, T. (2016). *The European Research Council.* Cambridge: Polity.

Kosmützky, A., & Putty, R. (2016). Transcending borders and traversing boundaries: A systematic review of the literature on transnational, offshore, cross-border, and borderless higher education. *Journal of Studies in International Education, 20*(1), 8−33.

Kropp, K., & Blok, A. (2011). Mode-2 social science knowledge production? The case of Danish sociology between institutional crisis and new welfare stabilizations. *Science and Public Policy, 38*(3), 213−224.

Labaree, D. F. (2017). *A perfect mess: The unlikely ascendancy of American higher education.* Chicago, IL: University of Chicago Press.

Leydesdorff, L., & Etzkowitz, H. (1998). The triple helix as a model for innovation studies. *Science and Public Policy, 25*(3), 195−203.

Leydesdorff, L., & Meyer, M. (2006). Triple Helix indicators of knowledge-based innovation systems: Introduction to the special issue. *Research Policy, 35*(10), 1441−1449.

Lotka, A. J. (1926). The frequency distribution of scientific productivity. *Journal of the Washington Academy of Sciences, 16*(12), 317−323.

May, R. M. (1997). The scientific wealth of nations. *Science, 275*, 793−796.

Marques, M., Powell, J. J. W., Zapp, M., & Biesta, G. J. J. (in press). How does research evaluation impact educational research? Exploring intended and unintended consequences of research assessment in the United Kingdom, 1986–2014. *European Educational Research Journal.*

Meo, S. A., Al Masri, A. A., Usmani, A. M., Memon, A. N., & Zaidi, S. Z. (2013). Impact of GDP, spending on R&D, number of universities and scientific journals on research publications among Asian countries. *PLOS One, 8*(10). Retrieved from http://dx.doi.org/10.1371/journal.pone.0066449

Meo, S. A., Usmani, A. M., Vohra, M. S., & Bukhari, I. A. (2013). Impact of GDP, spending on R&D, number of universities and scientific journals on research publications in pharmacological sciences in Middle East. *European Review of Medical and Pharmacological Sciences, 17*(20), 2697−2705.

Meyer, J. W. (1977). The effects of education as an institution. *American Journal of Sociology, 83*(1), 55−77.

Meyer, J. W., Ramirez, F. O., Frank, D. J., & Schofer, E. (2008). Higher education as an institution. In P. J. Gumport (Ed.), *The sociology of higher education: Contributions and their contexts* (pp. 187−221). Baltimore, MD: The Johns Hopkins University Press.

Mihai, I. A., & Reisz, R. D. (2017). STEM+ productivity, development, and wealth, 1900–2012. In J. J. W. Powell, D. P. Baker, & F. Fernandez (Eds.), *The century of science: The global triumph of the research university* (Vol. 33). International Perspectives on Education and Society. Bingley: Emerald Publishing Limited.

Miller-Idriss, C., & Hanauer, E. (2011). Transnational higher education: Offshore campuses in the Middle East. *Comparative Education, 47*(2), 181−207.

Mohrman, K., Ma, W., & Baker, D. P. (2008). The research university in transition: The emerging global model. *Higher Education Policy, 21*(1), 5−27.

Nowotny, H., Scott, P., & Gibbons, M. (2001). *Re-thinking science: Knowledge and the public in an age of uncertainty*. Cambridge: Polity Press.

Ntuli, H., Inglesi-Lotz, R., Chang, T., & Pouris, A. (2015). Does research output cause economic growth or vice versa? Evidence from 34 OECD countries. *Journal of the Association for Information Science and Technology, 66*(8), 1709−1716.

OECD.Stat. (2017). *Main science and technology indicators*. Retrieved from http://stats.oecd.org/Index.aspx?DataSetCode.MSTI_PUB

Oleksiyenko, A. (2014). On the shoulders of giants? Global science, resource asymmetries, and repositioning of research universities in China and Russia. *Comparative Education Review, 58*(3), 482−508.

Perkmann, M., Tartari, V., McKelvey, M., Autio, E., Broström, A., D'Este, P., ... Sobrero, M. (2013). Academic engagement and commercialisation: A review of the literature on university-industry relations. *Research Policy, 42*(2), 423−442.

Powell, J. J. W., Bernhard, N., & Graf, L. (2012). The emergent European model in skill formation: Comparing higher education and vocational training in the Bologna and Copenhagen processes. *Sociology of Education, 85*(3), 240−258.

Powell, J. J. W., & Dusdal, J. (2016). Europe's center of science: Science productivity in Belgium, France, Germany, and Luxembourg. *EuropeNow, 1*(2). Retrieved from http://www.europenowjournal.org/2016/11/30/europes-center-of-science-science-productivity-in-belgium-france-germany-and-luxembourg

Pritchard, A. (1969). Statistical bibliography or bibliometrics?. *Journal of Documentation, 25*(4), 348−349.

Riddle, P. (1989). University and state: Political competition and the rise of universities, 1200–1985. Unpublished doctoral dissertation. Stanford University, Stanford, CA.

Roberts, P. (2006). Performativity, measurement and research. In J. Ozga, T. Seddon, & T. Popkewitz (Eds.), *Education research and policy* (pp. 185−199). London: Routledge.

Romer, P. M. (1986). Increasing returns and long-run growth. *The Journal of Political Economy, 94*(5), 1002−1037.

Rüegg, W. (Ed.). (2004). *A history of the university in Europe. Vol. III: Universities in the nineteenth and early twentieth centuries (1800–1945)*. Cambridge: Cambridge University Press.

Rüegg, W. (Ed.). (2011). *A history of the university in Europe. Vol. IV: Universities since 1945*. Cambridge: Cambridge University Press.

Sarwar, R., & Hassan, S. U. (2015). A bibliometric assessment of scientific productivity and international collaboration of the Islamic World in science and technology (S&T) areas. *Scientometrics, 105*(2), 1059–1077.
Schofer, E. (2004). Cross-national differences in the expansion of science, 1970–1990. *Social Forces, 83*(1), 215–248.
Schofer, E., & Meyer, J. W. (2005). The worldwide expansion of higher education in the twentieth century. *American Sociological Review, 70*(6), 898–920.
Scott, W. R. (2015). Organizational theory and higher education. *Journal of Organizational Theory in Education, 1*(1), 68–76.
Shima, K. (2017). Changing science production in Japan: The expansion of competitive funds, reduction of block grants, and unsung heroes. In J. J. W. Powell, D. P. Baker, & F. Fernandez (Eds.), *The century of science: The global triumph of the research university* (Vol. 33). International Perspectives on Education and Society. Bingley: Emerald Publishing Limited.
Shin, J. C., Postiglione, G. A., & Huang, F. (Eds.). (2015). *Mass higher education development in East Asia*. Cham: Springer.
Slaughter, S., & Leslie, L. (1997). *Academic capitalism: Politics, policies and the entrepreneurial university*. Baltimore, MD: Johns Hopkins University Press.
Slaughter, S., & Rhoades, G. (2009). *Academic capitalism and the new economy: Markets, state, and higher education*. Baltimore, MD: Johns Hopkins University Press.
Solow, R. M. (1957). Technical change and the aggregate production function. *The Review of Economics and Statistics, 39*(3), 312–320.
Teodorescu, D. (2000). Correlates of faculty publication productivity: A cross-national analysis. *Higher Education, 39*(2), 201–222.
The Royal Society. (2011). *Knowledge, networks, and nations: Global scientific collaborations in the 21st century*. London: Author.
van Rooij, A. (2014). University knowledge production and innovation: Getting a grip. *Minerva, 52*(2), 263–272.
White, H. D., & McCain, K. W. (1989). Bibliometrics. *Annual Review of Information Science and Technology, 24*, 119–186.
Whitley, R., & Gläser, J. (Eds.) (2007). *The changing governance of the sciences: The advent of the research evaluation systems*. Dordrecht, NL: Springer.
Wiseman, A. W., Alromi, N. H., & Alshumrani, S. A. (Eds.). (2014). *Education for a knowledge society in Arabian Gulf countries*. Bingley: Emerald Group Publishing Limited.
Zapp, M., Marques, M., & Powell, J. J. W. (forthcoming). *European educational research (re-)constructed*. Oxford: Symposium Books.
Zapp, M., & Powell, J. J. W. (2017). Moving towards Mode 2? Evidence-based policy-making and the changing conditions for educational research in Germany. *Science and Public Policy*. doi:10.1093/scipol/scw091
Zhang, L., Powell, J. J. W., & Baker, D. P. (2015). Exponential growth and the shifting global center of gravity of science production, 1900-2011. *Change: The Magazine of Higher Learning, 47*(4), 46–49.
Zhang, L., Sun, L., & Bao, W. (2017). The rise of higher education and science in China. In J. J. W. Powell, D. P. Baker, & F. Fernandez (Eds.), *The century of science: The global triumph of the research university* (Vol. 33). International Perspectives on Education and Society. Bingley: Emerald Publishing Limited.
Ziman, J. (2000). *Real science: What it is, and what it means*. Cambridge: Cambridge University Press.
Zipf, G. K. (1949). *Human behavior and the principle of least effort: An introduction to human ecology*. Boston, MA: Addison-Wesley Press.

HIGHER EDUCATION EXPANSION AND THE GROWTH OF SCIENCE: THE INSTITUTIONALIZATION OF HIGHER EDUCATION SYSTEMS IN SEVEN COUNTRIES, 1945−2015

Mike Zapp

ABSTRACT

Purpose − This chapter explores the trajectories of higher education expansion and its political and social conditions in seven countries, namely China, Japan, Germany, Qatar, South Korea, Taiwan, and the United States of America.

Methodology/approach − The analysis relies on longitudinal and cross-sectional data gleaned from the World Higher Education Database, UNESCO, and the OECD.

Findings − The countries have seen remarkable higher education expansion in the 20th century in terms of enrollments and the foundings of universities, with particularly strong growth in the immediate post-WWII period and since 1990. For the particular case of STEM fields (science, technology, engineering, mathematics), the chapter shows that in those higher education systems in which growth took off relatively late, universities oriented toward *the STEM fields are more dominant than in those with a longer history. Countries with a more recent HE system stress technological development more than those that look back on multiple centuries of HE expansion with their canonical legacies.*

Originality/value — *Comparing these highly dissimilar countries nevertheless reveals important common patterns, and the variable paces of higher education expansion can be explained by national, social, and political factors driving the institutionalization of higher education and research.*

Keywords: Higher education expansion; STEM+; enrollment; university foundings; science; development

INTRODUCTION

Scientific activity is influenced by myriad political, economic, and cultural factors. Despite trends toward a more diversified organizational research landscape, public research and innovation systems continue to be the major contributors to fundamental scientific output, with the university as the most important institutional form (Fernandez & Baker, 2017; Powell & Dusdal, 2017). Previous research has shown the massive expansion in tertiary education around the globe, with developing nations catching up quickly with the historical forerunners (Schofer & Meyer, 2005). Everywhere in the world, (higher) education is regarded as the guarantor of national development and enshrined in national development plans (Drori, Meyer, Ramirez, & Schofer, 2003; Hwang, 2006). International organizations promote this model advocating innovation and research planning — despite the lack of solid evidence for the actual or immediate value of higher education (HE) to such progress (Finnemore, 1993; Ramirez, Luo, Schofer, & Meyer, 2006).

To analyze the relationship between HE expansion and the growth of science, this chapter explores the trajectories of such expansion and its political conditions in seven countries, namely China, Germany, Japan, Qatar, South Korea, Taiwan, and the United States. These countries have seen remarkable HE expansion over the 20th century, with particularly strong growth in the immediate post-WWII period and since 1990. For the particular case of the fields of science, technology, engineering and mathematics (STEM), the analysis shows that in those HE systems that took off relatively late universities with departments in all four fields are more dominant than in those systems with a longer history. Although with caution when interpreting such long-term trends, it seems that countries with a more recent HE system emphasize applied fields of technological development more than do those that reflect multiple centuries of HE expansion with their classic professions and canonical legacies. In organizational terms, universities' initial structures show the imprinting of external environments at their establishment and remain relatively stable (Stinchcombe, 1965), even as HE expansion rates increase and technology advances.

Moreover, while all countries display similar long-term HE growth, they differ in the types of organizations that account for the biggest share in that expansion. In the public-private continuum higher education systems analyzed here, the United States tends toward the highly privatized pole, while Germany defends its position as a predominantly public research and innovation system. It seems, however, that the public-private distinction matters less when explaining the similarly strong production of scientific papers in all the countries presented in this volume. In other words, global trends of rationalization and scientization seem to be more influential than the funding or governance status of individual organizations within the system (Drori et al., 2003). The building of research infrastructure, and its key produced outputs such as the peer-reviewed journal articles measured in this volume, are effects of the same macrosocial phenomenon: the worldwide institutionalization of science as the main principle of social organization.

NATION-STATE BUILDING AND THE INSTITUTIONALIZATION OF EDUCATION

Studying patterns of early mass educational expansion, neoinstitutionalists were puzzled by the fact that "despite much variation in level of industrialization, class structure, and political regime, the ideological and organizational responses of the various countries to challenges to state power were strikingly similar" (Ramirez & Boli, 1987, p. 9). These responses included national declarations of interest in mass education, compulsory enrollment legislation, establishment of public education agencies (ministries or departments) and public supervision. In explaining this puzzle, the authors rely on the notion of myth to characterize the key constructs of modern societies: the individual, the national, progress, socialization, and the state, in other words "the secular procedure for constructing the individual" (Boli, Ramirez, & Meyer, 1985, p. 150), the rise of the nation-state, and the construction of a national society (Ramirez & Boli, 1987). As the result of long centuries of Reformation and Counter-Reformation, the expansion of capitalism and the institutionalization of the state and interstate systems, these myths came to constitute the institutionalized environment surrounding and shaping the then-emerging nation-state identity, at whose core had been education, gradually replacing the faithful subject with the loyal citizen (Meyer & Jepperson, 2000).

The consequences of the worldwide institutionalization of such a state identity based upon the spread of schooling and each further level of education are well-documented – and indeed we have all grown up in such "schooled societies" (Baker, 2014). Studies on enrollment in primary and secondary education find universal compulsory primary education legislation worldwide and (formal) enrollment for more than 90% of the world's children, at extraordinary speed, especially in peripheral countries (Meyer, Ramirez, & Soysal, 1992). Primary education is now treated as a human right (Article 26 of the Universal Declaration of Human Rights). Secondary education has seen even more rapid expansion in most countries around the world. What was once understood as "school leaving" is now understood as "dropout" or "pushout" and is everywhere considered a major social problem (Baker, 2014). Even children and youth with disabilities are classified as having "special educational needs," are integrated in regular schools, and increasingly participate in all forms of education, including higher education (Powell, 2016) with the human right to inclusive education codified in the Convention on the Rights of Persons with Disabilities that has been ratified by most countries worldwide.

For higher education and science systems, findings are similarly beyond dispute. Schofer and Meyer (2005) show strikingly rapid and global growth in tertiary enrollment for the time after WWII, when enrollment expands by factors of 10 and 20. Less developed countries in Africa or Asia now have higher enrollments than did core member countries of the Organization for Economic Co-Operation and Development (OECD) like Germany or the United Kingdom 30 years ago (Powell & Dusdal, 2017). This trend is reflected in and propelled by a number of legislative efforts in countries worldwide to ensure access to tertiary educational opportunities to various once-underprivileged groups, such as women, people with special (educational) needs, rural populations, ethnic minorities, and so on (Bradley & Ramirez, 1996). Hence, the notion of the "non-traditional student" that deviates from the prototypical male, white, able-bodied, upper class, full-time student who directly entered higher education from secondary school (Schuetze & Slowey, 2000) is quickly losing its analytical appeal in countries like South Korea where almost the entirety of a cohort is enrolled in and almost 70% graduates from a higher education institution (Kim & Choi, 2017). With regard to political organization, ministries of education have become a universal reality, as have science ministries (Ramirez & Ventresca, 1992), and professionalized (and often state-controlled) teacher training is advancing rapidly everywhere in the world, even in places where local realities are far from favorable (Meyer, 1998).

After WWII, national and international discourses around development had increasingly become dominated by an instrumental view of education and science, with a premium on the economic value of education (or human capital). In such an education and science for development policy model, educational expansion is understood as a national, systemically planned, realist, economically viable and utilitarian tool to foster progress (Drori et al., 2003). National policymakers, often supported by international organizations, regard educational and scientific activity as a guarantor of national development (Chabbott, 2003; Finnemore, 1993; Hwang, 2006).

Along with a massive worldwide educational expansion in general, one of the chief consequences of such an instrumental view of education might be found in higher education expansion, which helps explain the striking enrollment boosts mentioned above. Such a view might also contribute to understand the worldwide proliferation of the university as the standard organizational form of educational and scientific activity (Fig. 1).

Such striking expansion over since the 1960s has multiple causes. Worldwide nation-building efforts, particularly in former colonies, "massification" of HE systems, particularly in Western countries, are certainly key reasons for early expansion in the second half of the 20th century (Schofer & Meyer, 2005). The more recent boost, mainly spurred by a "global revolution" (Altbach & Levy, 2005) in the private sector, is triggered by much regime change and higher education *glasnost* in former USSR countries and many East Asian countries (Slantcheva & Levy, 2007). In other countries, the response to a perceived advent of the global knowledge economy as well as technological change was met with massive "higher-educationalization," as policy priority, social norm, and individual choice, for example in Korea (Kim & Choi, 2017) and Taiwan (Fu, 2017).

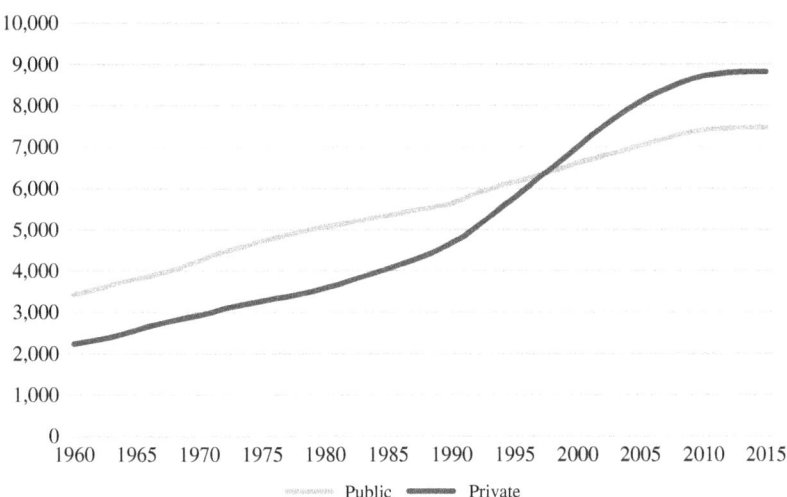

Fig. 1. Number of Higher Education Organizations Offering a First Terminal Degree Worldwide, 1960–2014. *Source*: Author's calculations of data from the World Higher Education Database (WHED).

THE NEW GLOBAL ENVIRONMENT OF HIGHER EDUCATION

Much of the expansion described in the previous section is supported by emerging global discourses and structures conducive of further higher education growth and integration. Here, I highlight some of these trends, from open borders and free markets to international organizations and systems of accountability, assessment, and research evaluation.

Open borders and *free markets* often go hand in hand and facilitate the mobility of students, faculty, and service providers. The most recent estimates available range from 2.8 to 3.2 million internationally mobile students worldwide, meaning an increase by more than 53% over the period 1999–2007 (OECD, 2011; United Nations Educationl, Scientific, and Cultural Organization, 2009). As student mobility increases, so do international branch campuses (IBCs) and international academic programs (Kosmützky & Putty, 2016). Within several years, the number of IBCs grew by 43% (Observatory on Borderless Higher Education, 2009; on Qatar, see Crist, 2017).

Further, frameworks and initiatives to facilitate *recognition* of vocational and HE qualifications have grown remarkably over the past two decades, now including almost 150 (sic) countries (European Centre for the Development of Vocational Training, CEDEFOP, 2013). Such work is often propelled by initiatives at the regional level where the overlapping European Qualifications Framework and the Bologna Process of higher education reorganization and standardization can be considered the most elaborate attempt (Powell, Bernhard, & Graf, 2012). Often neglected, however, is the fact that most regions in the world have started similar initiatives, with the first global convention on the recognition of HE qualifications has been drafted in March 2016 led by the United Nations Educational, Scientific, and Cultural Organization (UNESCO, 2016). Although General Agreement on Trade in Services (GATS) of the World Trade Organization (WTO) has stalled since 2008, the original framework foreshadows this global picture, while numerous bi- and multilateral treaties continuously spur the internationalization of education services (Altbach & Knight, 2016).

A *growing world polity* composed of ever denser and diverse networks of *international organizations* (IOs), intergovernmental and non-governmental alike, provide educational policymakers with benchmarks and best practices, along with goal-oriented and highly scientized reporting. In general, global educational discourses are now awash with much rationalized "good advice" on how to improve HE systems, with these organizations providing fora and nodes of diffusion for educational ideas (Chabbott, 2003; Jakobi, 2012; Zapp, 2017; Zapp & Dahmen, 2017). The first UNESCO-led global conference explicitly dedicated to higher education took place only in 1998, but the related Higher Education Network now regularly brings together over 100 IOs to discuss these issues (UNESCO, 2016). Every area in the world has now its own regional association of universities, which are, since 2000, represented on the Administrative Board of the International Association of Universities, UNESCO's organizational arm for HE.

Counting and *accounting* has forcefully reached HE systems worldwide. National and international ratings and ranking (e.g., German Center for Higher Education University Ranking; the pan-European "Multi-Rank," and the global Academic Ranking of World Universities, to name a few; see Hazekorn, 2011), research evaluations and performance-based funding (e.g., United Kingdom's Research Excellence Framework), national and cross-national HE teaching and learning assessments (e.g., US Collegiate Learning Assessment; OECD's Assessment of Higher Education Learning Outcomes (AHELO); the EU's Measuring and Comparing Achievements of Learning Outcomes in Higher Education in Europe) and the rise of an international quality assurance and accreditation sector are certainly phenomena increasingly germane, but certainly not unique to the HE field. Instead, they reflect the "metrological mood" (Power, 2004, p. 766) in the more recent period that has transformed organizations and a wide variety of social domains in general (Bowker & Star, 2000; Brunsson & Jacobson, 2003; Wiseman & Baker, 2005).

A NEW ROLE FOR THE STATE?

In such a transparent and permeable global higher education landscape, the state does not disappear as is sometimes feared. Indeed, it remains the "visible hand" (Baker, 2009) ensuring access through legislative decision-making, quality through accreditation, and infrastructure through resources. The paradox involved is that the strong isomorphism detected in many cross-national HE analyses may well be caused by environmental forces, yet the national level remains the primary transmission mechanism to translate and implement these external pressures.

One of the key findings in Buckner's (2016) work on national higher education discourses from 1960 to 2005 is that the first half of that period was marked by clear references to national development. Yet, there is an additional finding. In the second half of that period, a marked shift occurs toward a stronger emphasis on global competitiveness and the global knowledge economy, with states tending to view their role more as a regulatory agency.

The wider environment of HE organizations surely reflect national development and human capital investment, but also on human rights and human capabilities. Endowed with the quasi-sacred authority of science, case of education, and particularly HE, are perceived as highly viable tools (Drori et al., 2003). And, tellingly, in those rare cases where HE expansion stalls or even declines, authoritarian regimes were involved (Baker, Köehler, & Stock, 2007;

Lenhardt, 2002; Levy, 2013). Whenever nation-states facilitate access to HE, the expansion pathway is taken. In an ironical turn, perhaps, the emergence of the (neo)liberal evaluative or regulatory state (Neave, 1998; Scott, 1998) could mean restoring the original universality and autonomy of the university *vis-à-vis* the state found to be characteristic of the pre-Westphalian order (Riddle, 1996).

The analysis presented here contributes complementary insights into the relationship between the state and HE by (1) focusing on a more recent period (post-WWII), marked by dramatic HE expansion in terms of enrollments; (2) including particular fields of study, namely the group of STEM disciplines that are often considered the academic core of the science for development model, now even more so than at the beginning of nation-building, when humanities were dominant and before the rise of the social sciences (Frank & Gabler, 2006). A telling indicator of the current importance attached to STEM can be found in national education reports submitted to UNESCO World Conferences (UNESCO IBE, 2016). A key word search of national reports from the more recent period (since 2000) shows that *all* countries worldwide explicitly refer to STEM subjects as of paramount importance in fostering progress.

EXPANSION TRENDS IN CROSS-NATIONAL PERSPECTIVE

Looking at the main indicators of research and development (R&D) and science infrastructure, we find common longitudinal expansive trends although at different scales. Gross domestic expenditures on R&D (GERD) or "research intensity" for the five countries, for which data is available, show clear upward trends for the past two decades (Fig. 2). Although still below the four OECD countries, China has made the largest leap in the period 1996–2014 by tripling its GERD to 2%. South Korea leads the group with 4% or more than double the rate in 1996. Germany, Japan, and the United States show only gradual development with growth rates between 0.2% (US) and 0.8% (Japan).

R&D expenditures are not necessarily channeled toward HE systems because much research is done outside of universities in government research centers and publicly financed private research organizations (Fernandez & Baker, 2017; Powell & Dusdal, 2017). A more accurate indicator is higher education R&D expenditure (HERD). Here, the different shares change considerably. Although South Korea again shows the strongest increase, now matching the United States at roughly 0.4%, Germany and Japan have the largest share of their GDP invested in their intramural research systems. China, in turn, remains even further below in the group than for the GERD measure (Fig. 3).

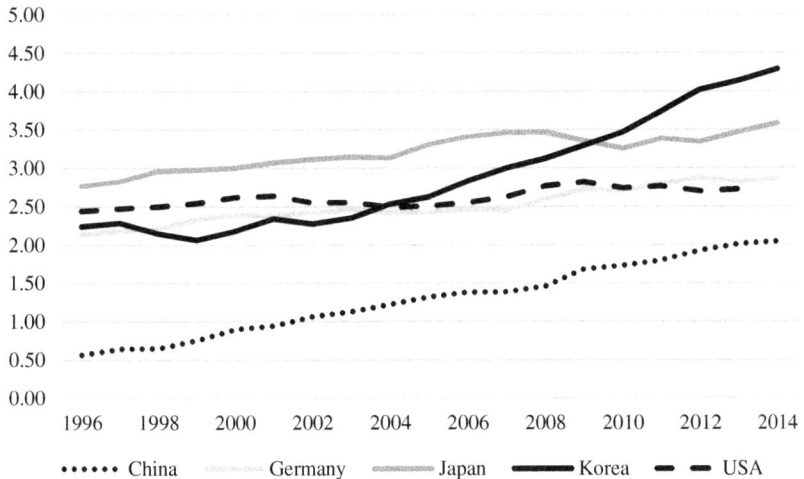

Fig. 2. Research Intensity (GERD as Percentage of GDP), Select Countries, 1996–2014. *Source*: Author's calculations of data from UNESCO (2016) and OECD (2016).

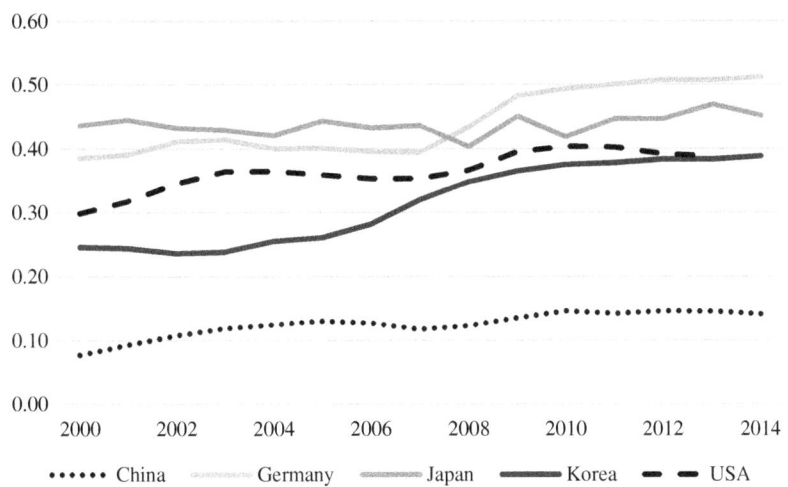

Fig. 3. Higher Education R&D Expenditure as Percentage of GDP, Select Countries, 1996–2014. *Source*: Author's calculations of data from OECD (2016).

Turning to the HE systems in more detail, Fig. 4 shows the total number of higher education organizations (HEOs) since 1945.[1] All countries show strong expansive trends in the post-WWII era, especially in countries where the HE system was limited prior to that period (China, Taiwan, South Korea). The

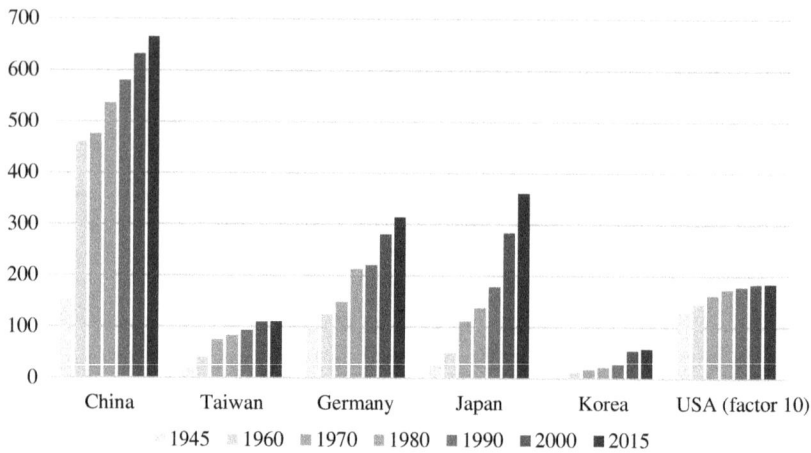

Fig. 4. Number of Universities, Select Countries, 1945–2015. *Source*: Author's calculations of data from the World Higher Education Database (WHED).

Table 1. Higher Education Institutions, General and STEM by Country and Type.

	Total Number of HEOs	Total Number of HEOs with STEM	STEM HEI Share of Total in %	Public/Private Ratio STEM HEOs[a]
China	886	788	90	12:1
Taiwan	148	136	92	1:2
Germany	333	233	70	5:1
Japan	749	37	50	1:2
Qatar[b]	1	1	100	1:0
South Korea	186	162	87	1:3
United States	1,993	1,651	83	1:4

Source: Author's calculations of data from the World Higher Education Database (WHED).
[a]Public and private are defined as a legal category in the IAU WHED.
[b]Only the national Qatar University is counted here since the IBCs of Education City are counted as part of their home campus (for more detailed information, see Crist, 2017).

United States has, by far, the largest number of universities, in fact with more than 1,800 HEOs, it exceeds the other countries combined. Interestingly, while the "massification" of HE in the 1960s is well documented, the numbers suggest a similarly strong surge in the more recent period with some countries like South Korea almost doubling their count. For the later period, growth has mostly resulted through expansion in the private HE sector (Table 1).

Higher education systems are the natural habitat of researchers, one could argue. In this sense, growing R&D investments and numbers of HEOs should be reflected in a rise of the number of researchers. Yet, other than the case of South Korea, where the number of researchers has almost tripled in the period 2000−2014, the trend is, while upward, not striking. Germany has seen an increase by 2%, while all other countries remain below that mark (Fig. 5).

Focusing on the position of STEM fields within the overall HE landscape, we can see that older HE systems such as those in Germany and Japan seem to display stronger academic diversity with only half or three-quarters of the HEOs having STEM departments. Systems that developed more recently are indeed more "STEM-heavy" with almost all HEOs having a STEM department (range 87−92%), according to the World Higher Education Database. Differences in the inter-sectoral distribution of these HEOs are striking. Private STEM HEOs outnumber public ones in all countries, except communist China, monarchist Qatar, and industrial pioneer Germany. The share of private HEOs is particularly large in the United States and the Republic of Korea, where every public HEOs is outmatched by 3−4 private ones.

Pairing data on organizational composition of the HE field with student data, we find considerable cross-national differences. Graduation ratios are much higher in OECD countries, with Germany having a traditionally lower ratio due to strong vocational education and training sector, although this has been rising due to challenged institutional barriers to higher education expansion (Powell & Solga, 2011). Gross enrollment ratio (GER) for STEM is highest in South Korea, Qatar, and Germany. Although HE expansion, both

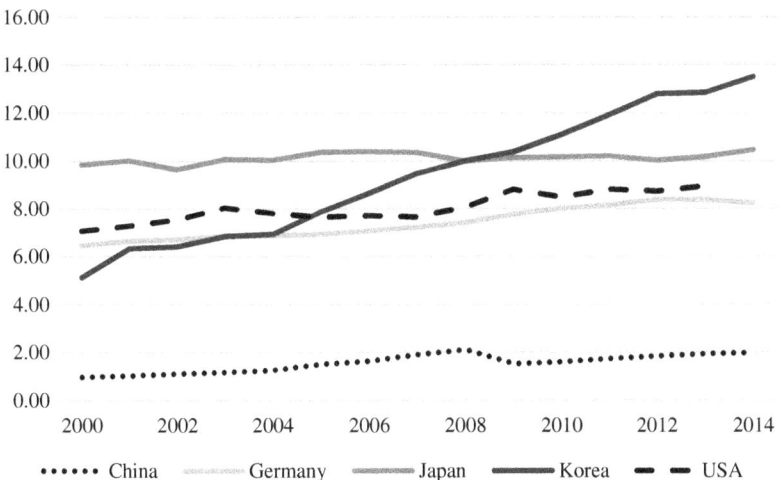

Fig. 5. Researchers per 1,000 Total Employment, Select Countries, 2000−2014. *Source*: Author's calculations of data from OECD (2016).

organizationally and in terms of student enrollments, occurs in all countries with similar momentum (Figs. 4 and 6), countries display varying student/HEO ratios. On average, German and American STEM HEOs receive between 327 and 339 STEM students, while South Korean universities host 5,255 students in STEM fields. This largely reflects the general HEO/student ratio, except for Japan improving and the USA scaling up their ratios (Table 2).

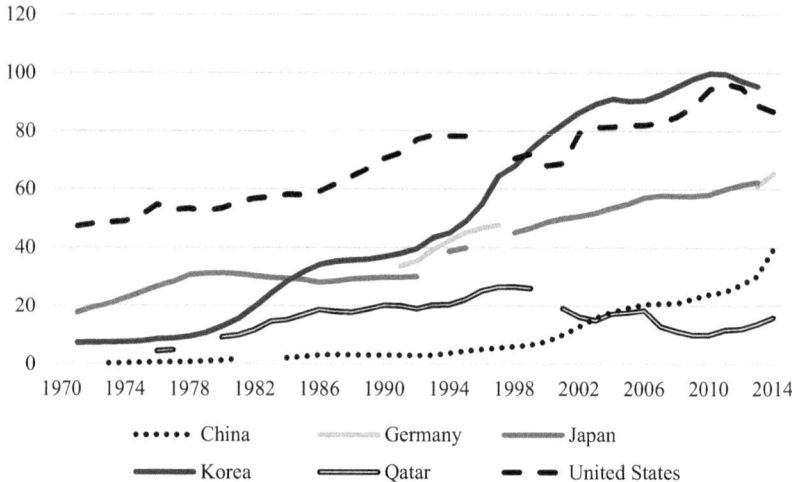

Fig. 6. Gross Enrollment Ratio, Tertiary, Both Sexes (%), Select Countries. *Source*: UNESCO UIS.

Table 2. Student Enrollment and Graduation Ratio, General and STEM, Select Countries.

Country (Year)	Graduates from Tertiary Education, Total (Gross Graduation Ratio, %)	Total Number of STEM Students and GER in STEM	STEM HEO/ STEM Student Ratio	HEO/ Overall Student Ratio
China (2013)	9,366,202 (17.3)	–	–	1:10,571
Germany (2002; 2013)	293,920 (32)	76.419 (26.1)	1:327	1:882
Japan (2014)	977,214 (44.1)	194,465 (19.9)	1:5,255	1:1,304
Qatar (2014)	2,569 (3.4)	706 (27.5)	1:706	1:2,569
South Korea (2012)	618,281 (48.4)	196,613 (31.8)	1:1,213	1:3,324
United States (2012)	3,784,640 (40.1)	560,126 (14.8)	1:339	1:1,898

Source: Author's calculations of data from UNESCO Institute for Statistics and U.S. Census Bureau.
Note: Data for Taiwan is not available. For Germany, data on graduates from 2002, on GER from 2013.

"ELEVATOR EFFECT" OR CONVERGENCE IN HIGHER EDUCATION EXPANSION?

Two contrasting ways of interpreting the shown cross-national developments in HE include the "elevator effect," in which all countries move up one floor, with each country improving its situation in absolute numbers, yet not in relation to each other. This requires that the unit of measurement is infinite. Obviously, this does not apply to the HE indicators presented here. Neither investments as a percentage of GDP nor HE enrollments do not represent infinite values as they are politically contested and demographically ceiled. In contrast, what we observe among this sample of expanded HE systems and strong STEM science producers is likely to resemble a gradual convergence of educational enrollment, occupational structure and social differentiation, with forerunners stagnating, but with latecomers catching up. South Korea is the most telling example, now championing in GERD, enrollment, number of researchers, and publications outstripping the other sampled countries (Kim & Choi, 2017). At a lower relative but much higher absolute level, China shows similar ambitions. Although HE expansion has not yet translated into rising numbers of researchers per capita, student enrollment is clearly on the rise signaling a historic turning point in education policy (Zhang, Sun, & Bao, 2017).

For the countries analyzed here, HE expansion occurs most strongly in times of political change. Qatar founded its only university one year after gaining independence (1971–1972). South Korea founded more than 27 universities in the years 1946–1948, almost as many as in the entire preceding history of the country combined. Together with the 23 foundings in the 1950s, public and private alike, this period represents the most expansive decade for South Korean HE. Similar trends can also be found for Japan, Germany, and Taiwan, with high leaps in university numbers in the immediate aftermath of WWII, although the two Asian countries display greater numbers for private HEOs with STEM departments. The two most dissimilar cases are China and the United States. The latter is the only country in the sample that has always had a stronger private STEM HEO share, with steep and steady growth throughout the second half of the 19th and the entire 20th century. Public universities have lost their momentum in the 1990s due also to state funding retrenchment and demographic trends. For China, there were virtually no private STEM HEOs (or HEOs in general) before the 1980s due to the Cultural Revolution. In the period after 1979, however, more than 35 private STEM universities were opened (Zhang et al., 2017).

CONCLUSION

Considering the catching up by HE "late comers" and the more modest growth in the more established HE systems, all countries show similar expansive trends for enrollments, organizational foundings, investments and, as shown in the following chapters in this volume, their scientific production. Such isomorphic expansion provides forceful evidence for the effects of higher education as an institution, to cite John Meyer's (1977) seminal contribution. In this sense, HE provides authoritative legitimacy for the "national project" based on education. Considering these wider macrosocial structures, it seems to matter little if science is mainly a national development tool or the baton in an inter-state or inter-organizational competition or if STEM expansion occurs through private or public HE. In both cases, the "externalist" perspective, to borrow from the sociology of science, outweighs the internalist perspective (Elzinga, 1984). If science is considered a necessary condition for individual and social development as is the case in the modern period marked by a belief in human capital and capabilities, opportunities to expand scientific production loom large in virtually all domains of social life (Zhang, Powell, & Baker, 2015).

Future research might trace the more large-scale trends presented in this and the other chapters in the volume at the micro-level. Here, institutional effects increasingly translate into the expansive professionalization of the researcher within a growing labor market segment in which PhD-trained scientists may work full time in often temporally determined, project-based contexts (Sahlin-Andersson & Söderholm, 2002). Here, publications as a form of legitimated knowledge and institutionalized cultural capital become a novel criterion of status allocation in the schooled society (Baker, 2014).

NOTE

1. Missing data on founding dates in the International Association of Universities' WHED lowers the numbers for HEOs in all countries (except the United States), especially Japan and South Korea by 10–30% (see Table 1 for total numbers).

REFERENCES

Altbach, P., & Knight, J. (2016). The internationalization of higher education: Motivations and realities. In P. Altbach (Ed.), *Global perspectives on higher education* (pp. 105–121). Baltimore, MD: John Hopkins University Press.

Altbach, P., & Levy, D. (2005). *Private higher education: A global revolution*. Rotterdam: Sense.

Baker, D. P. (2009). The invisible hand of world education culture: Thoughts for policy makers. In G. Sykes, B. Schneider, & D. Plank (Eds.), *American education research association's handbook of education policy research* (pp. 958–968). Washington, DC: AERA.

Baker, D. P. (2014). *The schooled society: The educational transformation of global culture*. Stanford, CA: Stanford University Press.

Baker, D. P., Koehler, H., & Stock, M. (2007). Socialist ideology and the contraction of higher education: Institutional consequences of state manpower and education planning in the former East Germany, 1949 to 1989. *Comparative Education Review*, *51*(3), 353–377.

Boli, J., Ramirez, F. O., & Meyer, J. W. (1985). Explaining the origins and expansion of mass education. *Comparative Education Review*, *29*(2), 145−170.

Bowker, G. C., & Star, S. L. (2000). *Sorting things out: Classification and its consequences.* Cambridge, MA: MIT Press.

Bradley, K., & Ramirez, F. (1996). World polity and gender parity: Woman's share of higher education, 1965-1985. *Research in Sociology of Education and Socialization*, *11*(1), 63−91.

Brunsson, N., & Jacobson, B. (Eds.). (2003). *A world of standards.* Oxford: Oxford University Press.

Buckner, E. S. (2016). The changing discourse on higher education and the nation-state, 1960–2010. *Higher Education*, 1–17.

Chabbott, C. (2003). *Constructing education for development: Education for all.* New York, NY: Routledge.

Crist, J. T. (2017). "A Fever of Research": Scientific Journal Article Production and the Emergence of a National Research System in Qatar, 1980−2011. In J. J. W. Powell, D. P. Baker, & F. Fernandez (Eds.), *The century of science: The worldwide triumph of the research university* (Vol. 33). International Perspectives on Education and Society. Bingley: Emerald Publishing Limited.

Drori, G. S., Meyer, J. W., Ramirez, F. O., & Schofer, E. (2003). *Science in the modern world polity: Institutionalization and globalization.* Stanford, CA: Stanford University Press.

Elzinga, A. (1984). The growth of science: Romantic and technocratic images. In *Essays on scientism, romanticism and social realist images of science* (Report No. 143) (pp. 51−90). Göteborg: Göteborg University, Institutionen for Vetenskapsteori.

European Centre for the Development of Vocational Training (CEDEFOP). (2013). *Global national qualifications framework inventory* (Resource document). Retrieved from http://www.cedefop.europa.eu/de/publications-and-resources/publications/2211

Fernandez, F., & Baker, D. P. (2017). Science production in the United States: An unexpected synergy between mass higher education and the super research university. In J. J. W. Powell, D. P. Baker, & F. Fernandez (Eds.), *The century of science: The worldwide triumph of the research university* (Vol. 33). International Perspectives on Education and Society. Bingley: Emerald Publishing Limited.

Finnemore, M. (1993). International organizations as teachers of norms: The United Nations educational, scientific, and cultural organization and science policy. *International Organization*, *47*(4), 565−597.

Frank, D. J., & Gabler, J. (2006). *Reconstructing the university: Worldwide shifts in academia in the 20th Century.* Stanford, CA: Stanford University Press.

Fu, Y. C. (2017). Science production in Taiwanese universities, 1980−2011. In J. J. W. Powell, D. P. Baker, & F. Fernandez (Eds.), *The century of science: The worldwide triumph of the research university* (Vol. 33). International Perspectives on Education and Society. Bingley: Emerald Publishing Limited.

Hazekorn, E. (2011). *Rankings and the reshaping of higher education: The battle for world-class excellence.* London: Palgrave Macmillan.

Hwang, H. (2006). Planning development: Globalization and the shifting locus of planning. In G. S. Drori, J. W. Meyer, & H. Hwang (Eds.), *Globalization and organization: World society and organizational change* (pp. 69−89). Oxford: Oxford University Press.

Jakobi, A. P. (2012). Facilitating transfer: International organizations as central nodes for policy diffusion. In G. Steiner-Khamsi & F. Waldow (Eds.), *World yearbook of education: Policy borrowing and lending* (pp. 391−407). London: Routledge.

Kim, H., & Choi, J. (2017). The growth of higher education and science production in South Korea since 1945. In J. J. W. Powell, D. P. Baker, & F. Fernandez (Eds.), *The century of science: The worldwide triumph of the research university* (Vol. 33). International Perspectives on Education and Society. Bingley: Emerald Publishing Limited.

Kosmützky, A., & Putty, R. (2016). Transcending borders and traversing boundaries: A systematic review of the literature on transnational, offshore, cross-border, and borderless higher education. *Journal of Studies in International Education*, *20*(1), 8−33.

Lenhardt, G. (2002). Europe and higher education between universalisation and materialist particularism. *European Educational Research Journal*, *1*(2), 274–289.
Levy, D. (2013). The decline of private higher education. *Higher Education Policy*, *26*(1), 25–42.
Meyer, J. W. (1977). The effects of education as an institution. *American Journal of Sociology*, *83*(1), 55–77.
Meyer, J. W. (1998). Training and certifying unqualified teachers in Namibia. In W. Snyder & F. Voights (Eds.), *Inside reform policy and programming considerations in Namibia's basic education reform*. Windhoek: Gamsberg Macmillan.
Meyer, J. W., & Jepperson, R. L. (2000). The 'actors' of modern society: The cultural construction of social agency. *Sociological Theory*, *18*(1), 100–120.
Meyer, J. W., Ramirez, F. O., & Soysal, Y. (1992). World expansion of mass education, 1870-1970. *Sociology of Education*, *65*(2), 128–149.
Neave, G. (1998). The evaluative state reconsidered. *European Journal of Education*, *33*(3), 265–284.
OECD. (2016). Online education database. Retrieved from http://www.oecd.org/education/database.htm. Accessed on April 5, 2017.
Organization for Economic Co-operation and Development. (2011). *Education at a glance, 2011*. Paris: Author.
Powell, J. J. W. (2016). *Barriers to inclusion: Special education in the United States and Germany*. London: Routledge.
Powell, J. J. W., Bernhard, N., & Graf, L. (2012). The emergent European model in skill formation: Comparing higher education and vocational training in the Bologna and Copenhagen processes. *Sociology of Education*, *85*(3), 240–258.
Powell, J. J. W., & Dusdal, J. (2017). The European Center of Science Productivity: Research Universities and Institutes in France, Germany, and the United Kingdom. In J. J. W. Powell, D. P. Baker, & F. Fernandez (Eds.), *The century of science: The worldwide triumph of the research university* (Vol. 33). International Perspectives on Education and Society. Bingley: Emerald Publishing Limited.
Powell, J. J. W., & Solga, H. (2011). Why are higher education participation rates in Germany so low? Institutional barriers to higher education expansion. *Journal of Education and Work*, *24*(1), 49–68.
Power, M. (2004). Counting, control and calculation: Reflections on measuring and management. *Human Relations*, *57*(6), 765–783.
Ramirez, F. O., & Boli, J. (1987). The political construction of mass schooling: European origins and worldwide institutionalization. *Sociology of Education*, *60*(1), 2–17.
Ramirez, F. O., Luo, X., Schofer, E., & Meyer, J. W. (2006). Student achievement and national economic growth. *American Journal of Education*, *113*(1), 1–29.
Ramirez, R., & Ventresca, M. (1992). Building the institution of mass schooling: Isomorphism in the modern world. In B. Fuller & R. Rubinson (Eds.), *The political construction of education* (pp. 47–60). New York, NY: Praeger.
Riddle, P. (1996). The university and political authority: Historical trends and contemporary possibilities. *Research in Sociology of Education and Socialization*, *11*, 43–62.
Sahlin-Andersson, K., & Söderholm, A. (2002). *Beyond project management: New perspectives on the temporary-permanent dilemma*. Mälmo: Liber Ekonomi.
Schofer, E., & Meyer, J. W. (2005). The worldwide expansion of higher education in the twentieth century. *American Sociological Review*, *70*(6), 898–920.
Schuetze, H. G., & Slowey, M. (2000). Traditions and new directions in higher education: A comparative perspective on non-traditional students and lifelong learners. In H. G. Schutze & M. Slowey (Eds.), *Higher education and lifelong learners: International perspectives on change* (pp. 3–24). London: Routledge.
Scott, P. (Ed.). (1998). *The globalization of higher education*. Buckingham: Society for Research into Higher Education and Open University Press.
Slantcheva, S., & Levy, D. (Eds.). (2007). *Private higher education in post-communist Europe: In search of legitimacy*. New York, NY: Palgrave Macmillan.

Stinchcombe, A. L. (1965). Social structure and organizations. In J. G. March (Ed.), *Handbook of organizations* (pp. 142–193). Chicago, IL: Rand McNally.

UNESCO. (2016). *UNESCO Institute of Statistics*. Higher Education. Retrieved from http://uis.unesco.org/en/topic/higher-education. Accessed on April 5, 2017.

United Nations Educational, Scientific and Cultural Organization. (2009). *Global Education Digest, 2009: Comparing education statistics across the world*. Retrieved from http://unesdoc.unesco.org/images/0018/001832/183249e.pdf

United Nations Educational, Scientific and Cultural Organization. (2016). *Global convention on the recognition of higher education qualifications project*. Retrieved from http://www.unesco.org/new/en/education/themes/strengthening-education-systems/higher-education/recognition/global-convention-on-the-recognition-of-higher-education-qualification-project/

United Nations Educational, Scientific and Cultural Organization, International Bureau of Education. (2016). *National reports on the development of education submitted by countries since 1933*. Retrieved from http://www.ibe.unesco.org/en/ibedocs/national-reports

Wiseman, A. W., & Baker, D. P. (Eds.). (2005). Global trends in education policy. *International Perspectives on Education and Society Series*, 6.

Zapp, M. (2017). The World Bank and education: Governing (through) knowledge. *International Journal of Educational Development, 53*, 1–11.

Zapp, M., & Dahmen, C. (2017). The diffusion of educational ideas – An event history analysis of lifelong learning, 1990-2015. *Comparative Education Review, 61*(3).

Zhang, L., Powell, J. J. W., & Baker, D. P. (2015). Exponential growth and the shifting global center of gravity of science production, 1900–2011. *Change: The Magazine of Higher Learning, 47*(4), 46–49, doi:10.1080/00091383.2015.1053777

Zhang, L., Sun, L., & Bao, W. (2017). The rise of higher education and science in China. In J. J. W. Powell, D. P. Baker, & F. Fernandez (Eds.), *The century of science: The worldwide triumph of the research university* (Vol. 33). International Perspectives on Education and Society. Bingley: Emerald Publishing Limited.

THE EUROPEAN CENTER OF SCIENCE PRODUCTIVITY: RESEARCH UNIVERSITIES AND INSTITUTES IN FRANCE, GERMANY, AND THE UNITED KINGDOM

Justin J. W. Powell and Jennifer Dusdal

ABSTRACT

Purpose — *Growth in scientific production and productivity over the 20th century resulted significantly from three major countries in European science — France, Germany, and the United Kingdom. Charting the development of universities and research institutes that bolster Europe's key position in global science, we uncover both stable and dynamic patterns of productivity in the fields of STEM, including health, over the 20th century. Ongoing internationalization of higher education and science has been accompanied by increasing competition and collaboration. Despite policy goals to foster innovation and expand research capacity, policies cannot fully account for the differential growth of scientific productivity we chart from 1975 to 2010.*

Approach and Research Design — *Our sociological neo-institutional framework facilitates explanation of differences in institutional settings, organizational forms, and organizations that produce the most European* research. We measure growth of published peer-reviewed articles indexed in Thomson Reuters' Science Citation Index Expanded (SCIE).

Findings — *Organizational forms vary in their contributions, with universities accounting for nearly half but rising in France; ultrastable in Germany at four-fifths, and growing at around two-thirds in the United Kingdom. Differing institutionalization pathways created the conditions necessary for continuous, but varying growth in scientific production and productivity in the European center of global science. The research university is key in all three countries, and we identify organizations leading in research output.*

Originality/value — *Few studies explicitly compare across time, space, and different levels of analysis. We show how important European science has been to overall global science production and productivity. In-depth comparisons, especially the organizational fields and forms in which science is produced, are crucial if policy is to support research and development.*

Keywords: Scientific productivity; university; research institute; France; Germany; United Kingdom

THE ORGANIZATION(S) OF SCIENTIFIC PRODUCTIVITY

Charting huge growth in scientific productivity over the 20th century in three European countries, we analyze the development and contemporary state of research universities and institutes that bolster Europe's position as a key region in global science. Ongoing internationalization (and Europeanization) of higher education (HE) and science challenges traditional nation-based studies. In response, neo-institutional analyses have explored the powerful diffusion of worldwide ideas and norms in science (Drori, Meyer, Ramirez, & Schofer, 2003). This framework emphasizes global similarities, with (HE) expanding worldwide (Meyer, 2009) and the development of the "super research university" a powerful contributor to the "schooled society" (Baker, 2014). Despite convergence pressures due to internationalization, comparative institutional analyses show persistent differences in higher education (HE) systems as well as the diffusion of a distinctly European model in skill formation (Bernhard, 2017; Graf, 2013; Powell, Bernhard, & Graf, 2012; Powell & Solga, 2010).

Our sample of three key countries reflects the history and development of the research university as well as independent research institutes as they host the most prestigious and productive science organizations worldwide. Historically, France, Germany, and the United Kingdom (UK) have led in organizational developments and scientific innovation. These countries differ in languages and cultures and in the resources devoted to education and science. In an era of internationalization, massive growth in the scientific output of these countries and globally simultaneously reflects competition and collaboration (Zhang, Powell, & Baker, 2015). Charting the last four decades since 1975, our comparison uncovers sustained and increasing scientific productivity in these three countries but variable institutionalization of HE and science systems, and contrasting investments in research and development (R&D).

Measured in papers published in leading peer-reviewed journals of the Science Citation Index Expanded (SCIE), the volume of scientific output differs, sometimes unexpectedly, according to institutionalized structures of HE and research. For example, the relative importance of universities, research institutes, and firms differs across the analyzed cases. The overall scientific output in science and technology disciplines, including health, increased dramatically over the 20th century, with Europe losing, but regaining its position as one of the global "center(s) of gravity" after WWII (Zhang et al., 2015). Together, these countries contribute considerably to global scientific production as their scientists publish a vast number of scientific papers. While all invest considerably in education and science at all levels, as measured in absolute terms and per capita (OECD, 2016), we find important differences in science production and productivity, especially over the post-WWII period. On the basis of comprehensive historical data of science, technology, engineering, mathematics disciplines, and health – thus, we note this dataset as representing STEM+ – we measure the volume of science produced, tracing in particular the development of research universities and research institutes, the two major organizational forms that host scientists producing peer-reviewed publications in specialized scientific journals.

The selected countries differ in research policies, HE and science systems, and internationalization. They manifest extensive collaboration and competition since the earliest academies and universities. Among all science-producing organizational forms, how much do universities and non-universities, for example, extra-university research institutes, government agencies, or companies, proportionately, contribute to scientific productivity? How do these countries, with varying institutionalization of universities, compare in their production of STEM+ research?

To address these questions, we proceed as follows: We first chart the historical evolution of different organizational forms in European science, from the first academies to universities and research institutes. Placed within global trends in science production, these strong producers have maintained their position at the core of the European center of science – and globally, despite the quantitative dominance of the United States and China (Fernandez & Baker, 2017; Zhang, Sun, & Bao, 2017). Reviewing our historical and quantitative data and methods, we present findings on developing research-producing structures and scientific productivity in France, Germany, and the UK, differentiating by organizational form where possible. Finally, we compare across countries to better understand institutionalized systems of HE and research largely responsible for scientific productivity, and we conclude by identifying further steps for comparative research.

EUROPE: A CENTER OF GLOBAL SCIENTIFIC PRODUCTIVITY

Higher education and research, transmitting and producing knowledge in the *lingua franca* of the day, are thoroughly worldwide activities. Along with changes in the "center" of science — France around 1800, Germany from 1840, and the United Kingdom and the United States since WWI (Ben-David, 1984) — the language of science shifted from French to German to English, leading to the current dominance of journals publishing contributions in the English language. The case selection portrays the shifting significance of these three official languages as it does the legacy of earlier eras of scientific communication. Today, English everywhere provides a (necessary) common communication platform, especially in STEM+ disciplines and multidisciplinary fields.

Analyzing millions of original articles published since 1900 manifests unprecedented growth in the global pursuit of science, beginning just after mid-century and built upon contrasting concurrent trends — rising competition between and international collaboration across national borders (Zhang et al., 2015). Home to many of the oldest research universities and other organizational forms, such as academies and research institutes, Europe is at the heart of scientific productivity between North America and East Asia (on Russia and China, see Oleksiyenko, 2014). Universities and extra-university research institutes provide spaces and support for intercultural collaboration and learning and for scientific discovery, extending the massive educational expansion in societies worldwide (Schofer & Meyer, 2005), as countries capitalize on the myriad benefits that research universities bring (Baker, 2014). The earliest organizations with continuous scientific activity, such as academies, universities, and hospitals, have been joined not only by science-based companies, but also by a variety of government agencies, associations, laboratories, the military, among others (Dusdal, 2017). While originally science was dominated by Church and State, scholars and scientific organizations have gradually gained considerable independence to pursue the questions science itself defines as relevant. If the early social forms of science have been rarely studied, the successful institutionalization of science in England and France can be understood as based on "scientific movements oriented to political and social reform. For these movements, science was a model for attaining progress, objectivity, and consensus in general" (Ben-David & Sullivan, 1975, p. 205).

Today, all countries invest in HE and research and development (R&D), part of the mega-trend of scientization embedded within the ongoing rationalization of diverse spheres of life (Bromley & Meyer, 2015). France, Germany, and the UK maintain differentiated systems of universities that vary in size and prestige, yet all three host some of the strongest knowledge-producing organizations in the world. Whereas France and Germany have significant extra-university research institutes, connected in large umbrella associations or coordinated by government agencies, the UK relies most heavily on its internationalized research universities (Graf, 2009). The establishment and maintenance of research universities requires considerable investment: "The most consequential scientific revolutions of our time could not have happened in universities without massive government and/or corporate support" (Kennedy, 2015, p. 314), whether medical breakthroughs such as treatments for life-threatening illnesses or knowledge transmission infrastructures like the Internet.

Alongside the key indicator for the quantitative measurement of science (publications), institutional, personnel, or financial indicators likewise facilitate estimates of scientific growth and development. Rising science production demands commensurate resources (Weingart, 2001/2015), regardless of the actual, difficult-to-measure impact of any individual scientific article. While research on the relationship between R&D funding and demonstrated knowledge production is limited, studies confirm the general positive relationship between research funding and publication output (see Rosenbloom, Ginter, Juhl, & Heppert, 2014 on chemistry). Increasingly, research evaluation systems and competitive funding mechanisms determine the flows of resources. The UK, for example, distributes public funds for research on the basis of extensive peer review in the "Research Excellence Framework," that many other countries seek to emulate.

First, we examine the inputs of these top science-producing countries, namely the "research intensity" measured as the gross domestic expenditures on R&D (GERD) as a proportion of GDP. This indicator across the countries shows considerable variance. In 2014, the OECD mean was 2.38% while the EU-15 mean was 2.09%. The UK, with rising absolute investments in R&D, reached only 1.70% GERD in 2014. France has been relatively stable above 2% since 2000 (2.26% in 2014), whereas Germany has increased its science investments to nearly 2.90%. Thus, none have fully reached the EU target of 3% to be invested in innovation − and these countries' investments vary by a factor of almost two (Fig. 1).

While competition amongst the strongest science countries has risen in an age of self-proclaimed excellence, comparative indicators, and research evaluation systems, collaboration has also grown dramatically across cultures and countries (Zhang et al., 2015). Our selection of countries reflects HE and science systems with differently institutionalized structures, enabling us to

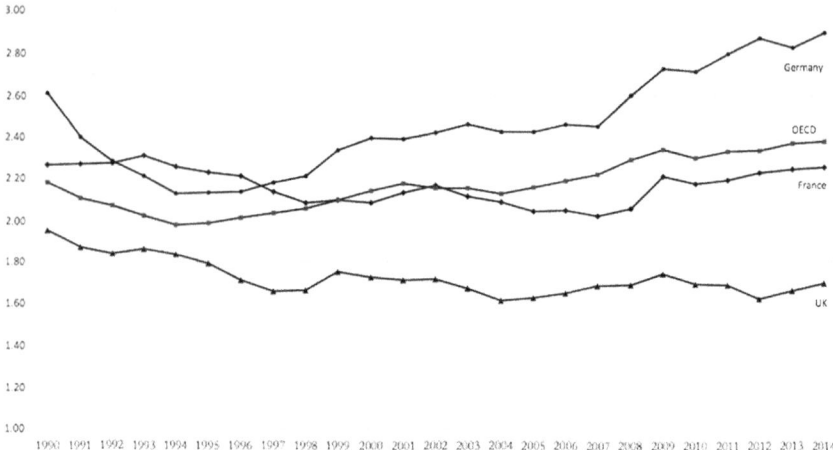

Fig. 1. Research Intensity in France, Germany, the United Kingdom, and OECD Average. GERD (as a proportion of GDP), 1990−2014. *Source*: OECD.stat. (2016): Main Science and Technology Indicators.

examine and compare, in the aggregate, those institutional setting(s) that provide favorable conditions for scientific productivity.

The institutional settings and organizational forms in which research is conducted affect overall capacity and scientific productivity. Establishing new organizations involves high costs and myriad challenges, with countries making challenging choices about which types of HE and research organizations will be most productive. State investment in science is often divided between universities and extra-university research institutes that have varying emphases (fundamental to applied) and with differing degrees of academic freedom. Research universities and institutes alike struggle to develop their reputations, which often requires generations of scholarship and exchange. Yet while research institutes may focus mainly on immediate scientific output, universities must balance research and teaching, the unity of which remains the foundational principle of the modern research university (Ash, 1999).

Universities receive around or less than a quarter of all R&D funds: only 18% in Germany, 21% in France, and 26% in the UK of the overall expenditures in R&D went to the HE sector (OECD.stat., 2016).[1] We might expect universities to produce proportionally more given their unique constellation of senior and junior academics across the disciplines. Alternatively, we might expect that research institutes selecting specialists in cutting-edge fields and devoted solely to research output will be more productive. This group of countries enables us to compare systems with varying constellations of science-producing organizational forms within diverse organizational fields — and varying importance of research universities within them.

While universities of all kinds experience "academic drift" and have many scientists intrinsically motivated to conduct research, universities in many countries are challenged by the lack of resources as many states retrench their commitments to public HE. This lack of support occurs even as the costs of tertiary education continuously rise (OECD, 2011). Increasing science budgets across Europe have, when calculated as a proportion of GDP, not kept pace with the rhetoric extolling the benefits of science and innovation (OECD, 2014). The rationale and vision shared by many governments of how to build capacity for science rests on the notion that infrastructure for research cannot be provided only by industry; that the state must invest in the so-called "knowledge triangle" — the beneficial combination of research activity, specialized education/training, and innovation that advances knowledge (European Commission, 2010, p. 3). Predictably, however, despite the state investments, HE and science systems and the resultant scientific productivity vary considerably across countries given long-term institutionalization (and intergenerational exchange) needed to build successful environments conducive to scientific discovery.

In Europe as elsewhere, the supranational dimension is becoming more influential, exemplified in intergovernmental processes leading to standardization in HE (Bologna process) and in such increasingly influential government initiatives (e.g., Horizon 2020, the EU's framework program for science) and organizations (European Research Council) that fund European science on the frontier (Hoenig, 2017). While the UK has been globally successful far beyond its size, with a well-rounded and impactful research base, and was the most successful host country for scientists in receiving European funding, the "Brexit" vote in June 2016 to rescind membership in the European Union has already done damage to the standing of UK universities and research collaborations (de Freytas-Tamura, 2016). France and Germany, as two of the largest HE and science systems in Europe, show how important national state funding is in providing the necessary infrastructure for science production. Focusing on countries in the European center of science production, we compare growth over time in their HE and research systems and the resulting scientific productivity. We analyze the institutionalization of their systems — following different models and compositions of organizational forms and fields structured over centuries — and research policies, especially their investments in R&D.

Methodologically, we measure science production on the basis of data purchased from Thomson Reuters (Web of Science), which we supplemented through extensive archival research and recoding (see introduction to this volume). The database consists of a stratified representative sample of published papers in selected science and technology disciplines, including health (STEM+) from 1900 to 1970 and a complete database of all papers through 2010, although we focus on the most recent period of expansion from 1975 to 2010 here. The increasing role of conference proceedings in STEM+ disciplines with high growth rates (e.g., computer sciences and engineering) is only partially reflected in the SCIE database. Nevertheless, peer-reviewed journal articles are the most important and traditional type of publications in these fields, next to patents — the growth rate of scientific publications is still increasing overall, with disciplinary differences (Olesen Larsen & von Ins, 2010). By including health-related disciplines, this dataset inflates somewhat the productivity of universities with academic teaching hospitals; however, medical research is genuine scientific output, furthermore with clear impact for society, a newer and stronger factor in research funding. Focusing on STEM+ disciplines, we examine research produced in universities and research institutes that rely heavily on public funds.[2] Selecting a set of disciplines is necessary, because disciplines form "the primary unit of internal differentiation of the modern system of science" (Stichweh, 1992, p. 4). While official publication figures under-represent the true extent of scientific production and SCIE data is biased toward the English language, nevertheless, peer-reviewed research articles indexed in the Web of Science or in Elsevier's Scopus—as the two main databases—are the key source for most bibliometric analyses (Glänzel, 2016).

INSTITUTIONALIZING SCIENCE: RESEARCH UNIVERSITIES AND INSTITUTES

Theoretically, we apply a sociological neo-institutional framework to explore and explain both the tremendous expansion of HE and science across Europe and considerable differences across time and space in the institutional settings, organizational fields and forms, and organizations that produce the most research (Scott, 1995/2014, 2015). Science, as a social institution that follows internal social norms and rules (Merton, 1942), in turn provides the foundations for the production of scientific knowledge (Weingart, 2003/2013). As communities of organizations, organizational fields reflect the interrelationships of diverse organizations sharing an environment (Aldrich & Ruef, 1999). Within a field, particular organizational forms share similar functions and organizations by a common network; this is quite true within scientific communities that, spanning the globe, rely on familiar organizational forms, such as the university. Organizations are defined as social structures established to achieve specific goals through the coalition of actors embedded in an institutional environment (Scott, 1995/2014). The focus on the organizational field and organization levels enables an analysis of differential contributions to scientific productivity.

Universities with their institutional character are assumed to be the most appropriate organizational form for creating significant scientific knowledge, providing the setting for research simultaneously with teaching each new generation of scientists. Alongside universities, diverse state-supported research institutes constitute another pillar of modern science. These various organizational forms undergird local, regional, and national economic development even as they expand human rights and individuals' capabilities (Meyer, 2009). Increasingly, individual well-being and societal futures rely on scientific discoveries, generated more than ever in research universities that remain key contributors of scientific outputs (Baker, 2014). Yet research institutes outside of universities constitute another crucial pillar of science. Despite numerous hypotheses regarding the transformation of knowledge production (Nowotny, Scott, & Gibbons, 2003), the variable contributions of different organizational forms across decades and in different countries have been rarely addressed in explicit comparisons (Zapp & Powell, 2017). We begin such exploratory analysis here, focusing on universities and research institutes as the primary organizational forms producing mainly state-funded research. Research universities are characterized by fundamental principles of the nexus of research and teaching, freedom to teach and to study, autonomy and commitment to science as well as the granting of doctoral degrees. In comparison, research institutes contribute less to teaching, instead focusing on research, often in well-resourced, cutting-edge, and specialized facilities.

These three countries differ in the scale and scope of their systems – and, as analyzed below – in the developmental pathways and distribution of their universities and research institutes. France, Germany, and the UK have centuries-old, world-renowned research universities. Both Germany and France also have well-established extra-university research institutes, often linked in extensive associations that contribute hugely to these countries' scientific output – and are world leaders (Oleksiyenko, 2014, p. 498). Especially in Germany and the UK, research universities are most significant organizations for producing science. In France, universities' research orientation has been strengthened over time, with research institutes and elite researchers producing STEM+ science in a range of organizational forms and, most recently, in research clusters (see Musselin, 2017).

According to the volume of produced STEM+ papers and to historical reach, we sketch the development of universities and research institutes in France, Germany, and the UK, showing how capacity for producing scientific papers has expanded. Europe has the oldest and leading universities worldwide such as the University of Oxford (teaching began around 1096), Paris-Sorbonne University (founded ca. 1150), or the University of Heidelberg (1386) that produce increasingly large numbers of publications and are globally interconnected. Research institutes – like those of France's *Centre national de la recherche scientifique* or Germany's Max Planck Society for the Advancement of Science – though founded in the 20th century, are similarly well-established. The countries differ in the time elapsed since establishment and in the differentiation of these organizational forms and fields. Comparing the three research university sectors, Germany and the UK are more highly institutionalized than that in France. By contrast, in research institutes, France and Germany have large, differentiated non-university research sectors, whereas the UK does not.

We begin with process-tracing in each country, based on synthesis of the research literature in multiple languages and emphasizing the founding dates of organizations and system institutionalization. Process-tracing helps us to understand sequential (historical) events and allows us to explore developmental processes in specific cases (Mahoney, 2004, p. 88f.). We pair the historical case analysis with quantitative analysis of bibliometric data. This combination facilitates analysis of how these organizational forms and fields evolved and provides results on their scientific productivity.

FRANCE: ELITE PROFESSIONAL HIGHER EDUCATION AND RESEARCH BETWEEN HIERARCHY AND ACCESS ISSUES

France's differentiated HE system consists of a range of universities, some very strong in research and others focused more on teaching and applied fields. Universities are challenged by the elite higher professional schools, the *grandes écoles*, to attract talent. And in research the *Centre national de la recherche scientifique* (CNRS) is dominant, though many of its researchers establish or work in research "laboratories" (research groups) physically located within universities. France finances and maintains prestigious extra-university research units and institutes, many but not all under the CNRS umbrella. With 79 universities, 205 *grandes écoles*,[3] and 14 foreign institutions, the professional school sector remains significant (METRIS, 2012). The Paris-Sorbonne University was among the first universities in Europe; for centuries the guarantor of academic excellence across diverse fields. Today's major concentration of universities in the capital city is built upon those ancient foundations. In 1970, shortly after the student protests of 1968, this institution was decentralized and divided into 13 autonomous universities (Musselin, 2007, p. 713). The national extra-university sector consists of seven larger umbrella research associations with more than 70 institutes, centers, or departments. Most recently, in what Musselin (2017) calls the "remodeling of French HE," consortia are being established to grow collaborations across organizational forms and aggregate research in stronger groupings of researchers and organizations. At Paris-Saclay, for example, bridges are being built between 18 research organizations, including two universities, an *Ecole Normale Supérieure*, six research organizations, ten engineering and business schools, and two educational clusters that host 10,000 researchers and 300 laboratories (organizational units of different size and structure).[4] Clearly, the underlying theory is that physical proximity matters for scientific exchange; however, this does run counter to some important features of the recent decades, namely globalization and intellectual exchange via virtual communication platforms.

Despite the principle of equivalence, France's tertiary education and research system exhibits stratification: the *grandes écoles*/university divide and the split between selective and non-selective segments as well as distinctions between CNRS researchers and academy members at the top and regular university faculty members below. While the key organizational form for research may be – increasingly – the university, CNRS laboratories and institutes play a key role within them and more generally in producing science (OECD, 2014). The *grandes écoles* constitute a diverse group of highly selective and prestigious institutions that train future elites: higher-level civil servants, professors and researchers, engineers, and company managers (Givord & Goux, 2007), but increasingly they also produce science. Widely criticized, this divide has often been blamed for the current crisis experienced by universities, as the *grandes écoles* attract high-achieving students and relegate universities to struggle for global reputation (Clark, 1995, p. 93). Thus, from 2006 "alliances" have been formed to join both organizational forms, such as in Centers for Research and Higher Education (PRES) (Le Deaut, 2013).

The contemporary university crisis also results from lack of resources, multiple incoherent reforms, lack of labor market forecasting, and increased bureaucratization (Bernhard, 2017). Universities' status is limited because neither are societal elites trained there nor are the most significant research projects initiated by them, thus they serve mainly as teaching bodies, even if some host influential research groups or laboratories. With notable exceptions and shifting recently, both *grandes écoles* and universities emphasize teaching more than they excel at research. The French HE system reflects an "education model," emphasizing professional preparation (Kreckel, 2008, p. 88).

Yet French universities are changing, not least due to global norms and European standards. Universities were responsible for general education (except for law, medicine, and pharmacy), while *grandes écoles* offered vocational preparation of elites or middle-range technicians. Research was long conducted primarily in separate research organizations. A fundamental shift, the Liberties and Responsibilities of Universities (LRU) bill, passed in August 2007, grants significant power to university presidents. The proclaimed aim: to meet the demands of the "knowledge economy" and to bring French universities to the level of excellence of major international competitors. The French "excellence initiative," designed to strengthen research collaborations and consortia of researchers within a differentiated HE system, cannot eliminate decades of specialization and uneven development. Ironically, the German Excellence Initiative aimed to do the opposite, creating more differentiation in a less stratified, less differentiated HE system (Münch, 2007). Along with the diffusion of "performance discourse" and new instruments such as "agencification" came national calls designed to identify the best researchers and encourage their collaboration; yet perhaps most significant is the requirement that all HEIs must be part of scientific consortia (Musselin, 2017).

Historically, some processes have successfully linked teaching and research in France. In the late 19th century, the new organizational form of *grands établissements* was established to support and develop education and research, including the *École pratique des hautes études* (1868) and the *Institut Pasteur* (1887), which has grown in capacity and influence (Hage & Mote, 2008). Founded in 1530, the *Collège de France* enjoys special status among the *grands établissements* (Kreckel, 2008).

Since 1939, fundamental research is predominantly financed by CNRS, the dominant association of research institutes, units, and laboratories. This state-funded, complex umbrella organization encompasses seven research institutes, three national institutes and 1,028 research units, with the vast majority (95%) joint laboratories with universities and industry. CNRS is significant for France's scientific development and international standing in a wide range of fields. Organized in associations, university faculty members may apply to establish collaborations with one of the national research institutes, or associated laboratories receive funding, and sometimes CNRS staff, while autonomous research units — called *unités propres* — have no university affiliation (Musselin & Vilkas, 1994, p. 129). The varying relationships of researchers to each other and the organizational forms in which they work confound analyses of affiliations and aggregate measurement of the impact of organizational conditions on outputs. Other publically funded extra-university research institutions conduct strategic research related to national needs, from infrastructure and energy to agriculture and health, all part of a powerful centralized state (Clark, 1995). The funding and organization of research has traditionally been the responsibility of separate organizations; with the institutional separation between HE and research difficult to bridge (Ben-David, 1977/1992, p. 107) — and continuously debated. Yet, this is precisely what French research policy seeks to accomplish today in establishing consortia connecting organizations and research groups. From 2009, the government's "Investments for the Future programs" aim to strengthen competitiveness through targeted investments in research, higher and vocational education, in particular enterprises, and in expanding sectors. Thus far, these programs have allocated €26.6 billion to HE and research (AFR, 2016). The traditional government-sponsored, largely autonomous research organizations operate alongside competitive project-based funding in large competitive programs (OECD, 2014). Thus, HE and research and development remain particularly complex in France, despite efforts are coordination and consolidation.

Turning now to output, we examine France's overall scientific productivity in STEM+. We find continuously rising output and strengthened university-based research. The non-university/university sectoral divide has been narrowed (Fig. 2). These sectors' output grew in parallel for decades, witnessing

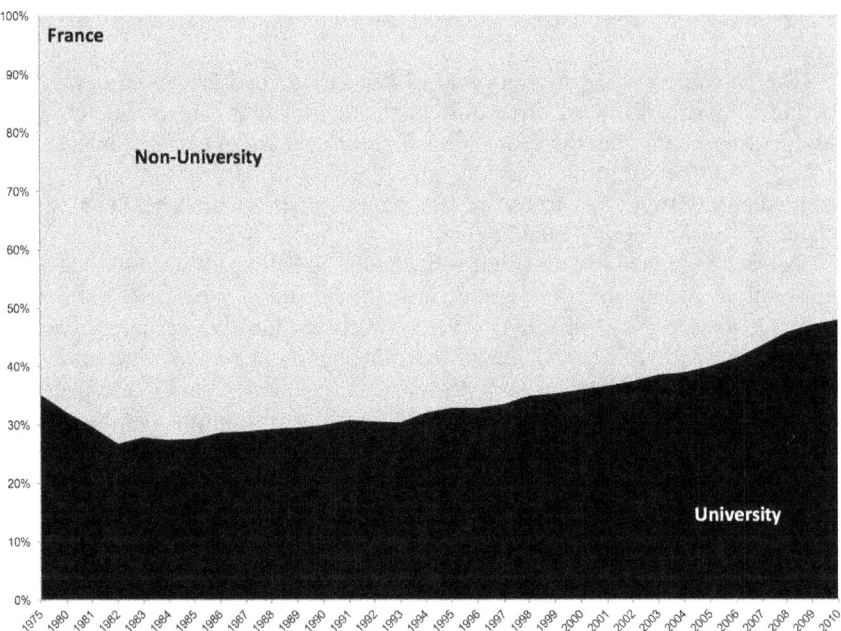

Fig. 2. Scientific Productivity in France: Universities versus Non-University Organizations, 1975–2010. *Note*: This representation is based on differentiating publications from organizations with the word "univ" from all others, thus is a rough measure of the productivity of the university versus non-university sector, which includes a range of science-producing organizations: firms, large government agencies, and academies. "Black" = university sector, "grey" = non-university sector. *Source*: SPHERE project database of SCIE publications (Thomson Reuters' Web of Science).

considerable expansion from 2004 onward. Today, the two pillars of French science are at parity, at least in terms of STEM+ article publications.

In individual organizational terms, if we consider the diverse branches of the University of Paris together, the aggregated output of 15,453 articles clearly led this centralized country. The capital city's university-based scientific output was produced by Paris VI Pierre and Marie Curie (4,714), Paris VII Diderot (3,165), Paris XI Sud (3,163) and Paris V Descartes (2,598). At a lower level of output were further branches, of Paris XII Est (1,036), Paris XIII Nord (392), and Paris IX Dauphine (135), with some authors listing their affiliations simply as University of Paris (undefined: 250).

By contrast, and unsurprisingly, the CNRS led the French research institute contribution in scientific productivity in 2010 with 6,497 research articles, collecting the intellectual products of the myriad research institutes, laboratories, and individual scientists associated with France's leading scientific organization.

The University of Lyon – located in France's second largest city and consisting of 16 organizations, from universities to *grandes écoles* to research institutes (without counting the *École normale supérieure* there) – contributed 3,605 articles. Another southern university, Toulouse, was very productive (2,674), combining contributions from the two natural sciences branches Toulouse 1 Capitole and Toulouse III Paul Sabatier.

Three government agencies that contribute heavily in peer-reviewed scientific publications are the medical research institute *Institut national de la santé et de la recherche médicale* (INSERM) with 2,534 articles, the atomic energy commission (CEA) with 2,352, and the *Institut national de la recherche agronomique* (INRA) with 1,758. Further strong producers include the southern university, Provence Aix–Marseille I and III Paul Cezanne (campuses in both cities), which 2,339 pieces of scholarship. Grenoble Alpes University (here: Grenoble I Joseph Fournier) produced 1,886 and the University of Montpelier I and II contributed 1,861 articles in SCIE journals.

This list reflects two important particularities. First, that institutional affiliations in France tend to be multiple, with many CNRS researchers working within universities and universities collaborating with national research institutes. Second, universities have different branches for different fields, but the actual organizational setting in which the research was produced is not always distinguished. In bibliometric databases such as Thomson Reuters' Web of Science or Elsevier Scopus, the primary affiliation is paramount. A methodological challenge that qualitative research should address at the organizational level is how resources are provided within these settings and what reputational logics guide scientists in noting their affiliation(s).

Now we turn to Germany, a country with a similar duality of research universities (relatively similar in resources and reputations) and extra-university research institutes, albeit without the centralization characteristic of France.

GERMANY'S DUAL PILLARS OF STRENGTH: THE SYMBIOSIS OF RESEARCH UNIVERSITIES AND EXTRA-UNIVERSITY RESEARCH INSTITUTES

Germany is home of the undisputed model of the research university and significant extra-university research institutes. Yet universities have been underfunded for decades (Pritchard, 2006), despite considerable increases in the proportion of each cohort entering HE, and the sector is divided into two, with research universities and universities of applied sciences. Paradoxically, policymakers have ignored this "institutional crisis" of underfunding HE even as they send ever more of their children into the system (Lenhardt, 2005): "Stagnation of public funds is particularly damaging to efforts toward fostering internationally competitive basic research in the universities, as they receive only a relatively small share of the entire national research budget" (Baker, 2014, p. 93). Here, there is a decoupling between rhetoric and policy reality.

Indeed, the German "Humboldtian" model of university-based science is among the oldest and influential conceptions of HE worldwide (Humboldt, 1809), reaching mythic proportions, despite the ongoing transformation of German HE – not least reunification that led to unforeseen, dramatic dynamics in academia (Ash, 1999; Clark, 2006; Pritchard, 2006). While the foundational principle of the nexus of research and teaching enjoys sustained attention worldwide, the relationship remains complex and ambiguous both within organizations and between the organizational fields of HE and research. The success story of German research-based teaching relies on self-government, institutional and organizational growth, and its generality, dealing with matters of general human interest and preparing students for a broad range of occupations (Ben-David, 1977/1992).

Germany's 126 research universities, 232 universities of applied sciences, and 51 art and music colleges operate alongside a research-intensive and powerful extra-university research institute sector of 300 institutes, most gathered in four large umbrella associations. With annual R&D investments among the highest in Europe (OECD, 2015), the Federal Ministry of Education and Research (BMBF) is the key actor in research policy, even as education is mostly the province of the *Länder*. Among public funding organizations, the German Research Foundation (DFG) is the main promoter of science as an peer-review organizing intermediary. Furthermore, the European Commission and more than 16,000 foundations offer innumerable possibilities to apply for financial support for education and research (Hinze, 2010).

Higher education devoted to research grew in Germany stronger than in more differentiated systems like that of France. This research-focused type of university continues to dominate German HE up to today, despite establishment of universities of applied sciences (*Fachhochschulen*) after massification of tertiary education. Since the 1960s, this new organizational form provides a more applied and praxis-oriented focus. Investments in (fundamental) research are less significant; however, increasingly their faculty members do conduct research, often collaborating with industry. Gradually, reflecting general trends of "academic drift," they have become more like research universities, even if the monopoly on granting doctoral degrees remains in universities (Teichler, 2005).

Around WWI, Germany established an alliance between representatives of science, research-intensive industry, and ministerial bureaucrats to found innovative research institutes outside universities. The 1911 founding of the *Kaiser-Wilhelm-Gesellschaft* (from 1948 Max Planck Society) challenged the German HE system as the dominant locale for fundamental research. In this sector, research was institutionally separated from teaching. Today, 83 Max Planck institutes are located in Germany and five institutes. After WWII, further competitors entered the growing organizational field of extra-university research: The Fraunhofer Society was established in 1949 to focus on applied sciences and industrial contract research (today: 67 institutes). The Leibniz Association was established in 1997, but had existed since 1977 known as the "blue list" (*Blaue Liste*), a collection of diverse research institutes with regional or national significance and varying emphases on fundamental or applied research (today: 89 institutes). The Helmholtz Association of German Research Centers (2001), dealing with research related to infrastructure (*Vorsorgeforschung*) comprises 18 very large research institutions (*Großforschungseinrichtungen*) and around 40 federal research institutions in a range of fields related to national interests (Hohn, 2010). Yet all of these research institutes and their umbrella associations continue to rely on universities for crucial aspects of their work, whether it be training of young scholars or certifying doctoral candidates. Thus, the competition must be considered more of a symbiosis, with elements of collaboration and competition continuously (re)negotiated.

Universities have come under threat due to declining funds and internationalization and Europeanization processes. Competition between universities and research institutes has increased as centers of excellent research outside universities intensify their activities, increase investment in cutting-edge research projects, and amass the best and brightest scientists. Their enviable funding derives from both Federal and *Länder* governments jointly providing funding, though in differing proportion (usually 50/50) (Hohn, 2010). Germany's dual pillars of mass universities and independent research institutes continue to boast prodigious scientific output – and the universities' central position has been maintained.

With the emergence of newer hybrid types of research (and teaching) as well as universities of applied science demanding the right to confer doctoral degrees, the German HE system confronts a new situation. The structural duality of the German system no longer seems unassailable or as sustainable. Examples of newer boundary-spanning organizations include the Karlsruhe Institute of Technology (KIT), an amalgam of the Karlsruhe Research Center (Helmholtz) and the Technical University of Karlsruhe, as well as the International Max Planck Research Schools (IMPRS) as examples for interinstitutional, international, and interdisciplinary collaboration (www.mpg.de/de/imprs). Because only research universities in Germany have granted doctoral degrees, others depend on close collaboration or "strategic partnerships." Furthermore, such collaborations have also been affected by three developments: massification, segregation of research and teaching, and growing third-party funded research.

Turning now to our examination of Germany's SCIE scientific output over the past several decades, we unsurprisingly find dual pillars of strength in science, with ultrastability in the university/non-university distribution, with about 60% of all STEM+ publications having at least one university-based author

(Fig. 3). Symbiosis of research institutes and research universities viewed in explicit collaborations is particularly strong in doctoral education and the conferral of doctoral degrees, for which the institutes have been wholly dependent on universities.

The Max Planck Society, with its dozens of institutes and emphasis on fundamental research, produced 6,374 research articles, with a further 225 more generally ascribed to the Max Planck Society itself. Among the leading 37 MPIs are those researching Astrophysics, Extraterrestial Physics, Solid State, Polymers, Astronomics, Biogeochemistry, Colloids and Interfaces, Radioastronomy, Nuclear Physics, Biophysical Chemistry, Physics of Complex Systems (all above 200 contributions in 2010).

The researchers in the large Helmholtz Association institutes together published 4,556 papers in 2010, with the leading organizations being the Jülich Research Center (871), the German Cancer Research Center Heidelberg (829),

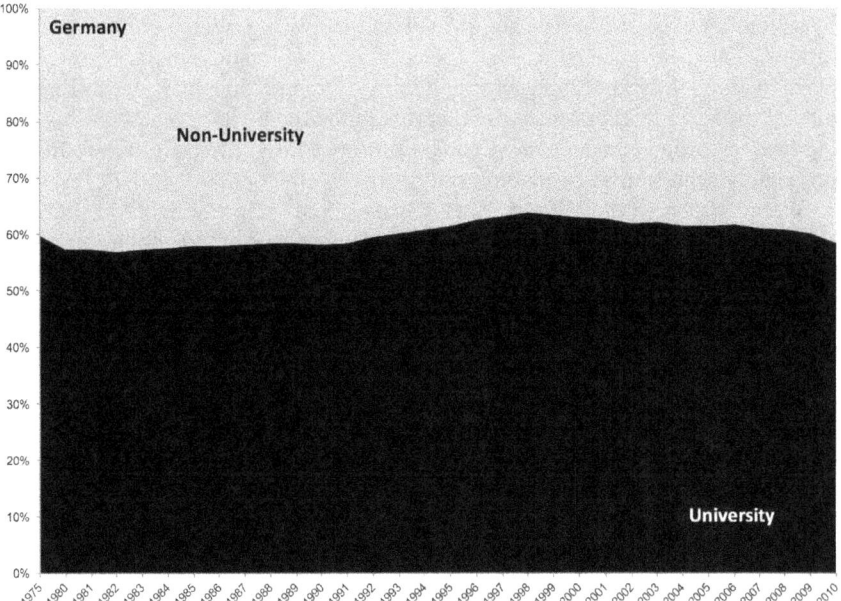

Fig. 3. Scientific Productivity in Germany: Universities versus Non-University Organizations, 1975−2010. *Note*: This representation is based on differentiating publications from organizations with the word "univ" from all others, thus is a rough measure of the productivity of the university versus non-university sector, which includes a range of science-producing organizations: firms, large government agencies, and academies (e.g., in the GDR). "Black" = university sector, "grey" = non-university sector. *Source*: SPHERE project database of SCIE publications (Thomson Reuters' Web of Science).

Helmholtz Center Munich (460), Polar and Ocean Research Alfred Wegener (348), Environmental Research (310), German Electron Synchroton (DESY) (290), Materials and Energy (208), and Max Delbrück Center for Molecular Medicine (206), along with several others under 200 contributions each.

The top three universities in the STEM+ fields are LMU Munich with 2,977; University of Heidelberg with 2,976; and the Technical University Munich with 2,712. Berlin's 300-year-old medical research and teaching center, the Charité – Universitätsmedizin Berlin which collaborates intensively with the universities in Berlin with medical faculties, produced 2,030 in 2010. Indeed, we find that medical research contributes considerably to many of the universities' output, with those universities with medical faculties producing significantly more STEM+ research, due to the publication intensity of medical fields. These include the University Erlangen-Nuremberg (1,956), the University of Freiburg (1,951), University of Tübingen (1,865), and the University of Bonn (1,827).

Thus, in both France and Germany, extra-university research institutes play an important role in research, as do the associations that directly fund research by selecting the best scientists and providing them with research-conducive conditions. The continued strength of Germany's two main pillars of research capacity mirror France's structural duality. Despite the dual structure that places emphasis and concentrates resources in the research institutes, with varying degrees of independence and collaborations across the institutional divide, both enjoy significant capacity and output.

We now turn to the UK, in which a strong and internationalized organizational field of universities contributes disproportionately to global scientific output.

UNITED KINGDOM: FROM UNDERGRADUATE COLLEGES TO LEADING INTERNATIONAL RESEARCH UNIVERSITIES

The UK enjoys a leading position in global science, as it is home to ancient learned societies, such as The Royal Society (founded 1660), and it continues to contribute far more than its size would suggest: although representing less than 1% of the world's population, it expends 3.2% of global R&D, and hosts 4.1% of the world's researchers (Elsevier, 2013). Like those of France and Germany, the history of HE in the UK begins many centuries ago; it is home to some of the world's oldest and most-renowned universities. With teaching in the city of Oxford documented as early as 1096, the University of Oxford can be considered the oldest university in the English-speaking world. Similarly, the University of Cambridge celebrated its 800th anniversary in 2009, charting its existence back to an association of scholars who gathered there in 1209. In Scotland, St Andrews, Glasgow, and Aberdeen were established in the 15th century, with the University of Edinburgh founded by royal charter in 1583. A first major expansion of HE occurred in the 19th century with further royal charters awarded to St David's College in Lampeter (1822; later becoming part of the University of Wales), Durham University, King's College London, and University College London. In Northern Ireland, Queen's University Belfast, which has its roots in the Belfast Academical Institution (founded 1810), is also among the UK's oldest universities. These institutions of higher learning in the UK continue to be recognized as leading universities not only in the English-speaking world.

The British model of HE reflects a system originally supporting classical education for a very select few to become "educated gentlemen" of the ruling class (Cummings, 1999, p. 424). Thus, as in France, the original target group was a tiny elite, many of whom had previously attended college preparatory boarding schools. These young men were provided a classical learning canon in the colleges of Cambridge and Oxford. These exemplary HE organizations became an attractive model around the world, in all the Commonwealth countries and in the United States (Powell et al., 2012).

The traditional images of British HE are, however, far removed from the system's contemporary reality, with the original colleges now part of a differentiated HE system educating a large minority of each cohort. While the autonomy of HEIs was long guaranteed under state guardianship, with governance decentralized, more recently emphases on markets (and quickly and considerably rising tuition fees) and individual responsibility have increased. The state has massively retrenched its support for HE, leading to privatization and marketization. Evidence of loose coupling between the rhetorics of Europeanization and the structures of education systems, UK HE has been active in the Bologna process from the start – with limited impact in the aims or practices of individual universities, many already operating very successfully internationally (Graf, 2009), including large proportions of (fee-paying) international students and international branch campuses. Currently, the planned exit of Britain from the EU poses a major further threat to the system. While the HE system in the UK includes prestigious institutions of higher learning, it also integrates dozens of universities, especially the former polytechnics, that remain oriented far more toward undergraduate education instead of research, similar to the French universities.

Originally, medical, science, and engineering colleges were founded across England in major industrial cities. Eventually, these colleges would be transformed into the so-called red-brick universities in cities such as Birmingham, Bristol, Leeds, Liverpool, Manchester, and Sheffield. The post-WWII period witnessed tremendous HE expansion responding to the demands of a growing population and supposedly to meet the needs of an increasingly technological economy. Governments expanded the HE sector by establishing new colleges of advanced technology, which were later awarded university status in the 1960s such as Aston, Bath, Bradford, Brunel, City, Loughborough, Salford, and

Surrey. In Wales, the University of Wales Institute of Science and Technology became a constituent part of today's Cardiff University. The academic drift and rebranding did not stop there. The former university colleges (Hull, Leicester) were granted university status and seven new universities – East Anglia, Essex, Kent, Lancaster, Sussex, Warwick, and York – were founded.

A further, most significant round of expansion occurred in 1992 with the *Further and Higher Education Act*, in which the UK government granted university status to 35 former polytechnics and other organizational forms, mainly colleges of higher and further education. In formally abolishing the binary divide between universities and polytechnics and fostering a unitary HE system, the number of universities almost doubled and the number of university students doubled virtually overnight (Halsey, 2000, cited in Boliver, 2015, p. 608). If in 1984 there were 48 HEIs with university status, after the policy reform in 1992 (the *Further and Higher Education Act*), the number rose to 86 (Tight, 2009). Finally, in the new century, several dozen additional universities were created. Collectively, these universities are referred to as "post-92" or "modern" universities, many building on extended histories as vocational training organizations.

A number of classifications of HEIs in the UK exist, including the self-selected association of 24 public research universities called the "Russell Group" since 1994. Three other associations, mainly representing post-1992 universities are (1) the "Million+" Association for Modern Universities since 1997 (originally the Coalition of Modern Universities that seeks to widen access to HE among its 17 members); (2) GuildHE, since 2006 representing 28 "smaller and specialist" post-1992 universities and university colleges; and (3) the University Alliance, since 2006, of 20 post-1992 and two Robbins-era universities with a science and technology focus (Boliver, 2015). Given its predominance in research, the Russell Group association views its mission as "supporting the nation's world-class universities and a diverse HE system [that] will help ensure the UK continues to enjoy the international recognition it rightly deserves for the quality of its educational provision and cutting-edge research" (Russell Group, 2012). Established in 1994, it represents members' interests, principally to government and parliament, of the most research-oriented UK universities that together receive around two-thirds of all university research grant and contract income in the UK, award the majority of doctorates, and serve around a third of all students studying in the UK from outside the EU.

In research funding, the UK has what is probably the most influential system worldwide, currently named the Research Excellence Framework, started in 1986: confirming its ever-stronger presence in UK HE, seven assessment exercises have been conducted, leading to selectivity in which scholars' work is evaluated and heightened stratification in HE. Other countries have begun to develop similar research evaluation systems to evaluate the quality of research and (re)allocate government funding for research. Such evaluations are related to "excellence initiatives" both France and Germany used to distribute research funds to the strongest universities or their organizational subunits − based on submitted proposals that undergo extensive peer review. These various programs attempt to promote and achieve "excellence" in research, to produce innovative knowledge, and develop technology for the advancement of economy and society.

In terms of the sectoral sources of total SCIE scientific output since 1975, the universities have even increased, from half to two-thirds of all STEM+ publications with a university-based author (Fig. 4).

In this university-dominated research system, with differentiation in the HE sector, it is important to distinguish groups of universities. In 2015/2016, following the latest research evaluation − 2014 REF − the 19 English universities with research funding allocations in excess of £20m (excluding transitional

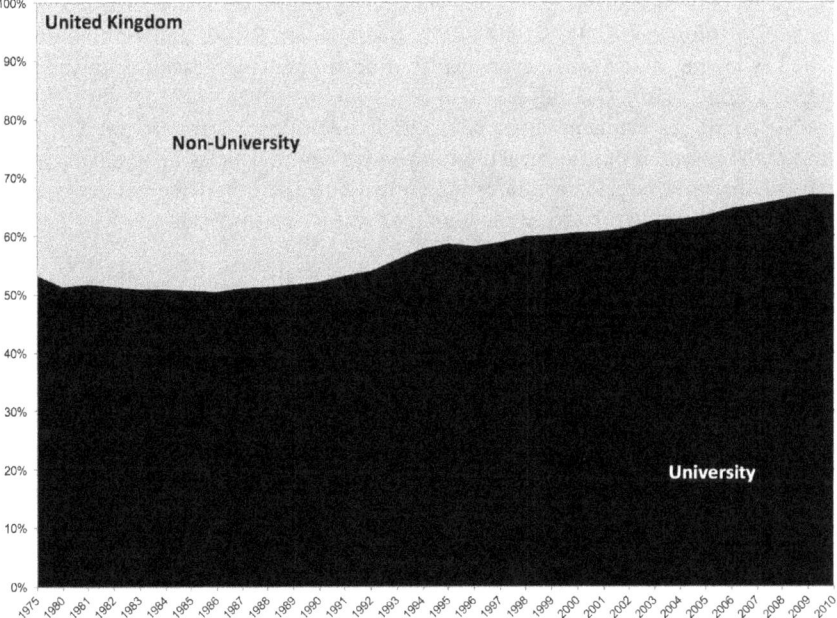

Fig. 4. Scientific Productivity in France, Germany, and the United Kingdom: Universities versus Non-University Organizations, 1975−2010. *Note*: This representation is based on differentiating publications from organizations with the word "univ" from all others, thus is a rough measure of the productivity of the university versus non-university sector, which includes a range of science-producing organizations: firms, large government agencies, and academies. "Black" = university sector, "grey" = non-university sector. *Source*: SPHERE project database of SCIE publications (Thomson Reuters' Web of Science).

funding) from the Higher Education Funding Councils (e.g., HEFC for England) were all members of the Russell Group. These universities together received four-fifths of the total HEFCE research funding allocation, emphasizing the concentration of research funding from the state among a small group of research universities. Examining the UK's SCIE scientific output in 2010, the Russell Group universities are the foundation for research in England. Boliver (2015) argues that Oxford and Cambridge remain distinct in their research intensity and publication output as individual organizations. Yet our results show that the associated colleges and universities of the University of London have a higher combined output of STEM+ research articles, with a total of 13,125, led by the most prolific university in our sample, namely University College London (UCL) with 5,596. Further London-based top producers include the second-ranked Imperial College (5,292); King's College London (2,868); Queen Mary (1,069); and London School of Hygiene and Tropical Medicine (946); among others. The University of Oxford contributed 5,161 and the University of Cambridge 4,854. Manchester produced 3,188 papers; Bristol 2,396; Nottingham 2,204; Leeds 2,201; Birmingham 2,174; and Southampton 2,033, showing a relatively even distribution among top research universities beyond London and Oxbridge.

No single government agency, research institute or firm in the UK can match the research output measured in peer-reviewed articles in academic journals of the universities, an interesting contrast to the other two countries analyzed here. We now turn to explicit comparison of the three cases.

COMPARING COUNTRIES' STRUCTURES AND SCIENTIFIC PRODUCTIVITY: FINDINGS AND OUTLOOK

The over time and cross-national comparisons emphasize that France, Germany, and the UK have varying research intensity and proportions of scientists of all employees. Their HE and research systems reflect varying involvement of the state and particular institutionalization pathways that have resulted in the differing significance of research universities and institutes, each organizational form contributing more or less to scientific productivity. In these countries, research universities and research institutes (often gathered in umbrella associations) contribute different proportions to overall scientific output, yet in all three the research university represents the key organizational form − even growing in significance over time.

We compare the scientific productivity in France, Germany, and the UK over the past three and half decades, beginning with the input-side of investments (GERD). We then turn to per capita indicators of output before examining the organizational forms that produce this science, emphasizing the distinction between the relative contributions of universities and non-university organizations. The latter category includes research institutes, government agencies, companies, and other research producers.

As mentioned above, in R&D spending per capita, Germany spent by far the most, followed by France, and the UK trailing behind. Cole and Phelan (1999) have argued that wealth strongly, but not completely, influences the volume of research produced by countries. Indeed, the number of researchers per thousand in the labor force in these countries does not vary markedly, from 8.2 in Germany to 8.9 in the UK to 9.9 in France (OECD, 2016). Differences between these three prosperous European countries in scientific productivity cannot be fully explained by differences of overall investments or the volume of researchers engaged in science. Rather, the institutionalization and distribution of organizational forms in which researchers produce science remain crucial factors to be examined further as are disciplinary emphases.

In contrast to these investments, in terms of outputs, measured here in SCIE publications per million inhabitants, the UK has the highest productivity, followed by Germany, and then France. All three countries witnessed continuously and steadily rising publication output per million inhabitants. Resources fully explain neither the expansion nor the country-level differences found. With targeted investments and much larger proportion of GDP going to R&D than the other two countries, Germany recovered from the shock of reunification. In fact, Germany's steady upward trend contrasts with a slight lowering of output per million inhabitants in 2005 in France and the UK, with Germany now slightly ahead of France. In 2010, France produced 856 SCIE articles per million inhabitants, Germany 908, and the UK 1,129. In the UK, factors such as the hegemonic language of English, international research collaborations, and the strong research-oriented universities factor in this surprising result given the lower level of research investment.

Analyzing the total number of SCIE publications for the three countries over the 20th century shows massive increases, especially since the 1970s and again over the past decade. With differences in scale, France, Germany, and the UK have all increased their output dramatically over the past four decades. As absolute numbers are difficult to interpret across cases of different size and science capacity, we calculated the scientific output per one million inhabitants (Fig. 5). This enables a more reliable comparative measure of the productivity based on SCIE publications in leading journals. While the long-term scientific strength of Germany (even during the division of West and East Germany) continues to the present day, it is the UK, with its highly internationalized and Anglophone research universities, that leads in per capita productivity, followed by Germany and France, although these two continental systems have had relatively similar production per capita throughout the period, with a similar, but slightly lower trend as that seen in the UK.

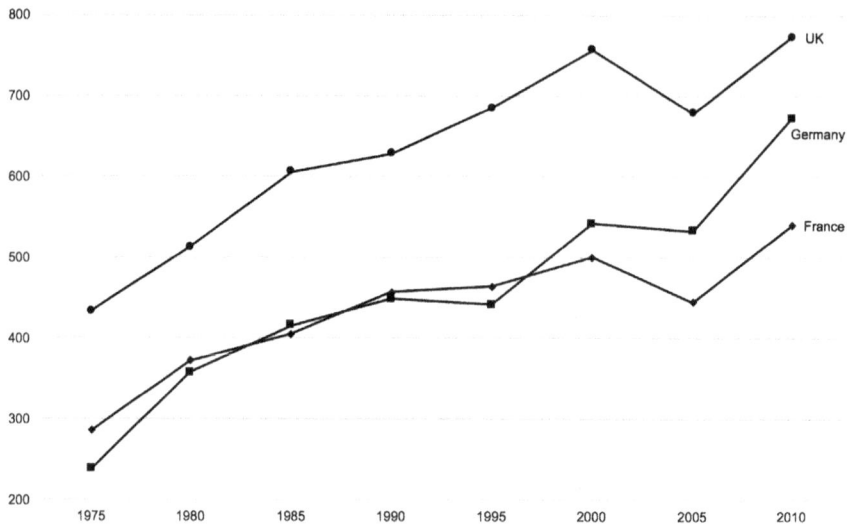

Fig. 5. Number of Publications from France, Germany, and the United Kingdom (per million iInhabitants), 1975–2010. *Source*: SPHERE project database of SCIE publications (Thomson Reuters' Web of Science).

Comparing the absolute productivity levels of countries historically manifests the dramatic rise of science. The three countries examined here have, since the 1980s, witnessed a veritable boom in the publication of scientific articles in STEM+ disciplines. Comparing cases, we must acknowledge issues of scale and scope. When analyzing the number of these publications standardized by population, we find an even more dramatic rise, especially over the past decade. This provides a more comparable indicator and also reorders the countries in terms of productivity.

Our study investigated the contributions of different research organizational forms to scientific output. We compared the production of STEM+ research papers in three countries in Europe since 1975. As discussed earlier, these countries achieve their scientific outputs having distinct and differently institutionalized HE and science systems, yet with the universities at the core in all countries (see also other country studies in this volume). Germany and the UK have long-established research universities that produce a large number of articles — more than do the equivalent organizations in aggregate in France. France, while relying on a group of strong universities, emphasizes teaching and has fewer such organizations than does Germany. But, France also funds a diversity of well-established research institutes and other organizational forms such as the researchers and laboratories of the influential and highly productive CNRS. Still, France follows Germany slightly in the total number of publications.

Our key finding is that the institutionalization of the research university sector and reliance on it seems to support high productivity. In fact, those large and dual structured systems with a larger institutionalized non-university sector, as in France and Germany, have less per capita output than the UK with its group of world-leading universities that has attracted top talent globally. From 1975 to 2011, we see stable (Germany) or rising university contributions (France, UK) (Figs. 2–4). France initially had a very low university contribution (around 30%), but that this has risen over the past decades. In the UK, the growth of university-produced science went from around half to just under 70%. By contrast, we find stability around 60% in Germany, despite the enormous growth of HE and the dual structure of universities (and universities of applied science) and the strong, elite research institutes.

Examining the three top contributors to the European center of science productivity, we found remarkable sustained growth, building on the evolving institutionalization of research universities and institutes and embeddedness in worldwide scientific networks. The elaboration and technology-driven expansion of scientific communication through a world of scientific journals built upon peer-review and rising (inter)national competition and collaboration in STEM+ fields spur global growth — with Europe still central to global science. Although in the past Germany and France were outpaced by the UK, it is questionable whether the country can maintain its high standard and extraordinary success in international collaborations post-Brexit, as scientists declared in a *Nature* (2016) poll.

Simply more investment in R&D does not necessarily yield more STEM+ research in international, mainly English language journals indexed by Thomson Reuters' Web of Science database, although its coverage is steadily growing. In analyzing what makes these European countries successful in science, but to varying degrees, we identified the long-term development yet differential elaboration of research universities and research institutes. Internationalization and the global *lingua franca* of English in which research must be reported in leading SCIE journals changes the attention paid to particular research or the measurement of productivity; more generally it shifts the conditions of the research enterprise and the publication strategies of individual researchers. These factors require further fine-grained analysis. Next steps in understanding better the publication patterns in the STEM+ fields include analysis of the contributions of various organizational forms in the diverse non-university sector and organization-level studies of the most productive organizations identified here.

In cross-national and historical comparison, neither solely size of country nor level of R&D investments account completely for the growth of scientific production and productivity. Newer entrants to the world of science can quickly increase their capacity and productivity by investing heavily in research infrastructure and recruiting talent worldwide (see the example of Qatar; Crist, 2017). Yet especially the older established universities and associations of research institutes have successfully driven the considerable increase in science production over the past several decades. The exploratory historical and comparative research reported here uncovered huge growth over time, due to academic drift, technology-facilitated communication, and collaborations. We also find relatively stable patterns of productivity of the universities within countries. In contrast to Germany's ultrastability, there has been strong growth in France and increases in the UK on an already high level from the mid-1970s. The center of science today reflects the strengthening of research in European universities, with France, Germany, and the UK contributing significantly to global science.

NOTES

1. OECD Main Science & Technology Indicators. Accessed on August 14, 2016.
2. We cannot here address in-depth ancillary questions of disciplinary differentiation, industrial investment in R&D or the fluctuating influence of academies of science.
3. Disagreement persists about the number of *grandes écoles*. The *Conférence des Grandes Écoles* notes 205 *grandes écoles* in France (http://www.cge.asso.fr/en/our-members/grandes-ecoles).
4. https://www.universite-paris-saclay.fr/en

REFERENCES

AFR. (2016). *Investments for the future*. Paris: Agence Nationale de la Recherche. Retrieved from http://www.agence-nationale-recherche.fr/en/about-anr/investments-for-the-future
Aldrich, H. E., & Ruef, M. (1999). *Organizations evolving*. Thousand Oaks, CA: Sage.
Ash, M. G. (Ed.). (1999). *Mythos Humboldt*. Vienna: Böhlau.
Baker, D. P. (2014). *The schooled society: The educational transformation of culture*. Stanford, CA: Stanford University Press.
Ben-David, J. (1977/1992). *Centers of learning: Britain, France, Germany, United States*. New Brunswick, NJ: Transaction.
Ben-David, J. (1984). *The scientist's role in society*. Chicago, IL: University of Chicago Press.
Ben-David, J., & Sullivan, T. A. (1975). Sociology of science. *Annual Review of Sociology, 1*, 203−222.
Bernhard, N. (2017). *Durch Europäisierung zu mehr Durchlässigkeit? Veränderungsdynamiken des Verhältnisses von beruflicher Bildung zur Hochschulbildung in Deutschland und Frankreich*. Opladen: Budrich UniPress.
Boliver, V. (2015). Are there distinctive clusters of higher and lower status universities in the UK? *Oxford Review of Education, 41*(5), 608−627.
Bromley, P., & Meyer, J. W. (2015). Hyper-organization. *Global organizational expansion*. Oxford: Oxford University Press.
Clark, B. R. (1995). *Places of inquiry*. Berkeley, CA: University of California Press.
Clark, W. (2006). *Academic charisma and the origins of the research university*. Chicago, IL: University of Chicago Press.
Cole, S., & Phelan, T. J. (1999). The scientific productivity of nations. *Minerva, 37*(1), 1−23.

Crist, J. T. (2017). "A Fever of Research": Scientific Journal Article Production and the Emergence of a National Research. In J. J. W. Powell, D. P. Baker, & F. Fernandez (Eds.), *The Century of Science: The Global Triumph of the Research University* (Vol. 33). International Perspectives on Education and Society. Bingley: Emerald Publishing Limited.

Cummings, W. K. (1999). The institutions of education: Compare, compare, compare! *Comparative Education Review*, *43*(4), 413–437.

de Freytas-Tamura, K. (2016). 'Brexit' may hurt Britain where it thrives: Science and research. *The New York Times*, October 17. Retrieved from http://www.nytimes.com/2016/10/18/business/international/brexit-may-hurt-britain-where-it-thrives-science-and-research.html?emc=eta1&_r=0

Drori, G. S., Meyer, J. W., Ramirez, F. O., & Schofer, E. (2003). *Science in the modern world polity*. Stanford, CA: Stanford University Press.

Dusdal, J. (2017). Welche Organisationsformen produzieren Wissenschaft? Expansion, Vielfalt und Kooperation im deutschen Hochschul- und Wissenschaftssystem im globalen Kontext, 1900-2010. Unpublished Doctoral Dissertation. University of Luxembourg.

Elsevier. (2013). *International comparative performance of the UK research base: A report prepared by Elsevier for the UK's Department of Business, Innovation and Skills*. Amsterdam: Author.

European Commission. (2010). *A vision for strengthening world-class research infrastructures in the European Research Area*. Luxembourg.

Fernandez, F., & Baker, D. P. (2017). Science Production in the United States: An Unexpected Synergy between Mass Higher Education and the Super Research University. In J. J. W. Powell, D. P. Baker, & F. Fernandez (Eds.), *The Century of Science: The Global Triumph of the Research University* (Vol. 33). International Perspectives on Education and Society. Bingley: Emerald Publishing Limited.

Givord, P., & Goux, D. (2007). France: Mass and class − Persisting inequalities in postsecondary education in France. In Y. Shavit, R. Arum, & A. Gamoran (Eds.), *Stratification in higher education* (pp. 220–239). Stanford, CA: Stanford University Press.

Glänzel, W. (2016). *Bibliometrics. A concise introduction*. Retrieved from https://www.ecoom.be/en/research/bibliometrics

Graf, L. (2009). Applying the varieties of capitalism approach to higher education. *European Journal of Education*, *44*(4), 569–585.

Graf, L. (2013). *The hybridization of vocational training and higher education in Austria, Germany and Switzerland*. Opladen: Budrich UniPress.

Hage, J., & Mote, J. (2008). Transnational organizations and institutional change: The case of the Institut Pasteur and French science. *Socio-Economic Review*, *6*(2), 313–336.

Halsey, A. H. (2000). Further and higher education. In A. H. Halsey & J. Webb (Eds.), *Twentieth century British social trends*. London: Macmillan.

Hinze, S. (2010). Forschungsförderung in Deutschland. In D. Simon, A. Knie, & S. Hornbostel (Eds.), *Handbuch Wissenschaftspolitik* (pp. 162–175). Wiesbaden: VS.

Hoenig, B. (2017). *Europe's new scientific elite: Social mechanisms of science in the European Research Area*. Abingdon: Routledge.

Hohn, H. (2010). Außeruniversitäre Forschungseinrichtungen. In D. Simon, A. Knie, & S. Hornbostel (Eds.), *Handbuch Wissenschaftspolitik* (pp. 457–477). Wiesbaden: VS.

Humboldt, W. (1809). *Antrag auf Errichtung der Universität*. Berlin: Königsberg.

Kennedy, M. (2015). *Globalizing knowledge*. Stanford, CA: Stanford University Press.

Kreckel, R. (2008). Frankreich. In R. Kreckel (Ed.), *Zwischen Promotion und Professur*. Leipzig: Akademische Verlagsanstalt.

Le Deaut, J. (2013). *Refonder l'université, dynamiser la recherche, mieux coopérer pour réussir*. Paris: Ministère de l'enseignement supérieur et de la recherche.

Lenhardt, G. (2005). *Hochschulen in Deutschland und in den USA*. Wiesbaden: VS.

Mahoney, J. (2004). Comparative-historical methodology. *Annual Review of Sociology*, *30*, 81–101.

Merton, R. K. (1942). Science and technology in a democratic order. *Journal of Legal and Political Sociology*, *1*, 115–126.

METRIS. (2012). *Social sciences and humanities in France* (Country Report). Luxembourg: European Commission, DG-Research.
Meyer, J. W. (2009). Universities. In G. Krücken & G. S. Drori (Eds.), *World society: A theory and a research program in context* (pp. 355–372). Oxford: Oxford University Press.
Münch, R. (2007). *Die akademische Elite*. Frankfurt/Main: Suhrkamp.
Musselin, C. (2007). France. In J. J. F. Forest & P. G. Altbach (Eds.), *International handbook of higher education* (pp. 711–728). Dordrecht: Springer.
Musselin, C. (2017). *La grande course des universités*. Paris: Presses de Sciences Po.
Musselin, C., & Vilkas, C. (1994). Interference between scientists and research policy in a French research institution: The case of the CNRS. In U. Schimank & A. Stucke (Eds.), *Coping with trouble* (pp. 127–162). Frankfurt/Main: Campus.
Nature. (2016). *Scientists say 'no' to UK exit from Europe in Nature poll*. Retrieved from http://www.nature.com/news/scientists-say-no-to-uk-exit-from-europe-in-nature-poll-1.19836
Nowotny, H., Scott, P., & Gibbons, M. (2003). 'Mode 2' revisited: The new production of knowledge. *Minerva*, *41*(3), 179–194.
OECD. (2011). *Education at a glance 2011: OECD Indicators*. Paris: OECD.
OECD. (2014). *OECD reviews of innovation policy: France 2014*. Paris: OECD.
OECD. (2015). *Education at a glance 2015: OECD indicators*. Paris: OECD.
OECD. (2016). *Main science and technology indicators*. Paris: OECD.
OECD.stat. (2016). *Main science and technology indicators*. Retrieved from http://stats.oecd.org/Index.aspx?DataSetCode=MSTI_PUB
Oleksiyenko, A. (2014). On the shoulders of giants? Global science, resource asymmetries, and repositioning of research universities in China and Russia. *Comparative Education Review*, *58*(3), 482–508.
Olesen Larsen, P., & von Ins, M. (2010). The rate of growth in scientific publication and the decline in coverage provided by Science Citation Index. *Scientometrics*, *84*(3), 575–603.
Powell, J. J. W., Bernhard, N., & Graf, L. (2012). The emergent European model in skill formation: Comparing higher education and vocational training in the Bologna and Copenhagen processes. *Sociology of Education*, *85*(3), 240–258.
Powell, J. J. W., Graf, L., Bernhard, N., Coutrot, L., & Kieffer, A. (2012). The shifting relationship between vocational and higher education in France and Germany: Towards convergence? *European Journal of Education*, *47*(3), 405–423.
Powell, J. J. W., & Solga, H. (2010). Analyzing the nexus of higher education and vocational training in Europe: A comparative-institutional framework. *Studies in Higher Education*, *35*(6), 705–721.
Pritchard, R. O. M. (2006). Trends in the restructuring of German universities. *Comparative Education Review*, *50*(1), 90–112.
Rosenbloom, J. L., Ginter, D. K., Juhl, T., & Heppert, J. (2014). *The effects of research & development funding on scientific productivity: Academic chemistry, 1990-2009*. NBER Working Paper No. 20595. Retrieved from http://www.nber.org/papers/w20595
Russell Group. (2012). *Jewels in the crown: The importance and characteristics of the UK's world-class universities*. London: Author.
Schofer, E., & Meyer, J. W. (2005). The worldwide expansion of higher education in the twentieth century. *American Sociological Review*, *70*(6), 898–920.
Scott, W. R. (1995/2014). *Institutions and organizations*. Thousand Oaks, CA: Sage.
Scott, W. R. (2015). Organizational theory and higher education. *Journal of Organizational Theory in Education*, *1*(1), 68–76.
Stichweh, R. (1992). The sociology of scientific disciplines. *Science in Context*, *5*(1), 3–15.
Teichler, U. (2005). *Hochschulstrukturen im Umbruch*. Frankfurt am Main: Campus.
Tight, M. (2009). *The development of higher education in the United Kingdom since 1945*. Maidenhead: Open University Press.
Weingart, P. (2001/2015). *Die Stunde der Wahrheit? Zum Verhältnis der Wissenschaft zu Politik, Wirtschaft und Medien in der Wissensgesellschaft*. Weilerswist: Velbrück Wissenschaft.

Weingart, P. (2003/2013). *Wissenschaftssoziologie*. Bielefeld: Transcript Verlag.
Zapp, M., & Powell, J. J. W. (2017). Moving towards Mode 2? Evidence-based policy-making and the changing conditions for educational research in Germany. *Science and Public Policy*. doi:10.1093/scipol/scw091
Zhang, L., Powell, J. J. W., & Baker, D. P. (2015). Exponential growth and the shifting global center of gravity of science production, 1900-2011. *Change: The Magazine of Higher Learning*, *47*(4), 46–49.
Zhang, L., Sun, L., & Bao, W. (2017). The Rise of Higher Education and Science in China. In J. J. W. Powell, D. P. Baker, & F. Fernandez (Eds.), *The Century of Science: The Global Triumph of the Research University* (Vol. 33). International Perspectives on Education and Society. Bingley: Emerald Publishing Limited.

SCIENCE PRODUCTION IN THE UNITED STATES: AN UNEXPECTED SYNERGY BETWEEN MASS HIGHER EDUCATION AND THE SUPER RESEARCH UNIVERSITY

Frank Fernandez and David P. Baker

ABSTRACT

Purpose — *During the 20th century, the United States rapidly developed its research capacity by fostering a broad base of institutions of higher education led by a small core of highly productive research universities. By the latter half of the century, scientists in a greatly expanded number of universities across the United States published the largest annual number of scholarly publications in STEM+ fields from one nation. This expansion was not a product of some science and higher education centralized plan, rather it flowed from the rise of mass tertiary education in this nation. Despite this unprecedented productivity, some scholars suggested that universities would cease to lead American scientific research. This chapter investigates the ways that the United States' system of higher education underpinned American science into the 21st century.*

Design — *The authors present a historical and sociological case study of the development of the United States' system of higher education and its associated research capacity. The historical and sociological context informs our analysis of data from the SPHERE team dataset, which was compiled from the Thomson Reuters' Science Citation Index Expanded (SCIE) database.*

Findings — *We argue that American research capacity is a function of the United States' broad base of thousands of public and broadly accessible institutions of higher education plus its smaller, elite sector of "super" research universities; and that the former serve to culturally support the later. Unlike previous research, we find that American higher education is not decreasing its contributions to the nation's production of STEM+ scholarship.*

Originality/Value — *The chapter provides empirical analyses, which support previous sociological theory about mass higher education and super research universities.*

Keywords: Higher education; Carnegie Classification; doctoral education; STEM+; science productivity; United States

> We should not forget how young the institution of graduate study was by World War II — hardly more than two generations old. Many of the students of the first graduate professors were themselves still active in 1940 and were only then beginning to turn the system over to *their* students. In that brief period, the graduate school had to accommodate itself to two large pressures: numbers of students, expansion of knowledge.
> — Bernard Berelson, *Graduate Education in the United States* (1960)

The United States has led the world as the largest producer of scientific publications in science, technology, engineering, mathematics, and health (STEM+) fields since the early 20th century. Until the late 19th century, Germany led the world in scientific research, largely because the Prussian government developed the modern research university model, but then the global center of scientific, scholarly publications shifted toward the United States (Ben-David, 1977; Zhang, Powell, & Baker, 2015). As access to higher education expanded rapidly after World War II, the number of publicly supported colleges[1] and universities swelled and university-based scientific production dramatically increased. Thus, during the 20th century, the research university became institutionalized in the United States (as well as across the world) as the primary site resourced for knowledge production (Geiger, 2009). Despite wars, economic recessions, energy crises, and tax revolts, the U.S. research university persisted as a strong producer of scientific knowledge (Baker, 2014; Labaree, 2017). And although a stunning rise in productivity of scientists in other nations since the 1980s, most notably in Western Europe and Asia, means that the United States is joined by other nations at the center of science, these nations are using some of the innovations first undertaken in American universities.

Toward the end of the 20th century, some observers sought to characterize universities as weakening or diverted organizations; they speculated that their share of scientific publications would decline, and that they would be outpaced by private industries (Gibbons et al., 1994; Godin & Gingras, 2000). Yet this prediction has proved wrong. University-based researchers continued to not only produce a majority of U.S. scientific publications, they also collaborated with non-university partners to author more than three-quarters of all STEM+ scholarly works. Research universities and inclusive educational practices originating out of public institutions over the last century serve as the backbone of American scientific production. Understanding why this is explains much of the country's scientific success as well as its emulation, accurately or not, through university development policies worldwide (Fu, 2017) for a discussion of the ways that Taiwanese policymakers were inspired by U.S. higher education policy.

We argue here that U.S. scientific production resulted from an unexpected and unintended synergy between the rise of research universities, particularly public ones, and the comparatively rapid development of mass schooling, including mass access to higher education (Baker, 2008a, 2008b). Beginning in the 19th century, expanding primary enrollments gave way to the creation of the comprehensive high school (Labaree, 1988). Then, during the 1920s, the percentage of America's teenagers who attended high school "more than doubled, from 20 to 50 percent" (Levine, 1986, p. 166). Eventually, near-universal secondary school enrollments led to mass enrollment in higher education as waves of high school graduates went on to enroll in higher education (Trow, 2007). Universities not only offered access to broad segments of the population, they also added to the U.S. stock of scientists by training new PhDs in STEM+ fields. Although elite, private universities were the early leaders of U.S. doctoral education, they were outpaced after World War II by large public universities that produced significant numbers of PhDs – thus supplying the human capital necessary for large-scale science production. All of which added to a deepening cultural acceptance and broad legitimation of universities and their products (epistemological, credentials, and human capital) throughout the American society. And, this is likely one key factor behind the high levels of public and private resources that have flowed to universities and enhanced their knowledge production mission.

To illustrate our argument is a brief sociological and historical description of highlights of the development of U.S. higher education and research capacity from the colonial period until the first decade of the 21st century. The section that immediately follows describes how American mass higher education developed as a result of limited national oversight and federal control. The subsequent section describes the origins of the American research university and the recent manifestation of the "super research university" (Baker, 2008a, 2008b, 2014). Then a brief analysis focusing on STEM+ publications written by university-based scientists and other indicators of university-based science capacity further illustrates our interpretation of American sociological-historical case, plus its implications for understanding develops in other nations in this larger SPHERE project found here.

THE UNITED STATES AS THE BIRTHPLACE OF MASS HIGHER EDUCATION

Americans borrowed the residential college model from England and adopted the vision of the research university from Germany, but they added a new element to their system of higher education – relatively unrestricted founding of institutions that evidentially lead to mass access (Baker, 2014; Kerr, 2001; Labaree, 2010, 2017; see also Powell & Dusdal, 2017). During the colonial period, colonists founded nine different colleges to train religious leaders in British North America, but only two colleges (Cambridge and Oxford) existed in England. After the revolution, American states were free to set their own charters without a Federal ministry of education, and local boosters founded colleges in new territories as settlers moved west. Although the national government did not financially support the growth of the higher education sector, it did nothing to impede the founding of new universities.[2] In the words of Joseph Ben-David: "There was only a general democratic pressure to make higher education accessible to all strata of society" (1977, p. 25). Thus, by the middle of the 19th century, U.S. higher education had expanded to include an array of 250 public and private colleges.

By contrast, the strong, centralized English government financially supported Cambridge and Oxford but limited the emergence of new universities, despite large population growth (Riddle, 1993; Stone, 1972). In France, there were more universities than in England, but unlike the American case, "the distinguishing characteristic" of the French "system was it complete subjection to the central government" (Ben-David, 1977, p. 16). Nearby, the German-Prussian government cultivated a relatively homogenous set of research universities, and "the middle classes had little political influence and no effective organization" to press for a different type of university or broadly accessible higher education (Ben-David, 1977, p. 21). See Powell and Dusdal (2017) for a more detailed discussion of the development of higher education in England, France, and Germany. Compared to its early European competitors, the U.S. system of higher education was unregulated, decentralized, and could rapidly expand to meet demand growing out of mass secondary education (Baker, 2008a).

During the American Civil War, the U.S. Congress took its first step in shaping (but note, not controlling) the country's system of higher education. Unlike many countries around the world, the federal government had never, and would never establish, established a national university, but instead it assisted in establishing public universities in states. Therefore, it was significant when legislators from the Union states (the Confederate states had seceded) passed the first Morrill Land Grant Act giving state governments large swaths of federal land, which they could sell to build universities. The only stipulation, which was loosely interpreted and inconsistently implemented – was that the newly erected universities must teach courses in agricultural and mechanical (A&M) fields. These so-called "land-grant" colleges opened access to higher education and helped set the expectation that universities should focus on dispensing applied knowledge that improves society (Baker, 2008a). After the Civil War, a second system of land-grant colleges was built in the American South (Geiger, 2000a). The land-grant bills helped finance the creation of new universities such as Cornell University and the Massachusetts Institute of Technology (MIT), as well a large number of institutions that are now known as state universities (e.g., Michigan State University; University of California) or "A&M" universities (e.g., Texas A&M University). Through a mix of federal legislation such as the Morrill Land Grant Acts, state initiatives, and the efforts of other entrepreneurs, the number of colleges and universities continued to grow. By the late 19th century, single American states had more colleges than whole countries; for example, in 1880 England had only doubled its number of universities to four. The public, land-grant universities became part of the foundation for mass higher education, the creation of a growing pool of new scientists, as well as a significant share of scientific publications.

At the start of the 20th century, the United States had almost 1,000 colleges and universities, while France, for example, had just 16. In the decades that followed, an entire class of normal schools (training colleges for primary school teachers) became regional state universities, many of which went on to be full-scale research universities, such as was the case with the University of California, Los Angeles (Levine, 1987). Although the growth of U.S. higher education slowed during the interwar period, and American colleges and universities were hit hard by the Great Depression in the 1930s, during the 1940s, universities were enlisted in the national war effort and they began to train soldiers and conduct war research (Geiger, 2014; Gillmor, 2004).

After the World War II, U.S. higher education continued to grow at a rapid pace. Open-access community colleges (subbaccalaureate colleges without selective admissions processes) opened "at a rate exceeding one per week" (Geiger, 2005, p. 62). The Servicemen's Readjustment Act of 1944 subsidized the costs of attending higher education for U.S. military veterans, and the broad system of colleges and universities continued to grow to accommodate demand for education and training. By the mid-1950s, over two million veterans attended higher education, and more than 400,000 engineers, 90,000 scientists, and 60,000 doctors were trained by U.S. universities (Katznelson, 2005). From the 1950s to the present, colleges and universities continued to grow and diversify with women, racial and ethnic minorities, older, and international students attending in greater numbers. This was mostly, however, not because of some national policy or even national vision; the nation's decentralized and state-level governance of education unintentionally yielded its large scientific capacity.

Mass Capacity Led to Mass Access to Institutions, Programs, and Degrees

As the number of colleges and universities increased, so did access to higher education, the breadth of academic fields of study, and types of degrees offered by universities. In the first four decades of the 20th century, the proportion of the U.S. age cohort that enrolled in higher education increased from 4% to over 15%. Mass undergraduate enrollments not only created a pool of potential graduate school applicants, but the percentage of students who earned baccalaureate degrees and went on to graduate schools also increased from approximately 6% to 15%. At the highest level of university study, the percentage of doctorates increased by 250% in the first two decades of the 20th century and by more than 500% in the subsequent two decades. These enrollment increases were all the more remarkable because they occurred in a generation where the population of young Americans grew at a relatively small rate (Clark, 1995).

As higher education expanded, professors began to assert their expertise in developing curriculums and academic programs – and even to define new areas of knowledge and scientific inquiry. For example, at land-grant Cornell University, faculty members were innovative in several academic fields. In 1881, a Cornell physics professor and inventor organized a full-fledged program of study in electrical engineering. Similarly, Cornell's chemistry program began to offer industrial chemistry courses, which led to studies of chemical engineering in 1891 (Geiger, 2014). Farther west, Iowa State College of Agricultural and Mechanical Arts had grown beyond its original name and mission. By the early 20th century, Iowa State spawned departments and programs in fields such as education, journalism, psychology, and the liberal arts (Levine, 1986). In summary, once universities were organized, they took on lives of their own. The large public and land-grant universities grew beyond their original mandates and began to produce knowledge and granting degrees in new fields.

Around the turn of the 20th century, a series of studies of university systems in Iowa, Washington, and more than a dozen other states recommended that state flagship universities should hold monopolies on graduate-level academic programs and that land-grant universities should not be allowed to offer courses or degrees in non-technical and agricultural fields. The same experts argued that state normal schools or teachers' colleges should not be allowed to provide instruction to those who would not enter the teaching profession. In California, the Carnegie Foundation for the Advancement of Teaching conducted a study of the state's burgeoning system of public higher education and concluded that the University of California, Los Angeles should not be allowed to grant doctorates. It was thought that if universities were allowed to grow without constraints on the numbers of students they educated and the types of degrees they awarded, public funds would be wasted and universities would overeducate state populations (Levine, 1986). Despite the dire warnings of the so-called experts, their proposed restrictions failed to come to pass, and the American system of mass higher education and graduate education thrived in its usual decentralized fashion.

America's universities not only offered degrees in innovative fields of study, many colleges and universities began offering doctoral degrees, unencumbered by any central authority governing higher education. In the late 1800s, 12 colleges or universities in just the state of Ohio – approximately one-third of the institutions in that state – offered doctoral programs (Geiger, 2000b). The only national attempts to regulate doctoral education came from networks of faculty or institutional peers. First, the American Philological Association and the American Association for the Advancement of Science adopted a resolution to crack down on the overly liberal distribution of honorary doctorates. Then, in 1900 the Association of American Universities (AAU) was formed to standardize doctoral education. Although many colleges or universities shuttered PhD programs after the AAU issued new standards for doctoral education, the goal of the AAU was not to create a monopoly on the production of graduate degrees. Instead, the AAU guidelines were meant to ensure that the PhD met a certain standard of rigor or quality. Although many of the doctoral programs that emerged in the late 19th century did not last, the fact that they existed demonstrates that the relative lack of government oversight provided leeway for colleges and universities to freely pursue graduate education and knowledge production (Geiger, 2000b). This open environment set the stage for the development of the American version of the intensive research university.

THE RISE OF THE UNIVERSITY RESEARCH MODEL

The birth of what has become emulated worldwide in the American research universities is best understood as a dynamic process that played out in this decentralized and somewhat unregulated environment (Baker, 2008b). Although university leaders borrowed from European models, the unique organizational form of the American research university was born out of competition between ambitious public and private universities seeking to reconcile mass undergraduate education and knowledge-producing research programs. Newer, well-endowed institutional entrants to the higher education landscape challenged the larger, older state universities, and regional rivalries broke out between public and private institutions. For example, Stanford University was a source of competition for the University of California, and the Universities of Illinois, Michigan, and Wisconsin were challenged by the University of Chicago (Levine, 1986). Several distinct components of the history of how public and private institutions came to produce doctorates and scientific research agendas illustrate the rise of the research university in the United States.

Distinguishing between Undergraduate and Post-Baccalaureate Education

When American universities sought to develop graduate education, they also needed to re-assess undergraduate instruction. For example, the University of Michigan was founded as a state institution in 1837, during an era when American colleges were more like secondary schools (the equivalent of the German *gymnasium*), but by the 1870s, the University of Michigan had standardized the requirements for master's degrees and began awarding PhDs (Turner & Bernard, 2000). Michigan's first president, Henry Tappan, realized that to build a true university, he needed to improve academic instruction. Under Tappan's leadership, Michigan instituted reforms to move beyond the classical curriculum, characterized by rote memorization of dead languages, and distinguish post-graduate education from undergraduate studies. Tappan called the new program for post-baccalaureate study the "university course." At this early state, Michigan did not offer formal graduate degrees, and Tappan's university course was not what we would recognize as a contemporary graduate school. However, "Tappan's much-discussed innovations at Michigan in the 1850s and early 1860s provided the first American model of a modern university," a model which was later emulated (Geiger, 2014; Turner & Bernard, 2000, p. 225).

Through the latter half of the 19th century, U.S. scholars who wanted to earn doctorates had to travel to Europe to complete their graduate studies. In fact, "until about the 1870s, German universities were virtually the only institutions in the world in which a student could obtain training in how to do scientific or scholarly research" (Ben-David, 1977, p. 22). Thus, the German model of research and scholarship inspired the American PhD. When Yale awarded the first PhD in the United States in 1861, it catalyzed American graduate education and university scholarship (Geiger, 1997). Cornell, a land-grant university founded in 1868, awarded its first PhD in 1872 (Geiger, 2014). The University of Michigan began awarding the PhD in the 1870s, followed by Wisconsin in 1892, and Illinois in 1903 (Geiger, 2014; Turner & Bernard, 2000). In their haste to develop graduate education, faculty members awarded doctoral degrees before their universities developed proper graduate schools to administer doctoral education. However, the graduate schools were not far behind.

Wisconsin founded a formal graduate school in 1904, replete with funding for graduate fellowships and teaching assistantships for its doctoral students. Although Illinois was late to award its first PhD, it established a graduate school in 1906, beating the University of Michigan by several years. Slow to begin graduate education, Illinois got a strong start through a $50,000 infusion from the state legislature. Even though the awarding of PhDs and chartering of graduate schools happened out of order, strong graduate education programs came together in the end. Wisconsin was the largest public producer of PhDs between 1898 and the outbreak of the World War II. Around the end of the World War I, Illinois was the ninth largest producer of PhDs in the United States (Geiger, 2014).³

Across the Atlantic, English universities did not even begin to award the PhD until the period between 1917 and 1920 (Bucock, Baston, Scott, & Smith, 2003; see also Simpson, 1983). Bucock et al. (2003) observed: "In America, with its significant private university sector, diverse institutional patterns of university education have long existed …. In the UK, on the other hand, where degree-awarding powers are regulated by Act of Parliament, a more unitary system has evolved" (p. 337). Although Bucock and colleagues correctly observed that private universities contributed to U.S. doctoral education, they did not fully appreciate the innovative capacities of American public universities. The creation of the public land-grant university system pre-dated by nearly a century the emergence of an English equivalent where curriculum and research would focus on practical sciences and technology. In the United States, authority was decentralized and state universities were relatively free to open new campuses, create new academic programs, and grant graduate degrees in new fields of study. By contrast, even into the 20th century, a royal charter was required in England to obtain university status (read degree-granting authority), and the creation of a "British MIT" was a much-debated, decades-long process that was heavily influenced by the Ministry of Education (Bucock et al., 2003).

Building Sustainable Research Universities Required Faculty and Finances

The research enterprise required two things from the new universities: reorganization and resources. The growth of the professoriate and the emergence of academic departments or disciplinary schools was a prerequisite to the rise of large research universities. Colleges that did not substantially grow their faculties, such as Princeton, stayed relatively small. Larger faculties allowed for differentiation between teaching and research roles as well as the ranking of faculty within departments based on assignments and productivity. In essence, larger academic departments created economies of scale that allowed some faculty to specialize and focus on research.

During the late 19th and early 20th centuries, faculty members were increasingly expected to publish academic research to receive advancement within the university (Levine, 1986, p. 176). As the faculty at Michigan embraced academic research, they pressed for changes within the university and in 1900 many senior faculty members formed "a Research Club" and "pressed the point that scholarly work should be the basis for faculty appointments and promotion" (Geiger, 2014, p. 357). The Research Club advocated re-organizing the administrative apparatus of the university to create a formal graduate school.

The senior faculty were joined by younger colleagues who chartered a "Junior Research Club" and female professors who started a "Women's Research Club" (Geiger, 2014, p. 356). By 1912, the University of Michigan, created a formal graduate school directed, at least in part, by the faculty-initiated Research Club (Geiger, 2014).

Although certain private institutions, such as Johns Hopkins and the University of Chicago, tried to focus nearly exclusively on graduate education and research, they found that model to be unsustainable. Public universities were able to hire more faculty because they admitted larger numbers of undergraduate students whose tuition helped pay faculty salaries (Geiger, 1997). Additionally, public universities in many states benefitted as state governments increased funding for higher education after state coffers rebounded from the recessions of the late 19th century. The large public universities used their increased state appropriations to hire more faculty members, growing their faculties more quickly than their student bodies (Geiger, 2014). Of the 15 largest universities (measured by number of students) in the United States in 1930, six were research universities, and half of those six were state universities: California, Minnesota, and Illinois. Ohio State also made the 1930 list of largest universities by enrollment, but at the time, it was not considered a research university (Geiger, 2009).

Donors complemented undergraduate tuition with generous philanthropy that made the emergence of new American research universities possible. As students went on to achieve success, many alumni later became prodigious donors who further subsidized university research (Geiger, 1997). Five of the top 11 most successful fundraising campaigns between 1919 and 1925 were conducted by state or land-grant colleges; the Universities of Illinois, Michigan, Minnesota, Wisconsin, and Cornell ranked among Harvard, Chicago, Princeton, Stanford, Johns Hopkins, and the University of Pennsylvania (Geiger, 2009). Also in the early 20th century, philanthropic endowments came to be organized and distributed through non-profit foundations such as the Rockefeller trusts. The directors of the Laura Spellman Rockefeller Memorial supported basic scientific research with the hope that it would yield advances that would improve society. Industry groups also came to support university research, albeit to a lesser extent (Geiger, 1997).

When the United States committed to full-scale involvement in World War II, new federal funds were disbursed for academic research. After the war, funding was also made available for universities to conduct military research, study atomic energy, and conduct applied research for improving public health. Funding for universities to conduct basic scientific research, that is, non-applied research, was not a federal priority until the launch of the Sputnik satellite caused panic and made policymakers determine not to allow American science to fall behind Soviet advances (Geiger, 1997). Between 1958 and 1968, inflation was relatively low, but the federal government increased funding for basic research by a factor of seven — from under $180 million to more than $1.25 billion (Clark, 1995).

Some have come to understand the creation of Johns Hopkins, Stanford, and Chicago as evidence that elite, private institutions dominate U.S. higher education. If the early age of the research university was dominated by the private sector, then the post-World War II era decidedly belonged to the large public sector. Although a few private research universities were founded in the 19th century, in the latter half of the 20th century, public universities continued to grow into large research powerhouses. Schools such as the University of Arizona and the Georgia Institute of Technology grew into prominent public research universities thanks to growing enrollments, the establishment of doctoral programs, and large amounts of federal research dollars (Geiger, 2004).

In the 1980s, 14 of the top 20 universities (and 12 of the top 15 — or 80%) with the highest levels of research and development (R&D) expenditures were public or land-grant universities (Clark, 1995). Not only were public and land-grant institutions highly ranked, but most of the large public universities outranked the Ivy League institutions on the list. For example, the University of Minnesota (7th), Texas A&M University (8th), and the University of Washington (11th) had higher levels of R&D spending than Harvard University (15th), University of Pennsylvania (18th), Columbia University (19th), and Yale University (20th). This is an additional metric that helps demonstrate that elite private American universities are important, but they are only part of the story of U.S. research production (Clark, 1995).

Research Universities Were Early Organizers of Scientific Efforts

The emergence of research universities and graduate education coincided with the organization and professionalization of academic disciplines. As universities grew and faculty members became increasingly specialized, the faculties of the academic disciplines created associations for formalizing knowledge production and disseminating research findings. In this way, disciplines become "communication systems" that use scientific publications to bring together communities of authors with similar areas of disciplinary research (Stichweh, 2001, p. 13728). According to Stichweh (2001), the disciplinary-publication process created "a kind of feedback loop" whereby "publications, as the ultimate form of scientific communication, exercised pressure on the scientific production process" and "scientific disciplines then became research disciplines based on the incessant production of novelties" (p. 13729).

Two disciplinary associations were founded before the start of the Civil War, but between 1865 and 1905 more than 20 disciplinary associations were founded in the United States. Many of these associations have endured to this day such as the American Mathematical Society (founded 1888) and the

American Society for Microbiology (founded 1899). Several disciplinary associations founded their own academic journals or scholarly publications, such as the *Bulletin of the American Mathematical Society*. Other publications entered into circulation without the sponsorship of a disciplinary association; some of these later merged with disciplinary associations, while others remained independent. Notable publications founded during the late 19th and early 20th centuries are recognizable names in academia today: *Science, Journal of Physical Chemistry*, and the *American Journal of Psychology*. By 1906, American research universities were home to many academic publications; the University of Chicago housed the *Journal of Geology*, and Harvard University was home to the *Annals of Mathematics* (Geiger, 2009). Not to be outdone, the public universities also helped publish academic work. For example, in 1893 the University of California launched its own press to support faculty authors (Geiger, 2014).

In France and Germany, many of the nations' prolific researchers worked for non-university research institutes (Powell & Dusdal, 2017), but historically, the lion's share of prominent U.S. scientists worked for American universities. In 1906, "James McKeen Cattell, the editor of *Science* ... attempted to identify the one thousand most eminent American scientists in a dozen fields" (Geiger, 2009, p. 38). Cattell found that more than 40% of the 1000 scientists were affiliated with just 15 research universities. Nearly 200 additional scientists were located at other colleges and universities. Thus, nearly 60% of the nation's leading scientists were affiliated with the higher education sector. Among public universities, the University of California had a plurality of these men of science (Geiger, 2014). Only about 10% were identified as working for the U.S. government, and 25 others were affiliated with non-university organizations.[4] This pattern set the precedent that in the United States scientists worked for universities. For example, in the decades that followed, physicists who immigrated to the United States during the World War II were often given academic appointments at American universities.

Faculty Professional Autonomy and Scientific Research

The university houses science production, but faculty members conceive of research studies, conduct laboratory experiments or data analyses, and circulate research findings. During the 20th century, U.S. faculty members were granted unparalleled professional autonomy. Previously, American faculty members had little job security and could be dismissed without cause and without recourse. However, during and after World War II, a tacit agreement emerged among government (i.e., through a series of court decisions), universities, and faculty to develop tenure, protect academic free speech, and, ultimately, allow faculty to pursue research with little oversight (Metzger, 1990). Faculty members were also given deference over the development of courses, programs of study, and graduate student admissions.

Because university researchers were granted significant professional autonomy, they have been able to focus on long-term knowledge production that led to the rise of new, interdisciplinary fields such as molecular biology and biotechnology (Etzkowitz, Webster, Gebhardt, & Terra, 2000). One notable example of biotechnology research comes from a partnership between the University of California, San Francisco (UCSF) and the private company, Genentech. Together, UCSF and Genentech pursued recombinant DNA research and synthesized the human gene for insulin. Some may assume that the industrial partner led the effort and the professors merely played a supporting role; however, Genentech sought out university research expertise. After the UCSF-Genentech success, many for-profit corporations sought to emulate the model of finding university partners (Geiger, 2004).

Hall, Link, and Scott (2003) noted that academic researchers have tended to be involved in knowledge production in emerging areas of scientific inquiry. By their nature, emergent fields of study were not established and research projects were often problematic. Although those projects "experience more difficulty and delay" the involvement of university partners meant that the studies were less likely "to be aborted prematurely" (Hall et al., 2003, p. 485). In part, these types of findings have been attributed to academic freedom as a central tenet of the research university and faculty members' prerogative to pursue research on new topics without corporate constraints (Aghion, Dewatripont, & Stein, 2008).

The Rise of the Super-Research University

The qualities of the mid-20th century research university have intensified to create a contemporary "super research university" (Baker, 2008a, 2008b). The new class of super research universities is small in number but large in influence. Super research universities are often household names and top international rankings of leading "world-class research universities." In addition to the system of mass higher education, it is important to understand the role of the super research university in U.S. science production because the super research university has become a global model.

Unlike the colonial colleges and the state universities of the 18th and 19th centuries, the super research university assumes a global mission. Instead of serving the state, region, or even federal government, super research universities consider themselves – and are looked upon by others – as global actors with a network of international peers. In the post-modern knowledge society, these universities are increasingly research-intensive. To foster science production, super research universities compete for funding from government or private sources and use multi-disciplinary research centers and laboratories to help faculty share capital-intensive resources. This movement from less-costly "little science" to an expensive "big science" model is justified by the widely held value that knowledge production is good for society (Baker, 2008a, 2008b, 2014; de Solla Price, 1963).

When super research universities adopted global missions, they intensified their recruitment efforts for international students, faculty, and administrators. Faculty members are recruited for research prowess and expertise. For example, the London School of Economics recruited more than 80% of its faculty from outside England. In addition, the emergence of the super research university has led to changing roles for faculty members. The stereotypical image of the lone professor holed up in an office for a lifelong career of solitary research is increasingly quaint (what de Solla Price, 1963 described as "little science"). Instead, more professors are members of interdisciplinary teams of researchers and often belong to global networks of scholars (Baker, 2008a, 2008b; Zhang et al., 2015).

Super research universities have achieved new levels of organizational complexity to support faculty as international purveyors of science. These universities have adopted new academic programs, established professional schools, and built offices to facilitate university−industry partnerships − often culminating in fully operational science parks that are jointly staffed by academic and private sector researchers. For example, companies in Silicon Valley have partnered with researchers at the University of California at Berkeley (public) and Stanford University (private) to produce innovative research with practical applications. Similar arrangements have been facilitated at the Research Triangle, which is a cooperation between businesses and industries, North Carolina State University (public), Duke University (private), and the University of North Carolina at Chapel Hill (public). These arrangements are paradigm examples of what Elzinga (2012) refers to as "megascience" projects or those that represent "a range of interests from science, state and regional bureaucracies as well as private corporations" (p. 417).

The management apparatus of the university has also expanded to include non-faculty professionals who oversee new patents, ensure protection for research involving human subjects, and facilitate government relations (Baker, 2008a, 2008b; see also Slaughter & Rhoades, 2004). Many U.S. super research universities, such as The Pennsylvania State University, have multi-billion dollar annual budgets that finance their rising costs of research and support offices. As federal funding declined from its Cold War zenith, super research universities have diversified their revenue sources. The contemporary blend of funding includes government appropriations, revenue from research grants, private philanthropy, undergraduate tuition and fees, student athletics, and profits from miscellaneous enterprises that are not part of the university's academic core. For example, Stanford University generates revenue by leasing land to host a shopping mall on its campus (Baker, 2008a, 2008b). The cost structure of the super research university has allowed American researchers to move beyond de Solla Price's "big science" model and embrace "megascience" projects (Elzinga, 2012).

Super research universities compare themselves to global peers and perpetuate globalization by acknowledging international rankings and building international campuses. In the pursuit of conducting large-scale research projects, super research universities simultaneously compete and cooperate for faculty and funding. Super research universities are a minority of U.S. colleges and universities, but they sit atop a broad base of thousands of other colleges and universities that offer mass (universal) college access and carry out knowledge production, albeit to a lesser extent. Super research universities set an example that many other institutions aspire to emulate both within the United States and around the world. This has been referred to as the Emerging Global Model (Mohrman, Ma, & Baker, 2008).

Mass higher education and the development of the research university (and its contemporary variant, the super research university) likely allowed the United States to produce a large share of the world's STEM+ publications since 1900. Employing Thomas Reuters' Science Citation Index Expanded (SCIE) data from the Science Productivity, Higher Education, and Research Economy (SPHERE) project, augmented with data on the production of PhDs, from the U.S. Doctorate Records File, and higher education enrollments, the mass education to major research universities argument is illustrated in how mass undergraduate enrollment, graduate education, and faculty scientific societies aligned with growing science production. Note, some publications were included more than once in the SCIE/SPHERE dataset. Duplicate entries for the same publications were not dropped from the SCIE/SPHERE dataset to preserve as much information about authors' affiliations and the role of different types of universities in science production.

SCIENCE PRODUCTION IN THE UNITED STATES

The U.S. research university was formed to produce knowledge. To do this, universities had to expand beyond undergraduate and into graduate education. New faculty were hired, and academic departments were organized to reduce teaching loads, foster specialization, and allow professors to devote more time and effort to research. To make all this possible, universities admitted greater numbers of undergraduates to pay tuition and fees, along with graduate students to teach course sections and provide research assistance. As greater numbers of research universities emerged, faculty created national societies that mirrored the nascent academic disciplines at the campus level. These four elements of U.S. higher education are included in Fig. 1.

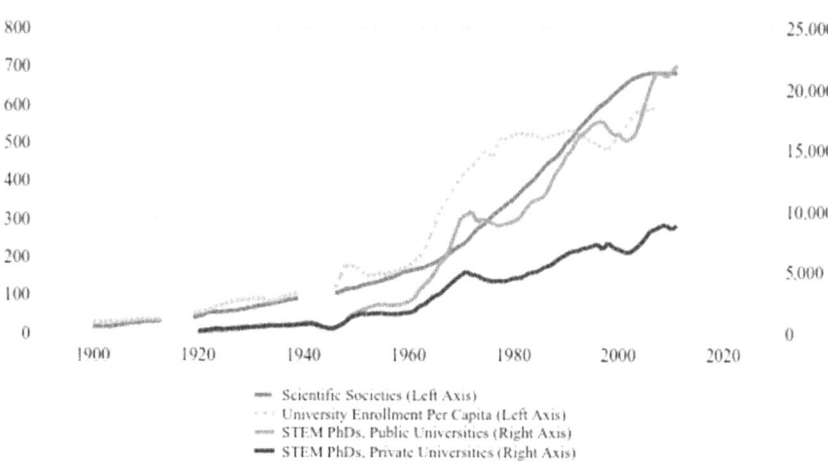

Fig. 1. Four Indicators of Scientific Research Capacity in the United States, 1900–2011. *Notes*: Trends in Fig. 1 were calculated by the authors. STEM PhDs include doctorates awarded in the following fields: Computer and Information Sciences; Engineering; Life Sciences; Mathematics; Physical Sciences, and Psychology. *Source*: Data on scientific societies and university enrollments per capita was shared by Evan Schofer.

Throughout the period of study, these four elements of U.S. mass higher education substantially increased. The scientific societies that tend to organize faculty members, create networks for peer-review, and produce flagship academic journals grew from less a few dozen at the beginning of the century to nearly 700 by the early 21st century. Whereas less than 5% of U.S. young adults attended higher education in 1900, the proportion increased to almost 60% by the mid-2000s. Although private universities (Stanford, Harvard, etc.) receive many accolades for their selective doctoral programs, both public and private universities trained large cohorts of PhD students, culminating in training tens of thousands of doctorates in STEM+ fields in recent years. Although public universities and private universities trained similar numbers of PhDs for the early part of the century, after World War II, public universities steadily out-produced their private counterparts and eventually more than doubled their PhD output.

Three Patterns of Science Publications

The analyses in this section reveal three patterns of scientific publishing in the United States. First, since 1900, universities have increasingly been responsible for science production in the United States. Second, throughout the century, university-based authors increasingly collaborated with scientists working for other types of organizations, such as industry and government labs. Third, overall American science production is led by a core group of super research universities that rely on a strong foundation of thousands of institutions of higher education, spanning public, private-non-profit, and private-for-profit sectors. These patterns reveal complex synergies and counter the narrative that American science is the product of a few private elite schools, such as Harvard and Stanford.

For each decade from 1900 to 2010, random samples of all scientific publications in the SCIE/SPHERE dataset were analyzed to determine whether STEM+ publications were produced by the higher education sector and to examine the proportion to which public and private higher education contributed to science publications. Universities were coded as either public or private using the Carnegie Classifications Data File (Carnegie Foundation, 2012). The Carnegie Foundation assigned unique identification numbers to U.S. universities and classified the universities along multiple dimensions, including whether they were publicly or privately controlled. The Carnegie Foundation also classified universities according to the types of degrees they offered (e.g., to distinguish between two-year colleges, baccalaureate institutions, master's degree-granting institutions, doctoral universities, and other special-purpose institutions). The SCIE/SPHERE data were manually coded to be merged with the Carnegie Classifications Data File.

The transition from "little science" to "big science" (de Solla Price, 1963) was accomplished through the efforts of university-based academic researchers. In 1900, 42% of STEM+ publications were produced by the U.S. higher education sector. In two decades, universities produced more than half (53%) of published STEM+ research. The proportion of research produced by the higher education sector remained relatively flat, and even slightly declined through 1950 (50%). However, as shown in Fig. 2, American universities increased their research production in the latter half of the 20th century. U.S. universities produced two-thirds of STEM+ research by 1980 and then 70% by 2010.

Fig. 2 also demonstrates that the balance of production shifted from private universities to public universities throughout the century. In 1900, private universities produced many more STEM+ publications than public universities. However, the proportion of public-private university science production began to flip around the middle of the 20th century. By the end of the period of study, the massive system of public universities produced more than twice as many publications as private universities.

Increasing Coauthorship with University-Based Scientists
To add to these statistical descriptions, in Fig. 3 the SCIE/SPHERE data were examined for author affiliations. When multiple authors wrote STEM+ publications the authors' affiliations were analyzed to determine whether at least one author was identified as working for a university. In 1900, universities produced

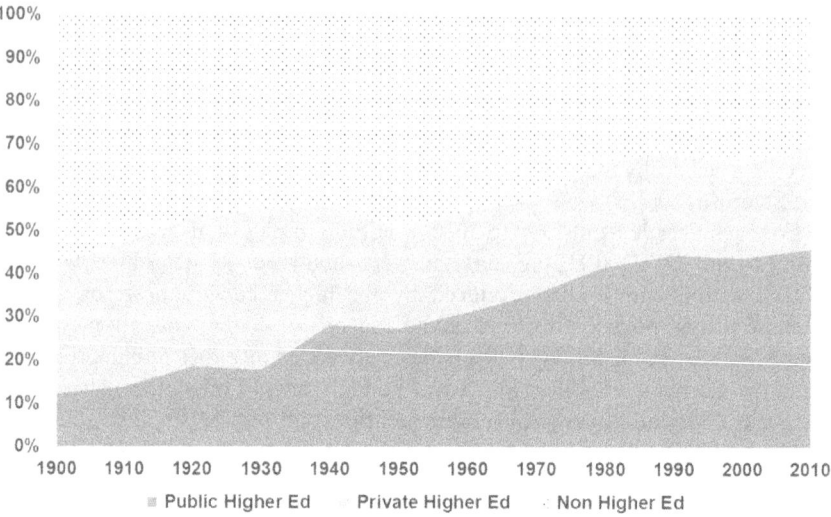

Fig. 2. Percent of Samples of U.S. STEM+ Publications Produced by Public, Private, and Non-Higher Education Organizations, 1900–2010. *Source*: SPHERE project database of SCIE publications (Thomson Reuters' Web of Science). Classification of Institutions of Higher Education as private or public based on the Carnegie Foundation for the Advancement of Teaching's (2012) Carnegie Classifications Data File.

over one-third of all U.S. STEM+ publications, and in the early part of the century, university-based authors were less likely to collaborate with non-university-based colleagues. Throughout the 20th century, university authors were more likely to publish with researchers who did not work at universities. Still, more than half of all U.S. STEM+ publications were written completely by university-affiliated scientists. In the United States, university-affiliated scientists produced a majority, and they collaborated with scientists in the non-higher education sector to produce a super-majority, of STEM+ publications.

The examination of SCIE/SPHERE data shows that more than 80% of the United States' 2011 STEM+ publications included at least one university-based author. The difference between the dashed and solid lines in Fig. 3 can be understood as representing the institutionalization of the university into American science production. Though the data are descriptive, the analyses suggest that university-based scientists were increasingly incorporated into the work done by non-university industries or research centers.

Synergy between Super Research Universities and Mass Higher Education
The previous two figures relied on samples of publications at different time points since 1900. Additional analyses were also conducted using one complete

Fig. 3. Percent of U.S. Publications Produced by University Authors, 1900–2011. *Source*: SPHERE project database of SCIE publications (Thomson Reuters' Web of Science).

cross-section of American STEM+ publications to determine how the different sectors of U.S. higher education contributed to the nation's science productivity. First, the dataset was sorted to generate a list of the top 20 university producers of STEM+ research publications in 2011. The list emphasizes the core group of "super research universities" (Baker, 2008a, 2008b, 2014) that produce the largest percentages of scholarly publications in STEM+ fields. Out of the top 20 universities, 13 (65%) were classified as public. In 2011, Harvard University had the highest percentage of STEM+ publications, and University of Michigan was the largest public university producer of STEM+ articles. In fact, Michigan out-produced the rest of the Ivy League universities and Stanford University. In another signal of the strength of the American public university sector, five of the 10 University of California campuses produced larger percentages of U.S. scholarship than Yale University. Together, the top 20 universities accounted for just over one-third (33.49%) of all U.S. STEM+ publications in 2011.

Analyses of the SCIE/SPHERE authorship data show a synergistic relationship between the small core of super research universities that produce disproportionately large percentages of publications and the large base of colleges and universities that offer mass or universal access to higher education, and produce smaller, but important numbers of scientific publications. The top 20 super research universities produced a large share of U.S. university-based STEM+ publications in 2011, but they were joined by a wide array of higher education institutions with varying levels of scientific research capacity. Analyses of SCIE/SPHERE data show that there were 26 universities that produced more than 5,000 publications, accounting for 39.91% of U.S. publications. Another 100 universities were credited with producing less than 5,000 but more than 1,000 publications (45.33% of the U.S. 2011 total). Additionally, 176 universities produced between 999 and 100 publications (11.55%), and the largest group of 1,313 institutions of higher education produced less than 100 publications for a total of 3% of the 2011 U.S. STEM+ publications (Table 1).

The 2011 cross-section of STEM+ publications was further analyzed to examine the roles of different types of colleges and universities, using the Carnegie Classifications of Institutions of Higher Education, including measures of institutional control – that is, whether the college or university was a public, private (not-for-profit), or private (for-profit) organization. As Table 2 shows, the small number of elite, private research universities sit atop a broad

Table 1. Top 20 University Producers of STEM+ Publications, 2011.

Rank	University Name	Private or Public	Percent of 2011 U.S. STEM+ Publications
1	Harvard University	Private	3.66
2	University of Michigan-Ann Arbor	Public	2.12
3	Johns Hopkins University	Private	1.94
4	University of Washington-Seattle Campus	Public	1.89
5	University of California-Los Angeles	Public	1.87
6	Stanford University	Private	1.77
7	University of Pennsylvania	Private	1.75
8	University of California-San Francisco	Public	1.66
9	University of Pittsburgh-Pittsburgh Campus	Public	1.66
10	Columbia University in the City of New York	Private	1.54
11	University of California-Berkeley	Public	1.49
12	Duke University	Private	1.47
13	University of California-San Diego	Public	1.45
14	University of Minnesota-Twin Cities	Public	1.38
15	University of Wisconsin-Madison	Public	1.38
16	University of California-Davis	Public	1.33
17	University of Florida	Public	1.33
18	Yale University	Private	1.31
19	University of North Carolina at Chapel Hill	Public	1.26
20	Ohio State University-Main Campus	Public	1.23

Source: SPHERE project database of SCIE publications (Thomson Reuters' Web of Science). Classification of Institutions of Higher Education based on the Carnegie Foundation for the Advancement of Teaching's (2012) Carnegie Classifications Data File.

Table 2. STEM+ Productivity Rates of Different Sectors of U.S. Higher Education, 2011.

Classification of Institution of Higher Education	Public Institutions	Private (Not-for-Profit) Institutions	Private (For-Profit) Institutions	Total Number of Publication-Producing Institutions	Number of Publications by Classification	Percent of Publications by Classification
RU/VH: Research universities (very high research activity)	73	35	0	108	397,153	73.8
RU/H: Research universities (high research activity)	70	25	0	95	51,184	9.5
DRU: Doctoral/research universities	29	43	5	77	6,541	1.2
Master's comprehensive colleges	262	268	9	539	15,827	3.0
Baccalaureate colleges	104	289	5	398	5,603	1.0
Medical and health professional schools	27	78	6	111	58,817	10.9
Associate's colleges	249	11	3	263	2,624	0.5
Other special focus institutions	5	64	9	17	720	0.1
Total	819	813	37	1,608	538,469	100.0

Source: SPHERE project database of SCIE publications (Thomson Reuters' Web of Science). Classification of Institutions of Higher Education based on the Carnegie Foundation for the Advancement of Teaching's (2012) Carnegie Classifications Data File.

base of public and private institutions with varying levels of productivity. Oftentimes, policymakers and researchers seek to replicate the "Stanford-Silicon Valley Model," but to characterize America's exceptional research production as a result of a few elite research institutions ignore the complex organizational field that undergirds American science.

The first row of Table 2 includes universities with very high research activity such as University of California, Berkeley (public) and Stanford University (private). The second row includes those universities that were classified by the Carnegie Foundation as having high research activity: for example, The University of Alabama (public) and Catholic University of America (private). Examples of Doctoral/Research Universities in the third row are University of Massachusetts, Boston (public) and American University (private). The fourth row represents three Carnegie classes of master's colleges and universities (smaller, medium, and large programs), which include San Francisco State University (public) and Suffolk University (private). Based on the Carnegie classifications, colleges that might be represented in the fifth row of baccalaureate-granting colleges include the United States Naval Academy (public) or Harvey Mudd College (private). The sixth row of medical and health professional schools includes the University of California, San Francisco (public) as well as Weill Cornell Medical College (private).

Each sector of the American higher education system includes both public and private actors. Among multiple sectors, including the three most research-intensive, there were more public than private universities contributing to the production of American science. There were only a couple more private than public universities, which contributed to STEM+ scholarship in the "master's comprehensive" category. Compared to public universities, private baccalaureate colleges, private medical and health professional schools, and private special focus institutions in other areas employed more scientists who published in STEM+ fields. The public two-year sector employed included more colleges with STEM+ research-producing scientists than the private two-year sector.

In addition to productivity, the SCIE/SPHERE data were used to calculate participation rates of different sectors of U.S. higher education in STEM+ publishing. First, the dataset was limited to identify the number of unique colleges and universities that hosted STEM+ authors. Then, the colleges and universities were aggregated using the Carnegie Classifications data file and indictors of institutional control. Participation rates were calculated by dividing the number of institutions with scientists whose publications appeared in the SCIE/SPHERE dataset by the total number of each group of institutions in the United States (in other words, including universities that did not employ scientists whose publications were included in the SCIE/SPHERE dataset). For example, 35 private universities with very high research activity contributed to 2011 U.S. STEM+ publications. Because there were only 35 private universities with very high research activity in the United States, this sector had a 100% participation rate.

Table 3. Participation Rates of Different Classes of Institutions in STEM+ Research Production, 2011.

Classification of Institution of Higher Education	Public Institutions (%)	Private (Not-for-Profit) Institutions (%)	Private (For-Profit) Institutions (%)	Total (%)
Associate's colleges	23.6	9.6	0.4	13.7
RU/VH: Research universities (very high research activity)	100.0	100.0	0.0	100.0
RU/H: Research universities (high research activity)	94.6	100.0	0.0	96.0
DRU: Doctoral/research universities	96.7	87.8	45.5	85.6
Master's comprehensive colleges	96.7	70.5	12.3	74.4
Baccalaureate colleges	75.9	54.1	3.6	49.1
Medical and health professional schools	90.0	56.9	11.8	50.9
Other special focus institutions	14.3	14.5	4.7	11.7
Total	48.1	47.4	3.0	36.0

Source: SPHERE project database of SCIE publications (Thomson Reuters' Web of Science). Classification of Institutions of Higher Education based on the Carnegie Foundation for the Advancement of Teaching's (2012) Carnegie Classifications Data File.

Small numbers of private, prestigious research universities are complemented by high participation rates of public colleges and universities across multiple sectors. In several sectors, STEM+ authors were more likely to be affiliated with public organizations. For example, compared to private institutions, public institutions that were classified as Doctoral/Research Universities, Master's Comprehensive Colleges, Baccalaureate Colleges, or Medical and Health Schools were more likely to participate in the production of "Big Science" (Table 3).

Table 3 shows that in many sectors, private institutions had lower participation rates than public institutions in STEM+ science production in 2011. The private-for-profit universities had the lowest participation rates. Taken together, Table 3 and Table 4 show that American science is based on a synergistic relationship between public and private institutions, as well as between super research universities and other, less research-intensive sectors of the higher education system.

CONCLUSION AND IMPLICATIONS

The U.S. system of higher education is a dynamic field of institutions that were started by a variety of public and private entrepreneurs (e.g., states, churches, independent philanthropists, and local boosters). The American system of mass higher education evolved across the American states relatively free from federal oversight or regulation. The disjointed system of colleges and universities offered something for everyone, and U.S. higher education thrived throughout the 19th and 20th centuries in an environment with widespread public support (Labaree, 2010, 2017). This unique synergy between public and private institutions of higher education, as well as mass higher education and super research universities, sets the United States apart from much of the world. Whereas countries such as China are relying primarily on public universities to grow science production (Rhoads, Shi, & Chang, 2014; Zhang, Sun, & Bao, 2017), the United States has a multi-faceted system capable of supporting "big science" and even "megascience" scientific research initiatives (de Solla Price, 1963; Elzinga, 2012). The future of U.S. science production − and its relation to economic competitiveness and national security − rests on the nation's ability to maintain a favorable environment for both public and private institutions to support STEM+ research.

In the early 20th century, the number of faculty members in the United States increased fivefold, enrollments in higher education increased sixfold, the number of bachelor's degrees awarded expanded sevenfold, the number of matriculated graduate students 13-fold, and the number of graduate degrees earned by 17-fold (Clark, 1995). In the first four decades of the 20th century, the United States experienced more than threefold increase in the number of universities that offered doctoral programs, and "the top twenty" doctoral granting institutions in the United States "individually offer[ed] a quantitative production of Ph.D.s hardly approached by more than a few institutions in all the rest of the world" (Clark, 1995, p. 129). When compared to the rest of the world, the comparatively short history of the United States can be understood as a rapid transition from "elite to mass to universal access" to higher education (Trow, 2007).

People mistakenly thought that American higher education was a weak institution and that the U.S. higher education sector would produce less of the nation's science in the 21st century (Gibbons et al., 1994; Godin & Gingras, 2000). If governments were to make policy decisions on this incorrect assumption (such as reducing funding for basic research), they could inadvertently slow U.S. scientific production. Instead of presuming that universities would succumb to for-profit, industrial organizations, U.S. higher education is a strong social institution that brings together different organizational actors and vast resources to facilitate capital-intensive "megascience" (Elzinga, 2012). In the absence of a strong national planning agency that oversees U.S. higher education, several organizational forms have committed themselves to supporting scientific research both through individual faculty efforts and through cross-organizational collaboration.

Many of the experts who predicted that universities would produce a declining share of scientific research were mistaken (Gibbons et al., 1994; Godin & Gingras, 2000). Although the non-higher education sector makes significant contributions to U.S. science production, America's public and private research universities have continued to account for a majority of the nation's scientific output. When universities coauthor publications with industry partners, the university-related publications make up more than 80% of all U.S. science. This supports the argument put forth by Aghion et al. (2008) that university-based authors often take the lead with risk-averse industry partners to produce knowledge in new fields.

This chapter tells one side of the story of U.S. science production. Early development of a broad system of public and private higher education created a solid foundation for science production in the United States. The loosely organized collection of U.S. colleges and universities spawned their own symbiotic relationships that created vast networks for scientific research. In the 20th century, the institutionalization of the research university model was followed by the emergence of the super research university, and the higher education sector produced vast proportions of American science. However, even as the United States continues to make year-to-year gains in the number of scientific publications it produces, the share of American science is in relative decline when compared to the emergence of huge global science. Asian and European countries have bought into the emerging global model (Mohrman et al., 2008) of mass higher education and university-based research. If the global center of gravity for science production continues to shift to the East (Zhang et al., 2015), the unique constellation of public and private research universities and other higher education institutions in the United States will be the keys to continued remarkable growth in American scientific productivity.

NOTES

1. In the United States, the term "college" is generally used to refer to post-secondary schools that do not award research doctorates. "University" refers to a post-secondary organization that grants PhD degrees.
2. American universities later received direct support through the Land Grant Acts, research grants, and grants or loans for students.
3. These brief historical highlights are not meant to provide an exhaustive summary of the development of graduate education in the United States. Instead, these points illustrate how quickly PhD education spread through American higher education, especially in the large public universities.
4. The survey could not identify the locations of 270 of those who had been identified as the "1,000 Leading American Men of Science" (Geiger, 2009, p. 39).

REFERENCES

Aghion, P., Dewatripont, M., & Stein, J. C. (2008). Academic freedom, private-sector focus, and the process of innovation. *The RAND Journal of Economics*, *39*(3), 617–635.

Baker, D. (2008a). Privatization, mass higher education, and the Super Research University: Symbiotic or Zero-sum Trends? *Die Hochschule: Journal für Wissenschaft und Bildung* [German Journal on Higher Education], *2*, 36–52.

Baker, D. (2008b). Mass higher education and the super research university: A symbiotic relationship. *International Higher Education*, *2*, 36–53.

Baker, D. (2014). *The schooled society: The educational transformation of global culture*. Palo Alto, CA: Stanford University Press.

Ben-David, J. (1977). *Centers of learning: Britain, France, Germany, United States*. Berkeley, CA: The Carnegie Foundation for the Advancement of Teaching.

Berelson, B. (1960). *Graduate education in the United States*. New York, NY: McGraw-Hill.

Bucock, J., Baston, L., Scott, P., & Smith, D. (2003). American influence on British higher education: Science, technology, and the problem of university expansion, 1945–1963. *Minerva*, *41*(4), 327–346.

Carnegie Foundation for the Advancement of Teaching. (2012, February). Carnegie Classifications Data File.

Clark, B. R. (1995). *Places of inquiry: Research and advanced education in modern universities*. Berkeley, CA: University of California Press.

de Solla Price, D. J. (1963). *Little science, big science, and beyond*. New York, NY: Columbia University Press.

Elzinga, A. (2012). Features of the current science, policy regime: Viewed in historical, perspective. *Science and Public Policy*, *39*(4), 416–428.

Etzkowitz, H., Webster, A., Gebhardt, C., & Terra, B. R. C. (2000). The future of the university and the university of the future: Evolution of ivory tower to entrepreneurial paradigm. *Research Policy*, *29*(2), 313–330.

Fu, Y. C. (2017). Science production in Taiwanese universities, 1980–2011. In J. J. W. Powell, D. P. Baker, & F. Fernandez (Eds.), *The Century of Science: The Worldwide Triumph of the Research University* (Vol. 33). International Perspectives on Education and Society. Bingley: Emerald Publishing Limited.

Geiger, R. L. (1997). Research, graduate education, and the ecology of American universities: An interpretive history. In L. F. Goodchild & H. S. Wechsler (Eds.), *The history of higher education* (2nd ed.). ASHE Reader Series, Simon & Schuster Custom Publishing.

Geiger, R. L. (2000a). *The American college in the nineteenth century*. Nashville, TN: Vanderbilt University Press.

Geiger, R. L. (2000b). The crisis of the old order: The colleges in the 1890s. In R. L. Geiger (Ed.), *The American college in the nineteenth century* (pp. 264–276). Nashville, TN: Vanderbilt University Press.

Geiger, R. L. (2004). *Research and relevant knowledge: American research universities since World War II*. New Brunswick, NJ: Transaction Publishers.

Geiger, R. L. (2005). Ten generations of American higher education. In P. Altbach, P. Gumport, & R. Berdahl (Eds.), *American higher education in the twenty-first century: Social, political, and economic challenges* (pp. 38–70). Baltimore, MD: Johns Hopkins University Press.

Geiger, R. L. (2009). *To advance knowledge: The growth of American research universities 1900–1940*. New Brunswick, NJ: Transaction Publishers.

Geiger, R. L. (2014). *The history of American higher education: Learning and culture from the founding to World War II*. Princeton, NJ: Princeton University Press.

Gibbons, M., Limoges, C., Nowotny, H., Schwartzman, S., Scott, P., & Trow, M. (1994). *The new production of knowledge: The dynamics of science and research in contemporary societies*. Thousand Oaks, CA: Sage.

Gillmor, C. S. (2004). *Fred Terman at Stanford: Building a discipline, a university, and Silicon Valley*. Stanford, CA: Stanford University Press.

Godin, B., & Gingras, Y. (2000). The place of universities in the system of knowledge production. *Research Policy*, *29*(2), 273–278.

Hall, B. H., Link, A. N., & Scott, J. T. (2003). Universities as research partners. *Review of Economics and Statistics, 85*(2), 485–491.

Katznelson, I. (2005). *When affirmative action was white: An untold history of racial inequality in twentieth-century America*. New York, NY: WW Norton & Company.

Labaree, D. F. (1988). *The making of an American high school: The credentials market and the Central High School of Philadelphia, 1838–1939*. New Haven, CT: Yale University Press.

Labaree, D. F. (2010). Understanding the rise of American higher education: How complexity breeds autonomy. *Peking University Education Review, 8*(3), 24–39.

Labaree, D. F. (2017). *A perfect mess: The unlikely ascendancy of American higher education*. Chicago, IL: Chicago University Press.

Levine, D. O. (1986). *The American college and the culture of aspiration, 1915–1940*. Ithaca, NY: Cornell University Press.

Metzger, W. P. (1990). The 1940 statement of principles on academic freedom and Tenure. *Law and Contemporary Problems, 53*(3), 3–77.

Mohrman, K., Ma, W., & Baker, D. P. (2008). The research university in transition: The emerging global model. *Higher Education Policy, 21*, 5–27.

Powell, J. J. W., & Dusdal, J. (2017). The European Center of Science Productivity: Research Universities and Institutes in France, Germany, and the United Kingdom. In J. J. W. Powell, D. P. Baker, & F. Fernandez (Eds.), *The Century of Science: The Worldwide Triumph of the Research University* (Vol. 33). International Perspectives on Education and Society. Bingley: Emerald Publishing Limited.

Rhoads, R. A., Shi, X., & Chang, Y. (2014). *China's rising research universities: A new era of global ambition*. Baltimore, MD: Johns Hopkins University Press.

Riddle, P. (1993). Political authority and university formation in Europe, 1200–1800. *Sociological Perspectives, 36*(1), 45–62.

Simpson, R. (1983). *How the PhD came to Britain. A century of struggle for postgraduate education* (SRHE Monograph 54). Guildford, England: Society for Research into Higher Education.

Slaughter, S., & Rhoades, G. (2004). *Academic capitalism and the new economy: Markets, state, and higher education*. Baltimore, MD: Johns Hopkins University Press.

Stichweh, R. (2001). History of scientific disciplines. In N. J. Smelser & P. B. Baltes (Eds.), *International encyclopedia of the social & behavioral sciences* (Vol. 20, pp. 13727–13731). Amsterdam: Pergamon.

Stone, L. (1972). *The causes of the English revolution 1529–1642*. New York, NY: Harper Torchbooks.

Trow, M. (2007). Reflections on the transition from elite to mass to universal access: Forms and phases of higher education in modern societies since WWII. In J. F. Forest & P. G. Altbach (Eds.), *International handbook of higher education* (pp. 243–280). Dordrecht: Springer Netherlands.

Turner, J., & Bernard, P. (2000). The German model and the graduate school: The University of Michigan and the origin myth of the American university. In R. L. Geiger (Ed.), *The American college in the nineteenth century* (pp. 221–241).

Zhang, L., Powell, J. W., & Baker, D. P. (2015). Exponential growth and the shifting global center of gravity of science production, 1900–2011. *Change: The Magazine of Higher Learning, 47*(4), 46–49.

Zhang, L., Sun, L., & Bao, W. (2017). The Rise of Higher Education and Science in China. In J. J. W. Powell, D. P. Baker, & F. Fernandez (Eds.), *The Century of Science: The Worldwide Triumph of the Research University* (Vol. 33). International Perspectives on Education and Society. Bingley: Emerald Publishing Limited.

CHANGING SCIENCE PRODUCTION IN JAPAN: THE EXPANSION OF COMPETITIVE FUNDS, REDUCTION OF BLOCK GRANTS, AND UNSUNG HEROES

Kazunori Shima

ABSTRACT

Purpose — *This chapter describes the changing nature of Japanese science production. The author explains Japan's rise to prominence as the country with the second largest number of annual research publications in the world, followed by its subsequent decline to fifth in the world. The chapter highlights implications for Japanese universities of shifts in research policy.*

Design — *The author examines bibliometric data as well as contextual data from Japan's Ministry of Education, Culture, Sports, Science and Technology to analyze the contributions of Japanese universities in STEM+ research from 1975 to 2010. The chapter examines changes in higher education funding policies and their relationship to university-based production of STEM+ research articles in recent decades. The chapter also includes brief comparative analyses with selected other countries, including highly productive countries in Asia (China, Korea, and Taiwan), Western Europe (France, Germany, and the United Kingdom), as well as the United States.*

Findings — *Bibliometric data show that Japan's second-tier research universities contributed to Japan's rise to the second largest producer of STEM+ scientific research. When these second-tier research universities received less money from the government, their scientific output declined and aggregate national research output declined relative to other countries.*

Originality/value — *The chapter uses more recent and comprehensive data than other studies of research output of Japanese universities and offers several implications for research policy and higher education funding. Indeed, the chapter argues that second-tier universities are the "unsung heroes" of Japanese science production. The chapter also suggests that Japanese policymakers may need to reconsider their reliance on competitive funding over block grants that sustain research universities.*

Keywords: Science production; national universities; research universities; higher education funding; research policy; Japan

In his book *The Age of Discontinuity* (1968), Peter Drucker coined the phrase "the knowledge economy." In the globalized knowledge economy, science production is critical for the future success of a country. In many countries, governments expect universities to play a key role in knowledge production, particularly in science, technology, engineering, mathematics, and health-related fields (STEM+). Japan is one such country. This chapter will clarify key changes related to science production in Japan over the past several decades. For this study, we define the production of science in Japan as the number of articles published by scholars affiliated with universities, research organizations, and other organizational forms in Japan. Clarifying the number of articles published by scholars affiliated with different forms of research organizations is as crucial for Japan's academic, social, and economic environments as it is for its global position as a top science producer. Therefore, trends in the number of articles produced in Japan will be analyzed from historical and international comparative perspectives.[1]

Highlighting key results in advance, I find that science production in Japan grew between 1980 and 2000, with Japan becoming the second largest science producing country in 1990. However, science production in Japan stagnated after 2000, with Japan's position declining to fifth largest science producing country in 2010. National universities have been the core of science production and helped drive changes in national scientific production and sustained competitiveness. From 1995 to 2000, national universities that were not among the top 10 expanded their number of articles published at similar rates as did the top 10 national universities. In particular, second-tier national research universities have been important in STEM+ science production. However, under the expansion of competitive funding programs and intensive allocation to first-tier national universities — Former Imperial Universities and universities that were founded prior to World War II — the number of articles published by second-tier national universities stagnated. Thus, the expansion of competitive funds is not a panacea for promoting science production. Furthermore, I argue for the continued importance of second-tier research universities for Japanese science production overall.

This chapter begins by explaining the expansion of higher education and the differentiating university system in Japan (Section "Expansion of the Japanese Higher Education and University System"). Second, data and methods applied in this analysis on science production are explained (Section "Data and Methods"). Third, I show the changing scientific production in Japan compared to several European countries, East Asian countries, and the United States (Section "Changes of Scientific Productivity in Japan and International Comparison"). Fourth, we show the changes of scientific production in Japan, focusing on types of research organizations (Section "Types of Research Organization"), types of national universities (Section "Types of National Universities"), and individual universities (Section "Article Production by Individual National Universities") (see Table 1, Typology of Universities in Japan). Then, I provide the policy context for changes in scientific production, focusing on the expansion of competitive funds and their allocation by the Ministry of Education, Culture, Sports, Science and Technology (MEXT) with the aim of establishing "world-class" research and education bases or world-class universities (Section "Expansion of Competitive Funds since 2000"). Lastly, I summarize the results of my analysis and argue that second-tier national universities are important actors which sustain the base of science production in Japan as "unsung heroes" (Section "Findings and Implications").

EXPANSION OF THE JAPANESE HIGHER EDUCATION AND UNIVERSITY SYSTEM

The number of students enrolled in the higher education system in Japan increased during two periods (1950 to mid-1970s and mid-1980s to mid-1990s) and experienced two stagnation periods (see Fig. 1). As a result, student enrollments in 2010 were about 15 times larger than in 1950. Many OECD countries have experienced this kind of expansion (OECD, 2013). There are several organizational forms in the Japanese higher education system — universities, junior colleges, technical colleges, and specialized training colleges — yet universities have clearly played the crucial part in expansion. Although the ratio has fluctuated during this period, universities enrolled a maximum of 94% of overall enrollments in 1950, compared to a minimum of 64% in 1992, and around four-fifths in 2010 (Fig. 1).

Table 1. Typology of National Universities in Japan.

Type	Prestige	Type of National University									
			Name of National University								
Type A: Universities which have multiple disciplinary schools	High ←←←←←←←→→→→→→ Low	Former Imperial University	Hokkaido University	Tohoku University	The University of Tokyo	Nagoya University	Kyoto University	Osaka University	Kyushu University		
		Pre-War University	University of Tsukuba	Chiba University	Nigata University	Kanazawa University	Kobe University	Okayama University	Hiroshima University	Nagasaki University	Kumamoto University
		Post-War University 1	Gunma University	Shinshu University	University of Toyama	Gifu University	Shimane University	Yamaguchi University	Kagawa University	Ehime University	Saga University	Oita University	Kagoshima University	University of the Ryukyus
		Post-War University 2	Hrosaki University	Akita University	Yamagata University	University of Yamanashi	University of Fukui	Mie University	Tottori University	The University of Tokushima	Kochi University	University of Miyazaki
		Post-War University 3 (without MedSchool)	Iwate University	Fukushima University	Ibaraki University	Utsunomiya University	Saitama University	Ochanomizu University	Yokohama National University	Shizuoka University	Shiga University	Nara Women's University	Wakayama University

Post-War College (Humanities/ Social Science)	Otaru University of Commerce	Tokyo University of Foreign Studes	Tokyo University of the Arts	Hitotsubashi University	National Graduate Institute for Policy Studes							
Post-War College (Education)	Hokkaido University of Education	Miyag University of Education	Tokyo Gakugei University	Joetsu University of Education	Aichi University of Education	Kyoto University of Education	Osaka University of Education	Hyogo University of Education	Nara University of Education	Naruto University of Education	Fukuoka University of Education	National Institute of Fitness and Sports in Kanoya
Post-War College (Engineering/ Agriculture)	Muroran Institute of Technology	Obihiro University of Agriculture and Veterinary Medicine	Kitami Institute of Technology	Tsukuba University of Technology	Tokyo University of Agriculture and Technology	Tokyo Institute of Technology	Tokyo University of Marine	The University of Electro-Communications	Nagaoka University of Technology	The Graduate University for Advanced Studes	Nagoya Institute of Technology	Toyohashi University of Technology
	Kyoto Institute of Technology	Japan Advanced Institute of Science and Technology	Nara Institute of Science and Technology	Kyushu Institute of Technology								
Post-War College (Medicine)	Asahikawa Medical University	Tokyo Medical and Dental University	Hamamatsu University School of Medicine	Shiga University Medical Science.								

Type B: Colleges which have one dsciplinary school

Source: Developed and modified from Yoshida (2002) by the author.

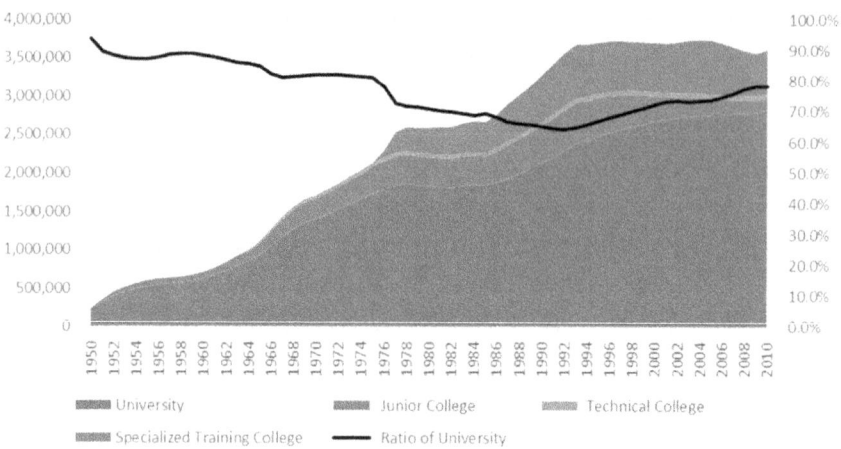

Fig. 1. Student Enrollments by Higher Education Organizational Form, Japan, 1950–2010. *Source*: School Basic Survey (MEXT).

Student enrollments are important as they exemplify the long-term expansion of the higher education system in Japan and its growing capacity for science production. Another indicator relevant to science production is the Grant-in-Aid for Scientific Research (KAKENHI) program, the largest and most prevalent competitive research grants in Japan. The ratio of universities among state-funded organizational forms is 87.7%. This shows that universities play the most crucial role in science production in Japan.[2] Within this funding stream, 68.2% of all KAKENHI grants were allocated to national universities, 4.8% to public universities, and 14.7% to private universities. From these numbers, it is clear that national universities are crucial to science production, even though less than 10% of all university students were enrolled in national universities in 2010.

DATA AND METHODS

This chapter applies the SPHERE project database (Powell et al., 2017)[3] to analyze changes in Japanese scientific productivity from 1975 to 2010, a period that witnessed shifts in the global positioning of Japanese science production. Regarding the Web of Science Science Citation Index Expanded data, I apply a narrower definition of scientific articles than do Saka and Kuwahara (2013), who in their analyses included "article," "article and proceedings," "reviews," and "letter and note." Thus, the present analysis is more selective, focusing only on full-fledged research articles, considered the "gold standard" in bibliometric studies.

In terms of counting, the "whole count" method is used to measure and allocate article publications in the cross-national analysis. In this manner, when one article has two authors, both of whom are affiliated with Japanese universities, I count this as one article produced in Japan. However, when one article has two authors and one author is affiliated with a Japanese university and the other author works for an American university, I count the same article once for Japan and once for the United States. I also apply this "whole count" method to the number of articles produced at the individual university level.[4]

CHANGES OF SCIENTIFIC PRODUCTIVITY IN JAPAN AND INTERNATIONAL COMPARISON

For decades, Japan has been a key country contributing to global science output. In international comparison, the number of articles produced in China (CHN), France (FRA), Germany (GER), Japan (JPN), Korea (KOR), Taiwan (TWN), the United Kingdom (UK), and the United States (USA) has grown from 1975 to 2010 in all countries (see also other chapters in this volume). However, increases in article production occurred at different rates (see Fig. 2, showing five-year intervals).

The United States and China have vastly increased their output of published articles since 1975, with the United Sates still the dominant world center of research, but with China increasing its output even more quickly since the turn of the century. The United Kingdom, Germany, France, and Japan increased their production of articles from 1975 to 2000. However, Japan increased the number of articles produced more rapidly than the United Kingdom, Germany, or France over the same period (1975–2000). Beginning in 1985 and continuing throughout the period of study, China, Korea, and Taiwan all rapidly increased the number of articles produced. While the United States continued to increase its level of article production through 2010, the United Kingdom, Germany, France, and Japan stagnated from 2000 to 2005. Japan is the only country of these that stagnated in the number of articles it produced from 2005 to 2010. Since 1995, the number of articles produced in China increased more rapidly than that in the United Kingdom, Germany, France, and Japan. In 2005, China became the second largest producer of STEM+ research articles.

As shown in Fig. 2, by 1990, Japan had become the second largest country in terms of science production; however, in 2010, Japan's rank had fallen to fifth. The number of articles produced in Japan has stagnated since 2000. On the other hand, the numbers from the United States, China, Korea, and Taiwan have continued to rise, and after 2005 the United Kingdom, Germany, and France escaped stagnation and again increased the number of articles produced. Based on this trend, Korea and Taiwan may surpass Japan in terms of article production in the coming decades.

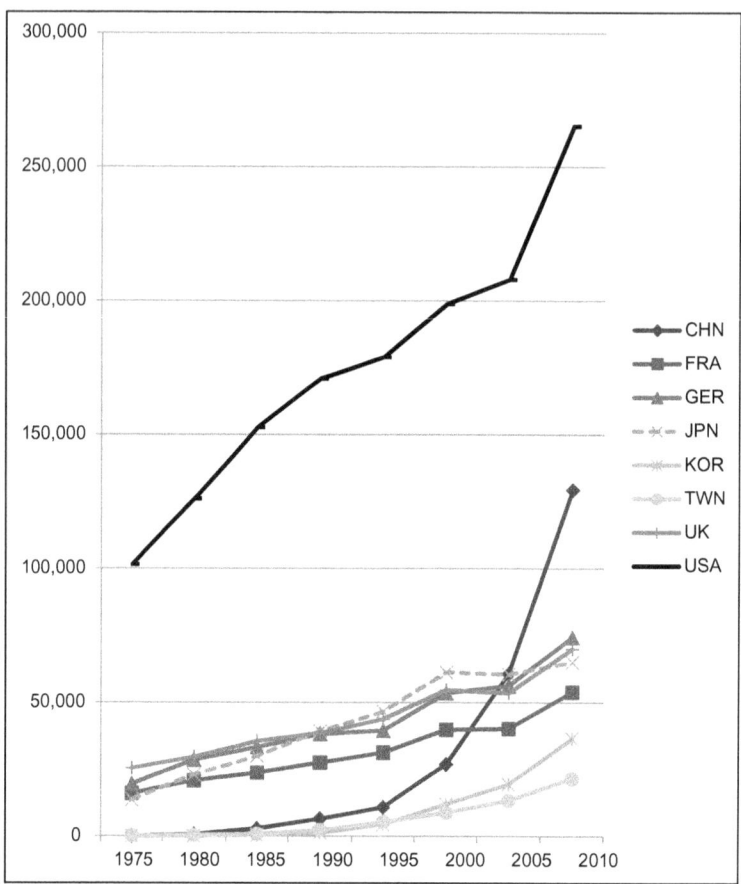

Fig. 2. Rise in Research Articles Produced, Japan and Selected Other Countries, 1975–2010. *Source*: SPHERE project database of SCIE publications (Thomson Reuters' Web of Science).

STRUCTURAL CHANGES IN HIGHER EDUCATION AND SCIENTIFIC PRODUCTIVITY IN JAPAN

Types of Research Organization

In Japan, large numbers and different types of organizations contribute to the production of research articles. The organizational forms producing science include (a) 86 national universities, which were established by the national government and were incorporated before 2004 (e.g., the University of Tokyo and Kyoto University); (b) 95 public universities, which were established by local governments, with most of these incorporated after 2004 (e.g., Tokyo Metropolitan University and Osaka City University); (c) 597 private universities established by incorporated educational institutions (e.g., Keio University and Waseda University); (d) inter-university research institutes that were established by the national government for research with the aim to promote the open use of advanced facilities among researchers throughout Japan; (e) national research institutes, which were established for research by the national government (e.g., Riken and New Energy and Industrial Technology Development Organization)[5]; (f) incorporated administrative agencies, which were established by the Act on General Rules for Incorporated Administrative Agency, which have research departments (e.g., National Hospital Organization); (g) other research-producing organizational forms, including private companies.[6]

It is apparent that national universities create the lion's share of science production in Japan (Figs. 3 and 4). National universities in Japan increased the number of articles they produced, although the proportion of articles they produced decreased from around 60% in 1975 to around 45% in 2010. Private universities increased the number of articles they produced from 1975, but the share of total articles produced is still less than 15%. Other producers, including business enterprises, constitute the second largest group, but the number of articles produced decreased between 2000 and 2005. Since 1995, incorporated administrative agencies have increased the number of articles they produce. Lastly, the analysis emphasizes that among all organizational forms, the university is the core producer of science in Japan, producing around 65% of science articles (similar in proportion to Germany, see Powell & Dusdal, 2017).

Types of National Universities

Although national universities are the largest producers of research articles, there are several types of national universities. In this section, I explain the different types of national universities in Japan, outlining a typology of nine national university types (see Table 1).

Initially, all national universities are divided into type A or B. Type A includes comprehensive universities with more than three types of disciplinary schools (e.g., humanities, social science, science and engineering, and medical science), and type B is composed of universities with only one type of disciplinary school. Type A universities include all universities that were established during Japan's imperial period and before World War II. Most other university types were established after World War II.[7] The ordering of the university types of type A represents a status hierarchy. As the oldest type, former imperial universities are the most prestigious universities in Japan, especially the University of Tokyo and Kyoto University.

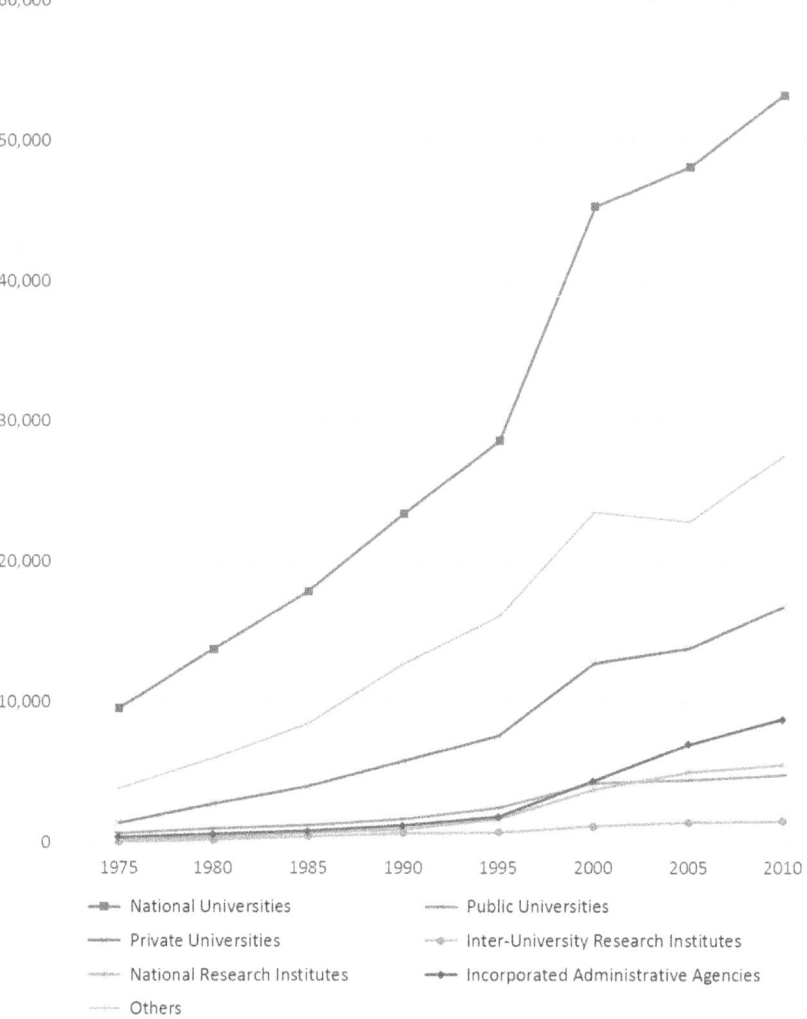

Fig. 3. Rise in Total Number of Research Articles Produced in Japan by Organization Type, 1975–2010. *Source*: SPHERE project database of SCIE publications (Thomson Reuters' Web of Science).

Regarding type B universities, each type of university has a different single disciplinary school. On average, type B universities are smaller in size (as measured by enrollments and university income) than type A universities, especially Post-War Colleges (i.e., those that focus on the Humanities/Social Sciences and Education). Nevertheless, there are some prestigious colleges among those of

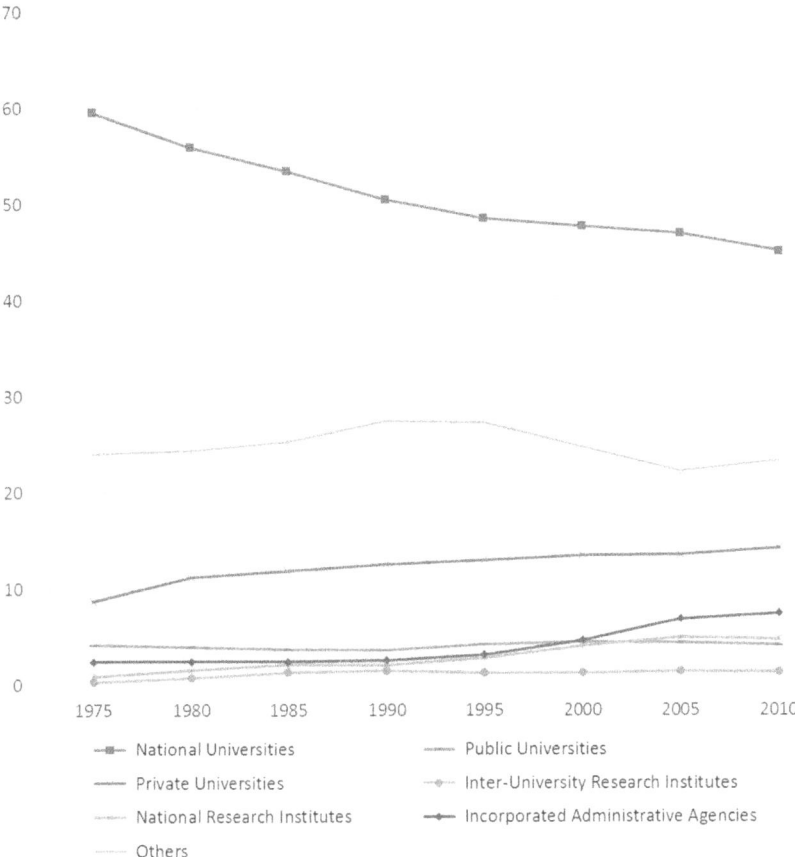

Fig. 4. Changes in the Share of Research Articles Produced in Japan by Organization Type, 1975–2010. *Source*: SPHERE project database of SCIE publications (Thomson Reuters' Web of Science).

type B, for example, Hitotsubashi University, Tokyo Institute of Technology, and Tokyo Medical and Dental University.

I will show changes in the number of articles produced according to the types of national universities (Figs. 5 and 6). Based on Fig. 5, since 1975, former imperial universities have been the core source of article production by national universities, and they have considerably increased the number of articles produced, although their share had been decreasing until 2000. Thereafter, imperial universities again started increasing their share. Pre-World War II universities also increased their number of articles; they increased their share of articles produced until 1990, but after that time their share has been stable. Post-World War II universities 1 and 2 also increased their number of articles and their

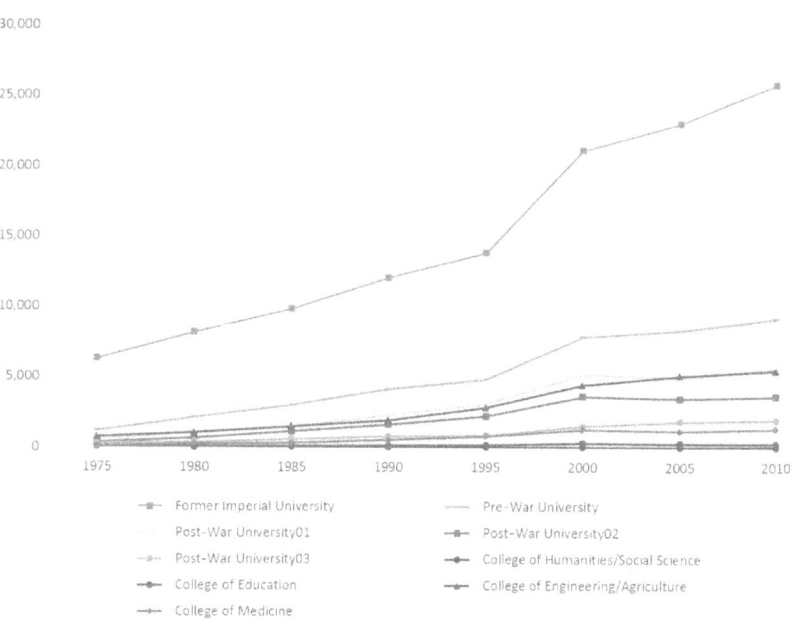

Fig. 5. Changes in Research Articles Produced in Japan by Types of National University, 1975–2010. *Source*: SPHERE project database of SCIE publications (Thomson Reuters' Web of Science).

share of articles produced until 2000, when their shares started to decrease or stagnate. In terms of share, former imperial universities and post-World War II universities 1 and 2 have moved in different directions, and the difference between these types of university had decreased through 2000 but increased after that.

Fundamentally, individual post-World War II colleges (engineering/agriculture) are much smaller institutions than individual type A universities. However, even they have increased the number of articles they have produced since 1975. Hence, post-World War II colleges (engineering/agriculture) have become one of the core producers of articles in Japan. In fact, their share of articles has been growing since around 1975, now reaching more than 10%.

Article Production by Individual National Universities

In this section, I show changes in the number of articles produced at the individual university level during three periods: from 1995 to 2000, from 2000 to 2005, and from 2005 to 2010 for more detail at the organizational level. I focus on these three periods because they include the years when Japan was the

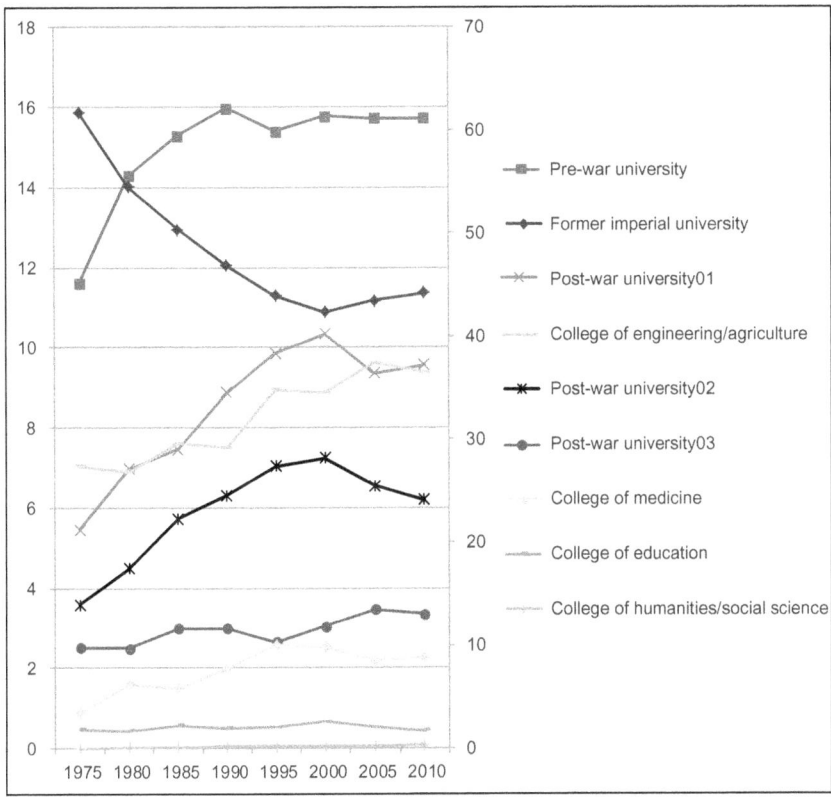

Fig. 6. Changes in Share of Research Articles Produced in Japan by Types of National University, 1975−2010. *Note*: The second Y-axis is used for Former Imperial Universities. *Source*: SPHERE project database of SCIE publications (Thomson Reuters' Web of Science).

second largest producer of scientific articles (after the United States) as well as the period that saw Japan drop to fifth largest producer. First, I show changes in the number of articles at the individual university level from 1995 to 2000. In Figs. 7 and 8, increases in the number of articles produced from 1995 to 2000 are plotted on the X-axis. The Y-axis represents increases in the ratio of articles produced from 1995 to 2000. Overall, the number of articles that most universities produced increased. Indeed, among the top 10 national universities, no university reduced the number of articles it produced during this period; instead, most increased their annual output by more than 500 articles, proportionally by between 35% and 65%. Indeed, the University of Tokyo increased its output during this period by around 1,750 articles.

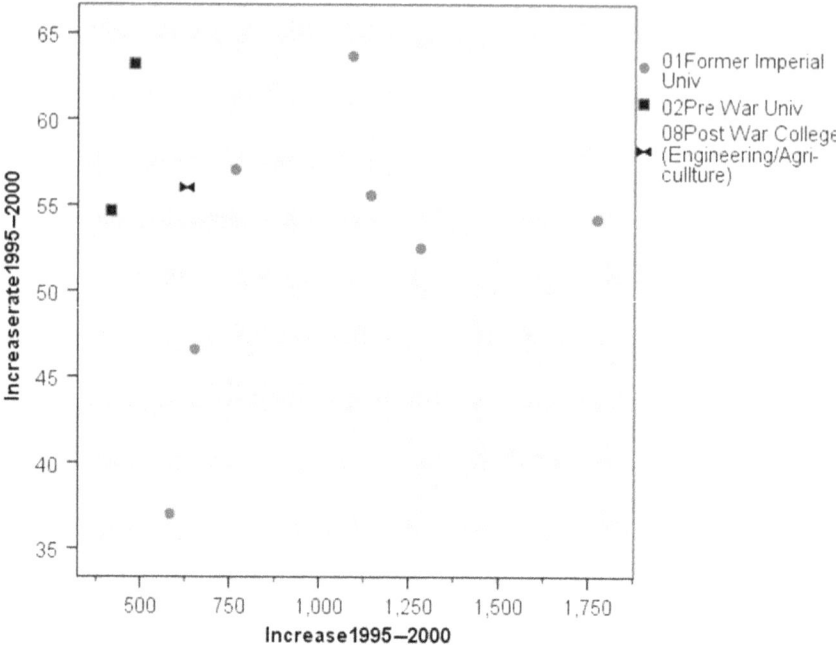

Fig. 7. Increases in Number × Ratio of Changes in Article Production among the Top 10 National Universities, Japan, 1995–2000. *Source*: SPHERE project database of SCIE publications (Thomson Reuters' Web of Science).

Most universities increased the number of articles they produced, yet many universities had larger increases in the ratio of articles they produced than the top 10 universities did (Fig. 8). In particular, most post-World War II universities 1 and 2 increased their output by more than 100 articles. Two post-World War II universities 1 increased their output by more than those produced by a pre-World War II university (which was ranked fifth highest in terms of increasing output) (see Fig. 9).

Second, I show changes in the number of articles produced at the individual university level from 2000 to 2005. The X-axis represents increases in the number of articles produced from 2000 to 2005, while the Y-axis represents increases in the ratio of articles produced from 2000 to 2005. Among the top 10 universities, there is no university that decreased the number of articles produced. However, all of them increased by less than 500 articles, including the University of Tokyo and University of Kyoto. In addition, increases in the ratio of articles produced from 2000 to 2005 were below 14% and much smaller than those from 1995 to 2000. But based on Fig. 10, the situation outside the top 10 is more serious, as many universities decreased the numbers of articles they produced. In fact, most post-World War II universities 1 and 2 were

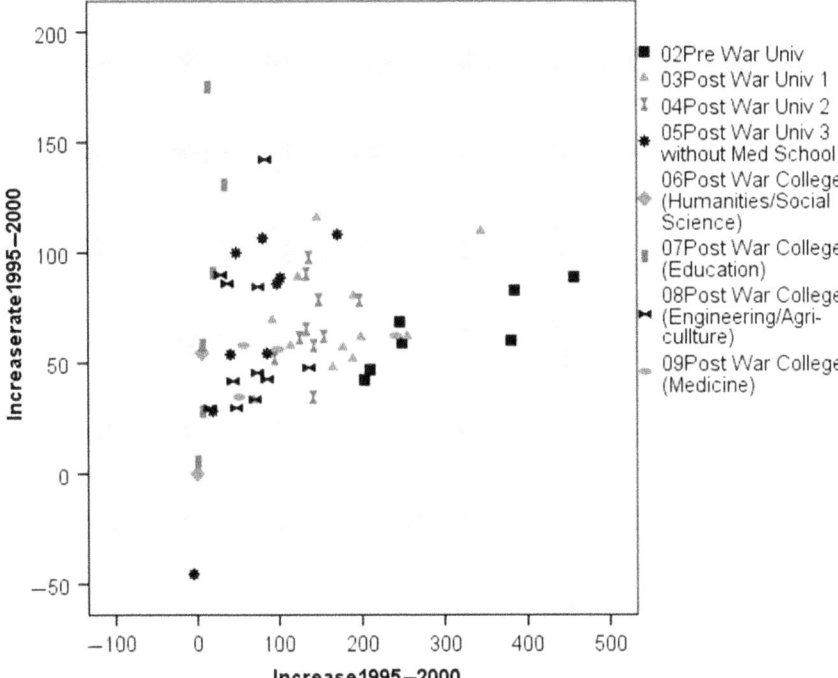

Fig. 8. Increases in Number × Ratio of Changes in Article Production among National Universities Outside the Top 10, 1995–2000. *Note*: This graph excludes five outliers. *Source*: SPHERE project database of SCIE publications (Thomson Reuters' Web of Science).

plotted around 0 (*X*-axis) and below 0% (*Y*-axis). This shows that the conditions for science production were less favorable for these post-World War II universities during the period.

Third, I clarify the changes in number of articles at the individual university level from 2005 to 2010 without graphs. Among the top 10 universities, no university decreased the number of articles produced. However, all of them increased by fewer than 500 articles, except for the University of Tokyo. In addition, increases in the ratio of articles produced from 2005 to 2010 are below 20% and much smaller than those from 1995 to 2000. The situation outside the top 10 is more serious from 2000 to 2005 and, many universities decreased the numbers of articles they produced. In fact, many post-World War II universities increased less than 50 articles (less than 25%). This shows that the conditions for science production were less favorable during this period.

Concerning the changes between 1995 and 2000, the top 10 universities published 8,824 additional articles. However, the universities outside the top 10

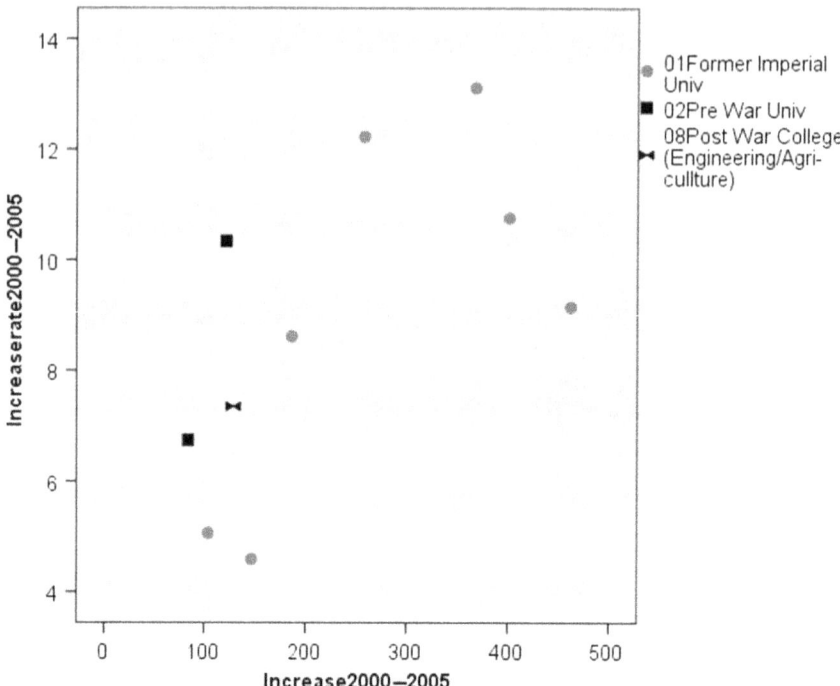

Fig. 9. Increases in Number × Ratio of Increase in Article Production among the Top 10 National Universities, Japan, 2000–2005. *Source*: SPHERE project database of SCIE publications (Thomson Reuters' Web of Science).

increased their article publication by 7,830 articles, around 88.7% of those produced by the top 10 universities. However, in the two latter periods (from 2000 to 2005 and from 2005 to 2010), the universities outside the top 10 increased only by 28% and 56% of those produced by top 10 universities. In addition, most universities that decreased the numbers of published articles from 2000 to 2005 in Type A are post-World War II universities 1 and post-World War II universities 2. Hence, since 2000, the total number of articles produced in Japan by national universities stagnated, and the differences among national universities have been growing.

EXPANSION OF COMPETITIVE FUNDS SINCE 2000

Reduction of Block Grants and Expansion of Competitive Funds

A reason for these changes may be that all national universities were incorporated in 2004. After being incorporated, block grants (Uneihi Koufukin) were

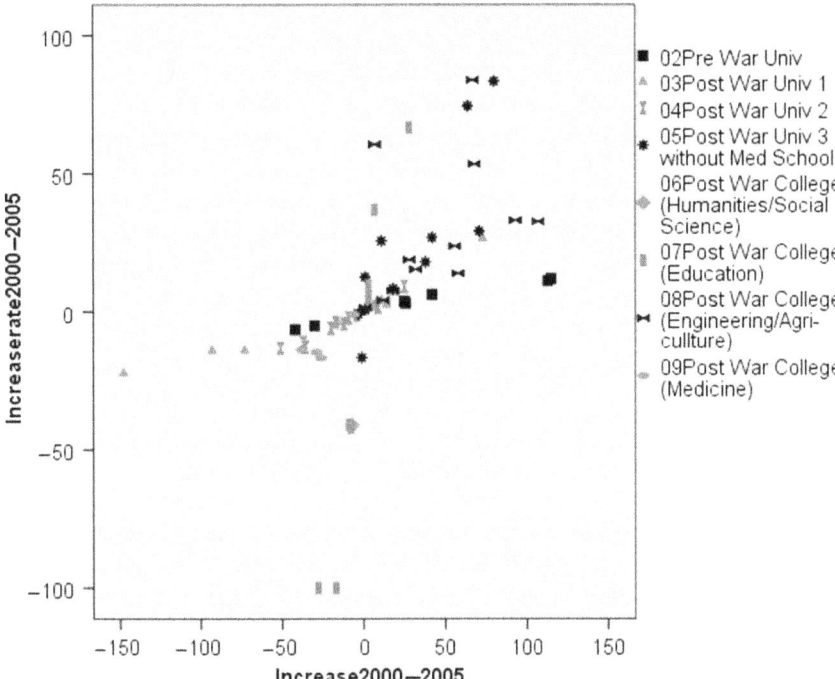

Fig. 10. Increases in Number × Ratio of Changes in Article Production among National Universities Outside the Top 10, Japan, 2000–2005. *Note*: This graph excludes two outliers. *Source*: SPHERE project database of SCIE publications (Thomson Reuters' Web of Science).

decreased by 1% for national universities and by 2% for university hospitals — each year.[8] Thus, during the six-year period between 2005 and 2010, many universities and university hospitals saw their budgets decrease by between 6% and 12%. This reduction in block grants pushed national universities, especially university hospitals, to raise money from private sources. However, not all universities have been able to succeed in this aspect (Shima, 2012). In fact, half of all national universities decreased their income levels after incorporation, excluding their hospital incomes. On the other hand, university hospitals have been able to succeed, but the faculties of medical schools have become focused on earning payments for medical services they provide.

On the other hand, what changes occurred in terms of competitive research funds since 2000 when science production in Japan stagnated and Japan's position in science production declined to fifth? The Basic Law on Science and Technology (Kagaku gijutsu kihon-hō), which is one of the most important laws on science and technology, was enacted in 1995. It prescribes a policy for promotion of science and technology. Based on the law, a science and technology promotion plan (Kagaku gijutsu shinkō keikaku) was settled on every five years, with the first such science and technology promotion plan lasting from 1996 to 2000 and the fifth such plan ongoing (2016–2020). The first two plans set numerical budget targets. In 2000, competitive research funds were $2,698 million ($1 = ¥110). But in 2010, competitive research funds had risen to $4,217 million. In addition, in 2000 there were 22 competitive funding programs offered by seven ministries, but by 2010 there were 39 competitive funding programs offered by eight ministries.[9] Thus, competitive funding has dramatically expanded since 2000, while national university block grants have decreased since 2005.

Intensive Allocation to First-Tier National Universities to Become "World-class Universities"

In preparation for – or reaction to – the globalized knowledge economy, MEXT started trying to create "world-class research" or "world-class universities." The starting point is a MEXT report entitled "A Policy for the Structural Reform of Universities" (2001), which proclaims that 30 universities were expected to become "highest standard world universities." Based on this policy, MEXT provided major competitive research funds to facilitate creation of such highly competitive universities; I discuss five related MEXT initiatives below.

(1) 21st Century COE[10] Targeted Support for Creating World-standard Research and Education Bases (Centers of Excellence) Program. Based on a MEXT report entitled "A Policy for the Structural Reform of Universities," this program was established in 2002 to cultivate a competitive academic environment among Japanese universities by giving targeted support to the creation of world-standard research and education bases (centers of excellence). MEXT selected 51 national universities.
(2) GCOE[11] (Global COE). Based on assessments of the '21st Century COE Program' and verifications of its results to date carried out by Japan's MEXT from FY2002, a decision was made to establish the 'Global COE (Centers of Excellence) Program'. The program will provide funding support for establishing education and research centers that perform at the apex of global excellence to elevate the international competitiveness of the Japanese universities. MEXT selected 27 national universities.
(3) PPERU[12] (The Program for Promoting the Enhancement of Research Universities) from 2013 targets building a cluster of world-standard universities to respond to the situation that the share of science production in Japan declined internationally (relatively). MEXT selected 17 national

universities. MEXT allocated approximately $1.6–3.2 million per year to each university for 10 years.

(4) Top Global University Project[13] (TG) from 2014 is designed to support internationally competitive universities as they aimed to achieve "globalization" in research and education. MEXT selected 13 Type A universities (those seeking to earn a ranking in the top 100 worldwide), 11 of them (84.6%) are national universities, and MEXT allocates about $4.1 million per year to each university for 10 years. MEXT also selected 24 Type B universities (i.e., universities that promote globalization) and allocated up to $2.4 million per year to each one for 10 years; 10 of these were national universities.

(5) MEXT's Classification of national universities into 3 types (2016)[14]: MEXT decided to re-categorize all national universities into three types in 2015 based on individual university application:[15] (1) Local universities[16] (55 national universities that primarily serve local communities), (2) Specific universities (15 national universities that primarily do world or national-level research and education in specific areas) and (3) World-class university (16 national universities that should compete with top world-class universities).

Highlighted parts of Table 2 shows which national universities received the above competitive funds to create "word-class research and education bases" or "world-class university" In addition to that, Table 2 only focuses on "comprehensive universities" (Type A) for simplification. As shown, MEXT gradually selected a limited number of national universities as "world-class universities" and allocated those competitive funds to only (1) Former Imperial Universities and some (2) Pre post-World War II universities, with Ochanomizu University and Nara Women's University, the two national women's universities, as exceptions.

I discussed competitive grant programs that were started after 2010 to show the trend and result of concentrating competitive funds among a limited number of national universities. Even in the 2002–2004 period, the allocation disparities of 21st COE funds among national universities were huge. The University of Tokyo got 28 funded projects in all research fields; on the other hand, Post-World War II university 3 got only one or two funded projects in limited research fields. In sum, since 2000, while the government expanded the competitive funds, it concentrated those funds within a limited range of universities (former Imperial Universities and pre-World War II universities). This means that "unsung heroes" (universities outside the top 10 or post-World War II universities, among others) were largely ignored as potential "world-class universities," even though they strengthened and sustained the base of science production in Japan during the country's rise to be come the second largest producer of scientific research between 1975 and 2000.

Table 2. List of Comprehensive Universities that Received Competitive Funds to Create "World-Class Research and Education Bases" or Achieve "World-Class University" Status.

Type	Type of National Universities	Prestige	21st COE								
Type A: Universities which have multiple disciplinary schools	Former Imperial University	High ←←←←←←←←→→→→→→→→ Low	Hokkaido University	Tohoku University	The University of Tokyo	Nagoya University	Kyoto University	Osaka University	Kyushu University		
	Pre-War University		University of Tsukuba	Chiba University	Nigata University	Kanazawa University	Kobe University	Okayama University	Hiroshima University	Nagasaki University	Kumamoto University
	Post-War University 1		Gunma University	Shinshu University	University of Toyama	Gifu University	Shimane University	Yamaguchi University	Kagawa University	Ehime University	Saga University	Oita University	Kagoshima University	University of the Ryukyus
	Post-War University 2		Hirosaki University	Akita University	Yamagata University	University of Yamanashi	University of Fukui	Mie University	Tottori University	The University of Tokushima	Kochi University	University of Miyazaki
	Post-War University 3 (without MedSchool)		Iwate University	Fukushima University	Ibaraki University	Utsunomiya University	Saitama University	Ochanomizu University	Yokohama National University	Shizuoka University	Shiga University	Nara Women's University	Wakayama University

	Prestige	Type of National Universities	GCOE						
Type A: Universities which have multiple disciplinary schools	High ↑↑↑↑↑↑↑↑↑↑↑↑↑↑ Low	Former Imperial University	Hokkaido University	**Tohoku University**	The University of Tokyo	Nagoya University	Kyoto University	Osaka University	Kyushu University
		Pre-War University	**University of Tsukuba**	**Chiba University**	Nigata University	Kanazawa University	**Kobe University**	Okayama University	Hiroshima University
			Nagasaki University	**Kumamoto University**					
		Post-War University 1	Gunma University	**Shinshu University**	University of Toyama	Gifu University	Shimane University	Yamaguchi University	Kagawa University
			Ehime University	Saga University	Oita University	Kagoshima University	University of the Ryukyus		
		Post-War University 2	Hirosaki University	Akita University	**Yamagata University**	**University of Yamanashi**	University of Fukui	Mie University	Tottori University
			The University of Tokushima	Kochi University	University of Miyazaki				
		Post-War University 3 (without MedSchool)	Iwate University	Fukushima University	Ibaraki University	Utsunomiya University	Saitama University	**Ochanomizu University**	**Yokohama National University**
			Shizuoka University	Shiga University	Nara Women's University	Wakayama University			

Table 2. (Continued)

Type	Prestige	Type of National Universities	PPERU									
Type A: Universities which have multiple disciplinary schools	High ↑↑↑↑↑↑↑↑→→→→→→→→ Low	Former Imperial University	Hokkaido University	Tohoku University	The University of Tokyo	Nagoya University	Kyoto University	Osaka University	Kyushu University			
		Pre-War University	University of Tsukuba	Chiba University	Nigata University	Kanazawa University	Kobe University	Okayama University	Hiroshima University	Nagasaki University	Kumamoto University	
		Post-War University 1	Gunma University	Shinshu University	University of Toyama	Gifu University	Shimane University	Yamaguchi University	Kagawa University	Ehime University	Saga University	Oita University	Kagoshima University	University of the Ryukyus
		Post-War University 2	Hirosaki University	Akita University	Yamagata University	University of Yamanashi	University of Fukui	Mie University	Tottori University	The University of Tokushima	Kochi University	University of Miyazaki	
		Post-War University 3 (without MedSchool)	Iwate University	Fukushima University	Ibaraki University	Utsunomiya University	Saitama University	Ochanomizu University	Yokohama National University	Shizuoka University	Shiga University	Nara Women's University	Wakayama University

Type	Prestige	Type of National Universities											
Type A: Universities which have multiple disciplinary Schools	High ← ← ← ← ← ← ← ← → → → → → → → Low	Former Imperial University	Hokkaido University	Tohoku University	The University of Tokyo	Nagoya University	Kyoto University	Osaka University	Kyushu University				
		Pre-War University	University of Tsukuba	Chiba university	Niigata University	Kanazawa University	Kobe University	Okayama University	Hiroshima University	Nagasaki University	Kumamoto University		
		Post-War University 1	Gunma University	Shinshu University	University of Toyama	Gifu University	Shimane University	Yamaguchi University	Kagawa University	Ehime University	Saga University	Oita University	Kagoshima University	University of the Ryukyus
		Post-War University 2	Hirosaki University	Akita University	Yamagata University	University of Yamanashi	University of Fukui	Mie University	Tottori University	The University of Tokushima	Kochi University	University of Miyazaki		
		Post-War University 3 (without MedSchool)	Iwate University	Fukushima University	Ibaraki University	Utsunomiya University	Saitama University	Ochanomizu University	Yokohama National University	Shizuoka University	Shiga University	Nara Women's University	Wakayama University	

TG

Table 2. (Continued)

Classification 3 Types

Type	Prestige	Types of National Universities	Universities
Type A: Universities which have multiple disciplinary schools	High ← ← ← ← ← ← ← ← ← ← → → → → → → → → → Low	Former Imperial University	Hokkado University, Tohoku University, The University of Tokyo, Nagoya University, Kyoto University, Osaka University, Kyushu University
		Pre-War University	University of Tsukuba, Chiba University, Nigata University, Kanazawa University, Kobe University, Okayama University, Hiroshima University, Nagasaki University, Kumamoto University
		Post-War University 1	Gunma University, Shinshu University, University of Toyama, Gifu University, Shimane University, Yamaguchi University, Kagawa University, Ehime University, Saga University, Oita University, Kagoshima University, University of the Ryukyus
		Post-War University 2	Hirosaki University, Akita University, Yamagata University, University of Yamanashi, University of Fukui, Mie University, Tottori University, The University of Tokushima, Kochi University, University of Miyazaki
		Post-War University 3 (without MedSchool)	Iwate University, Fukushima University, Ibaraki University, Utsunomiya University, Saitama University, Ochanomizu University, Yokohama National University, Shizuoka University, Shiga University, Nara Women's University, Wakayama University

Source: Created by author.

FINDINGS AND IMPLICATIONS

Japan's position as a leading producer of science publications (the second largest in 2000) among the globe's knowledge societies declined during the period of study (to fifth in 2010) and is at-risk moving forward. Universities remain at the core of science productivity in Japan. Although the share of science publications of national universities has been decreasing, national universities are still the primary actors within this core. Due to structural changes affecting science productivity from 2000 to 2005, second-tier national universities (post-World War II universities 1 & 2) decreased the number of articles they produced. Although the second-tier national universities are not as prestigious, they previously strengthened and underpinned the nation's scientific productivity. The declining share of research production among second-tier national universities has not been well recognized, but, I argue that it is crucial for the future of science productivity in Japan. Instead of strengthening the capacity of second-tier universities to contribute to STEM+ research, policymakers developed competitive grant programs that primarily benefitted Former Imperial Universities and pre-World War II universities.[17]

The result of these competitive funds seems to mean that post-World War II universities 1 and 2, which had strengthened and helped to sustain the position of Japan in science productivity, were largely ignored by the government as research-contributing universities. In addition, in 2015, MEXT categorized all national universities into three categories (world-class research universities, world and national-level research universities for specific areas, and universities which primarily serve their local community). As a result, all post-World War II universities 1 and 2 were categorized into category 3 (universities which primarily serve the local community), even though three of them were ranked in the world top 550[18] of the 2010 QS World University Ranking 500 and 11 of them were ranked in the Asian top 200 of the 2010 QS Asian University Rankings 200 (Shima, 2011b).

MEXT also began to decrease their governmental block grants to national universities beginning in 2005, just one year after incorporation of all national universities. Under this financial trend, Shima (2012) showed that the difference in total income of national universities increased, and more than half (51.8%) of national universities decreased their total income, excluding university hospital income. These results question whether investing large amounts of money only into most prestigious universities (either competitively or selectively) is the hoped-for panacea to improve overall scientific productivity. Building world-class research universities is certainly crucial; however, building thick clusters that sustain science production with stable block grants should also be considered.[19] In fact, even though there were rapid expansions of competitive funds and those funds were concentrated among a limited range of universities, the continuing reduction of basic block grants seemed to weaken the research activities of national universities. We should pay attention to other potential factors that could explain these results, but it is clear that expansion of competitive funds and concentration within a limited range of national universities provides no panacea for declines in science production in Japan. This would also entail paying more attention to the "unsung heroes" in the Japanese higher education system.

NOTES

1. There are some related preceding studies, for example, Kobayashi (2005), Shima (2011a), Saka and Kuwahara (2012a, 2012b, 2013), with details explained in this chapter.

2. It is important to note that KAKENHI does not cover all private companies' and hospitals' research activities, which are important actors in science production in Japan (see Section "Types of Research Organization"). Retrieved from https://www.jsps.go.jp/j-grantsinaid/27_kdata/data/3-3-1/3-3-1_h22.pdf

3. This analysis is based on the "Science Productivity, Higher Education Development, and Knowledge Society" (SPHERE) project database of Thomson Reuters (TR) Web of Science publication data (Science Citation Index Expanded; hereafter "SCIE") from 1900 to 2012. Data included every five years from 1900 to 1980 and every year from 1980 to 2012. For this analysis, only data for 1975, 1980, 1985, 1990, 1995, 2000, 2005, and 2010 were used.

4. For more detail, refer to Baker et al. (2015, pp. 14–15 and Powell et al. (2017).

5. National research institutes were established by the national government.

6. I used "NISTEP Dictionary of Names of Universities and Public Organizations" to categorize. Retrieved from http://www.nistep.go.jp/research/scisip/data-and-information-infrastructure. Accessed on April 11, 2015. In addition to that, in terms of national universities, I recoded some of the raw data's original categorization.

7. Hitotsubashi University and Tokyo Institute of Technology are exceptions.

8. During the first Midterm Target and Plan period (2004–2009), except in 2004, the government's block grants for national universities were reduced by 1% every year. In addition, the block grants for university hospitals were reduced by 2% every year, causing national universities with university hospitals to face a difficult financial situation. During the second MTP (2010–2015), the block grants for national universities without university hospitals were reduced by 1% every year, and those for national universities with university hospitals were reduced by 1.6% every year.

9. http://www.mext.go.jp/b_menu/shingi/chousa/shinkou/039/shiryo/__icsFiles/afieldfile/2015/03/04/1355560_10.pdf

10. https://www.jsps.go.jp/english/e-21coe/index.html

11. http://www.jsps.go.jp/english/e-globalcoe/index.html

12. http://www.mext.go.jp/a_menu/kagaku/sokushinhi/

13. http://www.jsps.go.jp/j-sgu/gaiyou.html

14. http://www.mext.go.jp/b_menu/houdou/28/03/__icsFiles/afieldfile/2016/03/09/1367853_01.pdf

15. There is a possibility that each national university decides its portions based on past competitive funds, an important topic of research for the near future.

16. Authors named "Local University," "Specific University," and "World-Class University" based on the policy, but "Local University" is also expected to foster world/national-level education and research on specific research areas.

17. Ida and Fukuzawa (2013) showed that COE research grants had positive impacts on science productivity, but unfortunately they did not pay attention to the decrease of block grants and the effects of incorporatization of national universities in 2004.

18. In that ranking, there were bands ranking in categories such as 501−550, 550−600, and 601+.

19. In this chapter, I did not do statistical analysis to examine the relationship between the research funds, including block grants, and number of articles. Certainly, this presents an important opportunity for future research.

ACKNOWLEDGMENTS

This chapter was rewritten and updated with many changes and new components based on Shima (2015). This work was made possible by NPRP grant #5-1021-5-159 from the Qatar National Research Fund (a member of the Qatar Foundation). The statements made herein are solely the responsibility of the author.

REFERENCES

Baker, D. P., Crist, J. T., Zhang, L., Powell, J. J. W., Shima, K., & Stock, M. (2015). *Science productivity, higher education development, and the knowledge society*. NPRP Report: 5-1021-5-159. Qatar National Research Fund.

Drucker, P. F. (1968). *The age of discontinuity: Guidelines to changing society*. New York, NY: Harper & Row.

Ida, T., & Fukuzawa, N. (2013). Effects of large-scale research funding programs: A Japanese case study. *Scientometrics, 94*(3), 1253−1273.

Kobayashi, S. (2005). Chishikino Sozoukyoten toshiteno Kokuritsu Daigaku. In The Japan Association of National Universities (Ed.), *21seiki Nihon to Kokuritsu Daigaku no Yakuwari: JANU Quarterly Report* (pp. 1−21). (in Japanese).

OECD. (2013). *Science, technology and industry scorecard*. Retrieved from http://www.oecdilibrary.org/science-and-technology/oecd-science-technology-and-industry-scoreboard-2013_sti_scoreboard-2013-en

Powell, J. J. W., & Dusdal, J. (2017). The European center of science productivity: research universities and institutes in France, Germany, and the United Kingdom. In J. J. W. Powell, D. P. Baker, & F. Fernandez (Eds.), *The century of science: The global triumph of the research university* (Vol. 33). International Perspectives on Education and Society. Bingley: Emerald Publishing Limited.

Powell, J. J. W., Fernandez, F., Crist, J. T., Dusdal, J., Zhang, L., & Baker, D. P. (2017). Introduction: The worldwide triumph of the research university and globalizing science. In J. J. W. Powell, D. P. Baker, & F. Fernandez (Eds.), *The century of science: The global triumph of the research university* (Vol. 33). International Perspectives on Education and Society. Bingley: Emerald Publishing Limited.

Saka, A., & Kuwahara, T. (2012a). *Benchmarking research and development capacity of Japanese Universities 2011: Improving universities research activities by identifying characteristics and strength of each university*. National Institute of Science and Technology Policy (NISTEP), MEXT. (in Japanese).

Saka, A., & Kuwahara, T. (2012b). *Benchmarking scientific research 2011: Bibliometric analysis on dynamic alteration of research activity in the world and Japan.* National Institute of Science and Technology Policy (NISTEP), MEXT. (in Japanese).
Saka, A., & Kuwahara, T. (2013). *Benchmarking scientific research 2012: Bibliometric analysis on dynamic alteration of research activity in the world and Japan.* National Institute of Science and Technology Policy (NISTEP), MEXT. (in Japanese).
Shima, K. (2011a). Research function of national universities by types of university. In R.I.H.E. (Ed.), *Empirical study on functions of national universities: Strategic research project series 3* (pp. 33–38). (in Japanese).
Shima, K. (2011b). Functions and self-images of national universities. *Reviews in Higher Education, 113*, 33–38. (in Japanese).
Shima, K. (2012). Changes in national university finances in Japan: After incorporation. *Japanese Journal of Higher Education Research, 15*, 49–70. (in Japanese).
Shima, K. (2015). Changes of scientific productivity in Japan from 1975 to 2010: Focusing on second-tier research universities. *Turkish Journal of Sociology, 3*(30), 119–138.
Yoshida, A. (2002). Types of national university. *Structural differentiation and community service of national university* (pp. 183–193). Center for National University Finance and Management. (in Japanese).

THE RISE OF HIGHER EDUCATION AND SCIENCE IN CHINA

Liang Zhang, Liang Sun and Wei Bao

ABSTRACT

Purpose — *This chapter provides a thorough historical overview of policies that have governed and guided scientific research in China since 1949 and illustrates changes in scientific publications that accompanied these policy reforms and programs.*

Design — *We divide this historical period into four stages, each with distinct R&D policies: (1) 1949−1955, a period of socialist transformation; (2) 1956−1965, a period of struggle for higher education and research development in a rapidly changing political environment; (3) 1966−1976, the lost decade of the Cultural Revolution; and (4) 1976−present, a period when major national policies have significantly promoted scientific research in China. We use the SPHERE project's comprehensive historical dataset based on Thomson Reuters' Web of Science and data from a set of research universities in China to analyze changes in scientific publication rates concurrent with these policy reforms and programs.*

Findings — *The analysis suggests a tight connection between national policy and scientific research productivity in higher education. The central government controlled scientific research through direct administration in early periods and has guided research activities through funding specific programs in recent decades. Due to their resource dependency on the central government, higher education institutions have been quite responsive to the common goals set by the central government. As a result, what is measured tends to be accomplished.*

Originality/value — *The chapter provides an in-depth description about the rise of higher education and science in China and produces recommendations for future development.*

Keywords: China; higher education; scientific productivity; research and development; science and technology

INTRODUCTION

In examining data on scientific research and development in recent decades, researchers have quickly identified rapid growth in research publications from BRICK[1] nations as one of the most significant forces changing the landscape of scientific research around the world (Adams, Pendlebury, & Stembridge, 2013). Among the five BRICK nations, scientific productivity in China is especially impressive. According to publication data published by Thomson Reuters (hereafter TR) and recoded and analyzed by members of the SPHERE research project, research output from China, as measured by the number of journal articles in journals included in the Science Citation Index (SCI), accounted for about 14% of worldwide research publications in 2011, up from slightly over 1% in 1990.[2] In some fields, such as material sciences and chemistry, more than 20% of all research papers produced globally have authors or coauthors affiliated with Chinese institutions. By comparison, while the authors or coauthors of 35% of all papers contained in TR in 1990 were affiliated with institutions in the United States, this proportion fell to 26% in 2011. This emphasizes the relative decline of the United States and the relative advance of China in these fields.

The dramatic increase in research output from China raises many questions: What has spurred research productivity in China in recent decades? In particular, which policy initiatives might be responsible for this growth? What is the current status of research production and international collaboration in China? Will this pattern continue into the near future? In this chapter, we aim to shed light on these questions by reviewing research and development (R&D) policies and examining research productivity in China since the mid-20th century.

We are particularly interested in higher education institutions because both in China and elsewhere research universities have played an important role in promoting innovation, economic development and core competencies in their home countries (Geiger & Sá, 2008). During the second half of the 20th century, research universities in the United States transformed into entrepreneurial institutions that combine basic research and education with industrial innovation. Such universities, represented by Stanford and MIT, have established a mode of virtuous interaction with industries and governments, and have significantly contributed to economic and social development. With the rise of this successful model, other countries realized the power of knowledge and attached great importance to developing their capacity in science and technology (S&T). R&D plays a crucial role in providing knowledge for innovation and S&T competence. Therefore, the governments of many countries, including all of the countries examined in this volume, have created various R&D policies in which universities play important roles.

In this chapter, we provide a thorough historical overview of policies that have governed and guided scientific research in China since 1949. We divide this historical period into four stages, each stage with distinct R&D policies. In the section "Building a New Higher Education System and S&T Workforce (1949–1955)," we briefly introduce relevant policies and their effect on Chinese higher education from 1949 to 1955, a period of socialist transformation in China. In the section "A Messy Marriage between Politics and Science (1956–1965)," we discuss the struggles of higher education and scientific development in the changing political environment from 1956 to 1965. In the section "The Cultural Revolution: A Lost Decade (1966–1976)," we describe the stagnation of education and science during the Cultural Revolution from 1966 to 1976. In the section "Reform and Modernization (1977–2012)," we concentrate on major national policies implemented in China from the reform to the present day. For the last stage, from the latest reform to the present day, we use both publication data from TR and university-level data that we collected to examine scientific research production at the national and institutional level. We conclude by summarizing major themes gleaned from our historical review and empirical analyses, examine the implications of our data and identify themes related to the future of scientific research in China.

BUILDING A NEW HIGHER EDUCATION SYSTEM AND S&T WORKFORCE (1949–1955)

After a century of unrest that culminated in the Sino-Japanese War (1937–1945) and the Chinese Civil War (1945–1949), the newly established communist government that took power in China in 1949 finally "had a chance to build the nation along a self-chosen socialist track" (Hayhoe, 1996). From 1949 to 1955, China transformed from a nationalist society into a socialist nation. To stabilize the nascent regime and recover the national economy, the Chinese government called upon people from all walks of life to devote themselves to economic construction and received wide support from members of the ardent public who expected a strong nation and a better life. During this period of time, China restructured its higher education system and built a new

S&T workforce. In particular, China modeled itself after the Soviet Union, and benefited greatly from its assistance (Hayhoe, 1996; Oleksiyenko, 2014).

Restructuring China's Higher Education System

In September 1949, the Common Program of the Chinese People's Consultative Conference was passed and temporarily played the role of constitution. As such, the Common Program guided every aspect of the new nation's construction. In Chapter 5, "Culture and Education Policies," Article 43 stipulated that China would "strive to develop natural science to serve the construction of agriculture, industry and national defense; reward scientific discovery and invention; and popularize scientific knowledge." Article 46 further stipulated that "the educational method shall be based on consistent theory and practice; the People's Government of the People's Republic of China shall systematically renovate the old educational system, content and pedagogy" (People's Network, 2006).

The new Ministry of Education was formed in November 1949 to lead the restructuring of the higher education system. Universities and other research organizations financed by individuals, corporations, or foreign churches were all taken over by the new government and remolded into new institutions. For example, the Central Research Institute, Peking Research Institute, and their affiliates became the Chinese Academy of Sciences in Beijing. Meanwhile, government sectors related to industry, agriculture, transportation, public health and so forth set up their own affiliated institutions for scientific research. Using peers in the Soviet Union as models, Chinese universities consolidated scientific research efforts after "the reordering of colleges and departments" that dismembered comprehensive universities and redefined curricular patterns and institutional identities (Hayhoe, 1996). The administration system for higher education was characterized as being highly centralized and united as it shared responsibilities with other central governmental sectors in supervising non-comprehensive colleges (Dong, Dan, & Chen, 2007). By the end of 1955, a new S&T system was established with the Academy at its center and surrounded by higher education institutions and the governmental sectors.

During this period of time, the role of S&T was to serve the common interests of the nation and the public, as stipulated in the Common Program. In August 1950, a national representative conference on science and technology was held in Beijing. The conference followed the guidelines set by the Common Program and suggested that "scientific work of the new China should be an enterprise of the masses, and the scientific community should serve the national construction and the public." Another government file commenting on a report from the Academy of Sciences to the central government in 1954 heavily emphasized the significance of science in national construction: "As the economic construction has begun, [we shall] strive to develop natural science so as to promote the development of production technology and fully know and utilize national resources" (Cui, 2000).

Building a New S&T Workforce

Scientific talents were scarce in the People's Republic of China (PRC) after several decades of war and social unrest. The new government adopted several measures to build an S&T workforce to address urgent economic needs. These measures included educating existing talent, training a new cadre of intellectuals, and attracting scientists from abroad. Although a socialist polity had been established in China, a large number of intellectuals remained skeptical of the Communist Party of China (CPC). Since the construction of the new nation depended upon these intellectuals, ideological change was required. In a movement to "remold intellectuals," training focused on creating positive political attitudes. Intellectuals were indoctrinated that "socialism provides the broadest space for, and is in great need of scientific and technological development" and that "scientists should serve their people" (Cui, 2000).

At the same time, a new cadre of intellectuals was trained. The restructuring of colleges and departments during this period of time significantly improved and enhanced the status of colleges devoted to engineering in the higher education system. Enrollment increased dramatically in these engineering colleges, supplying a new stream of S&T workers. In a guideline issued by the central government to the Academy of Sciences in 1954, it was emphasized that "new blood is crucial in developing the scientific cause in our country, and [we require] that higher education institutions get engaged in scientific research" (Cui, 2000). Later in 1955, the Academy began to enroll graduate students. In response to this great enthusiasm for developing scientific education, the number and quality of new scientists rapidly increased. Moreover, the new government invited Chinese scientists who lived and worked overseas to return and serve the new nation. By the end of 1955, over 1,000 scientists had returned to China; eventually played leading roles in their fields and made important contributions to the country's development.

Because of these efforts, the scientific workforce grew rapidly during this period of time. By the end of 1955, there were over 840 S&T institutions and 425,000 people working in related fields (Cui, 2000). During the early 1950s, as the Chinese government created favorable policies and heavily emphasized the role of intellectuals in social development, the value of intellectuals was widely acknowledged and respected. Therefore, this period was also called "the golden age for intellectuals" (Wu, 1997).

Learning from the Soviet Union

Due to political and ideological similarities, China used the Soviet Union as a model during these formative years, which significantly influenced many aspects of Chinese society, including its education, cultural, and economic patterns. Particularly, China learnt the Soviet expertise in industrial and technology development, and imitated the Soviet higher education which was characterized by strong and centralized governmental interests (Hayhoe, 1994). In 1950, Chairman Mao gave a speech at a national conference in which he emphasized that "all of us should seriously learn from the advanced experience of Soviet Union, not only political theories, but also their science and technology, and make use of it to build our own country" (Cui, 2000). Mao's speech sparked a movement among the citizenry to accept the Soviet Union as a role model, and led to official cooperation between the two countries. In October 1954, the Cooperative Agreement of Science and Technology of China and the Soviet Union was co-signed in Beijing, which signified formal cooperation between the S&T fields of the two countries in the forms of scientific research exchange, consultancy, cooperative research, and conferences.

The cooperation was, however, lopsided to say the least. The Soviet Union provided enormous scientific and technological assistance to China by sending thousands of experts to supervise scientific and technological work and providing over 8,400 items of scientific information and data. In addition, China sent over 1,000 experts and over 6,000 students to the Soviet Union to learn advanced knowledge and skills (Cui, 2000). Moreover, the Chinese government imported technology and equipment directly from the Soviet Union.

A good example of the Soviet influence on China is the afore-mentioned restructuring of colleges and departments. In fact, before the founding of the PRC, many universities had developed fairly comprehensive academic programs and were comprised of separate colleges with different specializations. During the restructuring, some university departments were moved from relatively developed regions of China to the backward northwest. New colleges or universities were established in less developed areas to rebalance the distribution of higher education geographically. University's regulations, academic programs, and teaching plans also followed the Soviet model. (This process would be reversed some 40 years later, as we will discuss in the following sections.)

A MESSY MARRIAGE BETWEEN POLITICS AND SCIENCE (1956–1965)

With assistance from the Soviet Union, the PRC quickly built up its S&T infrastructure and workforce. At the dawn of the new nation's second decade, the socialist higher education system featuring governmental control and centralization was fully implemented across the country. This decade, however, did not go smoothly, and was characterized by both great achievements and serious drawbacks. As the political environment kept changing, S&T policies were constantly in flux.

The Honeymoon: "Marching toward Science"

The late 1940s marked the beginning of the Third Scientific Revolution in the United States, which soon spread to Western Europe and Japan (Cui, 2000). This global industrial revolution showed its power in changing the way we live and accelerating national economies in the 1950s. Having realized the vast gap between China and developed countries, the government held a national conference to discuss policies for intellectuals in January 1956. The conference report highlighted the idea of "marching toward science." The report clarified the importance of science and technology as a key component of national construction, and set a goal of catching up to match the highest levels of science and technology in other countries — as soon as possible. Detailed strategies included learning from the Soviet Union; mobilizing the most talented students and scholars in scientific research; emphasizing the leading role of the Academy of Sciences; strengthening the research base in universities; and attaching importance to the application of research results. To enable intellectuals to "march toward science" without political concerns, Chairman Mao suggested "a hundred flowers should bloom in arts, a hundred schools of thought contend in academics" (Hayhoe, 1996). This powerful endorsement of academic freedom mobilized positive attitudes toward the arts and scientific work. This principle was welcomed by intellectuals and greatly encouraged scientists to devote themselves fully to research.

This favorable political climate ushered in a short period of scientific and technological flourishing. The Scientific and Technological Development Plan (1956–1967) was enacted by the end of 1956. The plan's purpose was to focus national research strength on key areas so as to catch up to the world's most advanced level. These key areas included nuclear power, semiconductors, computers, remote control technologies, production automation, oil exploration, smelting, agriculture, prevention and treatment of major diseases, and basic theoretical research. With resources generously allocated by the central government, this plan was smoothly implemented in 1957, resulting in fast R&D expansion in terms of both workforce and outputs. For example, by the end of 1962, the number of research institutions had increased from 381 to 1,296, and the science and technology workforce had grown from 62,000 to 200,000 (Cui, 2000). This rapid development laid a solid foundation for future achievements, particularly the successful detonations of an atom bomb in 1964 and a hydrogen bomb in 1967 as well as the launch of satellites in 1970.

An Adversarial Stance: The Anti-Rightist Movement

Unfortunately, the honeymoon between politics and science did not last very long. Since intellectuals felt greatly encouraged by government policies, they began to express critical views of the existing sociopolitical system. With regard to higher education, they complained about mechanical copying from the Soviet Union, narrow teaching programs, and the neglect or repression of the social sciences. Wider social criticism was associated with the authoritarian role of the communist party in all policy decision making, the bureaucratic working style of cadres of the party and the government, and problems between the cadres and the public (Hayhoe, 1996). These criticisms were initially well received by the government because the party also wanted to improve its governance. Before long, however, socialism and the leadership role of the party were openly criticized, and the anti-rightist movement was started.

The movement started in universities, among scholars in literature, the arts, and sciences, and spread to secondary and primary schools as well as among the cadres of the party and the government. Without a clarified definition of "rightist," the anti-rightist movement expanded quickly. Over 550,000 people were treated as rightists and were publicly criticized for opposing the government and the leadership of the CPC. As a result, the movement seriously impeded the development of scientific work and education.

Political Dominance: The Great Leap Forward

Encouraged by the achievements of socialist transformation and construction during the first decade, government leaders became overly confident that the new nation could rapidly move forward and fully realize communism if they worked as hard as possible. This belief ushered in the "Great Leap Forward" period nationwide. The Great Leap Forward in science started at the beginning of 1958 and lasted until the end of 1960 and was embodied mainly as boasting and exaggeration in scientific and technological work. Guided by the spirit of the movement, people in science and technology showed a strong ambition to realize the goals set by the central government. Researchers prioritized speed over quality, and neglected the principles of science. They announced astonishing "achievements" in honor of the government, national conferences, National Day, and so on. For example, it was reported that the Institute of Geology of the Academy of Sciences completed 10 years' worth of work in 10 months; the Institute of Applied Physics announced 22 contributions on the opening day of a national conference, and announced another 45 accomplishments at the end of the conference by working hard for 3 days and nights.

Another, more concrete, result of the Great Leap Forward policy in science was the rapid expansion of research institutions. Research institutions set up various affiliations to instantly enlarge their research teams. For example, the University of Science and Technology of China was established within just 3 months. Such institutions all lacked solid foundations and thus their achievements were very limited. As a result, most of them were unsustainable.

Fortunately, the movement was short lived. The failure of the movement suggested that scientific activities have their own principles, that is, scientific exploration demands long-term investments and efforts while results cannot be planned. The intention to accelerate scientific progress without considering these principles not only impeded the development of science and technology, but also countered the progress that had already been made.

Adjusting S&T Policies

The anti-rightist movement and the Great Leap Forward inflicted great harm on the country and caused an economic recession, which made immediate changes necessary. In January 1961, the party conference officially issued a new guideline, "adjust, consolidate, replenish and improve" (Cui, 2000), which was to inform new policies related to education and S&T. A policy regarded as the "Constitution of Science" at that time, the "14 Articles in S&T," was implemented. It regulated the missions of research institutions, acknowledged the principles of scientific work, and established mechanisms to guarantee appropriate time, quality, and stability of scientific work. After its implementation, the number of scientific research institutions was decreased to a more appropriate level, the number of research personnel and college students was adjusted, and the quality of research and education improved. Furthermore, the government reversed its position toward the intellectuals who had been defined as rightists, and even provided advantageous living conditions and special care for scientists in key fields. These measures reestablished the confidence and motivation of intellectuals as they pursued scientific work.

During this second decade, China made some developmental progress in S&T, despite fluctuating policies. From 1955 to 1965, the number of research institutions grew from 800 to 1,714, while the number of full-time research personnel increased from 8,000 to 120,000 (Cui, 2000). Progress was made not only in terms of quantity, but also in terms of quality. By 1965, China had many high-level scientists whose achievements met the world standard of excellence. Thus, a solid foundation was in place for the future modernization of the country.

THE CULTURAL REVOLUTION: A LOST DECADE (1966–1976)

Extreme leftism reigned in China during the Cultural Revolution. The whole nation was struggling ideologically; riots were common. No S&T policies were implemented during these tumultuous 10 years, and scientific activities came to a halt. Instead, politics and class struggle became the main theme of people's lives. As such, the Cultural Revolution caused immeasurable damage to the causes of education and science.

Scientific research institutions were destroyed and intellectuals were attacked. Represented by the "Gang of Four," leftists preached that the rightists had caused science to be monopolized by the capitalist class and that proletariats should fight against them. The leftists not only destroyed valuable instruments and materials within scientific institutions, but also disturbed their organizations by creating administrative chaos. Many scientists and professors were persecuted; they were humiliated in public, physically punished, and had their property confiscated. Many were left permanently disabled or dead; some committed suicide. As scientific and educational institutions were destroyed, the normal order of teaching and learning was interrupted. Even worse, students in cities were sent to rural areas to learn from farmers. As a result, a whole generation lost the opportunity to receive formal education, which was an inestimable loss to the reserve of scientists and the cause of science and technology. Exchange activities with foreign countries also were cut off. The leftists attacked the policy of learning advanced knowledge and skills from foreign countries and stigmatized it as submitting to imperialism. They advocated secluding the country from the outside world. Therefore, all communication with other countries ceased, including academic exchanges of students and scholars, research collaborations, and sharing advanced technology and equipment.

Thus, the Cultural Revolution was a period of stagnation and regression for China. Leftist policies completely reversed the policies set up before 1966 for maintaining the autonomy of scientific work, respecting intellectuals, and learning from foreign countries. It did irrevocable harm to education and science. Indeed, it was only after the downfall of the "Gang of Four" and Deng Xiaoping's rise to power in 1976 that scientific research gradually got back on track.

REFORM AND MODERNIZATION (1977–2012)

The year 1978 was a turning point in China's modern history. The past 35 years have been characterized by unprecedented growth in China. Fueled by cheap labor and scientific and technological advancements, the economy has grown by nearly 10% each year. A series of R&D policies enacted during this period have promoted impressive achievements in science and technology.

Putting the House Back in Order

At the National Science Conference in 1978, Deng Xiaoping put forth the idea that "science and technology is the primary productive force," and that the central mission of government is to "modernize science and technology." After this conference, the "bring order out of chaos" policy was soon implemented in science and technology circles. The reputations of intellectuals who were stigmatized during the Cultural Revolution were restored, the National Committee of Science and Technology was established to manage scientific institutions across the country, and the education of scientific talent was resumed and accelerated.

Deng attached great importance to higher education since intellectuals suffered a huge loss during the Cultural Revolution and new scholars were urgently needed. The first step was to resume the National College Entrance Examination and enroll high school graduates based on merit rather than ideological correctness. Second, graduate students were recruited once again; 10,500 graduate students were recruited in 1977 and 1978. Third, a new study abroad policy was implemented. In 1978, 50 students were sent by the Chinese government to study in the United States. Beginning in 1981, students were allowed to study abroad at their own expense (Cui, 2000). Fourth, to enhance the status of intellectuals and teachers and reverse people's attitude toward science, instructional documentation was issued requiring all local governments and institutions to implement policies for intellectuals that provided them with good working and living conditions, and calling on all members of society to protect and respect intellectuals. This "bringing order" policy enabled educational and scientific work to resume.

Developing Comprehensive S&T Policies

In 1978, the government issued a new guideline, "adjust, reform, reorganize, and improve," to revive the national economy. As the relationship between economic development and S&T became clear in China, the development of more comprehensive and systematic S&T policies was pursued. In 1981, the government issued a guideline for S&T stipulating that: facilitating economic development is the foremost mission of S&T; research on production technology should be strengthened; technological development at the frontlines of agriculture and industry should be strengthened and promoted; basic research should be developed steadily; and learning foreign S&T achievement should be emphasized.

Several specific policies were initiated to integrate the economy with S&T. *The Blue Book of Science and Technology*, which introduced technological policies for major sectors of the national economy, was issued from 1986 to 1989. In addition, recommendations from the National Commissions of Science, goals of the National Plan, and economic considerations together informed the development of the *Long-Term Plan of Science and Technology of China*

(1986–2000), which illuminated the current status of S&T development at home and abroad and plans for future S&T development in China.

The pace of reform for the S&T system accelerated as well. S&T achievements were expected to be widely and swiftly applied, leading to production, and the role of S&T personnel was expected to be elevated so that the S&T productivity would be liberated to promote economic and social development. More specifically, efforts were made to strengthen the links between research institutions and companies, encouraging those active in research, design, education, and production to work together. To ensure this reform would run smoothly, a series of supportive policies and regulations were created as well, from patent protection and evaluation and reward systems to a scientific funding system and the establishment of nongovernmental research institutions.

During the 1980s, three S&T development plans were especially notable. The goal of the "Spark Program" of 1985 was to guide rural enterprises and farmers in the utilization of science and technology in agriculture. Created in March 1986, the goal of the "863 Program" was to facilitate the development of technology by documenting foreign high-tech achievements. The "Torch Program" of 1988 focused on promoting the commercialization, industrialization, and internationalization of high-tech by establishing special development zones and encouraging the S&T personnel in universities and research institutions to join high-tech enterprises. Taken together, this series of comprehensive S&T policies greatly promoted the link between S&T research and economic development and encouraged ties among universities, research institutions, and industry. These policies created a positive atmosphere and paved the way for stronger S&T development in the 1990s.

Revitalizing the Nation through Science and Education

The rapid economic growth throughout the 1980s, which was largely attributed to intensive use of labor and natural resources, gave rise to the issue of economic sustainability, that is how to achieve a sustainable mode of economic development and how to utilize science and technology. Based on the ideas that "science and technology is the primary productive force" and "the promotion of science and technology entails the promotion of education," the chain effects of education-talent-S&T-economy were recognized. Education, therefore, was seen as the primary driver of economic and social development at the dawn of the 1990s.

In May 1995, the government announced its *Decision on Expediting Progress in Science and Technology*, based on a strategy of "revitalizing the nation through science and education." Implementing this strategy entailed creating specific S&T policies. The foremost mission was to set up an S&T system that accommodated the principles of a market economy. S&T reform in the 1990s followed a "stabilizing and opening" principle; the goal was to expose the market to a great number of technological developments so that service organizations and commercial enterprises could become competitive and participate in the market economy. At the same time, a few key universities and research institutions remained engaged in basic and applied research. Due to the brain drain in basic research that originated in the study abroad craze that began in the 1980s, the role of universities in sustaining basic research was particularly emphasized in the *Decision*. Scientific research bases were set up in key areas of research and academic talent gradually gathered there. For example, as of 1999, Tsinghua University had invited 18 faculty members from abroad to its base for biology, and Peking University had hired dozens of faculty members with doctoral degrees and had recruited eight overseas returnees to teach at its base for geology (Dong et al., 2007).

Increasingly, R&D was viewed as a productive investment because the outputs of S&T activities, such as scholarly papers, project achievements, and patents, consisted of knowledge that could enhance productivity. Accordingly, a goal was set that R&D expenditures would grow from less than 0.6% to up to 1.5% of GDP in China before 2000 (The State Council of China, 1995), which was finally fulfilled in 2008 (World Bank, 2016).

S&T activities in China are categorized into R&D, the application and promotion of S&T achievements, and S&T services. R&D, as the core of these three categories, is "central to the capacity to adopt and adapt technologies through technology transfer" (UNESCO Institute for Statistics, 2010). Thus, other than the ratio of total S&T expenditure to GDP, the ratio of R&D expenditure to GDP is considered the most important international indicator of the S&T input of a country. In addition to the provision of governmental resources, efforts were made to increase R&D investment from other sources, such as private companies, nongovernmental organizations, international loans and investment. Policies were stipulated to facilitate financing and to encourage private enterprises and individuals to participate in R&D investment (Cui, 2000).

Re-Investing in Universities: The "211" and "985" Projects

Higher education in China has dramatically expanded in recent decades, with the number of higher education institutions increasing from 1,041 in 2000 to 2,358 in 2010. Total enrollment increased from about 5.56 million in 2000 to 22.32 million in 2010. The system is predominantly public, with private institutions serving a minor, supplemental role.

A strategy of "revitalizing the nation through science and education" has set the tone for S&T development and education since 1995. To accelerate S&T development, higher education institutions were evaluated and re-endowed.

Among various efforts and initiatives, the "211 Project" and "985 Project" have been most notable. The "211 Project," launched in 1995, refers to the expectation that at the beginning of the 21st century, China would have 100 elite higher education institutions. The project goal was to build national elite universities by improving their capacity in teaching, research, and public service. The government selected universities according to their status and strength in academic disciplines. The project eventually included 116 universities. Among all higher education institutions, a subset of most comprehensive and prestigious institutions, a total of 116 institutions, received special funds from the "211 project." Thirty-nine of these institutions further distinguished themselves as part of the "985 project."

Universities selected for the "211" project received special grants from both central and local governments. From 1995 to 2000, the "211 Project" provided almost CNY 10.9 billion (about USD 1.3 billion) to Chinese universities. As resources flowed into these institutions, they were able to consolidate their advantageous positions in China's higher education system. The value of equipment, the number of books, and the amount of research funds associated with these institutions respectively accounted for 54%, 31%, and 72% of resources held by all higher education institutions in the country. Moreover, the "211" institutions gained a distinct advantage in fostering new talent. These universities trained 84% of all doctoral students and 69% of all master's students nationwide (Dong et al., 2007).

Based on the "211 Project," the "985 Project" was proposed in May 1998 and implemented the same year to construct and develop world-class research universities in China. Compared with the "211 Project," the "985 Project" was stricter in its selection criterion. To be awarded a grant from the project, a university had to be ranked first in a specific discipline or be the only institution to offer a specific sub-discipline nationwide. The "985 Project" included just 34 universities during the first phase, and an additional five during the second phase. The goal was to build world-class research universities by funding institutions with specific academic disciplines that were already the best in China. To achieve this grand goal, "985" institutions were granted much more support and resources from the Chinese government than those participating in the "211 Project." "985" institutions in Phase I (1998–2003) were awarded as much as CNY 25.5 billion (about USD 3 billion) from the central government, and grants during Phase II (2004–2009) were as high as CNY 42.6 billion (about USD 5.3 billion) (Yang, 2009).

One (unintended) consequence of the "985" and "211" projects has been heightened stratification within China's higher education systems. For example, 8,214 of the patent applications submitted by Chinese universities were approved in 2007; over 50% were submitted by "985" institutions, and 25% by the top nine universities in that group (Gao & Zhao, 2010). Both the "211" and "985" projects have enabled a select group of Chinese universities to improve their capacity in education and scientific research. In turn, these institutions have contributed to S&T development by promoting the creation and application of knowledge.

Attracting Talent: "100 Talents" and "1,000 Talents" Schemes

The "100 Talents" program was implemented by the Chinese Academy of Sciences (CAS) in 1994 to address the lack of prominent scientists and world-class researchers in China who could play a leading role in domestic scientific research. To attract and motivate young talent, CAS decided to recruit 100−200 promising young scientists from China and abroad by the end of 1999. A special office was set up to manage the recruitment plan, admission, and evaluation. Research centers and institutes within CAS reported to the office about the number and description of positions they intended to fill. Recruitment information and guidelines were publicized at certain time of the year and applicants submitted their application materials to the research center or institute directly. Intention of admission was reported by each research center or institute to the office, and later would be approved and publicized by the office. Each scientist selected would be placed in the research center or institute they applied to and receive a grant of CNY 2 million (about USD 230,000 in 1994) to fund research, experimental equipment, and a housing allowance. The office would conduct evaluation of these scientists' work on a regular basis. Through application and approval, 14 researchers were accepted by this program in 1994. In 1998, as the National Knowledge Innovation Project was being piloted at CAS, the Chinese government appropriated CNY 200 million (about USD 24 million in 1998) to this program. With this additional funding, the program developed rapidly and CAS was able to recruit more scientists than its original goal (Zhao, 2009).

With support from the Chinese government, CAS launched "The Plan of Introducing Foreign Outstanding Talent" and "The Well-Known Overseas Scholars Program" in 2001 as part of the "100 Talents" program. By the end of 2005, 1,443 elite scientists had been recruited into the program and worked in CAS. By the end of 2009, over 1,200 scientists had been introduced from overseas, among which 29 became CAS academicians,[3] 53 assuming the positions of chair scientists in key national scientific research projects, and 371 playing a leading role in national high-tech development projects (Zhen, 2013). Following the success of the "100 Talents" program, the Ministry of Education launched the "Yangtze River Scholar Scheme" in 1998. Among the 1,107 Yangtze River Scheme scholars recruited between 1998 and 2006, 94% had education or work experiences abroad.

A larger program, "The Recruitment Program of Global Experts," also known as the "1,000 Talents" program, was launched in 2008. The goal of the program was to recruit about 2,000 scientists from overseas within 5−10 years to work in key national innovation projects, key subjects and laboratories, national industrial and financial enterprises, or science parks. The selected experts are expected to make technological breakthroughs, lead emerging disciplines and develop high-tech industries.

This program has a high selection threshold; an expert must have obtained a doctoral degree overseas, be less than 55 years old, and be able to work in China for at least 6 months every year. The selection pool includes professors at prestigious foreign universities or research institutions, high-level technical or management talent in renowned international companies or financial institutions, and entrepreneurs with intellectual property rights or core technology experience who are familiar with related industry and international rules. Selected experts will work in the employing unit they apply to, including CAS, universities, national enterprises, and other research institutions.

To attract persons of interest, this program provides preferential working and living conditions. Those selected are able to immediately assume lead positions in their employing unit. Selected experts with foreign citizenship can be granted permanent residence or long-term multiple-entry visas. Selected experts with Chinese citizenship are free to reside in any city in China and are awarded CNY 1 million with tax exemption (about USD 144,000 in 2008) (The Recruitment Program of Global Experts, 2008). Between 2009 and 2013, 3,319 people were recruited from abroad, including over 40 scholars from developed countries. Under this program, Chinese provincial governments also have launched their own "1,000 Talents" programs and have successfully attracted more than 20,000 people from overseas (Zhao, 2013).

The last 35 years have been a period of rapid growth in China. Although it is difficult to establish a causal relationship between S&T development and economic growth, it is safe to say that S&T development has been playing a partial but increasingly important role. In return, S&T development has also greatly benefited from overall economic development, because the government has had the resources to continue to invest in academic and research institutions and R&D personnel. This mutually beneficial relationship has been most evident recently as the country has strived to upgrade its industries.

WHAT SCIENTIFIC PRODUCTIVITY DATA REVEALS ABOUT CHINESE INVESTMENTS IN R&D

What effects have national S&T and higher education policies had on the production of scientific research in China, especially during the past 35 years? Resource dependence theory provides insights into this particular question. The theory posits that an educational institution engages in direct exchange relationships with external agents in order to acquire the resources necessary to accomplish its mission (Pfeffer & Salancik, 1978; Slaughter & Leslie, 1997).

Agents who control critical resources can impose preferred values and practices by linking compliance with resource allocation. Since the government is either the only or the primary resource provider for institutions involved in scientific research, one would expect that higher education institutions would have done their best to comply with the common goals set by the central government.

In this section and the next, we attempt to examine the change in scientific productivity using the SPHERE dataset and some institutional level data we collected from a set of research universities in China. It is important to note that the SPHERE dataset is heavily weighted toward basic research, as opposed to other research activities such as patenting and research commercialization. Also, given the time span and the varied nature of policies, this is not intended to be a rigorous causal analysis (i.e., the effects of specific policies). Instead, we try to broadly describe trends in scientific research among scholars in China and the rest of the world. At the institutional level, we compare the performance of the Chinese Academy of Science and higher education institutions in China.

Although R&D productivity can be measured in a variety of ways, research publications are a primary R&D productivity metric for higher education institutions. In this section, we use SCI publication data from TR to study publication productivity patterns in China. TR collected the author names and institution addresses listed on each article published in SCI journals since 1980. While a selective database, TR has the most comprehensive data on journal publications available. Since much of the information on publications before 1980 either has not been digitalized or is simply missing, we drew a random sample of journals every 5 years to obtain estimates of publications from each country, going back to 1900. We counted the number of publications adopting uniform criteria that helped to establish a unique historical dataset of peer-reviewed publications over the 20th century (see introduction to this volume).

Table 1 shows the number of SCI articles for China. Due to China's resumption of sovereignty over Hong Kong and Macau in 1997 and 1999, respectively, we created two columns here, with one excluding and the other including Hong Kong and Macau when counting the number of publications in China. TR data for the United States and the world total are reported as a basis for comparison. Between 1900 and 1950, the total number of publications from China was small and grew slowly, from essentially zero in 1900 to about 200 in 1950. During the two decades following the birth of new China, there were no publications from China recorded in our sample due to the turbulent political climate. Since the reform and modernization era from 1980 to 2010, the total number of publications from China (including Hong Kong and Macau) has increased more than 150-fold, averaging over 18% annual growth. This growth is even more impressive when Hong Kong and Macau are excluded, with an overall increase over 200 times the number of publications in 1980 and an annual growth rate of 19.3%. During the same period, the total number of world publications has merely tripled, with an annual growth rate of 3.8%.

Table 1. Number of SCI Publications by Country/Region.

Year[a]	China Excluding HK and Macau[b]	China Including HK and Macau[c]	USA[d]	World Total[e]
1900	2	2	1,960	9,503
1905	0	0	1,797	10,637
1910	7	7	4,004	11,695
1915	0	0	5,557	10,679
1920	12	12	5,486	14,059
1925	41	41	6,627	19,586
1930	53	53	11,789	25,428
1935	266	266	13,972	25,531
1940	72	72	9,661	23,057
1945	170	170	16,092	20,523
1950	178	192	5,295	22,489
1955	0	10	14,627	36,315
1960	0	0	33,958	49,455
1965	0	122	43,127	94,216
1970	0	184	102,225	223,980
1975	48	209	101,447	259,998
1980	733	999	125,906	351,794
1985	2,866	3,337	152,704	424,519
1990	6,524	7,356	170,800	488,492
1995	10,796	12,287	178,906	527,388
2000	26,909	27,228	198,776	622,842
2005	60,697	60,697	207,862	690,535
2010	129,361	129,361	265,149	988,522
2011	152,397	152,397	281,613	1,073,552

Source: SPHERE project database of SCIE publications (Thomson Reuters' Web of Science).
[a]Data between 1900 and 1970 are from SPHERE project. Year-to-year variations could be due to sampling errors. Data after 1975 are from Web of Sciences.
[b]Because China reassumed sovereignty over Hong Kong and Macau in 1997 and 1999, respectively, we created two columns here, one excluding Hong Kong and Macau and the other including both.
[c]Since Hong Kong and Macau became part of China after 1997 and 1999, respectively, numbers after year 2000 between excluding and including Hong Kong and Macau are close or identical.
[d]This includes all articles with a U.S. author or coauthor.
[e]Total number of publications worldwide. Multiple-authored papers are not double-counted.

The growth in the United States is lower than the world average, with an overall growth of 2.24 times the number of publications in 1980 and 2.7% annual growth rate.

The growth rate, however, was not constant throughout the entire 30-year period. Fig. 1 shows the proportion of SCI publications authored or

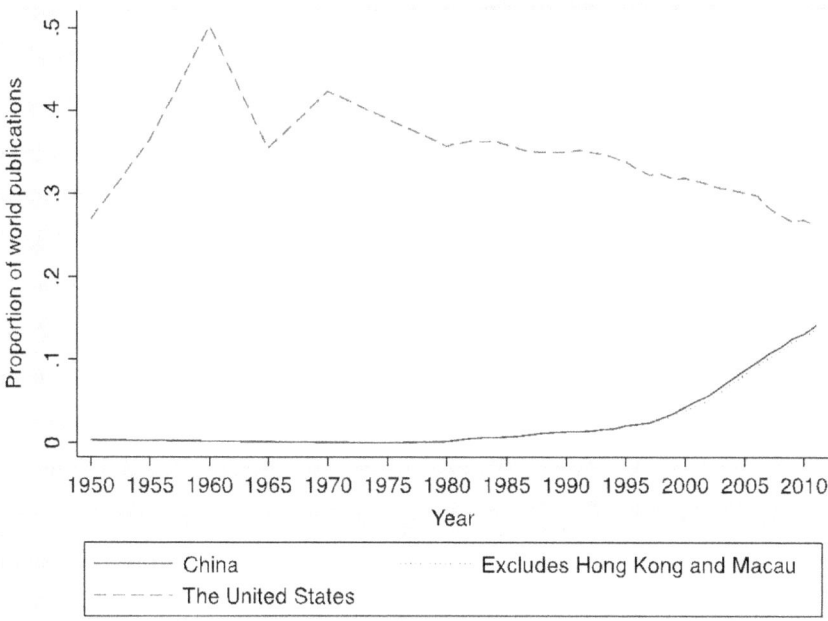

Fig. 1. Proportion of SCI Articles (Co-)Authored by Researchers from China and the United States. *Source*: SPHERE project database of SCIE publications (Thomson Reuters' Web of Science).

coauthored by researchers from China and the United States. This figure shows that before 1980, the number of SCI publications by researchers who resided in China was essentially zero. This is not surprising, given that the Cultural Revolution had just ended and S&T development was marred by political turmoil and setbacks. Of course, this does not mean that there was no R&D activity in China before 1980. Much of the limited R&D activities at that time focused on research projects that were significant for national development. Another possible reason for this low level of publishing activity during this period was the dominance of the Russian language within China's academic circle. As a result, many of their publications fail to appear in TR data, because the SCI consists of journals that, increasingly over time, have published in the English language.

The gradual growth in publishing activities came right after the reform and the adoption of an open-door policy in 1978. For the first 15 years after 1980, growth was gradual. The proportion of world SCI articles authored or coauthored by researchers from China grew from essentially zero (about 0.2% to be exact) to about 2% in 1995. This modest growth increased significantly over the next 5 years. In 2000, Chinese researchers authored or coauthored about 3.3% of world SCI articles. Since then, the proportion of world SCI articles authored or coauthored by Chinese researchers has been increasing at about 1% per year, culminating in an impressive 13.7% in 2011.

It appears as though the period between 1995 and 2000 was one of transition and acceleration. Incidentally this period coincided with the "211" and "985" projects, which provided enormous investment and incentives for higher education institutions to improve their research capacity. Although it is impossible to establish a causal relationship between these policy reforms and initiatives and the overall research output measured by SCI articles from China, the multiple coincidences between changes in major national policy – the reform and open-door policy in 1978, the "211" and "985" projects between 1995 and 2000, and increased investment in the higher education sector in recent years – and research outputs suggest a tight association.

In comparison, the proportion of SCI articles authored or coauthored by researchers from the United States has been on a downward trend during last 30 years or so, starting at about 35% in 1980 and ending at about 26% in 2011. This relative decline is partly due to the dramatic increase in publications from scholars in China (and thus an increased world total); however, even when excluding China from the analysis, the growth of SCI articles from scholars in the United States has not been able to keep pace with that of scholars from the rest of the world. Our calculations suggest that if the growth pattern of the last 10 years continues apace, the United States and China will be on par in terms of proportion of world SCI articles authored or coauthored by their researchers in 2020, with both contributing to about 22% of world SCI articles.

International collaborations are vastly increasing; a crucial aspect of scientific research. How has the trend of international collaboration and its relationship with overall research output affected China? Fig. 2 shows the proportion of internationally collaborated articles by scholars from institutions in China, the United States, and the rest of world since 1980. The trend shows a distinct jump between 1997 and 1998 because of a change in address data sources at TR. Despite this data problem, it is still possible to make some general observations based on the trends before and after 1997/1998. In general, international collaborations have increased over the past 30 years. In 1980, only 2% of the world's total SCI articles were coauthored by scholars from two or more countries (this figure could well underestimate collaboration due to data issues). By 2011, this proportion reached 23%. Thus, nearly one in every four papers resulted from international collaboration.

The United States has a consistently higher collaboration rate than the world average and the gap has been increasing over time. For example, in 1980, about 3% of all articles authored or coauthored by scholars in the United States had at least one coauthor from another country. This figure reached 35% in 2011, dwarfing the 23% world average. The international collaboration

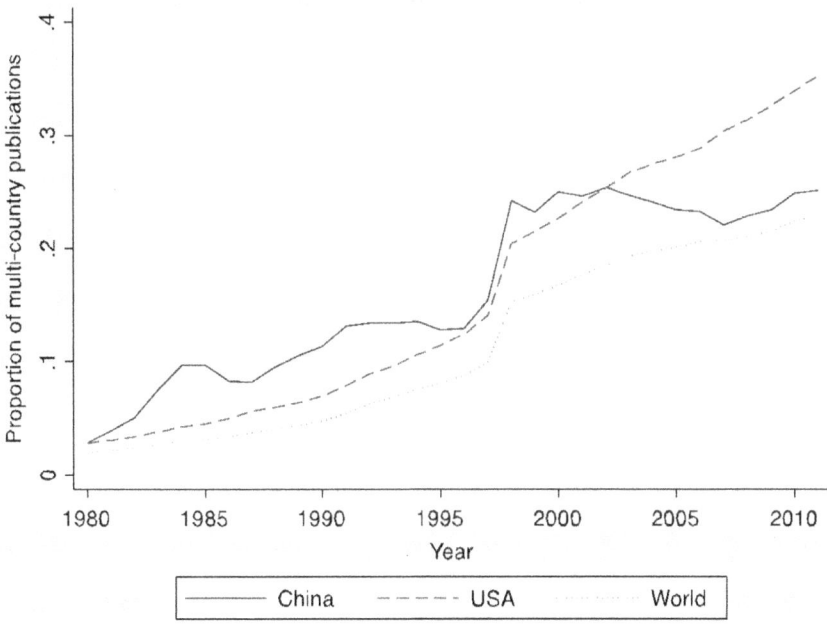

Fig. 2. Proportion of Internationally Collaborated SCI Articles (China, USA, the World). *Source*: SPHERE project database of SCIE publications (Thomson Reuters' Web of Science).

pattern of researchers in China is distinctly different from that of researchers in the United States. Before 1997, the collaboration rate for Chinese researchers was slightly higher than that for researchers in the United States. However, the rate has stagnated since 1998, hovering around 25%. This trend suggests that international collaboration benefited research output for China in the 1980s and 1990s, perhaps especially due to returning scholars through the active recruitment policies. During the most recent decade these collaborations have not grown at the same rate as overall production from within an expanding national system. Fig. 3, which shows the average number of countries on a research article, presents another way to look at international collaboration. The general observation is similar to that for Fig. 2, with the average number of countries on a research article worldwide increasing from 1.02 in 1980 to 1.32 in 2011. In the United States, these two numbers were 1.03 and 1.55, and in China, 1.03 and 1.37. Again, this number has not increased much in recent years for China.

Because China and the United States produce the largest number of SCI articles, it is interesting to examine collaboration between the two countries.

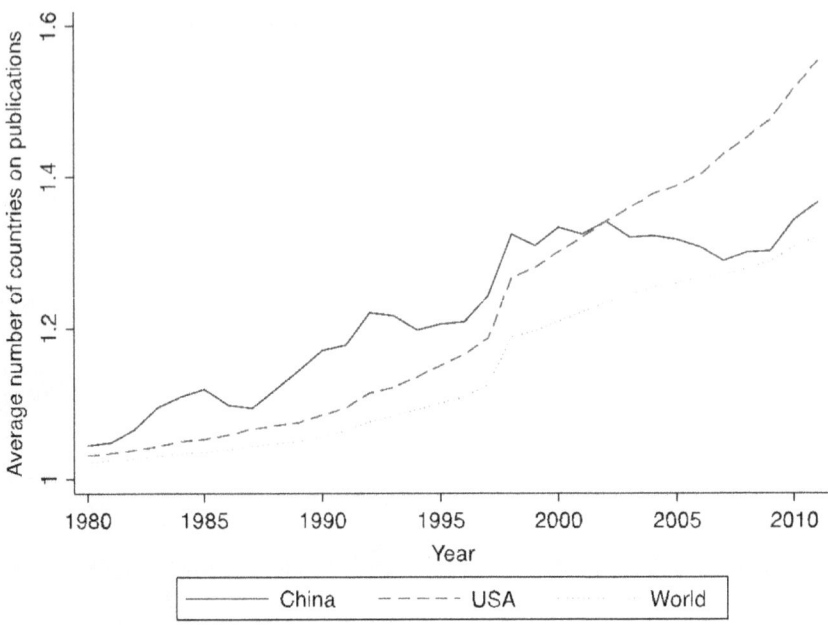

Fig. 3. Average Number of Countries on SCI Publications (China, USA, the World). *Source*: SPHERE project database of SCIE publications (Thomson Reuters' Web of Science).

Fig. 4 shows the proportion of China–U.S. collaborated articles among all internationally collaborated articles from the two countries. The dominant form of international collaboration among Chinese researchers is collaboration with researchers from the United States. During the 1980s, collaborations with researchers in the United States accounted for approximately 50% of all international collaborations for Chinese researchers. The proportion decreased significantly in the 1990s due to a series of diplomatic and economic sanctions imposed by the United States and its allies immediately after the 1989 Tiananmen Square event. The proportion began to increase in 2000 and reached 40% in 2011. On the U.S. side, collaborations with Chinese researchers were inconsequential in early years; however, they have become increasingly important recently. The proportion of U.S.–China collaborations among all international collaborations of researchers in the United States has increased from less than 5% in 2000 to nearly 16% in 2011. In other words, about one in every six articles coauthored by a researcher in the United States has been coauthored by a researcher affiliated with a Chinese institution.

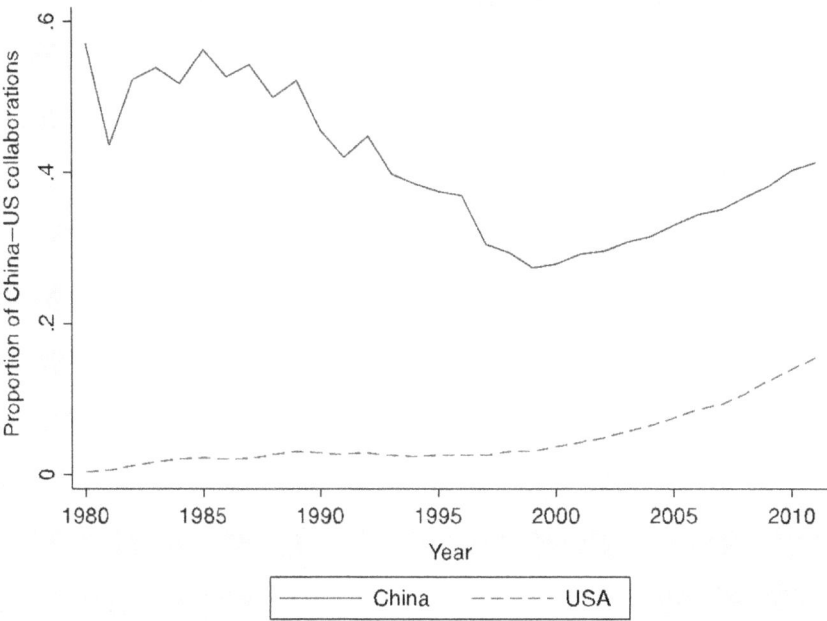

Fig. 4. Collaborations between Scholars from China and the United States. *Source*: SPHERE project database of SCIE publications (Thomson Reuters' Web of Science).

COMPARING THE PERFORMANCE OF THE CHINESE ACADEMY OF SCIENCE AND OTHER HIGHER EDUCATION INSTITUTIONS

A discussion about scientific research in China would not be complete without examining the role of the Chinese Academy of Science (CAS), which is, historically, the single most prolific research institution in China. CAS was established in November 1949, as an affiliate of the Government Administration Council of China (which later became State Council of China). At first, CAS consisted of 14 institutes, one observatory, and one industrial laboratory. In 1955, these units were consolidated into four academic divisions (i.e., physics, mathematics and chemistry; biology and geology; technology; and philosophy and social science) and each began enrolling graduate students. A total of 233 most influential scientists in China were elected as committee members of the divisions. (The title "academician" was bestowed on these scientists beginning in 1993.) The academic divisions of CAS began to advise the government on science-related policies, and CAS was regarded as the center of the science and technology system of China. Its first research missions centered on the utilization of atomic power, iron and steel alloys, petroleum and other key national priorities. With political support and ample appropriations from the central government, CAS swiftly expanded and set up branches across the country (Cui, 2000).

In the national administrative system of science that was formed in China during the 1950s, the Chinese government created the missions and goals of scientific development, organized the research teams and provided the funds for all scientific activities. Playing a "locomotive" role in national development schemes, CAS was tightly coupled with the Chinese government and, as discussed above, could not avoid the influence of political movements in China from the late 1950s to the 1970s.

In 1977, when the Cultural Revolution came to an end, CAS was permitted to resume its graduate education program. CAS established China's first graduate school in 1978 at the University of Science and Technology of China (an affiliated institution founded in 1958). CAS was also the pilot institution for university degree regulations in China. Among the first 18 graduates to obtain doctoral degrees in China, 12 were educated at CAS. In addition, CAS was the first institution to resume international academic exchanges when it sent visiting scholars abroad in 1978. Among the 20,000 students going abroad from 1978 to 1984, 85% studied in the fields of science and technology, among which one-fifth were from CAS. Moreover, CAS was the first institution to resume the evaluation system for academic ranks and scientific research grants and awards. In 1982, the Chinese government created an endowment to establish the Science Foundation of CAS, which provided research funds for basic research nationwide. Based on this foundation, the National Natural Science Foundation of China was founded in 1986 as an affiliate of the State Council of China, no longer within CAS structure. CAS also recruited the first postdoctoral scholar in China in 1984 and established more grant and award programs for young scientists, including The Research Foundation for Young Scientists and the CAS Young Scientists Award; since 1987, both have contributed significantly to training scholars for research teams (Li, 2011).

Unlike most universities and colleges which are in the charge of the Ministry of Education or other ministries, CAS is a direct affiliate of the State Council of China and runs independently of the regular higher education system. CAS was built up and given major research resources by the government to be the national center for scientific research and to provide scientific-related policy counseling, while universities played a more comprehensive role with an emphasis on education and had not been adequately valued in R&D until their role in boosting research was well recognized in 1980s. Thus, CAS had more advantages than higher education institutions in research on the starting line.

However, the boundary between CAS and higher education institutions seems quite blurred, because CAS cooperates with universities in research nationwide and also has set up its own affiliate universities, including University of Science and Technology of China, and Shanghai University of

Science and Technology. These two universities are considered higher education institutions in the analysis below, because they function as same as other higher education institutions in education and research rather than research-only institutes. They also receive funding from Ministry of Education and other governmental departments in addition to CAS, and their research team contains both CAS scholars and non-CAS employees.

Fig. 5 shows that number of SCI articles authored or coauthored by researchers from the Chinese Academy of Science and higher education institutions. It must be noted that because names of colleges and universities had various forms and changed over time, it is almost impossible to accurately count articles produced by higher education institutions. Here, we used two rough criteria. In the first approach, we counted all organizations with either "university" or "college" in their names. In the second approach, we also included those organizations with "institution" or "institute" in their names. "Institutions" and "institutes" could be higher education institutions (e.g., the well-known Harbin Institute of Technology), but could also be research institutions under the supervision of different state departments. Unfortunately, it is difficult to tell whether these institutions/institutes are research organizations

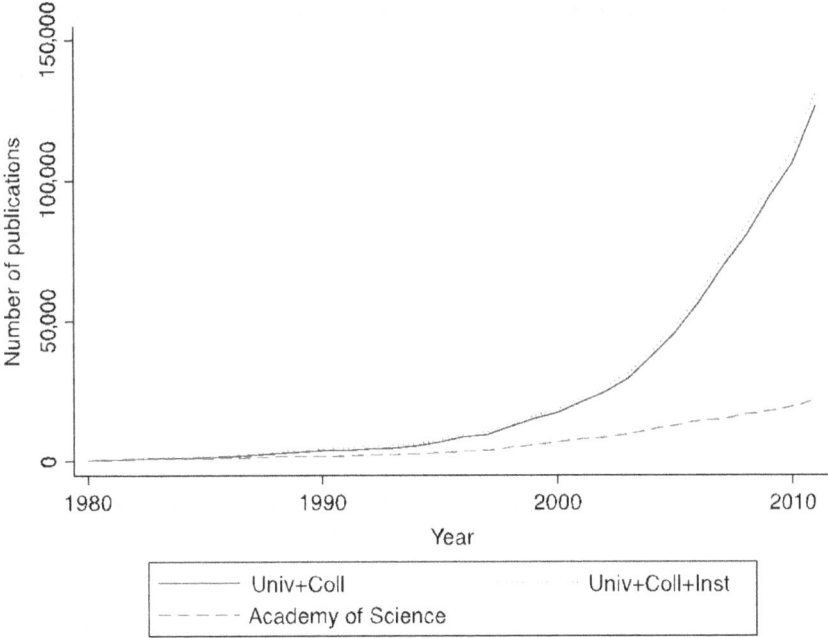

Fig. 5. Publications by Scholars from the Chinese Academy of Science and Other Higher Education Institutions. *Source*: SPHERE project database of SCIE publications (Thomson Reuters' Web of Science).

or academic institutions. Nonetheless, these two different approaches should approximate the contribution of the higher education sector to scientific research.

Clearly, the CAS and higher education institutions have followed two very different paths. In the case of CAS, the increase in research production has been gradual and constant over the years. By contrast, research production in the higher education sector experienced a gradual increase during 1980s, accelerated during the 1990s, and has grown dramatically since 2000. It is clear that the overall trend depicted in Fig. 1 has been largely driven by the higher education sector. In 1980, CAS produced approximately 300 of the 733 total articles by Chinese scholars, attributable almost entirely to the higher education sector. Fast-forward to 2011, CAS produced about 22,000 out of 148,000 articles, of which all other higher education institutions combined produced about 126,000. Articles produced by the industrial sector and various agencies of the government only account for a small fraction of the total.[4]

Fig. 6 clearly shows the changing landscape of scientific research over the past 30 years or so. CAS produced about 40% of all research articles from China, but this proportion has been decreasing over time, especially from 2000

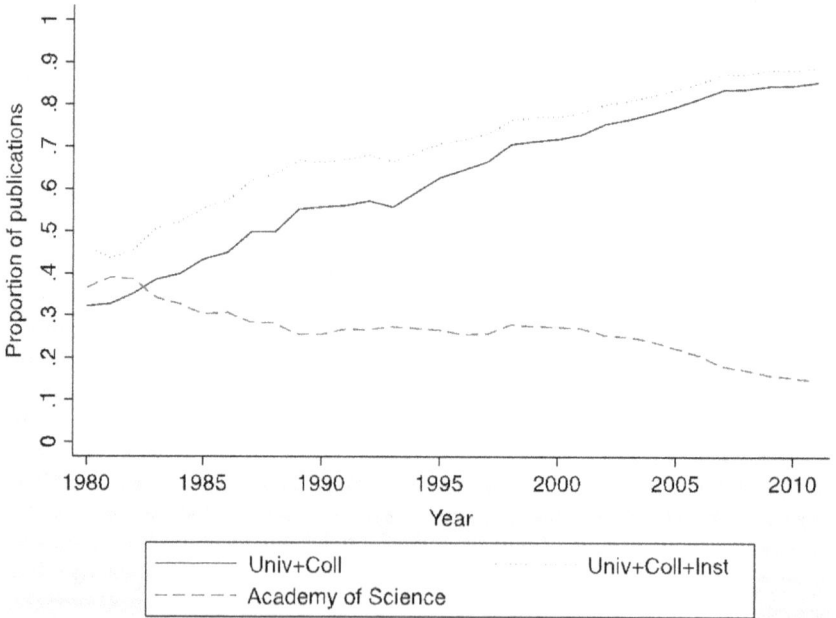

Fig. 6. Proportion of Publications by Scholars from the Chinese Academy of Science and Other Higher Education Institutions. *Source*: SPHERE project database of SCIE publications (Thomson Reuters' Web of Science).

to 2010. In 2011, the proportion of articles produced by CAS decreased to about 15%. Not surprisingly, during the same period of time the higher education sector has played a more prominent role; in the 1980s, higher education institutions (not including CAS) produced about 40% of all articles by Chinese scholars, but in 2011, they produced approximately 85%.

In order to gain a better understanding of institutional level R&D production in higher education, we collected the number of publications by scholars affiliated with a subset of higher education institutions in China. Theoretically, one can develop such an index from the TR publication data; however, because institution names changed over time and also appeared in different forms, it is difficult to directly count number of publications. As an alternative, we collected data on a subset of the most comprehensive and prestigious institutions, a total of 72, which are funded and supervised by the Ministry of Education. These are the most research-intensive higher education institutions in China that produce the vast majority of SCI articles. We collected data on various aspects of these 72 institutions every year between 2000 and 2008.

Table 2 reports the average number of publications in this set of universities between 2000 and 2008. One important aspect of this additional data collection is that the total number of publications from each institution is disaggregated by fields of study (i.e., Science and Engineering (SE) vs. Non-SE) and publishing venues (i.e., domestic and international journals). The average number of publications by scholars from these institutions increased from 2,136 in 2000 to 4,123 in 2008, an overall increase of 93% at an annual rate of 8.8% during this 9-year period. The increase was slightly more pronounced for SE fields with an overall increase of 96% at an annual rate of 8.8%, than for non-SE fields, with an overall increase of 84% at an annual rate of 8%.

Investigating where these papers were published reveals some interesting patterns. For SE publications, domestic journals represented the largest category in all years, but the gap between domestic and international journals has shrunk considerably. During this 9-year period, the number of domestic SE publications increased by 57% at an annual rate of 6%, while the number of international SE publications increased by 272% at an annual rate of 18.3% – more than three times the annual rate of increase for domestic SE publications. These data suggest that elite Chinese institutions prioritized publishing in international journals during this period.

One way to examine the increase in research publications is to compare it with increases in research inputs. To illustrate, we included the average research expenditure at those institutions from 2000 to 2008. (We do not argue that research expenditure is the only factor that matters. However, this simple comparison does provide useful information on how the increase in research publications stacks up against increases in other input factors.) The last column in Table 2 indicates that average research expenditures at our sample institutions increased from approximately CNY 90 million in 2000 (USD 1 was worth approximately CNY 8.3) to CNY 481 million in 2008 (USD 1 was worth

Table 2. Comparison of Average Number of Research Papers and Research Expenditures among a Subset of Chinese Research Universities, 2000−2008.

Year	Total	Domestic SE	International SE	Domestic Non-SE	International Non-SE	Research Expenditure
2000	2,136	1,323	289	509	16	90
2001	2,305	1,347	320	629	10	104
2002	2,550	1,488	354	694	14	127
2003	2,873	1,683	434	740	17	149
2004	3,098	1,712	574	791	20	171
2005	3,276	1,814	649	792	21	196
2006	3,841	2,136	803	874	28	217
2007	3,870	2,065	900	875	30	218
2008	4,123	2,082	1,075	931	36	481[a]
Overall change	92.99%	57.32%	272.46%	83.03%	124.03%	142.84%
Annual rate	8.78%	5.97%	18.33%	8.04%	10.88%	13.51%

Source: SPHERE project database of SCIE publications (Thomson Reuters' Web of Science).
[a]The jump in research expenditure in 2008 is mainly due to two factors. First, the Chinese government published a *National Medium and Long-Term Science and Technology Development Plan (2006−2020)* in 2006 and revised the *Law of China on Science and Technology Progress* in 2007 to increase investment in science and technology research activities and the proportion of expenditure on science and technology relative to GDP. Second, a reform of government revenue and expenditure classification was implemented in 2007 and was applied to the field of science and technology, that is, more accounting items related to research activities were added to the research expenditure category.

approximately CNY 6.8). The sharp increase between 2007 and 2008 was due to increased national investments in science and technology and a reform of government revenue and expenditure classifications in 2007. Even after excluding data from 2008, research expenditures increased at an annual rate of 13.5% after adjusting for inflation. Although it is difficult to establish a formal causal relationship between the financial investment in higher education institutions and their research output, we do find enhanced government investment and growth in research output, which also corroborates our historical review of various government policies that have aimed to increase research funding in the higher education sector.

CONCLUSIONS AND IMPLICATIONS

In this chapter, we reviewed major policy reforms and programs in China since its foundation in 1949, with a focus on the past 35 years of extraordinary growth. Data from TR were used to illustrate changes in scientific publications that accompanied these policy reforms and programs. Given the descriptive nature of this chapter, it is impossible to identify the effects of specific programs on scientific research productivity; nonetheless the analysis does suggest a tight connection between national policy and scientific research productivity in higher education. In this section, we summarize our main findings and also discuss implications of these main findings for the future of scientific research in China, particularly at Chinese universities.

The central theme from our policy review and data collection is that the higher education sector in China is a centralized system; it is an important part (and thus serves the interest) of national development. The central government controlled scientific research through direct administration in early periods and has guided research activities through funding specific programs in recent decades. Therefore, the higher education sector in general and scientific research in particular have been vulnerable to the larger political climate. When the priority was to build a new national economy right in the decade after the founding of the PRC (1949–1955), the higher education system was restructured and scientific work forces were trained. However, when a political agenda dominated all aspects of life, from 1956 to 1965, scientific research experienced a series of setbacks. As class struggle become the paramount focus of Chinese society during the Cultural Revolution (1966–1976), scientific research came to an abrupt halt. Scientific infrastructure and human resources were gradually restored only after the reform was implemented and an open-door policy was adopted (1978). Throughout the 1980s and 1990s, there was gradual growth in scientific research outputs as reflected in the TR data. Finally, under the general guideline of "constructing world-class universities" proposed in the "985 Project," investment in the higher education sector increased substantially, which consequently ushered in a period of rapid growth in scientific research (Yang, 2009).

A centralized system has its pros and cons. When well planned, a centralized system can mobilize limited resources and maximize overall output. There are, however, many downsides of a centralized system. The biggest risk, as history has shown (e.g., the Great Leap Forward movement, the Cultural Revolution), is that it is prone to catastrophic failures, because there are no checks and balances built into the system. As China becomes more open to the world and its citizens become more educated, particularly through the development of information technology that allows information to quickly flow across national borders, the probability of system-wide catastrophe seems less likely. Even when well planned, a centralized system may constrain innovation that is vital in current scientific research and economic development. As such, scholars in the Chinese higher education system, especially in general and scientific research, tend to be followers instead of leaders. The higher education system in China has historically modeled itself after other nations (e.g., first the former USSR, and then the United States). Similarly, although China recently ranked second in number of SCI publications, its share of highly cited papers lagged significantly behind the United States (Wang & Levitt, 2012). Clearly, alternate or supplemental policy instruments are needed if China is to truly become a world leader in scientific research.

Being a centralized system means that higher education institutions have been quite responsive to the common goals set by the central government. The recent surge in SCI publications can be seen as a response to incentives provided by the central government – and vastly expanded capacity. This is not surprising given the fact that the government was historically the sole resource provider for these institutions; even with recent hikes in student tuition and fees that began in the early 1990s, the government still provides the vast majority of funds for these institutions.

What is measured tends to be accomplished; however, not all goals can be easily achieved. The Great Leap Forward is an important footnote to this. Although the recent grand scheme of constructing "world-class universities" has ushered in a period of dramatic growth in scientific research as measured by the quantity of SCI publications, the quality and originality of these publications have not kept pace. This growth, in our view, is lopsided. The imbalance exists not only between the quantity and quality of research in sciences, but also between sciences and social sciences (and humanities and arts for that matter). Finally, due to the limitation of the SPHERE dataset, we were not able to address the imbalance between applied and basic research. For example, Liao (2010) found that as recently as 2007, the vast majority (95.3%) of R&D expenditure in China went to experimental and applied research, with only 4.7% allocated to basic research, while in the United States for example, 18.6% of R&D expenditure went to basic research in 2006 (Liao, 2010). While this chapter has examined the growth of scientific research in recent decades, further studies are warranted to seek a balanced growth path for R&D development in China.

NOTES

1. The acronym "BRIC" was coined by O'Neill (2001) to refer to Brazil, Russia, India, and China. Sometimes it is extended into "BRICK" to include South Korea.

2. Publication counts are not weighted by the number of coauthors on a paper. Each country gets one publication as long as there is at least one coauthor from that country. These numbers do not include papers published in Chinese-media journals. Because China resumed sovereignty over Hong Kong and Macau in 1997 and 1999 respectively, we also included publications from Hong Kong and Macau when calculating publications from China in order to make numbers comparable over the years.

3. CAS academician is considered the highest honor in academia in China. They are selected nationwide and do not necessarily hold positions within CAS. They can be researchers who work in CAS, but also may come from universities, national enterprises, or other research institutions.

4. For example, in 2011, higher education institutions and CAS account for more than 90% of all authors and coauthors of research papers in China. Examples of these

other organizations include various central government agencies (e.g., Ministry of Education, Chinese Center for Disease Control and Prevention), provincial and local agencies (e.g., Shanghai Mental Health Center, Zhejiang Academy of Agriculture Science), medical centers (e.g., Chinese People's Liberation Army General Hospital), and industries (e.g., SINOPEC, Microsoft Research Asia).

REFERENCES

Adams, J., Pendlebury, D., & Stembridge, B. (2013). *Building bricks: Exploring the global research and innovation impact of Brazil, Russia, India, China and South Korea.* Philadelphia, PA: Thomson Reuters.

Cui, L. C. (2000). *A study on the S&T policies of the CPC since 1949.* Doctoral thesis, The Party School of the Central Committee of C.P.C. Retrieved from https://vpn.ccnu.edu.cn/kns/brief/,DanaInfo=epub.cnki.net+default_result.aspx (in Chinese).

Dong, B. L., Dan, Z. B., & Chen, Q. (2007). *The modern history of higher education in China.* Wuhan: Huazhong University of Science and Technology Press (in Chinese).

Gao, L., & Zhao, W. H. (2010). A comparative study on the R&D expenditure and entrepreneurship between Chinese and American research universities. *China Higher Education Research, 2010*(5), 39−42 (in Chinese).

Geiger, R., & Sá, C. M. (2008). *Tapping the riches of science: Universities and the promise of economic growth.* Cambridge, MA: Harvard University Press.

Hayhoe, R. (1994). Ideas of higher learning, east and west: Conflicting values in the development of the Chinese university. *Minerva, 32*(4), 361−382. Retrieved from http://www.jstor.org.ezaccess.libraries.psu.edu/stable/41820949

Hayhoe, R. (1996). *China's universities 1895-1995: A century of cultural conflict.* New York, NY: Garland Pub.

Li, H. F. (2011). The experience of Chinese Academy of Sciences in talents building. *China's Talents, 397*(6), 30−32.

Liao, W. (2010). A comparative study on the R&D input of China and OECD countries. *Special Zone Economy, 259*(8), 107−109 (in Chinese).

Oleksiyenko, A. (2014). On the shoulders of giants? Global science, resource asymmetries, and repositioning of research universities in China and Russia. *Comparative Education Review, 58*(3), 482−508. doi:10.1086/676328

O'Neill, J. (2001). *Building better global economic BRICs.* Global Economics Paper 66. New York, NY: Goldman-Sachs.

People's Network. (2006). Common Program of the Chinese People's Consultative Conference. *People's Network*, December 31. Retrieved from http://www.hnredstar.gov.cn/yueyang123/djgz/dj_zywx/t20061230_84917.html (in Chinese).

Pfeffer, J., & Salancik, G. R. (1978). *The external control of organizations.* New York, NY: Harper & Row.

Slaughter, S., & Leslie, L. (1997). *Academic capitalism: Politics, policies and the entrepreneurial university.* Baltimore, MD: Johns Hopkins University Press.

The Recruitment Program of Global Experts. (2008). *The Recruitment Program of Global Experts*, December. Retrieved from http://www.1000plan.org/qrjh/section/2?m=rcrd (in Chinese)

The State Council of China. (1995). *The decision on expediting progress in Science and Technology.* Beijing: The State Council of China.

UNESCO Institute for Statistics. (2010). *Measuring R&D: Challenges faced by developing countries.* Technical Paper no. 5. Montreal: UNESCO Institute for Statistics. Retrieved from http://www.uis.unesco.org/Pages/default.aspx

Wang, J., & Levitt, J. M. (2012). The contribution to highly cited articles by authors from BRIC countries. *Proceedings of 17th international conference on science and technology* indicators, Science-Metrixd and OST, Montreal.
World Bank. (2016). *World development indicators*. Retrieved from http://databank.worldbank.org/data/
Wu, W. H. (1997). A historical study of Chinese scientific and cultural policies. *Scientific Management Research, 15*(5), 16−20 (in Chinese).
Yang, C. G. (2009). The national strategy of establishing world-class universities. *China Education Daily*, September 28. Retrieved from http://www.jyb.cn/high/gjsd/200909/t20090928_313808.html (in Chinese).
Zhao, L. J. (2013). Talk in the conference of The Recruitment Program of Global Experts. *The Recruitment Program of Global Experts*, September. Retrieved from http://www.1000plan.org/qrjh/article/40679 (in Chinese).
Zhao, Y. H. (2009). Sixty years of Chinese Academy of Sciences. *Renmin Daily*, October 31. Retrieved from http://www.gov.cn/jrzg/2009-10/31/content_1453257.htm (in Chinese).
Zhen, Q. L. (2013). The Hundred Talents Program of the Chinese Academy of Sciences. *ScienceNet*, September 24. Retrieved from http://talent.sciencenet.cn/index.php?s=Info/index/id/8598 (in Chinese).

SCIENCE PRODUCTION IN TAIWANESE UNIVERSITIES, 1980−2011

Yuan Chih Fu

ABSTRACT

Purpose − *Taiwan serves as a case study to investigate the association between the expansion and reform of higher education and the growth of science production. More specifically, what driving forces facilitated the growth of science production in different types of Taiwanese universities and other sectors, from 1980 to 2011.*

Design − *The contribution charts differential contributions to overall production. Taiwanese data from Thomson Reuters' Science Citation Index Expanded (SCIE) is analyzed to show the expansion of the higher education system and its relationship to the production of science. The author uses sociological organization theories to facilitate our understanding of how and why the landscape of science production changed.*

Findings − *Results show that the growth of science production is associated with processes of isomorphism and competition within the higher education system. Findings also suggest that universities quickly seized upon external opportunities and turned themselves into what is known as the "knowledge conglomerate." Unique organizational features bolster universities' position as the driving force behind advancing national innovation.*

Originality/value — *This study extends previous research by examining multiple sectors of higher education, using longitudinal and recent data, and highlighting themes that have been ignored or overlooked, such as competition and collaboration among universities and industry partners.*

Keywords: Higher education; university; reform; national innovation system; science production; Taiwan

INTRODUCTION

In today's knowledge society, the value of higher education for knowledge creation and technological advancement is well-recognized (Baker, 2014; Goldin & Katz, 2009; Zhang, Powell, & Baker, 2015). However, the association between higher education policy reform and the growth of science production has not been fully investigated. Taiwan has one of the highest participation rates in higher education globally — a higher percentage of young people attend universities in Taiwan than in most other countries in the world (OECD, 2016). For its size, Taiwan also produces a relatively large percentage of scientific publications compared to many other countries in different regions of the world. In recent years, Taiwan has instituted several policies to encourage university-based researchers to publish scientific research. Thus, the Taiwanese experience offers insights for understanding the relationship between higher education reform and the growth in scientific publication output.

In this chapter, Taiwan serves as a case study to explore the impacts of changes in higher education policy since the Second World War, but from 1980 in particular, on the growth of scientific production at national level. I examine changes to the internal dynamics of the higher education system that accompanied university reforms. Sociological organization theories will be used to interpret the longitudinal data analyzed. Then, I consider how changes to the external environment transformed university research and supported what is called the university-based "knowledge conglomerate."

The Taiwanese longitudinal data is drawn from millions of publications that are included in Thomson Reuters' Science Citation Index Expanded (SCIE), spanning from 1980 to 2011. The "whole count" strategy was applied to calculate the science production at chosen unit levels. I divided this longitudinal dataset into two key measures. The first measure represents the number of SCIE papers that were produced by an organization in a given year. The second measure is the frequency of coauthorship that represents the number of SCIE papers that were produced through collaboration across organizations. The former indicator reveals the productivity of each organization; the latter illustrates the types of partnerships among organizations. I conclude by arguing that the growth of university-based science production resulted from a series of national policy reforms affecting higher education.

HISTORICAL BACKGROUND

The history of Taiwanese higher education begins in 1928 when the first university, Imperial Taipei University, was established by a Japanese colonial government (Chang, 2001). As with other Japanese universities of the time, Taiwanese higher education took German higher education as its model. The central, colonial government took full responsibility for the administrative control of higher education, and the system was constructed with public institutions as central. Public higher education institutions were one part of this administrative structure and were completely dependent on the government for funding.

Soon after the end of the Second World War, Taiwanese higher education faced its first model transition. In 1945, the Republic of China (Taiwan) reclaimed its sovereignty. Because of the political alliance between the Republic of China (Taiwan) and the United States during the Second World War, followed by the Cold War, the American model of higher education was an important reference for the reconstruction of the Taiwanese higher education system (Xu, 2002).

The complexity of Taiwan's higher education system results from taking an idealized German system as a model, while at the same time developing a strong affinity with the American model. The result is a system of prestigious public universities that rely heavily on the central government for funding and which are, to a great extent, insensitive to market forces as well as to the very large private university sector.

In the following, I provide a brief historical review of Taiwanese higher education after the Second World War. I show that similar to the path taken by most advanced countries during the 20th century, Taiwan experienced a systemic transition from elite to mass to universal higher education (Table 1; see also Trow, 2007).

1945–1960: Transitioning from the German to the American Model

During the 15-year period that followed the end of the Second World War, Taiwanese higher education transitioned from following primarily a German to an American model of university development. As Taiwanese leaders transitioned away from Japanese governance, the higher education system that was implemented by that colonial government was either abandoned or modified (Chang, 2001; Ou, 2006; Xu, 2002). The practices that were implemented in contemporary American universities were adopted by Taiwanese universities.

Table 1. Number of Higher Education Institutions in Taiwan, 1950–2013.

Year	University		College		Junior College		Tertiary Education	
	Public	Private	Public	Private	Public	Private	GER	NER
1950	1	0	3	0	3	1	N/A	N/A
1955	3	1	3	3	4	1	N/A	N/A
1960	6	1	2	6	6	6	N/A	N/A
1965	8	2	1	10	15	20	N/A	N/A
1970	6	3	4	9	20	50	N/A	N/A
1975	6	3	7	9	20	56	15%	10%
1980	9	7	5	6	21	56	16%	11%
1985	9	7	6	6	21	56	21%	14%
1990	13	8	13	12	13	62	30%	19%
1995	16	8	18	18	16	58	39%	28%
2000	25	28	24	50	4	19	56%	39%
2005	41	48	10	46	3	14	82%	57%
2010	45	67	6	30	3	12	84%	67%
2013	47	75	3	22	2	12	84%	70%

Source: MOE (2016).
Notes: GER: Gross Enrollment Rate; NER: Net Enrollment Rate.

For example, the chair-based system for appointing university faculty, as is still the practice in Germany, was abandoned. Instead, the departmental system was introduced as the basic unit of university operations, as is the case in the United States. Furthermore, the credit system was used to organize students' course-taking activities. New degree systems, comprised of bachelor, master, and doctoral programs – and the duration of study for completing these degrees – were modeled on American universities (Ou, 2006).

Yet in one important sense, Taiwanese higher education did not follow the American model. In the United States, the national government did not and does not exert significant control over the higher education system (Fernandez & Baker, 2017). Although the reforms related to academic departments and degrees followed the American model, the governance of Taiwanese higher education continued to follow the German, state-dominated model. The new national government strictly controlled the operation of universities through government appropriations, administrative regulation, and appointing university leaders (Dong, 1997).

On the other hand, higher education continued to expand in Taiwan. A group of universities which were established in China were moved to Taiwan after 1949. Additionally, the number of private universities increased, and the higher education system was able to accommodate more students. A decade after the end of the Second World War, Taiwanese higher education comprised six public and four private higher education institutions (MOE, 2016). During this early stage, the net enrollment rate (at schooling age of 18–21 years old) at tertiary education level was below 10%. Based on Trow's (1973) structural-historical theory, Taiwan's higher education system was reserved for the nation's elite.

1960–1985: Higher Education Expands to Fill the Need for Skilled Labor

The period between 1960 and 1985 can best be described as a period of tertiary education expansion, spurred by social demands for a skilled workforce (Chen, 1999). During this period, Taiwan's economy was transformed into an industry-based one. The demands for well-educated and highly skilled workers were driven by growing economic development; in turn, changing labor demands accelerated the expansion of postsecondary education. Most of the expansion took place through the establishment of new junior colleges. The newly established junior colleges provided vocational training courses and prepared graduates with skills that were demanded by the labor market (Wu & Jian, 2008). This wave of expansion not only expanded the capacity of postsecondary education, it also resulted in the formation of a binary system of tertiary education, again similar to the system in Germany and many other countries with two tiers.

On the one hand, the academic-oriented track of tertiary education was comprised of 28 universities and colleges. On the other hand, the 77 junior colleges constituted a vocationally oriented track. Even though the whole educational system remained at the stage of elite education (Trow, 1973), the tertiary education system accommodated 14% of school-aged youth, approaching the threshold of mass higher education.

1985–1995: Transitioning from Elite to Mass Higher Education

In many countries, the pace of growth of higher education accelerated in the second half of the 1980s, and Taiwan was no exception. At the beginning of the 1990s, Taiwanese higher education started rapidly moving toward mass higher education. Two driving forces facilitated this transition. First, encouraged by political democratization and rising average family incomes, the public urged the government to increase the accessibility of higher education. The Taiwanese public tended to believe that higher education should be a general right with guaranteed access, rather than a privilege of the few. Second, the transformation of the economy toward a postindustrial structure went hand-in-hand with the education sector training more professionals, not just technicians (Chen, 1999; Wu & Jian, 2008).

However, the rapid expansion of tertiary education quickly met its financial and structural limits. In a country such as Taiwan, where the national government controls higher education, the treasury bore the rising costs of creating and maintaining new campuses. The solution was to foster structural diversification of the higher education system. This was achieved through two ways. The first was through upgrading the junior colleges, with these new postsecondary institutions, mostly technological and vocational, established at relatively low cost. Moreover, by turning junior colleges into universities, the government was able to decrease the time-lag between it took to graduate students who could enter the labor market (Goedegebuure, 1992). The second way the government diversified the Taiwanese higher education system was through the establishment of private universities that share the costs of expanding the higher education system and increasing access.

The expansion during this period was indeed dramatic. In 1995, the number of postsecondary education institutions increased to 134. Among them, the number of universities and colleges that conferred bachelor's degrees increased to 60. The whole system accommodated 28% of school-aged youth and entered the stage of mass higher education (MOE, 2016; Trow, 1973).

1995–2005: A Transition from Mass Education to Universal Education

Between 1995 and 2005, higher education expansion in Taiwan occurred at the same time that public funding was cut and neo-liberal or market-oriented policies were adopted (Tai, 2000). Through a series of governance reforms, the national government reduced its controlling grip on universities and granted them greater institutional autonomy. The most remarkable change came from reforms related to financial autonomy. The public universities, which used to heavily rely on state appropriations, diversified their financial resources mainly through engaging in commercial activities (e.g., licensing university-developed technology and incubating spin-off companies). The concept of the "entrepreneurial university" (Slaughter & Rhoades, 2004) became very fashionable during this period (Chang, 2006).

Between 1995 and 2005, the pace of higher education expansion was even more rapid than during previous decades. Within less than 10 years, the net enrollment rate increased from less than 28% to approximately 57%, or what Trow (2007) referred to as "universal" higher education. This expansion was accomplished mainly through the upgrading of private junior colleges. During this period, almost all of the junior colleges that were established during the 1980s were transformed to full-fledged technological universities. These were granted the privilege to issue bachelor's degrees. Some of them were even granted the privilege to provide master's- and doctoral-level education. By 2005, the Taiwanese system of higher education was comprised of 147 universities and colleges, while the number of junior colleges declined to 17.

The transition to universal higher education caused chaos in the operation of Taiwanese higher education. Without a well-established coordination system, old and new universities were competing with each other for student resources, research funding, and any possible resources that could sustain them. The line between old universities and newly upgraded universities – in terms of course offerings and mission of the schools – was blurred. As a result, the binary system that was created during the 1960s became less and less recognizable, leading to the blurred boundaries between types of HEI seen elsewhere.

2005–Present: The Stratification of Higher Education

As Taiwan achieved universal tertiary enrollments, there had been two driving forces reshaping the landscape of higher education. The first was a demand for the classification of the higher education to avoid the duplicate efforts dedicated by the higher education institutions. The second was the competitive pressure resulting from the popularity of the World Class University Ranking System (Song & Tai, 2007; Tai, 2006).

These two driving forces led to a transformative change with respect to how the state appropriation should be allocated. The principle of the even distribution was abandoned and the institutional-based competition was adopted. The World Class University Project of 2006 (hereafter, WCUP) is the first remarkable case presenting this paradigm shift. The idea behind the implementation of the WCUP is to concentrate the resource on a small group of elite universities, bolstering their research capacity. These funded universities were called as "World Class Universities" in Taiwan context. At the same time, the Teaching Excellence Project of 2006 was also instituted simultaneously to lead another group of universities toward teaching-oriented universities. Two projects together facilitated the formation of stratification of higher education, with research universities on the top of reputation ladder and teaching-oriented universities in the middle.

The expectation of the new policies is to classify the universities into different mission groups based on the result of competition. However, the label of "excellence" attached to the "World Class Universities" and "non-excellence" to the Non-World Class Universities stimulated more intense competition as well as the isomorphism of non-research universities on research counterparts. See Table 1 for a descriptive breakdown of the ways that Taiwan transitioned from elite to mass to universal higher education by creating HEIs and increasing student enrollments. Within less than four decades, the net enrollment rate rose dramatically from 10% (1975) to 67% (from 2010).

The Reform of Higher Education and the Growth of Scientific Production

The capacity of science production in Taiwan is remarkable. In 2011, with less than 24 million inhabitants — or less than 0.004% of the world's estimated population — Taiwan produced 2.6% of the world's scientific papers. To investigate the contribution of scientific production in the different sectors, I classify these science producers into five sectors based on their special missions. These five sectors include higher education institutions (HEIs), medical care institutes (Hosp.), Academia Sinica,[1] national laboratories (Lab.), and for-profit companies (Corp.). Table 2 and Fig. 1 display results from longitudinal analysis for the period between 1980 and 2011.

In 1980, when the Taiwanese system of higher education was relatively small, the scientific papers produced by the higher education sector already accounted for 69% of national production. With the expansion of higher education since 1990s, the portion of scientific publication produced by the higher education sector climbed, such that by 2011, the higher education sector accounted for nearly four-fifths (78%) of national publications. Compared to the higher education sector, the scales of science production in other sectors were relatively small. After the higher education sector, the first two sectors (medical care institutes and national laboratories) that produced most papers accounted for less than 20% of science publications in the higher education sector. This landscape indicates that the higher education sector has been the main producer and driving force in national scientific publications.

In Taiwan, the growth of science production should not be attributed only to the increasing number of HEIs. I argue that structural changes, mainly

Table 2. National Share of SCIE Publications by Sector, 1980–2011.

Year	World	TWN	Percent	Sectors				
				HEIs	Hosp	Lab	Sinica	Corp.
1980	373,238	363	0.10	251	9	70	42	7
1985	447,383	815	0.18	563	93	96	86	15
1990	505,936	2,414	0.48	1,744	221	275	222	46
1995	548,883	5,658	1.03	4,340	522	544	407	92
2000	640,493	10,112	1.58	7,702	1,124	1,032	695	226
2005	702,825	15,829	2.25	11,910	1,869	1,708	996	388
2010	997,113	25,741	2.58	20,186	3,185	3,082	1,598	573
2011	1,080,981	28,540	2.64	22,248	3,695	3,746	1,907	595

Source: SPHERE project database of SCIE publications (Thomson Reuters' Web of Science).
Notes: HEIs: Higher Education Institutions; Hosp: Medical Care Institutes; Lab: National Laboratories; Sinica: Academia Sinica; Corp.: For-Profit Companies. Whole count at national and sectoral levels.

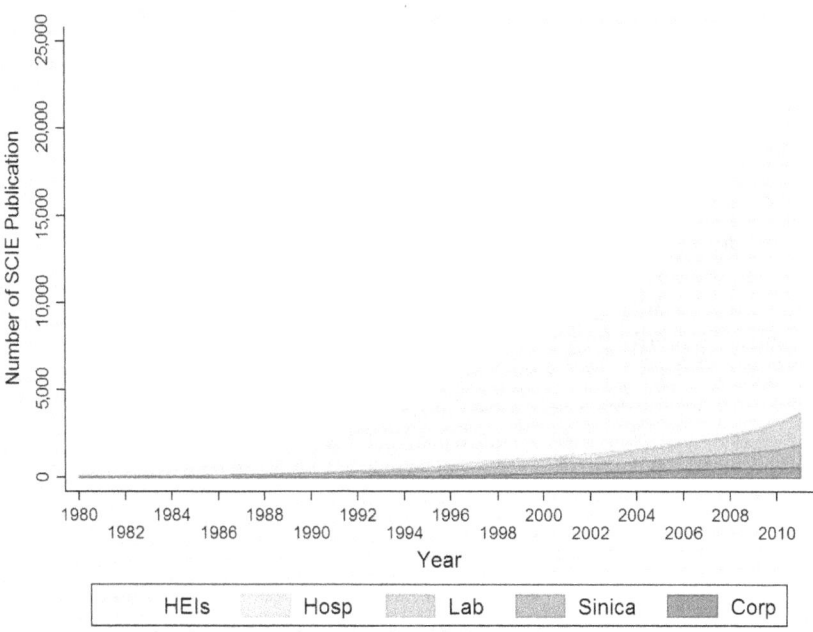

Fig. 1. SCIE Publications by Sector, 1980–2011. Notes: HEIs: Higher Education Institutions; Hosp: Medical Care Institutes; Lab: National Laboratories; Sinica: Academia Sinica; Corp.: For-Profit Companies. Whole count at national and sectoral levels. Source: SPHERE project database of SCIE publications (Thomson Reuters' Web of Science).

driven by policy reforms of higher education and the expansion of higher education enrollments, had direct impact on the transformative growth in scientific production that occurred over several decades. This argument is based on perspectives derived from sociological theory and organizational theory. In the following section, I highlight and explore those influential policy changes, which had close association with science production in the higher education sector.

From a Seniority-Based toward a Merit-Based Personnel System

After the end of the Second World War, Taiwan followed the American model to reconstruct its national innovation system. While the mission of Chinese universities was mainly limited to teaching (Zhang, Bao, & Sun, 2016), the Taiwanese government chose to provide public R&D funding to universities and to support university-based research projects. The National Science Council (hereafter, NSC), the government's leading R&D funding agency built in 1956, was created to coordinate and allocate public research funding to universities. At that time the private sector rarely supported research, thus research funding that was obtained through the NSC's project-based peer competition constituted the major portion of universities' research resources. Even though public R&D funding was available for the higher education sector since the late 1960s, universities' research output was not really impressive before the 1990s. Most faculty spent more time on knowledge delivery (i.e., teaching) instead of knowledge production.

Faculty members' lack of interest in research was associated with the contemporary personnel system. In Taiwan, faculty members were retained through a seniority-based system. The seniority-based system emphasized personal qualifications and duration of service. Personal research performance, which would have been highly appreciated under a merit-based system, did not play a decisive role in promotion decisions (Tien, 1999).

The seniority-based personal system faced its first reform in 1994 when the "University Act" created a new faculty ladder system (Ministry of Education, 1994). The new faculty ladder system followed the American university system by adding the rank of assistant professor into the promotion ladder. The rank of associate professor used to be the initial status for new faculty members, but after the adoption of the "University Act" new PhDs were hired as assistant professors. Under this new personnel system, junior faculty members could be quickly promoted to associate professor if their research (i.e., publishing) expectations were satisfied. This arrangement created an incentive for new faculty to actively engage in the research activities after they were recruited.

By 2005, the faculty personnel system faced its second transformative change. This transformative change was the introduction of periodic review of faculty members' performance (Ministry of Education, 2005). This change, to a certain extent, pressured faculty and encouraged them to be involved in research activities. The periodic review of faculty members' performance was used on campuses to dismiss faculty whose research performance did not meet institutional expectations. This new practice essentially canceled the job security that faculty had long enjoyed under the seniority-based system.

In 2010, threatened by "brain drain" in the global academic job market, the national government further reformed the faculty personnel system through differentiation of faculty compensation. This reform action was referred to as the "Flexible Wage System." Under the new personnel system of 2010, universities were granted the privilege to provide globally comparable compensation to those faculty members whose research had the potential for "excellence" (MOE, 2010). The 2010 reform broke the foundational principle constructed by the seniority-based personnel system. Between 1997 and 2010, Taiwan universities transitioned to rewarding their faculty based on personal performance, particularly on research performance.

Taiwanese Academic Drift: Technological Universities Emulating Research Universities

Faculty members' (individual) behaviors are subject to changes of organizational preferences and missions, but they are also subject to changes of the external environment. Such change can lead universities to adjust their strategic plans correspondingly (Pfeffer & Salancik, 1974). The transformation of technological universities over past decades provides a paragon case of this.

As mentioned earlier, the expansion of higher education in the 1990s was mainly completed through the upgrading of junior colleges to technological universities. No doubt, by increasing number of "new" technological universities the government was also able to increase the scale of national research manpower by creating new faculty position in the new universities. Nevertheless, there was no guarantee that all new technological universities should have or would have participated in scientific production. After all, research is a long-term investment, and not all universities could quickly benefit from the research, especially for those technological universities that were established to provide vocational education. However, in Taiwan's case, the technological universities that were founded in the 1990s showed very strong commitments to research.

In Fig. 2, the solid line indicates the number of technological universities that published at least one paper in international journals in a given year, while the dashed line indicates the number of elite, public universities that did so. The solid line in Fig. 2 rose steeply during the 1990s. Referring to Table 3, the number of technological universities producing science publications increased from 14 in 1990 to 70 in 2000. The portion of the national share of publications in STEM fields that was produced by the group of technological universities also increased from 5.2% in 1990 to 13.7% in 2000. The growth rate was a staggering 1,300%. By 2011, the group of technological universities had 91 schools involved in science production and contributed 20.2% of publications in the higher education sector.

The increasing number of technological universities that were involved in science production almost paralleled the increasing number of technological universities. In other words, the faculty in most of the junior colleges that became technological universities produced scientific publications. Additionally, the research capacity of this group has become a non-ignorable strength in Taiwan's science production, as these technological universities have become deeply engaged in research activities.

What forces drove this transformation? To answer this question, I draw on several classic arguments derived from the sociological literature. First, I argue that what we observe in Taiwan's case reflects the phenomenon of "academic drift" (Riesman, 1956). Horta and colleagues (2008) extended this concept, claiming that in the higher education sector academic drift is a consequence of

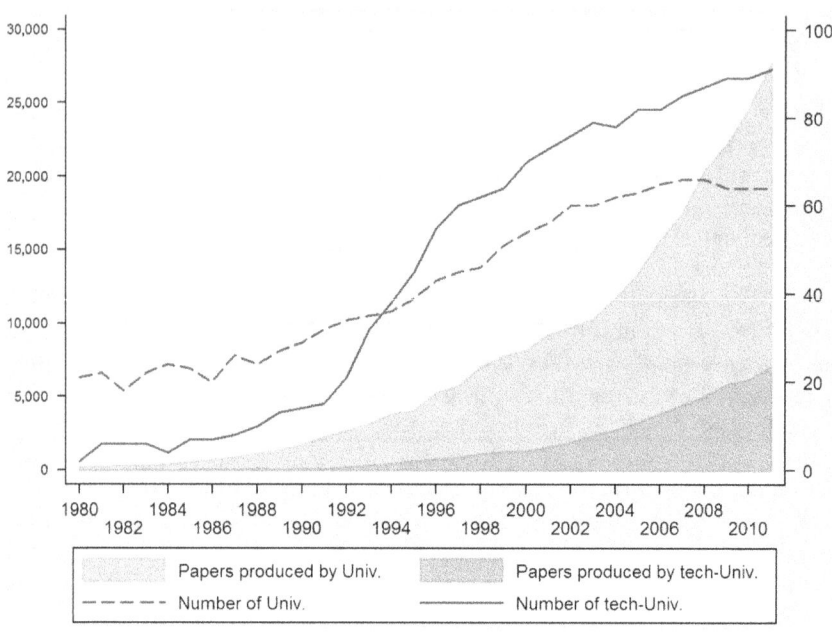

Fig. 2. SCIE Publications by Univ. and Tech-Univ. Groups, 1980−2011.
Source: SPHERE project database of SCIE publications (Thomson Reuters' Web of Science).

Table 3. National Share of SCIE Publications by University Types, 1980−2011.

Year	HEIs	University			Tech-University		
		School	Count	Share (%)	School	Count	Share (%)
1980	258	21	256	99.2	2	2	0.8
1985	573	23	549	95.8	7	24	4.2
1990	1,816	29	1,721	94.8	14	95	5.2
1995	4,613	39	4,040	87.6	45	573	12.4
2000	9,441	54	8,146	86.3	70	1,295	13.7
2005	16,593	63	13,378	80.6	82	3,215	19.4
2010	30,810	64	24,634	80.0	89	6,176	20.0
2011	34,720	64	27,716	79.8	91	7,004	20.2

Source: SPHERE project database of SCIE publications (Thomson Reuters' Web of Science).
Note: Whole count at institutional level.

increasingly shared values or attempts by non-university sector institutions (e.g., junior colleges) to become structurally and programmatically more similar to universities. I argue that, in Taiwan, the concept of academic drift is reflected in the intensifying engagement of technological universities to pursue the research activities that were formerly practiced solely by the elite, public universities.

But, why were the technological universities willing to institutionalize this value system that was not originally their own? From the perspective of neo-institutionalism, the "isomorphic" forces played a decisive role in this process. Neo-institutionalism emphasizes the idea that new organizations, as they seek legitimacy, shape themselves to be more like those that are already established in the field (DiMaggio & Powell, 1983; see also Meyer & Rowan, 1977). Following DiMaggio and Powell (1983, 1991) and Scott (2013), I analyze institutionalization processes reflecting cultural-cognitive, normative, and regulative mechanisms driving reproduction and change. Each of these dimensions suggests a different rationale for legitimacy, either by virtue of being legally sanctioned (coercive), culturally supported (mimetic), or morally governed (normative).

First, the academic drift of technological universities was motivated through coercive isomorphism. This means the behaviors of technological universities were the result of compliance with the external requirements. In Taiwan, if junior colleges wanted to be upgraded to technological universities, they had to meet requirements set by the national government. During the 1990s, the criteria used to evaluate universities' performance were directly transplanted and used to evaluate technological universities without thoroughly considering the special mission of technological universities. Among these criteria, the research capacity of the individual institution was brought into the review process.

In accordance with governmental requirements, research capacity referred to two aspects. The first was the qualification of faculty members. The second was the research performance of the individual institution. In order to fulfill these requirements, the junior colleges sent their instructors to research universities to complete PhD training. Also, they preferred to hire new PhD graduates with promising research performance instead of instructors with practical experiences (Wu & Jian, 2008).

Second, the academic drift of technological universities was motivated through mimetic isomorphism. Mimetic isomorphism occurs when an organization's goals or means of achieving these goals are unclear (DiMaggio & Powell, 1983). In this case, mimicking another organization that is perceived as legitimate becomes a safe way to proceed. During the transformation process, the world-renowned technological universities, such as MIT or Caltech, were frequently referred to as models by Taiwan's technological universities.

Third, the academic drift of technological universities was motivated by normative isomorphism. Normative isomorphic change is driven by pressure brought by professional norms. During the transition process, technological universities recruited a lot of new PhD graduates from leading research universities to improve the quality of faculty departments. Because these new faculty were educated in leading research universities, their behaviors and value systems tend to be similar with their counterparts or mentors who were faculty at those leading research universities. Faculty members' value systems ultimately affected how they defined good performance. This professional value system inevitably framed the core of the faculty's evaluation system and, as a result, guided many faculty members' behavior. All three mechanisms driving isomorphism can be found in the process of institutionalization in which technological universities were upgraded.

Competition: Research Universities versus Non-Research Universities

While isomorphism transformed the technological universities into active science producers, the competition derived from the implementation of the World Class University Project in 2006 has spurred the rise of a new group of universities as research intensive universities. In this section, I investigate how the implementation of the World Class University Project (WCUP) affects the scientific production of leading research universities. I also discuss how non-research universities are affected by being directly exposed to such a competitive environment. To address this question, I first introduce the WCUP and its connection with scientific production.

In the early 21st century, the idea of a knowledge society had swept almost the entire world (Salmi, 2003). Along with the transformation of economic production, the capacity to produce knowledge had become a decisive parameter to predict a country's prosperity (Drori, 2000). In accordance with my survey through searching the governmental reports worldwide, from 1995 to 2013, more than 23 countries initiated special funding schemes to invest in research universities through varied ways. These special funding schemes shared a common feature: the use of institutional-based competition for budgetary allocations. Meanwhile, these special funding schemes also share a similar perspective – valuing the research university as a way to improve national scientific and economic innovation (Salmi, 2009). The WCUP in Taiwan was created in this global context.

The implementation of the WCUP brought several remarkable changes to Taiwanese higher education and research funding system. First, the WCUP is an institutional-based funding program. Before the WCUP, universities only obtained research funding from faculty members' projects or grants. Even though faculty have been encouraged to conduct research by their host universities, in reality, it was rare to see universities strategically organize their faculty as a team to compete and seek external research funding. In other words, before the WCUP, seeking research funding was more dependent on faculty members' personal research agendas instead of universities' strategic actions.

However, the WCUP was designed to facilitate the formation of research clusters, and the institutionally based competition rewards the perceived quality and influence of research projects. Therefore, to do well in the WCUP competition, university administrators led departments and faculty in organizing interdisciplinary research groups. In this way, a university's research activities were transformed from personal matters to institutional matters. Once universities were selected as World Class Universities, they developed a reputation for "Excellence." The financial and prestigious incentives together led universities to see "excellence on research" as a crucial strategy to thrive in a competitive funding environment.

How did the WCUP affect scientific production in Taiwanese higher education? To appropriately address this question, I make comparisons between groups of universities including those that won the funding competition and received status as World Class Universities and another group of universities, which participated in the competition but lost the competition. The former group is the first tier group, while the latter is called the second tier group. Besides the group of first tier universities and the second tier universities, I gather the remaining universities together in the third tier group. The exact number of universities in this group has varied across the years but it reached a maximum of 125 in 2011. This arrangement is aimed to provide another reference base to observe historical trends.

The group of first tier universities is comprised of 10 universities: nine elite, public universities and one technological university. They are the oldest universities with the highest reputations for producing research over the past several decades. The group of second tier universities is comprised of 14 universities: 12 elite, public universities and two technological universities. They are relatively new, and most of them were established during the 1960s. I group these 14 universities based on their research performance and their efforts to compete with the first tier of leading research universities. To ensure that the two groups are comparable in terms of their research capacity, I calculate the number of scientific publications produced by Taiwanese universities between 2001 and 2005. I choose the top 30 universities that produced the largest numbers of scientific publications and matched these universities with the list of universities that participated in the funding competition for the World Class University Project. There was likely a delayed effect between the implementation of the WCUP and the time frame that it would take for research results to be published. To account for this issue, I adopt a practice that has been previously used in several empirical studies (Seong, Popper, Goldman, & Evans, 2008; Shin, 2009; Zhang, Patton, & Kenney, 2013). I calculate a two-year lag effect for the longitudinal analyses. In other words, I assume that any changes in research production that were caused by the WCUP occurred after 2008.

Based on observations from 2002 to 2011, I find that the absolute number of scientific publication increased for both first tier universities and second tier universities. In terms of the national share of research, the group of second tier universities roughly accounted for 19% of the national share before 2008 (i.e., before the implementation of the WCUP). Thereafter, the group of second tier universities continued to steadily, but gradually increase their national share. By 2011, the group of second tier universities accounted for more than 20% of Taiwan's scientific research production. See Table 4 for an annual breakdown of university-based scientific research. Additional statistical examination may support a causal relationship between the implementation of the WCUP and the change I observed in terms of producing scientific publications. However, the trend observed here clearly reveals that after the policy implementation, first tier universities steadily increased their number (but not share) of scientific publications, but the growth of scientific production in the second tier universities was slightly stronger.

How did this scenario develop? Organizational theory provides a good framework for interpreting these findings. First, the revenue theory of costs (Bowen, 1980) points out that the dominant goals of HEIs are educational excellence, prestige, and influence. In higher education, the quality of education is always hard to be measure. However, the World Class University Project confers a select group of universities with the title of "excellent." Therefore,

Table 4. National Share of SCIE Publications by HEI Tier Groups, 2002−2011.

Year	HEIs	First Tier Univ. (10)		Second Tier Univ. (14)		Third Tier Univ. (125)	
		Count	Share (%)	Count	Share (%)	Count	Share (%)
2002	11,575	6,932	59.9	2,079	18.0	2,564	22.15
2003	12,588	7,174	57.0	2,373	18.9	3,041	24.16
2004	14,471	7,998	55.3	2,757	19.1	3,716	25.68
2005	16,593	8,778	52.9	3,142	18.9	4,673	28.16
2006	19,428	10,288	53.0	3,635	18.7	5,505	28.34
2007	21,940	11,482	52.3	4,075	18.6	6,383	29.09
2008	25,473	13,127	51.5	4,885	19.2	7,461	29.29
2009	27,975	14,129	50.5	5,433	19.4	8,413	30.07
2010	30,810	15,482	50.2	6,145	19.9	9,183	29.81
2011	34,720	17,253	49.7	7,162	20.6	10,305	29.68

Source: SPHERE project database of SCIE publications (Thomson Reuters' Web of Science).
Note: Whole count at institutional level.

winning the WCUP became a simply and clear goal for university leadership to pursue.

The "Excellence" label not only awarded status to universities that won the WCUP competition, it also brought unique advantages for universities to compete for the most academically prepared students and talented faculty. This advantage became even more apparent as the higher education system faced an imbalance between supply and demand. That is, when higher education became universal, more universities competed for the limited share of the best students. Thus, universities have little choice but to differentiate themselves from other universities if they hope to have a recognizable profile that can attract talent. Harwood (2010) argued that when universities compete as they do in Taiwan, the most avid status-seeking institutions are in the middle of the status ladder, where administrators are particularly desperate to be recognized by their "superiors." Academic leaders at mid-tier institutions are more eager to differentiate themselves from their counterparts.

Second, resource dependence theory also provides a perspective to understand the behavior of the unfunded universities. Resource dependence theory posits that as universities pursue external resources, HEIs are confronted with various, often incompatible demands from external actors (Pfeffer & Salancik, 1974). From this perspective, the strategies of higher education institutions are constrained by external pressures since their survival is dependent upon their responsiveness to external demands and expectations (Horta, Huisman, & Heitor, 2008).

Since the 2000s, Taiwan's national government has frozen tuition increases. This policy made it hard for universities to increase their revenue through raising tuition levels. Yet the cost of university operations continually increased, and it became urgent for universities to obtain external financial support to thrive. The funding from the World Class University Project provided funding beyond the annual government appropriations – and it was all the more attractive because it was a long-term funding commitment.

The importance of receiving the additional WCUP funding for institutional operations is phenomenal. For example, in 2011 National Taiwan University received 27% of its revenues through state appropriations, and tuition accounted for 11% of the university's income. The funding received from the WCUP accounted for another 11% of the university's budget – equal to the amount generated by tuition payments (National Taiwan University, 2011). For any Taiwanese university, losing such a significant portion of funding would slow the development of the university and make the institution less competitive. The combination of financial incentives provided by the WCUP and the financial shortage that universities faced made it inevitable that most universities would participate in the national competition and expect faculty to publish scholarly articles.

COLLABORATION WITHIN HIGHER EDUCATION

In the previous section, I explored how isomorphism and competition changed the landscape of scientific production in the higher education sector; in this section, I focus on how universities collaborate with each other. For the nation's innovation system, collaboration could be much more meaningful than competition. In this subsection, I analyze three aspects that may be reflected in cross-tier collaborations.

First, collaboration may indicate the sharing of resources, and collaboration patterns may show how resources are shared. Resource sharing could include knowledge, data, and laboratory equipment, which may benefit all participants. Second, researchers tend to work with collaborators with comparable research capacity. At the institutional level, if certain universities received more invitations to collaborate, we may assume that their research capacities were well recognized by other counterparts — that is, universities with greater research capacity are more likely to be sought after for research collaboration. Third, collaboration may not only be for scientific production. The value system regarding the definition of good research could be passed from one participant to another participant; in other words, the prevailing norms in a highly successful or legitimate organization may be adopted by a less-successful organization (Wagner, Brahmakulam, Jackson, Wong, & Yoda, 2001).

Taiwan's HEIs are again analyzed in three groups or tiers. I investigate coauthorship patterns between 1980 and 2011 to reflect their scientific research collaborations (Fig. 3 and Table 5). Table 5 shows that collaboration among different tiers of higher education institutions increased dramatically over the past two decades. In 1980, there were four collaborative works, accounting for less than 2% of the scientific production in the higher education sector. By 2011, the number increased to 8,546 and accounted for 38% of the scientific production in the higher education sector. That is, over one-third of all works produced in higher education were the fruit of collaboration across HEIs.

Extraordinary growth in collaboration occurred from 1995 to 2000, the same period when the higher education system expanded at its fastest rate. Collaborative scholarly publications increased from 247 in 1995 to 1,484 in 2000, and the percentage of collaboratively written publications increased from 5% to 19%. Most of this growth came from collaborations involving the participation of the third tier group of universities. Fig. 3 shows that between 1996 and 2005, the third tier group increased its portion of cross-tier research collaborations, reaching a peak of 63.1%.

What forces have driven the growth of cross-tier group collaboration in the third tier group during this period? I argue that at least two forces helped the third tier group reach out to members of the other two tiers of universities for collaboration. The first is the alumni linkage. During the 1990s, while higher

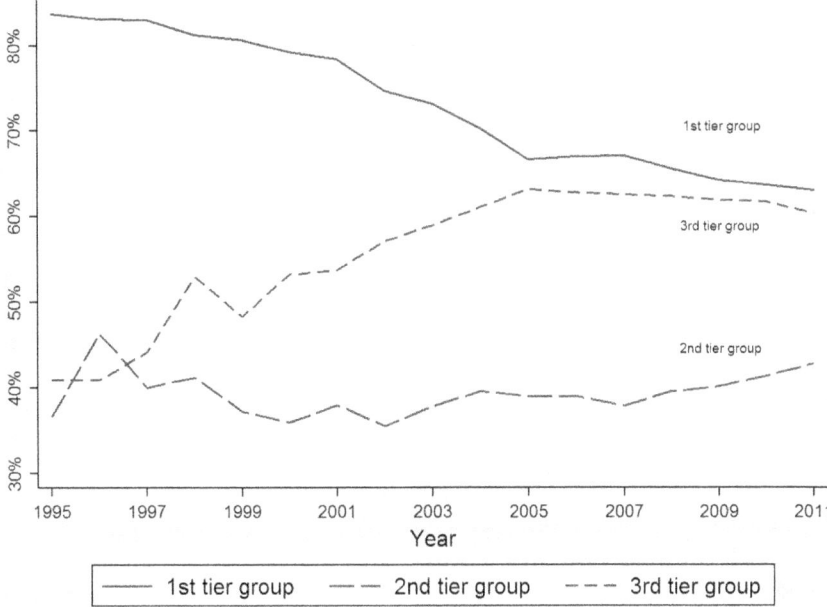

Fig. 3. Portion of Cross-Tier Collaboration, 1995−2011. *Source*: SPHERE project database of SCIE publications (Thomson Reuters' Web of Science).

Table 5. Co-Authorship among Different HEI Tier Groups, 1980−2011.

Year	HEIs	N	Percent	Co-Authorship Patterns (HEI Groups)					
				First tier−first tier	First tier−second tier	First tier−third tier	Second tier−second tier	Second tier−third tier	Third tier−third tier
1980	251	4	1.59	1	3	1	2	1	0
1985	563	10	1.78	4	4	0	0	0	2
1990	1,744	66	3.78	39	18	10	1	1	0
1995	4,340	247	5.69	89	62	80	12	27	6
2000	7,702	1,484	19.27	384	347	593	51	203	94
2005	11,910	3,559	29.88	658	836	1,464	142	751	586
2006	13,608	4,338	31.88	792	1,060	1,889	228	891	726
2007	15,189	4,939	32.52	963	1,225	2,147	232	991	901
2008	17,307	5,929	34.26	1,152	1,512	2,536	320	1,302	1,102
2009	18,750	6,702	35.74	1,337	1,732	2,731	371	1,525	1,337
2010	20,186	7,446	36.89	1,486	2,046	3,079	450	1,800	1,530
2011	22,248	8,546	38.41	1,754	2,468	3,420	590	2,129	1,765

Source: SPHERE project database of SCIE publications (Thomson Reuters' Web of Science).
Note: Whole count at sectoral and organizational type level; N indicates the number of papers produced through HEIs' collaboration.

education expanded, many faculty positions were opened at third tier universities. PhD holders who graduated from the traditional leading research universities quickly received job offers at the new universities and filled these vacancies. These individual connections laid the groundwork to facilitate the formation of collaboration partnerships at the institutional level.

In addition to the social or alumni networks, the accessibility of high-end laboratory equipment also pushed the third tier group to collaborate with the other two tier groups. A well-established laboratory required a long-term investment of personal energies and financial support (Geiger, 2004). For the universities in the third tier group, the laboratory equipment was often too expensive. Therefore, researchers needed to forge partnerships with researchers in universities that were willing and able to provide laboratory resources.

Fig. 3 also reflects another emerging change in the landscape of collaboration patterns. It is clear that the first tier group of universities shared the biggest portion of cross-tier group collaborations. This is because the first tier group is comprised of traditional research universities that have unique advantages in attracting collaborators. While the third tier group reached saturation in 2005 and did not expand their share of collaborated works in more recent years, the second tier group of universities continued expanding their share of collaborative works. This change is particularly apparent during the transition from 2007 to 2008. The portion of second tier group accounting for the cross-tier group collaboration increased from 25.4% in 2007 to 26.3% in 2008. After 2008, the growth continued climbing to 28.7% in 2011.

Fig. 4 reveals the landscape change in coauthorship pattern among groups. In Fig. 4, I compare the coauthorship pattern between the first tier group and the second tier group. The upper part of Fig. 4 shows that, since 2008, the number of collaborative publications between the first tier group and the second tier group increased more rapidly than the collaborative works within the first tier group. I interpret this scenario from two perspectives. First, the research capacity of the second tier group improved during this time period. Thus, the first tier group was more willing to collaborate with the researchers from the second tier group. Second, as previously mentioned, the accessibility of high-end laboratory equipment is an important incentive for researchers to collaborate. Because of the World Class University Project, the first tier group was able to upgrade their laboratory equipment. The unique advantage that the first tier group gained through the WCUP likely attracted the second tier group to seek more collaboration. The intensifying collaboration between the first tier group and the second tier group could help the second tier group to grow its research capacity and gradually become a strong competitor.

The intensifying collaboration between the second tier group and the third tier group to a certain extent supports this observation. In the lower part of Fig. 4, I compare the number of collaboration works between two coauthorship

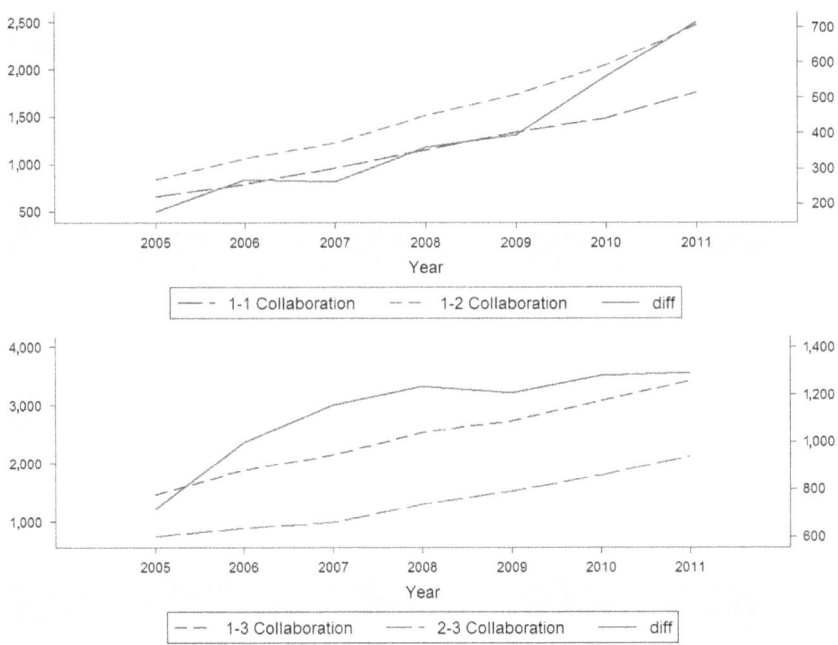

Fig. 4. Co-Authorship Patterns among Groups, 2005−2011. *Source*: SPHERE project database of SCIE publications (Thomson Reuters' Web of Science).

patterns: the first tier group and the third tier group; the second tier group and the third tier group. The purpose behind this comparison is to ask: *if we assume the third tier group is inferior to the other two tier groups, which group did they tend to collaborate with? Is there any change over the years?*

The lower part of Fig. 4 shows that since 2008, the number of collaboration works between the second tier group and the third tier group rapidly increased. Although the number of collaboration works between the first tier group and the third tier group was still greater than the collaboration works between the second tier group and the third tier group, the difference between two collaboration patterns stabilized. Based on the findings from Figs. 3 and 4, I argue that along with the improvement of research capacity in the second tier group, the importance of first tier group as the collaboration hub for the whole higher education system is weakening. Instead, the second tier group is challenging the status of first tier group and turning the collaboration structure from solo hub to dual hubs. In other words, the pyramid structure of scientific production in the higher education sector is becoming flatter.

THE TRANSFORMATION OF UNIVERSITIES: TOWARD THE KNOWLEDGE CONGLOMERATE

In this section, I focus on the transformation of university-based research due to changes in the external environment. Gibbons et al. (1994) argued that a new form of knowledge production began emerging in the mid-20th century, which was context-driven, problem-focused, and interdisciplinary. This new form of knowledge production required the formation of multidisciplinary teams that allow researchers to work together for short periods of time on specific, real world problems. They named this new form of knowledge production as "Mode 2." In contrast to Mode 2, the earlier Mode 1 is seen as academic, investigator-initiated, and discipline-based knowledge production. In Gibbons et al.'s (1994) prediction, universities that produce knowledge ("Mode 1") would gradually lose their importance in scientific production. However, referring to my longitudinal data, this prediction was incorrect. In Taiwan's case, while other non-higher education sectors continued to expand their commitments on research, the key importance of the higher education sector for scientific production never faded (Table 1).

How can the higher education sector retain its considerable strength in today's knowledge society? The organizational characteristics of universities help address this question. Geiger (2004) used the term "knowledge conglomerate" to describe the operation of the modern university. Today, science requires a diverse array of activities and significant resources. However, Gibbons and colleagues underestimated the adaptability of the modern university. The modern university is an adaptive system, and university-based researchers are driven by their own interests and commit their efforts to research projects in highly flexible ways. This special organizational structure allowed the modern university to quickly respond to the perceived needs or opportunities of society.

Baker (2014) found that in recent years, research universities have significantly increased the complexity of their internal organization to reflect changes in science, including differentiation and specialization. Research universities launched new research centers, encouraged interdisciplinary units, and created offices focused on corporate research projects (Baker, 2008). The availability of competitive funding for scientific R&D has made such units essential for any HEI that aims to become a high-quality research university. Through their autonomous research roles inside universities, these organized research units have intensified universities' knowledge production capabilities (Geiger, 2004).

In Taiwan's case, I find that over the past two decades, universities quickly seized external opportunities and transformed themselves through collaboration with external sectors. Figs. 5 and 6 and Table 6 reveal the historical trajectory of collaboration between HEIs and other external sectors in different time periods. First and the foremost, foreign institutions, mostly universities, have been the main collaboration partner of Taiwanese universities over the past two

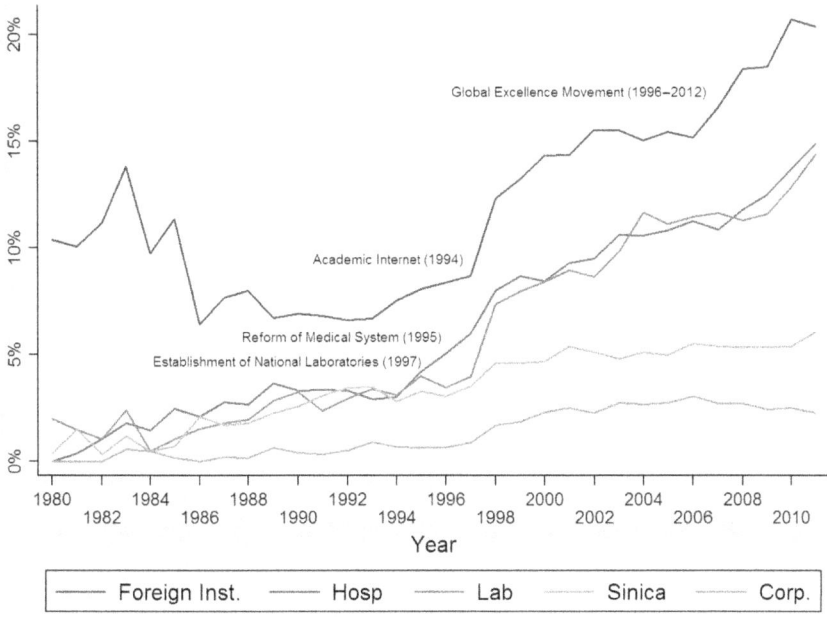

Fig. 5. Proportions of Co-Authored Papers (HEI and Non-HEI Authors) Accounting for Articles Produced in HEIs, 1980–2011. *Source*: SPHERE project database of SCIE publications (Thomson Reuters' Web of Science).

decades. The frequency of coauthorship with foreign institutions indicates the degree of connectivity between Taiwan and the global community. Looking back to the historical trajectory, the extent of partnership between the Taiwan's higher education sector and foreign institutes varied in different decades.

From 1980 to 1985, while the higher education sector produced small amounts of papers, nearly 10% of scientific papers were the products of cross-national collaboration. These works were mainly accomplished through Taiwanese visiting scholars hosted by foreign institutions. At that time, traveling was very expensive, and cross-national partnerships through on-site collaboration had practical limitations that hindered expansion. During the 1990s, when scientific production in the higher education sector started expanding, the portion of cross-national collaboration decreased to less than 10%. During this period most scientific works were independently completed by Taiwanese researchers. This scenario lasted until the late of 1990s.

The first transformative change appeared in 1998. In 1997, only 8.7% of scientific papers produced in the higher education sector were the fruits of international collaboration. In 1998, the portion increased to 12.3% with the number of scientific papers with international collaborators increasing from 522 in 1997

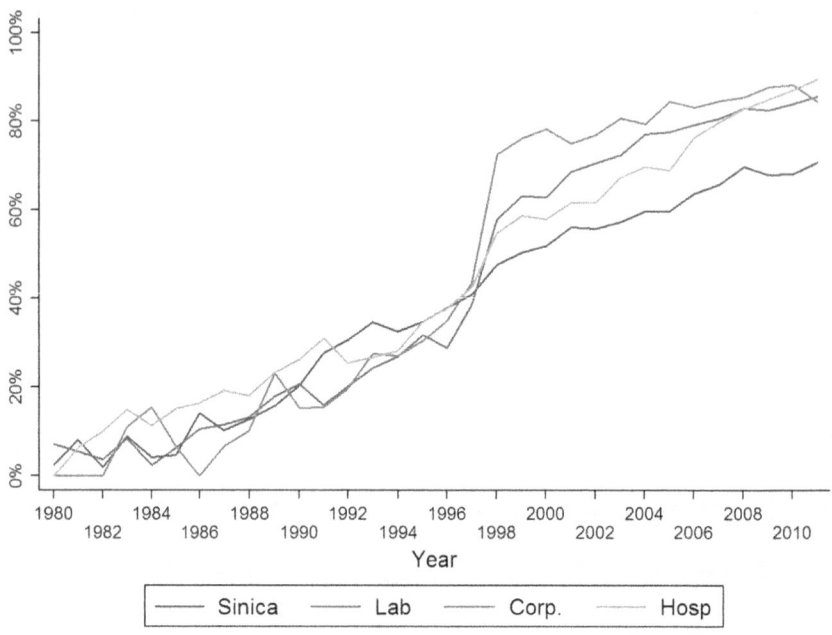

Fig. 6. Proportions of Co-Authored Papers (HEI and Non-HEI Authors) Accounting for Articles Produced in Non-HEIs Sector, 1980−2011. *Source:* SPHERE project database of SCIE publications (Thomson Reuters' Web of Science).

Table 6. Collaboration Patterns between HEIs and Other Sectors, 1980−2011.

Year	HEIs	Foreign Inst.		TWN							
				Hosp		Natl. Lab		Sinica		Corp.	
		Count	Share (%)	Count	Share (%)	Count	Share (%)	Count	Share (%)	Count	Share (%)
1980	251	26	10.4	0	0.0	5	2.0	1	0.4	0	0.0
1985	563	64	11.4	14	2.5	6	1.1	4	0.7	1	0.2
1990	1,744	121	6.9	58	3.3	57	3.3	45	2.6	7	0.4
1995	4,340	351	8.1	182	4.2	173	4.0	142	3.3	28	0.6
2000	7,702	1,103	14.3	651	8.5	649	8.4	360	4.7	177	2.3
2005	11,910	1,840	15.4	1,289	10.8	1,325	11.1	594	5.0	328	2.8
2010	20,186	4,181	20.7	2,771	13.7	2,589	12.8	1,088	5.4	505	2.5
2011	22,248	4,529	20.4	3,309	14.9	3,204	14.4	1,349	6.1	503	2.3

Source: SPHERE project database of SCIE publications (Thomson Reuters' Web of Science).
Note: Whole count at sector level.

to 844 in 1998. One of the leading forces driving this change is universal access to academic information technology and the Internet. The transformative improvement of such infrastructure significantly reduced the costs of cross-national communication, thus increasing efficiency.

During the 1990s, plenty of new Taiwanese PhD holders educated abroad chose to return to take faculty positions in Taiwan. The connections they built abroad can be maintained through modern communication technology. From 1998 to 2005, the portion of cross-national collaboration accounted for 15% of scientific production from the higher education sector. The significance of modern communication technology on scientific production has been well documented by the World Bank (1999) and is supported by this study.

After the foreign institutions, Taiwan's national laboratories (Lab.) and medical care institutes (Hosp.) were significant collaborators with the higher education sector. The historical trajectory indicates that before the late-1990s, their contributions were minor, accounting for less than 5% of scientific works in the higher education sector. The landscape changed because of the implementation of new policies in medical care. In 1995, the national government launched a new medical care system, classifying medical care institutes on four levels: medical center, regional hospital, local hospital, and clinic (Executive Yuan, 1995). The new medical care system created a pyramid structure with high-prestige medical centers at the top of the status hierarchy and less prestigious clinics at the bottom. The capacity to conduct medical research was given significant weight in status rankings. This policy change not only affected medical institutes, it also bolstered the extent of research collaboration between the medical sector and researchers in higher education.

As presented in Fig. 5, in 1995, the portion of collaboration between the higher education sector and the medical care institutes accounted for 4.2% of research works in the higher education sector. By 2000, the portion of collaboration had climbed to 8.5%. The pace of growth continued rapidly during the 2000s. By 2010, the portion had reached 15%. From the medical care institutes' perspective, the importance of the higher education sector as a research partner was transformed during this period. Before 1994, collaborating with the higher education sector accounted less than 40% of the publications that were produced by the medical care sector (Fig. 6). In 1998, this portion increased to about 60%. By 2011, this portion has climbed to 85%. This huge proportion shows that for medical institutes, the higher education sector has become an irreplaceable strategic partner to conduct medical research.

A similar transformative change was observed in the collaborations between the national laboratories and the higher education sector. During the same period, the development of the national laboratories facilitated the transformation of university-based research. In the late-1990s, Taiwan expanded its national innovation system through the establishment of national laboratories. These new national research institutes included the National Institute of Health (built in 1996) and six national laboratories (built in the late of 1990s). The new national laboratories were not affiliated with the universities in regard to organizational operation; however, they had very close ties with universities in many aspects.

The national laboratories were founded by scholars who had faculty positions in universities. Even today, the directors of the national laboratories come from universities and keep their faculty positions. While choosing the location of the national laboratories, geographical proximity to research universities was taken into consideration. As a result, these national laboratories were set adjacent to university campuses, or even were located within campus buildings. This arrangement embraced the idea proposed by the famous US report: *Scientific Progress, the Universities, and the Federal Government* (1960) or Seaborg Report.

The Seaborg Report argued that the close ties between research universities and national laboratories can create mutual benefits for collaborators. First, national laboratories can offer university researchers expensive equipment that universities find it hard to afford and maintain. Second, national laboratories provide spaces for PhD students to receive advanced scientific training by engaging in the research activities of national laboratories.

The national laboratories also benefit from partnerships with universities. The new research topics brought by university researchers can stimulate the intellectual growth of researchers working in the national laboratories. Besides, interdisciplinary collaborations are possible when researchers in national laboratories continually exchange ideas and concepts with university-based researchers (President's Science Advisory Committee, 1960).

The longitudinal data for Taiwan shows that the collaboration between the university and research institute sectors intensified because of their close connection. In 1997, before the national laboratories were fully operational, collaboration between universities and national laboratories accounted for only 3.9% of scientific publications produced in the higher education sector. By 1998, the portion increased to 7.4%. In 2011, the portion of scientific publications increased to 14.4%. From the perspective of national laboratories, the importance of the higher education sector for collaborative research was steadily enhanced. In 1997, collaboration between the two sectors accounted for 30% of research publication produced in national laboratories. By 1998, this portion climbed to 60% and continued growing. In 2011, this portion reached 80%. This portion indicates that the majority of scientific works in national laboratories were completed with the involvement of university-based researchers.

Last but not least, I discuss collaboration between industry and the university sector, which is always of interest to policymakers. In today's knowledge society, economic prosperity relies on linkages between innovation and production. In 1999, modeled on the Bayh-Dole Act of 1980 in the United States, the national government of Taiwan passed the Fundamental Science and Technology Act of 1999 (National Science Council, 1999), granting universities the authority to commercialize research findings supported through public research funding. The purpose of this legislative action was to encourage the commercialization of research findings and to facilitate academia–industry partnerships on research activities. Under this legislative framework, Taiwan's leading research universities started to establish technology transfer offices to bridge academia and industry.

In Fig. 5, the portion of collaborative works between the higher education sector and the industry sector did not appear to be increasing after 1999. In 1999, the collaboration works between the higher education sector and the industry sector accounted for roughly 5% of research publication produced in the higher education sector, and this portion basically remained unchanged until 2011. In contrast, only slight growth occurred between 1996 and 1998, a few years before the passage of the "Fundamental Science and Technology Act." Thus, from the higher education sector's perspective, there is no clear evidence for an association between passing the "Fundamental Science and Technology Act" and the growth of academia–industry collaboration in scientific publications.

Given that the academy and industry have contrasting cultures and interests, it might not be surprising that academia–industry collaboration only accounted for such a small portion of research publications produced in the higher education sector. However, it might not be accurate to claim that the academia–industry linkage is weak in Taiwan, either. Compared to the United States and Japan, the higher education sector in Taiwan maintains significant collaboration with industry (National Science Board, 1998; Pechter & Kakinuma, 1999).

Pechter and Kakinuma (1999) investigated coauthorship patterns between academia and industry in Japan. They found that in 1995, roughly 40% of Japan's publications produced in the industrial sector were coauthored by researchers in industry and the academy. This figure was remarkably close to corresponding figures in the United States (National Science Board, 1998). Fig. 6 demonstrates that in 1995 the portion of Taiwan industry publications that were coauthored with domestic universities was 32%, slightly less than those proportions in Japan and the United States. Yet this rapidly climbed to 75% and continued growing thereafter. By 2011, more than 80% of Taiwan's industry publications were coauthored with domestic universities. Our longitudinal data show very clearly that the academia–industry linkage has intensified over the past decades. The importance of the higher education sector to support industry's innovation is increasing.

To sum up the discussion in this section, I find that Gibbons et al.'s (1994) prediction did not occur in the Taiwan, given the centrality of the research university. Gibbons et al. (1994) argued that the importance of the higher education sector for scientific production would be reduced mainly because its discipline-based knowledge production cannot appropriately fit the demands of today's society. However, what Gibbons et al. (1994) did not expect is that the mode of knowledge production in the higher education sector is evolving.

Along with the increasing collaboration with external sectors and intensified involvement in searching for solutions to problems in the real world (such as climate change, food shortage, and disease treatment), the higher education sector has continued expanding and has transformed to include transdisciplinary research. The formation of interdisciplinary research centers or clusters within research universities reflects this tendency.

CONCLUSIONS

Before the start of 21st century, there were two famous predictions about the growth of scientific production. The first prediction suggested that the growth of scientific production would soon reach its saturation limit and stop increasing (De Solla Price, 1986). The second prediction claimed that the emergence of a new mode of knowledge production ("Mode 2") would make universities less important in knowledge creation (Gibbons et al., 1994). With the help of bibliometric data, Zhang et al. (2015) showed that the growth of science production continued exponentially – and at an accelerating pace. Among the key driving forces behind this wave of growth is the rise of East Asian higher education and science systems, such as China's (Zhang, Sun, & Bao, 2017) and Korea's (Kim & Choi, 2017).

The staggering growth of science production in Asia has attracted scholars' attention (Altbach & Balán, 2007); however, less attention has been paid to the longitudinal study of internal dynamics driving growth in national and local contexts. This chapter shows that in Taiwan, the growth of science production is mainly driven by the higher education sector, which counters Gibbons and colleagues' (1994) prediction. The analyses presented also explain that the growth of science production in the higher education sector results from a series of higher education reforms and rising investments. Some policies were explicitly designed to spur science production (World Class University Project, for example), while others were not (e.g., the general expansion of the higher education and enrollments). Some policies were developed to accommodate the needs of the higher education system, while others were created following other social interests, such as demand for higher education participation. Yet, they all came together to advance scientific production in the higher education sector, even though some outcomes were unintended or unexpected.

Sociological and organizational theories help explain how university behaviors changed to accommodate these external environmental changes. Universities in Taiwan used and modified their organizational characteristics to build strength in science production. Researchers and organizations not only competed, but increasingly collaborated across tiers of the higher education sector and across sectors to produce more science, measured here in peer-reviewed journal articles. This case study provides an example of the investigation of the association between the expanding higher education and scientific production in national contexts that could be usefully compared to the dynamics found in other countries.

NOTE

1. Academia Sinica is the most preeminent academic institution in the Republic of China (Taiwan). It was founded in 1928 to promote and undertake scholarly research in sciences and humanities. In 1949, Academia Sinica was re-established in Taipei as an independent public research institute.

REFERENCES

Altbach, P. G., & Balán, J. (Eds.). (2007). *World class worldwide: Transforming research universities in Asia and Latin America*. Baltimore, MD: Johns Hopkins University.

Baker, D. (2008). Privatization, mass higher education, and the super research university: Symbiotic or zero-sum trends? *Die Hochschule [German Journal on Higher Education]*, 2, 36−52.

Baker, D. (2014). *The schooled society: The educational transformation of global culture*. Stanford, CA: Stanford University Press.

Bowen, H. R. (1980). *The costs of higher education: How much do colleges and universities spend per student and how much should they spend?* San Francisco, CA: Jossey-Bass.

Chang, L. L. (2001). *The development of Imperial Taipei University*. Ph.D. Dissertation. National Taiwan University, Taipei.

Chang, Y. N. (2006). Developmental trends and problems of the entrepreneurial university and the implications for higher education management. *Education Policy Forum*, 9(4), 77−100.

Chen, D. H. (1999). The reform of Taiwan higher education. *Education Research Information*, 7(3), 1−12.

De Solla Price, D. J. (1986). *Little science, big science... and beyond*. New York, NY: Columbia University Press.

DiMaggio, P., & Powell, W. W. (1983). The iron cage revisited: Collective rationality and institutional isomorphism in organizational fields. *American Sociological Review*, 48(2), 147−160.

Dong, B. C. (1997). *Education law and academic freedom*. Taipei: Yuedan Press.

Drori, G. S. (2000). Science education and economic development: Trends, relationships, and research agenda.

Executive Yuan. (1995). *National Health Insurance Act*. Taipei City: Republic of China (Taiwan).

Fernandez, F., & Baker, D. P. (2017). Science production in the United States: An unexpected synergy between mass higher education and the super research university. In J. J. W. Powell, D. P. Baker, & F. Fernandez (Eds.), *The century of science: The worldwide triumph of the research university* (Vol. 33). International Perspectives on Education and Society. Bingley: Emerald Publishing Limited.

Geiger, R. L. (2004). *Knowledge and money: Research universities and the paradox of the marketplace*. Stanford, CA: Stanford University Press.

Gibbons, M., Limoges, C., Nowotny, H., Schwartzman, S., Scott, P., & Trow, M. (1994). *The new production of knowledge: The dynamics of science and research in contemporary societies*. New York, NY: Sage.

Goedegebuure, L. C. (1992). *Mergers in higher education: A comparative perspective*. Utrecht: Lemma.

Goldin, C. D., & Katz, L. F. (2009). *The race between education and technology*. Cambridge, MA: Harvard University Press.

Harwood, J. (2010). Understanding academic drift: On the institutional dynamics of higher technical and professional education. *Minerva, 48*(4), 413−427.

Horta, H., Huisman, J., & Heitor, M. (2008). Does competitive research funding encourage diversity in higher education? *Science and Public Policy, 35*(3), 146−158.

Kim, H. R., & Choi, J. H. (2017). The growth of higher education and science production in South Korea since 1945. In J. J. W. Powell, D. P. Baker, & F. Fernandez (Eds.), *The century of science: The worldwide triumph of the research university* (Vol. 33). International Perspectives on Education and Society. Bingley: Emerald Publishing Limited.

Ministry of Education. (1994). *University Act*. Taipei City: Republic of China (Taiwan).

Ministry of Education. (2005). *University Act*. Taipei City: Republic of China (Taiwan).

Meyer, J. W., & Rowan, B. (1977). Institutionalized organizations: Formal structure as myth and ceremony. *American Journal of Sociology, 83*(2), 340−363.

MOE. (2010). *Operation directions governing application for flexible wage system*. Taipei: Ministry of Education.

MOE. (2016). *The digest of education statistics*. Taipei: Ministry of Education.

National Science Board. (1998). *Science & Engineering Indicators—1998*. Arlington, VA: National Science Foundation.

National Science Council. (1999). *Fundamental Science and Technology Act*. Taipei City: Republic of China (Taiwan).

National Taiwan University. (2011). *The finance report*. Retrieved from http://www.ntu.edu.tw/about/statistics.htm. Accessed on March 12, 2013.

OECD. (2016). *Population with tertiary education*. Retrieved from https://data.oecd.org/eduatt/population-with-tertiary-education.htm

Ou, S. Y. (2006). *The history of National Taiwan University (1945−1950)*. Taipei: Wunan Press.

Pechter, K., & Kakinuma, S. (1999). Co-authorship linkages between university research and Japanese industry. In L. M. Branscomb, F. Kodama, & R. Florida (Eds.), *Industrializing knowledge: University-industry linkages in Japan and the United States* (pp. 102−127). Cambridge, MA: MIT Press.

Pfeffer, J., & Salancik, G. R. (1974). Organizational decision making as a political process: The case of a university budget. *Administrative Science Quarterly, 19*, 135−151.

President's Science Advisory Committee. (1960). *Scientific progress, the universities, and the federal government*. Washington, DC: The White House.

Riesman, D. (1956). *Constraint and variety in American education*. Lincoln, NE: University of Nebraska Press.

Salmi, J. (2003). Constructing knowledge societies: New challenges for tertiary education. *Higher Education in Europe, 28*(1), 65−69.

Salmi, J. (2009). *The challenge of establishing world-class universities*. Washington, DC: World Bank Publications.

Scott, W. R. (2013). *Institutions and organizations: Ideas, interests, and identities*. Thousand Oaks, CA: Sage.

Seong, S., Popper, S. W., Goldman, C. A., & Evans, D. K. (2008). *Brain Korea 21 Phase II: A new evaluation model*. Santa Monica, CA: Rand Corporation.

Shin, J. C. (2009). Building world-class research university: The Brain Korea 21 project. *Higher Education, 58*(5), 669−688.

Slaughter, S., & Rhoades, G. (2004). *Academic capitalism and the new economy: Markets, state, and higher education*. Baltimore, MA: JHU Press.

Song, M. M., & Tai, H. H. (2007). Taiwan's responses to globalisation: Internationalisation and questing for world class universities. *Asia Pacific Journal of Education, 27*(3), 323−340.

Tai, H. H. (2000). *Massification and marketization in the higher education*. Taipei: Yangchih Press.

Tai, H. H. (2006). *World class universities: Excellence and innovations*. Taipei: Higher Education Press.

Tien, F. F. (1999). The impact of research productivity on promotion of college faculty in Taiwan: An application of event history analysis. *Journal of Humanities and Social Sciences*, *11*(3), 359−394.
Trow, M. (1973). *Problems in the transition from elite to mass higher education*. Berkeley, CA: Carnegie Commission on Higher Education.
Trow, M. (2007). Reflections on the transition from elite to mass to universal access: Forms and phases of higher education in modern societies since WWII. In J. F. Forest & P. G. Altbach (Eds.), *International handbook of higher education* (pp. 243−280). Netherlands: Springer.
Wagner, C. S., Brahmakulam, I., Jackson, B., Wong, A., & Yoda, T. (2001). *Science and technology collaboration: Building capability in developing countries* (No. RAND/MR-1357.0-WB). RAND CA.
World Bank. (1999). *World development report 1998/1999: Knowledge for development*. Washington, DC: World Bank.
Wu, C. S., & Jian, H. M. (2008). The analysis of vocational education in Taiwan, 1996−2007. *Journal of Education Research*, *1167*, 47−67.
Xu, N. H. (2002). *The history of Taiwan education*. Taipei City, TW: National Taiwan Normal University Press.
Zhang, H., Patton, D., & Kenney, M. (2013). Building global-class universities: Assessing the impact of the 985 Project. *Research Policy*, *42*(3), 765−775.
Zhang, L., Bao, W., & Sun, L. (2016). Resources and research production in higher education: A longitudinal analysis of Chinese universities, 2000−2010. *Research in Higher Education*, *7*(57), 869−891.
Zhang, L., Powell, J. J. W., & Baker, D. P. (2015). Exponential growth and the shifting global center of gravity of science production, 1900−2011. *Change: The Magazine of Higher Learning*, *47*(4), 46−49.
Zhang, L., Sun, L., & Bao, W. (2017). The Rise of Higher Education and Science in China. In J. J. W. Powell, D. P. Baker, & F. Fernandez (Eds.), *The Century of Science: The Worldwide Triumph of the Research University* (Vol. 33). International Perspectives on Education and Society. Bingley: Emerald Publishing Limited.

THE GROWTH OF HIGHER EDUCATION AND SCIENCE PRODUCTION IN SOUTH KOREA SINCE 1945

Hyerim Kim and Junghee Choi

ABSTRACT

Purpose — *This chapter provides a historical overview of policies on higher education in South Korea since 1945 and illustrates growth of science production based on expansion of higher education.*

Design — *We divide higher education policies into three historical time periods: (1) 1945−1950s, a period of developing modern higher education system; (2) 1960s−early 1990s, a period of rapid expansion of higher education, while government establishing a few research-focused science and technology institutions aimed at better quality research production; and (3) since mid-1990s, a period of fostering the workforce and raising science productivity in universities using targeted investments in research. We use the SPHERE project's comprehensive historical dataset based on Thomson Reuters' Web of Science and data from Higher Education in Korea to analyze growth in scientific publication in national and organizational level.*

Findings — *The analysis suggests that the combined private and public investments in the expansion of higher education, and sequential policy intervention facilitated the massive and ongoing growth of science production in Korea.*

Originality/value — *The chapter provides a thorough description about the growth of higher education and science production in South Korea and draws lessons for developing capacity for producing science.*

Keywords: South Korea; higher education policy; science production; research and development; science and technology

INTRODUCTION

At a remarkable pace over the second half of the 20th century and until today, the Republic of Korea or informally South Korea (hereafter Korea) has developed public education up through higher education. In 1945, after four decades of Japanese rule, the majority of its people were illiterate (Lee, 2005). The Korean War (1950–1953) further devastated social infrastructure, including school facilities, and resulted in one of the poorest countries. Yet this agrarian country embarked on a national development program based on investments in human capital production through formal education, and achieved one of the world's most rapid economic growth and social development (Kim, 2002). Within three decades, Korea made primary schooling universal, expanded secondary schooling considerably, and dramatically expanded access to higher education (Kim et al., 2015). In fact, the higher education system's age-cohort enrollment rate grew from 11.4% to 70.5% from 1980 to 2008. Initially focusing on developing basic education, by the new century Korea funded all levels of education on par with many other high-income countries (OECD, 2015). In addition, Korea consistently places among the top countries in international assessments of secondary school achievement in reading, mathematics, and science competencies (OECD, 2014). Based on these remarkable developments in the creation of human resources, Korea joined the trillion-dollar club of world economies in 2004 and its 2016 gross domestic production (GDP) ranked 14th in the world (The World Factbook, 2017).

The huge expansion of higher education simultaneously led to unparalleled research capacity, which in turn led to an exponential increase of researchers and science production. It was only in 1957 when the first doctoral program opened in Korea (Lee, 1999). By contrast, in 2015, Korea ranked fourth in number of researchers per 1,000 employed among 35 OECD member countries. In 2013, Thomson Reuters published a special report on the marked, outstanding growth of scientific publication in five countries, the so-called BRICK countries, including Brazil, Russia, India, China, and Korea (Adams, Pendlebury, & Stembridge, 2013). Examining the growth of research production in these five countries, Korea is particularly noteworthy as it has a much smaller population than other four countries. Research production in Korea has continuously increased, with an extraordinary annual growth rate of 21.8% between 1980 and 2011, higher than all other countries. Research output in Korea, as measured by the number of articles in journals included in the Science Citation Index Expanded (SCIE), was more than 40,000 in 2011, accounting for 3.8% of worldwide science production.

The extraordinary Korean development raises several questions: How was the expansion of higher education possible within such a short period of time? How did Korean higher education sustain its continuous growth, also in the provision of researchers? What led to the exponential growth of science production? What lessons can be learned from Korea?

In order to answer these questions, we review policies on higher education and science production in Korea since 1948 that set up and reformed the current education system. Government and its policies play a distinctive role, especially in developing countries. In contrast to developed countries, often in western world, in newly developing countries, such as Korea, social institutions are often translated and transplanted from elsewhere by strong leadership, mostly under the influence and with the aid of international agencies or foreign countries (Dolowitz & Marsh, 1996). As we will discuss subsequently, Korea also went through such a process of policy transfer. National government policies have played a crucial role in the ongoing expansion of higher education as well as science production (Amsden, 1992). In particular, we argue that the Korean government's sequential approach has been key to this development, higher education institutions were built with private investment at early stage, while public investment has been more focused on specific leading institutions. In the later stage, government exercised policy tools to enhance science production among all higher education institutions through project funding programs that led to competition between researchers and institutions. In addition to taking the lead on national policy for science development and providing the necessary resources, the government also made efforts to cultivate a social culture that is conducive to the education and training of scientists and the development of science overall.

In this chapter, we divide higher education policies into three historical time periods. In the section, "Establishment of the Higher Education System in Korea, 1945–1950s," we introduce how the foundations of the current Korean higher education system were developed. This period covers from 1945 to end of the 1950s. Then, we examine relevant policies from 1960 to the early 1990s. Meanwhile, higher education had expanded rapidly, with the government establishing a few research-focused science and technology institutions aimed at better quality research production. Toward the end of this period, new ideas, such as targeted investments in research and funding distribution based on evaluations, arose. In the section, "Investment in Research: Toward the World-Class Research University (since Mid-1990s)," we examine policies designed to foster the science workforce and raise science productivity in universities that have been implemented since the mid-1990s. One landmark policy of this period presented in detail here is "Brain Korea 21." Our policy review will be followed by the analysis of publication data combining figures from the SPHERE project database and from the Korean Ministry of Education that chart the tremendous growth of science production in Korea. We conclude by summarizing the major themes from the policy review and empirical analyses, drawing some lessons learned related to the impact of policies on science capacity-building and production in Korea since the middle of the 20th century.

ESTABLISHMENT OF THE HIGHER EDUCATION SYSTEM IN KOREA, 1945–1950S

Korea was liberated from almost four decades of Japanese colonial rule in 1945. However, the peninsula was occupied and divided by the Allied victors, the United States and the Soviet Union, on a temporary basis. The United States was responsible for territory south of the 38th Parallel, and its military administration ruled for three years. The Republic of Korea, often informally called South Korea, was established in August 1948. The Democratic People's Republic of Korea, informally known as North Korea, was established one month later. In June 1950, the North began a full-scale invasion of the South, with this war lasting for three years.

Thus, this period was a time of chaos and turbulence. Nonetheless, a nascent education system was established and partially implemented during this period of time. People were full of expectations and hope for their newly established independent country, and the government strived to provide education to its citizen as much as possible. While policy resources were mostly invested to expand primary education, the foundations for the modern higher education system were also set up during this period.

Establishing the Higher Education System

When Korea gained its independence in 1945, higher education was extremely limited, due to the colonial Japanese government's policy of restricting educational opportunity. In this sense, liberation in 1945 could be taken as the beginning of higher education in Korea (Kim, 2008). Plans for the higher education system were mainly formulated under the U.S. Military administration, with this influence suggesting to replace the former restrictive educational policies with liberal, laissez-faire policies (Kim, 2008; Lee, 1999). The Seoul National University, the first comprehensive university in the country, was established by an Ordinance of the U.S. Military administration in 1946. In that same year, three private colleges were officially recognized as four-year universities.[1]

After the Korean national government was established in 1948, the first Education Act was enacted at the end of 1949. This key policy defined educational ideals, established the basis for the education system, and set basic operating rules. The 6-3-3-4 structure for schooling and higher education was established, with universities (degree programs lasting four or six years), teachers' colleges (two or four year programs), and junior colleges (offering two year programs). The enactment of the Education Act also marked the beginning of government control over higher education (Lee, 1999). Even though the system was established based largely on the model of American higher education, the Act stated clearly the overarching authority of the government to oversee operations of public as well as private institutions, including decisions on the substantive academic issues, such as conferring degrees.

The most notable higher education policy initiative during the Korean War (1950–1953) was the establishment of the Wartime Associated University. The Education Ministry proclaimed the Special Decree on University Education and set up the Wartime Associated University system, consisting of institutions that had been closed or evacuated due to war. Through this system, in spite of the war, more than 6000 university students could take classes in dispersed temporary campuses outside Seoul (6.25와 전시연합대학 (Korean War and the Wartime Associated University), 2004, April 4). After the armistice agreement was signed in July 1953, those temporary campuses were used as the basis for provincial national universities, which played a major role in the early growth of science production later.

In 1957, the first doctoral program in the country was opened at Seoul National University (SNU). Two years later, SNU established the Graduate School of Public Administration and the Graduate School of Public Health. These were the first professional graduate schools that later became one of the streams of graduate education for cultivating professionals and application of theories to practice. Two other streams are general graduate school for academic research, and special graduate schools for continuous education for workers and adults.

The Rapid Growth of Private Institutions

During this period, policy efforts concentrated on expanding basic educational opportunities to include all eligible children and most of the resources were allocated to primary education (Lee, 2008). Publicly funded national universities alone could not accommodate the surging demand for higher education and this led to the rapid establishment of numerous private institutions. These also played an important role in providing science researchers, even though policy efforts were legitimated through the promise of expanding access to higher education rather than the production of new knowledge.

From 1945 to 1950, the U.S. Military administration and the Korean government carried out a land reform whereby Koreans with large landholdings were obliged to sell most of their land cheaply. In order to avoid this legal obligation, landowners established private schools, by which educational foundations became the new owners of the land. This creation of new private institutions was also encouraged by the government. As a result, private institutions began to make up an increasingly large share of Korean higher education (Oh, 2004). Indeed, by the academic year 2016, almost 80% of college students were enrolled in private institutions.

With the establishment of these private institutions, the overall number of higher education institutions rapidly grew from 19 to 74 within the decade ending in 1955. In this short period, the number of students also massively expanded – to more than 10 times the number in 1945. However, many of the new institutions must be considered substandard. The Education Ministry announced the Decree on University Establishment Standards in 1955 to ensure certain quality of university education. This decree set minimum standards for the establishment of new institution in terms of facilities and instructors and required already existing institutions to meet the criteria within a certain time period. As a result, the number of new institutions fell dramatically after the decree was introduced. However, the decree provided criteria mainly related to teaching. The other functions of higher education, such as research and social services, were not considered in the regulation (Lee, 1999).

EXPANSION OF THE HIGHER EDUCATION AND THE RESEARCH WORKFORCE (1960s–EARLY 1990s)

After the April Revolution in 1960,[2] the new government strove to create a democratic education system, part of its efforts to build a democratic society. Eagerness for liberalization and democratization pervaded the education sector; however, only a year after the Revolution, the government was overthrown by a military coup and the country was led by the military government for the next three decades. The military government introduced a series of five-year economic development plans from 1962, with the primary goal of education planning the provision of an educated workforce for the economy (Kim, 2002). During this period, primary and secondary education became universal. Higher education also expanded. At the end of this period, the net enrollment rate in higher education was about 35% (Kim, 2008).

University policy shifted from liberal and laissez-faire to strict control. Government tried to adjust the number of university students to fit workforce demand agendas and to control university quality, especially private institutions. However, demand for higher education grew ever greater, with the number of students increasing accordingly. On the other hand, the government established research-focused institutions with a majority of researchers returning from overseas.

Continuous Expansion under Policies of Quality Control

In the early 1960s, the government imposed various policies in order to control the number of institutions and guarantee education quality. Higher education was expected to provide a skilled workforce required for implementation of the ambitious economic development plans. The government wanted to decrease studies in the humanities and increase industrial training. Guided by these principles, policymakers attempted to systematically foster talent by setting the total number of university enrollments and massively overhauling national, public, and private universities. In 1963, the Private School Act was enacted, placing private institutions under public control (Kim, 2008). Subsequently, restrictive policies were implemented, such as the 1966 Decree on University Student Quota, designed to curb the quantitative growth of the student population. A university entrance preparatory exam system was introduced in 1969 to maintain a certain quality of newly admitted students and ameliorate social ills associated with severe competition for college entrance. Several measures to control the quality of higher education were also implemented during this period. Graduate schools were evaluated for the first time in 1977, and program evaluation was also conducted in that year. These evaluations were initiated by the government, but were handed over to the university association in the 1980s.

Even though the government attempted to control the expansion of higher education, the number of higher education institutions continuously increased during this period. While there were 80 institutions in 1960, by 1990 the number had risen to 265. The student population also increased almost 12-fold, partially due to the failure of the above-mentioned policies. As the excessive competition for college entrance became a major social issue, the government introduced a system in 1980 to manage the graduating population – instead of limiting the number of admitted students. Through this policy, an additional 30% of applicants were admitted annually, under the assumption that colleges and universities would drop this amount of students through rigorous academic criteria before graduation. However, policymakers faced serious criticism from institutions as this selection goal was not deemed pedagogically desirable. In practice, colleges and universities did not select out nearly as many students as policymakers had planned. As a result, considerably more students were allowed to graduate. The policy was virtually abolished by 1985.

Beyond the extraordinary expansion, another important characteristic of Korean higher education is that no distinctive classification of all higher education institutions exists. In the United States the Carnegie Classification of

Institutions of Higher Education provides a framework to categorize individual organizations by their mission and other characteristics (Fernandez & Baker, 2017). Such classification can serve as an effective tool to develop organization-level policies or to control for institutional characteristics in academic research. While policymakers and researchers in Korea have much interest in classifying HEIs, this is a very sensitive issue (Shin, 2009b) because the majority of four-year institutions in Korea aspire to be research universities. Despite criticism of the lack of such classification, the widespread model and goal-setting to become research universities led to broadened access to graduate education and contributed to the rapid expansion of science production through the expansive education and training of researchers.

Illustrating the expansion of higher education with the number of tertiary-level undergraduate students by their major, Table 1 shows that more than one-third have majored in science and engineering fields since 1965. From 1965 to 2010, the growth in undergraduate enrollments in science, engineering, and medicine grew by more than 20times (Table 2).

Significant development was also made in the number of researchers. Whereas in 1965 only 105 doctoral degrees were awarded by Korean higher education institutions by 1990 the annual number had increased to 1,400 doctoral degrees awarded, reflecting a 10.9% annual rate increase. Indeed, this represents faster growth than the undergraduate student population. The expanded research workforce functioned as key capacity for the continuous growth of science production.

Science and Technology Policies

In addition to expanding general higher education, the Korean government pursued policies designed to enhance the country's overall capacity in science and technology that set the stage for the experienced growth in scientific production by Korean colleges and universities. As mentioned, Korea relied heavily on international aid from the international community, mainly the United States, following the Korean War. However, Korea's strong desire to achieve economic growth through industrialization was met by doubt and skepticism from the U.S. and international aid agencies. Such doubt regarding developing countries' capacity for science development was quite prevalent at the time, including questions about feasibility (Birdsall, 1996) and skepticism about whether such investments would necessarily lead to technological and economic growth (Goldemberg, 1988). To address such doubts, Korea needed to show the world that it had the necessary human capital and capacity to pursue its plans for industrialization. The first step was to enhance its own capacity in science and technology. The desire to validate and legitimate its long-term economic and social development plans, amid doubts from foreign

Table 1. The Number of Undergraduate Students by Major, 1965–2010.

	1965	1970	1975	1981	1985	1990	1995	2000	2005	2010
Science & Engineering	37,634	59,798	74,702	210,822	373,643	452,576	561,270	909,353	911,502	887,084
Medicine	11,136	12,925	16,813	25,679	39,408	40,430	53,655	81,118	79,995	96,933
Humanities & Social Sciences	48,841	55,048	60,090	196,062	512,045	562,190	610,025	940,107	995,298	1,073,995
Others	11,113	21,352	60,374	120,152	195,652	173,527	191,397	289,187	370,044	400,003
Total	108,724	149,123	211,979	552,715	1,120,748	1,228,723	1,416,347	2,219,765	2,356,839	2,458,015

Source: Hong et al. (2013).

Table 2. Korean Scientists Returning from Overseas via Government Program Sponsorship, 1968–1990.

	Permanent Return			Temporary Return		
	1968–1980	1981–1990	Subtotal	1968–1980	1981–1990	Subtotal
University	139	355	494	21	203	224
Research institutions	130	387	517	182	360	542
Industry and others	7	33	40	74	287	361
Total	276	775	1,051	277	850	1,127

Source: Moon (2006).

aid-providing entities, boosted Korea's efforts to enhance its capacity in science and technology.

Importantly, the Korean government's science and technology policy has focused on shifting cultural values, meaning the change in the general public's perception of working in engineering and technology. Korean society traditionally treated technicians, such as engineers, as people on the lower end of the occupational hierarchy, while holding in high regard lawyers, government officials, and scholars in the humanities and social sciences. Believing that such social perceptions would discourage talented people from entering the fields of science and technology, the government made several efforts to shift such views held by the public through what is known as the Learning Science Movement. Science learning programs were provided to nearly all constituents of society, including students and adults, farmers and fishers in rural areas, and even prisoners. Since 1967, April 21 has been officially designated as "National Science Day," on which talented scientists are recognized with national awards and science competitions take place in K-12 schools all across the country. In various ways, the government made explicit efforts to raise the social status of natural scientists and cultivate in people the idea that science and technology is crucial for the country's economic and social development.

Underscoring the influence of global researcher mobility in developing higher education and research in Korea, the Korea Institute of Science and Technology (KIST) played an important role in bringing capable Korean researchers living abroad back to Korea – diminishing brain drain and fostering worldwide brain circulation. Due to Korea's low standard of living and lack of infrastructure for advanced research after decades of occupation and war, Koreans who obtained advanced degrees in science from foreign universities mostly opted not to return to their home country. Thus, in order to bring talented scientists back to Korea, KIST, established in 1966, provided immense incentives for researchers. In addition to guaranteeing strong support for research, the researchers were provided with free housing, an income equivalent to three times the average salary of a college professor, a car and chauffeur, personal secretaries, and other amenities. The salary of many researchers exceeded the salary of Korea's President, a rarity for a developing country under a military dictatorship. Although there was much resentment from the domestic academic community toward this extremely favorable treatment of KIST researchers, the government was steadfast in its provision of strong incentives to bring back talent from abroad. In 1967, 25 overseas Korean scientists were finally selected among about 800 applicants and returned to join KIST. Based on this success, the government embarked upon a general program to bring back Korean scientists from overseas in 1968, with this program sustained until 1990.[3] More than 1000 such scientists returned to Korea permanently through this program.

Another institute worth noting is the Korea Advanced Institute of Science (KAIS), which later became Korea Advanced Institute of Science and Technology and now known simply as KAIST, is considered to be the first research university in Korea. While KIST focused on bringing in talent from abroad, KAIS was a graduate school designed to develop and train engineers and researchers domestically. In its initial design phase, the Korean government brought in Professor Frederick Terman of Stanford University, widely recognized as the father of Silicon Valley, to assist in designing the school. One of its main features is the high level of autonomy provided by the government. Indeed, existing laws on education did not apply to KAIS, giving it the freedom to creatively and flexibly (re)design curriculum. Although the government provided funding, it did not intervene in operational affairs. Also, students were provided with many benefits, including the option for specialized military service. The number of graduates of KAIS grew rapidly, starting from 92 master's degrees in 1975 to 548 in 1986, and two doctorate degrees in 1978 to 72 doctorate degrees in 1986 (Table 3), but this was just the beginning. The number of doctoral degrees exceeded 100 in 1987, 200 in 1994, and 400 in 2000. In 2015, KAIST celebrated its 10,000th doctoral degree awarded (KAIST, 2015, February 12). In 2016, KAIST awarded 1,314 master's degrees and 570 doctoral degrees. As of 2006, KAIST graduates composed approximately 10% of domestic professors in STEM fields, worked in more than 100 different governmental research institutes and 2,000 corporations, thus playing a leading role in

Table 3. The Number of Graduates of KAIS in the Early Years.

Type	1975	1976	1977	1978	1979	1980	1981	1982	1983	1984	1985	1986	Total
Master's	92	145	139	142	181	219	297	294	317	356	694	548	3424
PhD	–	–	–	2	17	13	21	18	49	43	64	72	299
Prof. Master's	–	–	–	–	44	87	89	75	54	56	–	–	405

Source: Hong et al. (2013).

the development of science and technology in Korea (Hong, Jeon, & Kim, 2013).

Other than utilization of government-funded institutes, the government also actively encouraged private companies to contribute to science research (Arnold, 1988). For example, large private firms were required to have their own research institutes and small- and medium-sized companies were required to form research consortia. Financial support and various tax incentives were directed toward the private sector to expand their research capacities (Arnold, 1988).

At the end of the 1980s, the government began to pay more attention to the production of research in universities and tried to undertake a policy reform to further cultivate the research-focused university. The Presidential Committee on Education Reform was formed in 1985 and proposed a reform agenda that included the expansion of basic science research within universities and graduate schools. However, this policy was not fully implemented as the country went through political turmoil in 1987.[4]

INVESTMENT IN RESEARCH: TOWARD THE WORLD-CLASS RESEARCH UNIVERSITY (SINCE MID-1990s)

The policy paradigm for education went through a sharp change in the 1990s. While priority had been given to the expansion of educational opportunity to accommodate the extensive demands during the 1980s, educational policy from the mid-1990s became more focused on the "excellence" and specialization of each higher education institution (Lee, 1999). Global competitiveness of universities was also emphasized in an era of globalization and large-scale research funding projects, such as Brain Korea 21, based on the competition strategy initiated by the Education Ministry.

University Reform Policy (Mid-1990s)

The number of institutions and their enrollments kept growing. In 1990, higher education enrollment rate of an age-cohort was 23.6%. It doubled within a decade, reaching 52.5% in 2000. Despite the quantitative expansion, the quality of university education and research remained a significant concern. As mentioned earlier, most four-year institutions pursued the goal to become research universities, all with similarly broad composition of academic departments. This phenomenon was often criticized as the "department store" model of higher education, and was perceived by some as individual institutions lacking unique characteristics or specializations – and substandard quality in general.

Accordingly, the government began to initiate special efforts to improve the quality of higher education and tried to cultivate world-class research university with new policy approach.

During this period, educational policy went through changes that emphasized "customer choice" based on the belief that autonomy and competition would, eventually, raise overall quality.[5] This led to a new approach in higher education as well: funding based on competition and evaluation. Basing financial support on evaluation results was a very new approach in educational policymaking in Korea (Ahn & Ha, 2015). The government expected evaluation to increase the quality of universities based on specialization and by bringing about diversity among higher education programs across the country. Indeed, a number of specific projects were initiated by the Ministry of Education during this time period, including two special projects for science and technology (Table 4).

In addition, the government also promoted basic research activities through establishing "centers of excellence," namely the Engineering Research Centers (ERC) and Science Research Centers (SRC) (Choung & Hwang, 2013). With the goal of more effective utilization of limited resources, such centers were established within universities, and were actively used to pursue industry–academy collaborations and interdisciplinary research (Choung & Hwang, 2013). Trends in research funding during the 1990s indicate the emphasis put on such collaborations, as team-based research funding more than doubled from 22% to 51%, while funding for individual research diminished from 78% to 49% (Choung & Hwang, 2013) (Table 5).

Table 4. Government Funding Program for University Reform (1994−2001).

Project	Budget in 1997 (in Korean Won)	Total Budget (in Korean Won)	Project Period	Recipients
Special Funding Project for Science & Engineering Colleges	40 billion	200 billion	1994−1998	8 universities
Special Funding Project for Graduate Schools	20 billion	100 billion	1995−1999	5 universities
Cultivating Global Talents Project	20 billion	100 billion	1996−2000	9 universities
Specialization Project of HEIs located outside of Seoul and its vicinity	20 billion	100 billion	1997−2001	28 universities
Upgrading Research Centers of Science & Technology	17 billion	150 billion	1997−2000	200 research centers

Source: Ahn and Ha (2015).

Table 5. Production of SCI Publications, Korea, 2007−2015.

	2007	2008	2009	2010	2011	2012	2013	2014	2015
Number of SCI publications									
Nationwide	14,362	14,624	16,157	18,258	20,678	23,868	25,250	27,179	28,965
Top 15 universities	8,272	8,311	8,806	9,826	10,794	12,177	12,554	13,243	13,759
Top 15 proportion	57.6%	56.8%	54.5%	53.8%	52.2%	51.0%	49.7%	48.7%	47.5%
Per professor publication									
Nationwide	0.237	0.233	0.250	0.272	0.296	0.333	0.345	0.365	0.388
Top 15 average	0.679	0.614	0.615	0.668	0.701	0.755	0.764	0.788	0.839

Source: HEIK.

Brain Korea 21 (1999−2005)

Stemming from the belief that quality of research is most crucial for enhancing the global competitiveness of Korean higher education institutions, the Ministry of Education (MOE) in 1998 announced a new research funding program called Brain Korea 21 (or BK 21). The first phase of the program (1999−2005) invested more than 1,300 billion Korean Won (approximately 1.1 billion US dollars) (Ministry of Education, 2006). Unlike regular research support that focused on research publications, BK 21 was designed to support the development of research personnel, such as master's and doctoral students, post-doctoral researchers, and visiting professors as well as project teams within graduate schools to increase overall education and research capacity in Korea. BK 21 included the vision of creating "world-class" graduate schools, setting the foundation for graduate school development, fostering the enhancement of regional universities, and improving research staff working within graduate schools.

As a university reform policy, BK 21 had dual policy objectives: to cultivate research capacity among research universities and to ameliorate social ills related to excessive competition for college entrance. In order to achieve these purposes, the MOE set up several preconditions for BK 21 funding, such as to reduce the number of undergraduate students, to introduce a multi-departmental admission system, and to admit a certain number of graduate students from other universities (Ministry of Education, 2006). The MOE also encouraged institutions to implement more transparent management of research fund as well as to evaluate professors participating in BK 21 (Ahn & Ha, 2015).

BK 21 can be considered as the first policy to apply the "choice and concentration principle" to higher education, created an environment supportive of research at universities, which has increased university research output while fostering outstanding research personnel (Lee, 2008). Although BK 21 has a subprogram for humanities and social sciences, the program's main focus has been on natural sciences and technology, which have been and are still perceived as crucial for nation development and succeeding in global competition. BK 21 aimed to build a self-sustaining system of knowledge production in science and technology disciplines. Nine times more funding went to projects and researchers in science and technology than those in the humanities and social sciences.[6] Partially as a result of such programs, the absolute number of peer-reviewed articles in journals indexed in the Science Citation Index Expanded published with an author based in Korea rose from 9,854 in 1998 (18th in the world) to 23,297 in 2006 (13th in the world). In the same period, the percentage of Korean SCIE research in global proportion rose from 1.13% to 2.05%. In addition, the number of SCIE papers published by professors who took part in BK 21 science projects doubled during the program. And, the ratio of students to docents has improved due to the introduction of further research positions, such as contract professors and post-doctorates.

Based on the success of the first phase of BK 21, a second phase was implemented in the period from 2006 to 2012. Currently, BK 21 is in its third phase, from 2013 until 2019.

ANALYSIS OF KOREA'S SCIENCE PRODUCTIVITY DATA

Growth in the Number of Researchers

In this section, the growth in the number of researchers since 1995 is elaborated based on OECD data. Calculating the number of researchers per 1,000 employed persons in Korea, as Fig. 1 shows the continuous increase since 1999 when BK 21 started – it has almost tripled since then. In 1995, number of researchers as a proportion of the overall workforce in Korea was slightly below the OECD average. However, it began to exceed the OECD average in 2003. In 2014, Korea ranked fourth among all OECD countries in this indicator, following three Nordic countries, namely Finland, Denmark, and Sweden. This indicator increased even faster than tertiary education attainment among younger cohorts, which is impressive in itself. In the context of the higher education expansion, BK 21 provided a crucial opportunity to increase the pool of researchers as well (Fig. 1).

Research Production between 1980 and 2011 (Country Level)

Analysis of the SPHERE data for Korea shows that the number of SCIE papers produced by researchers affiliated with Korean institutions grown from 90 in 1980 to 40,824 in 2011, a growth of more than 400% over the span of 30 years. In terms of organizational forms producing Korean science, colleges

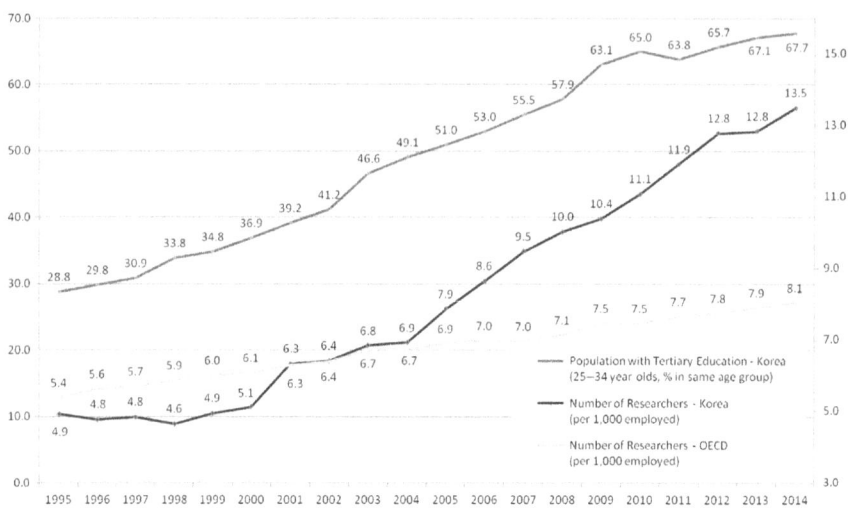

Fig. 1. Population with Tertiary Education and Number of Researchers. *Source*: https://data.oecd.org

and universities have accounted for more than 90%, without any signs of this dominance declining. In addition, from 1990 to 2010, the number of papers published in three most distinguished science journals (*Cell, Nature*, and *Science*) by Korean researchers increased from two to 47, indicating that improvements occurred not only in quantity, but also in quality (Choung & Hwang, 2013). However, this should not lead to the conclusion that colleges and universities have always played the leading role in Korea's science production. In the earlier phases of Korea's expanding science production, government research institutes were major players in science and technology research. However, because the focus in these institutes was primarily on enhancing the country's industrial capacity, such efforts resulted less in the production of academic papers in favor of patents and products (Figs. 2 and Fig. 3).

Science Production between 2007 and 2015 (Organizational Level)

In his research on the effects of BK 21, Shin examined the frequency of article publications in SCIE journals during the period from 1995 through 2005 and found significant growth in research publication from Korean research universities since BK 21 was implemented (2009a). In addition, he also identified the emergence of four research universities alongside three renowned research universities, Seoul National University (SNU), KAIST, and Pohang University of Science and Technology (POSTECH). These four universities are Korea

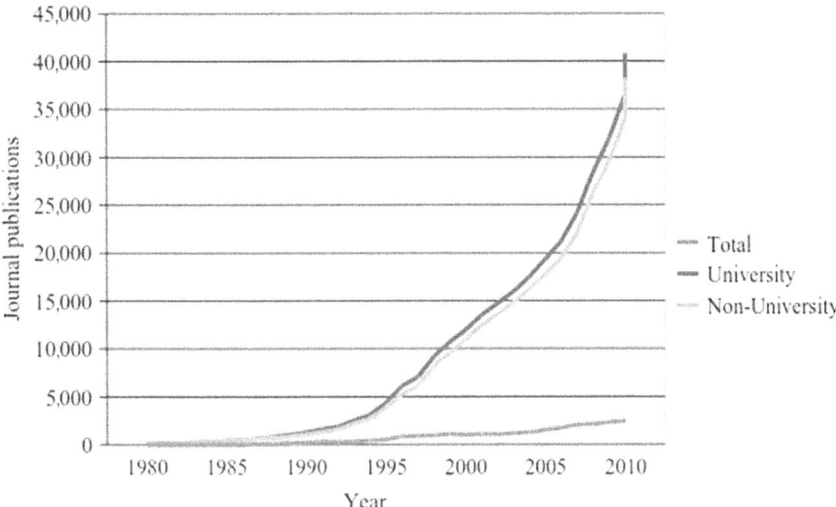

Fig. 2. Korea's Production of SCIE Journal Articles by Organizational Form (University and Non-university), Absolute, 1980–2011. *Source*: SPHERE project database of SCIE publications (Thomson Reuters' Web of Science).

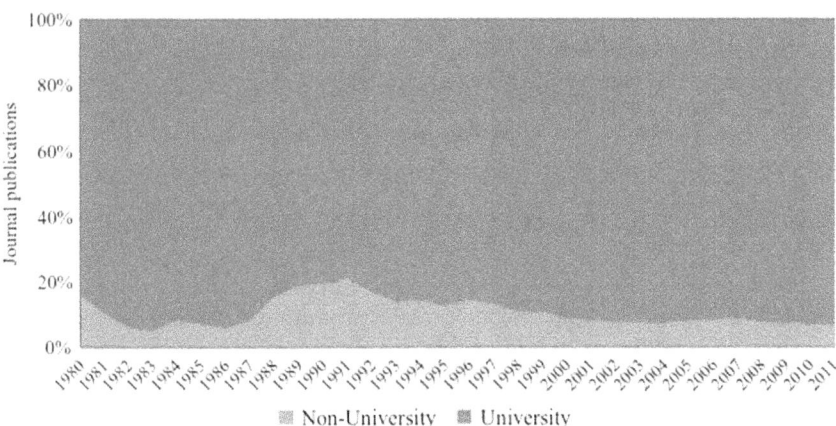

Fig. 3. Korea's Production of SCIE Journal Articles by Organizational Form (University and Non-university), Proportional, 1980–2011. *Source*: SPHERE project database of SCIE publications (Thomson Reuters' Web of Science).

University, Yonsei University, Syungkyunkwan University (SKKU), and Hanyang University. According to Shin, during the first phase of BK 21, these four universities grew faster than others in terms of research production and came to define themselves as research universities. Based on Shin's finding, we examined changes and trends in research production at the level of organizations, using the number of research publication in SCI journals between 2007 and 2015 – based on the "Higher Education in Korea (HEIK)" data (http://academyinfo.go.kr/).[7]

During the period between 2007 and 2015, SCI publication doubled nationwide.[8] The national average of SCI publication per full-time faculty, that is assistant, associate or full professor has also continuously increased from 0.237 in 2007 to 0.388 in 2015. Whereas the total number of papers and per professor publication rate among the top 15 universities also increased during this period, the rate of increase was slower than the national average. In addition, the proportion that the top 15 universities contribute to overall research production nationwide has continuously decreased. These mean that other universities that are less productive or participated less in research have become stronger and more engaged in producing research in the top peer-reviewed journals included in the Science Citation Index.

Among the highly ranked universities, we identified those five universities that grew faster than the national average (Table 6). While Shin's four universities lagged behind the national average in terms of rate of increase between 2007 and 2015, SCIE publications produced by members of new five universities increased considerably, including Kyung Hee University (almost quadrupled), Kyungpook National University, Catholic University, Ulsan University, and Chonbuk National University. Considering that BK 21 aimed to develop 10 "world-class" universities, the expansion of research-focused universities seems a most relevant result of the BK 21 and more general policies aimed at expanding higher education.

CONCLUSIONS

In this chapter, we reviewed the historical development of higher education policy and science production in Korea. After liberation from Japanese colonial rule in 1945 and after going through a three-year war with North Korea, Korea was one of the poorest countries in the world. However, aggressive investment in education led to very rapid education expansion, and this built the capacity for further extraordinary development of higher education and science production.

In the earlier stages of Korea's higher education development, public investment was focused on a few highly selective universities and research institutes, while broad-based private contributions were relied upon for the remaining organizations. This combination of investments resulted, between 1945 and 1955, in the rapid increase in the number of institutions from 19 to 74.

Further expansion of higher education took place simultaneously with active efforts to develop science and technology. While the government initially tried to control the growth of higher education, the enormous demand for college

Table 6. Growth of SCI Publications among Highly Ranked Universities,[a] Korea, 2007–2015.

	2007	2008	2009	2010	2011	2012	2013	2014	2015	Increase 2007–2015 (%)
SNU	1,341	1,671	1,603	1,767	1,786	1,935	2,007	2,043	2,139	59.5
Yonsei	1,184	936	1,039	1,107	1,164	1,253	1,271	1,354	1,447	22.2
SKKU	778	823	783	1,045	1,072	1,169	1,254	1,245	1,403	80.5
Korea	827	733	792	863	955	1,210	1,166	1,223	1,124	36.0
Kyung Hee	161	234	366	459	741	932	907	888	939	483.4
Kyungpook National	321	379	445	492	540	628	652	732	767	139.3
Pusan	677	446	483	504	545	640	606	738	766	13.2
Hanyang	453	480	494	468	629	694	723	769	754	66.6
KAIST	508	492	533	592	565	594	621	691	711	39.9
Catholic	321	331	425	473	497	532	625	612	687	114.3
Ulsan	330	357	344	451	538	606	629	655	669	102.8
Chonbuk National	258	329	334	363	410	525	585	619	606	135.4
Nationwide	14,362	14,624	16,157	18,258	20,678	23,868	25,250	27,179	28,965	101.7

Source: SPHERE project database of SCIE publications (Thomson Reuters' Web of Science).
[a] Universities in this table were the top 12 in 2015. All of them remained in the top 15 between 2007 and 2015.

enrollment and attainment by the general public played a large part in its ongoing expansion. For example, public demand led to the abolishment of the national admissions quota in 1980, and not long after graduation quotas were also abolished. By 1990, the number of colleges and universities in Korea reached 265. Simultaneously with the growing private investments, the Korean government perceived science and technology to be a crucial part of its overall development strategy. A variety of economic and social incentives were awarded to scientists, and the government heavily invested in organizations designed to conduct research and develop future researchers.

In terms of quantity and quality, Korea made significant strides in science production. Once Korea's higher education system had sufficiently developed quantitatively, the government utilized selection and concentration strategies to fund certain institutions with the goal of cultivating "world-class" research universities. While no causal impact of public policies can be analyzed here, descriptive statistics and previous research findings suggest that the combined private and public investments in the expansion of higher education facilitated the massive and ongoing growth of science production in Korea, which could provide lessons for other countries seeking to develop their capacity for producing science.

NOTES

1. Three universities are Ewha Womans University (former Ewha College), Yonsei University (Yonhi College), and Korea University (Bosung College).

2. The April Revolution, or April 19 Revolution, was a democratic uprising in April 1960, led by student and labor groups, which overthrew the autocratic government under the president Syngman Rhee. The uprising was triggered by the discovery in Masan Harbor of the body of a student killed by a tear-gas shell in protest against the rigged general election of March 1960.

3. Throughout the 1980s, the capacity of Korean institutions to cultivate researchers was continuously strengthened. In addition, increasing numbers of overseas Korean scientists voluntarily returned to Korea. Accordingly, the government program to bring back overseas scientists was suspended in 1991.

4. In June 1987, a nationwide democracy movement, known as the June Democracy Movement, formed in Korea to demand that the ruling government to hold elections and institute other democratic reforms. The Presidential election was held in December 1987 and thus the Presidential Committee on Education Reform (formed in 1985) couldn't fully implement its policy agenda.

5. The then president Kim Young Sam organized the Presidential Commission on Education Reform (PCER), which drafted an education reform plan, known as the 5.31 Education Reform Proposals (ERP). The ERP has enormously influenced Korean education policies since it was released in 1995 (Ahn & Ha, 2015). It required an overhaul of the entire education system from its users' viewpoints, and based on market principles (Kim, 2002).

6. During first phase of BK 21 (1999–2005), 547 billion Won was invested in S&T while 56 billion in humanities and social sciences (MOE, 2006).

7. HEIK provides the annual data on the number of publications in SCI journals that are published by the assistant, associate, and full professors. Papers published by lecturers are not counted in the number of publications.

8. In HEIK data, numbers are weighted by the rank in authorship sequence, that is papers of authors other than the first author are counted less than one. This is a difference from how we counted papers included in the SPHERE dataset used in the earlier section.

REFERENCES

Adams, J., Pendlebury, D., & Stembridge, B. (2013). *Building BRICKS: Exploring the global research and innovation impact of Brazil, Russia, India, China and South Korea*. Philadelphia, PA: Thomson Reuters.

Ahn, B. Y., & Ha, Y. S. (2015). *5.31 Education reform and 20 years*. Seoul: Hakjisa (in Korean).

Amsden, A. H. (1992). *Asia's next giant: South Korea and late industrialization*. Oxford: Oxford University Press.

Arnold, W. (1988). Science and technology development in Taiwan and South Korea. *Asian Survey*, 28(4), 437–450.

Birdsall, N. (1996). Public spending on higher education in developing countries: Too much or too little? *Economics of Education Review*, 15(4), 407–419.

Choung, J. Y., & Hwang, H. R. (2013). The evolutionary patterns of knowledge production in Korea. *Scientometrics*, 94(2), 629–650.

Dolowitz, D., & Marsh, D. (1996). Who learns what from whom: A review of the policy transfer literature. *Political Studies*, 44(2), 343–357.

Fernandez, F., & Baker, D. P. (2017). Science production in the United States: An unexpected synergy between mass higher education and the super research university. In J. J. W. Powell, D. P. Baker, & F. Fernandez (Eds.), *The century of science: The worldwide triumph of the research university* (Vol. 33). International Perspectives on Education and Society. Bingley: Emerald Publishing Limited.

Goldemberg, J. (1988). What is the role of science in developing countries? *Science*, 279, 1140–1141.

Hong, S., Jeon, C., & Kim, J. (2013). *2012 Economic development modulation: Korea's development in science and technology*. Sejong: Ministry of Science, ICT and Future Planning. (in Korean).

Kim, G. J. (2002). Education policies and reform in South Korea. In *Secondary education in Africa: Strategies for renewal* (pp. 29–39). Washington, DC: World Bank.

Kim, J., Cho, W., Moon, M., Park, H., Cho, J. M., Park, J., & Song, J. (2015). *Education for all 2015 national review: Republic of Korea*. Paris: United Nations Educational, Scientific, and Cultural Organization.

Kim, Y. C. (2008). *Universalization of tertiary education*. Seoul: Korean Educational Development Institute (in Korean).

Korea Advanced Institute of Science and Technology [KAIST]. (2015). KAIST cultivated more than 10,000 doctors. *KAIST News*, February 12. Retrieved from www.kaist.ac.kr (in Korean).

Lee, C. J. (2005, September). Korean model of secondary education development: Approaches, outcomes and emerging tasks. In WBI "*Seminar on Growth Strategies for Secondary Education in Asia*", Kuala Lumpur, Malaysia.

Lee, H. H. (1999, July–August). Trends in higher education policy after liberation. *Higher Education*, 100, 12–19 (in Korean).

Lee, S. J. (2008). *National development strategy and education policy*. Seoul: Korean Educational Development Institute (in Korean).

Ministry of Education. (2006). *Development of graduate schools and research-oriented universities (BK 21)*. Seoul: Ministry of Education (in Korean).

Moon, M. Y. (2006). Korea's 'Brain-Drain' and the role of KIST (The Korean Institute of Science and Technology). *Korean Culture, 37*, 229–261 (in Korean).

Oh, S. B. (2004). Exploration of private university expansion process: Based on land reform after the liberation. *The Journal of Korean Education, 31*(3). 53–73 (in Korean).

Organization for Economic Cooperation and Development [OECD]. (2014). *Lessons from PISA for Korea, strong performers and successful reformers in education*. Paris: OCED Publishing.

Organization for Economic Cooperation and Development [OECD]. (2015). *Education at a glance 2015: OECD indicators*. Paris: OECD Publishing. doi:10.1787/19991487

Shin, J. C. (2009a). Building world-class research university: The Brain Korea 21 project. *Higher Education, 58*(5), 669–688.

Shin, J. C. (2009b). Classifying higher education institutions in Korea: A performance-based approach. *Higher Education, 57*(2), 247–266.

The World Factbook. (2017). Retrieved from https://www.cia.gov

6·25와 전시연합대학 (Korean War and the Wartime Associated University). (2004). *Daily UNN*, April 4. Retrieved from http://www.unn.net/ColumnIssue/Univ50Detail.asp?idx=14&n4_page=1&n1_category=1 (in Korean).

"A FEVER OF RESEARCH": SCIENTIFIC JOURNAL ARTICLE PRODUCTION AND THE EMERGENCE OF A NATIONAL RESEARCH SYSTEM IN QATAR, 1980–2011

John T. Crist

ABSTRACT

Purpose — *Although its contributions to global science date from 1980, Qatar embarked on an ambitious plan in 2009 to position itself as an important hub for global research production. This paper assesses Qatar's contribution over the past three decades to global research output and science productivity in STEM+ fields, as measured by scientific journal article production.*

Design — *The core of the analysis is based on a specially coded dataset of all peer-reviewed journal articles in the STEM+ disciplines with at least one author whose primary affiliation was a Qatar-based research organization. The original data source is Thomson Reuters' Science Citation Index Expanded (SCIE). Analyzing trends between 1980 (the first year in which a paper with a Qatar-based author appeared in these selected leading journals) and 2011, the chapter documents how scientific journal article production in Qatar has developed over three decades.*

Findings — *Between 1980 and 2002, rates of journal article production were relatively low. From 2003, reflecting considerable investments in higher education and research, the annual number of journal article publications increased dramatically. Most publications were authored by university-based scientists (58%) and scientists based at research hospitals or other medical research facilities (30%). By 2011, over 83% of scientific journal articles published with at least one Qatar-based author were the result of collaboration with international partners. European, North American, and Middle Eastern research scientists and organizations were the most common international collaborators.*

Originality/value — *This is the first comprehensive empirical study of Qatar's contributions to global scientific production in the STEM+ disciplines.*

Keywords: Higher education; research; science productivity; STEM+; Qatar

INTRODUCTION

Qatar is among the most recent entrants into the global game of knowledge production — and also among the youngest. Having declared its independence in 1971, Qatar is the world's largest producer of liquid natural gas (LNG) and, according to the World Bank and the CIA, the country with the highest GDP per capita. After decades of investment in its education system and consecutive reforms, in the expansion of the national university, and in an innovative cluster of highly regarded international branch campuses known as Education City, the ruler of Qatar, Sheikh Hamad bin Khalifa Al-Thani, announced in 2009 that Qatar would devote 2.8% of GDP annually to research and development (R&D). World Bank estimates put Qatar's GDP at $202.5 billion in 2013, which translates into $5.67 billion in R&D annually.[1] By 2010, Sheikha Moza, the Emir's wife and the Chairperson of Qatar Foundation, felt the "fever of research in Qatar" (*The Peninsula*, 2010). To understand the extraordinary scale of Qatar's investment, it must be compared. The U.S. National Science Foundation estimated that global R&D expenditures were in excess of $1.4 trillion in 2011 and averaged a 6.7% increase annually during the previous 10 years (NSF, 2014). Following the successes of the world's older and more established research economies, R&D investment and the pursuit of a knowledge economy (or society) has become a popular strategy for national development among small and medium-size states (Dill & Van Vught, 2010). For example, the Republic of Korea devoted 4% of GDP to R&D in 2011; Israel, 3.9%;

Iceland, 2.60%; Slovenia, 2.47%; Singapore, 2.23%; and Luxembourg, 1.41% (World Bank, 2015). Qatar's investment is thus substantial, matching many European countries with developed higher education and science systems and historically high scientific productivity. In contrast, "the 57 member states of the Organization of the Islamic Conference (OIC) averages just .38% of gross domestic product" (The Royal Society, 2011). Such investment is envisioned to have a variety of direct and indirect benefits for the economy and society. Depending upon the country, these may include profits from the commercialization of scientific innovations, diversification of the economy and reduced dependence on non-renewable resources or commodities sold in volatile markets, increases in global investment, an educated and professional workforce, as well as the reputational value that accrues to states that are successful in the highly competitive global scientific and knowledge enterprise.

This chapter will summarize Qatar's efforts to build a national research economy as a vehicle – one of several – to achieve this economic and social transformation. The goal was first announced to the public in 2009, although there were important antecedents, such as the founding of a national research funding agency in 2006 and the opening (from 1998) of branch campuses of elite North American and European universities with substantial research facilities. After a review of the discourse about the goals of such funding, the chapter will analyze data about journal article production in Qatar to understand how investments in R&D have transformed the research landscape in Qatar within just a few short years.

One important caveat is in order. In their excellent volume of case studies about national research economies, Dill and Van Vught (2010) identify common stumbling blocks to a full analysis of how funding and other contextual factors influence science production in all countries or any particular country:

> It is quite difficult for several reasons to assess the impact and outcomes of policy on higher education and its research effort. Data is often sporadic, out of date, and difficult to obtain. But, more importantly, the effects of particular policies often take a considerable amount of time to appear. (p. 50)

These impediments are especially insurmountable in Qatar. Estimates of funding for R&D are limited to irregular announcements about planned funding. Precise figures about actual expenditures generally are not available consistently over time. National budgets are not available to the public in detailed form, and generally, Qatar's ministries do not have a tradition of sharing policy data with the public, except for limited purposes. On top of these concerns, the fact that Qatar's research economy is so young makes a quantitative assessment of long-term policy impacts impossible. However, given the ambitious policy-making and tremendous investments in research infrastructure as well as the international collaborations upon which Qatar has built its higher education and research systems, analysis is needed more than ever. Thus, using scientific journal article production as an indicator of growing science capacity, this chapter will describe the strategies, outputs, and context of Qatar's nearly unparalleled research capacity building effort.

LOCAL, REGIONAL, AND GLOBAL ASPIRATIONS FOR A NATIONAL RESEARCH SYSTEM IN QATAR

Qatar is a small desert country situated on a peninsula jutting into the Persian Gulf, along the coast of Saudi Arabia. As a consequence of the booming liquid natural gas industry, migration to Qatar has been high since the mid-1990s and especially since 2005. This population growth is almost entirely due to immigration of non-Qataris. The government announced in 2014 that Qatar's population size passed the 2 million mark, but most estimates of the ethnically Qatari population range from 250,000 to 300,000, or about 15% of the total. After a sustained campaign to promote literacy, Qatar's illiteracy rate is low (3.2%), but Qatari students consistently rank at or near the bottom on global standardized tests compared to students in other countries (Khatri, 2013; OECD, 2014). In 2010, there were 14,000 ethnically Qatari students enrolled at 13 universities (Qatar Statistics Authority, 2011). Only one of these universities was home grown — the others were international branch campuses of North American and European universities. Almost all of these students were enrolled in undergraduate programs, as there are only a small number of postgraduate programs in the country.

However, unlikely this context may seem for the pursuit of a national research system, there are nonetheless powerful motivations — economic, strategic, and aspirational — for this policy in Qatar. As for economic motives, Qatar's national development strategy is laid out in *Qatar National Vision 2030* (QNV), first published in July 2008 by the General Secretariat for Development Planning. With its acknowledgment that "the country's hydrocarbon resources will eventually run out," the document argues that "future economic success will increasingly depend on the ability of Qatari people to deal with a new international order that is knowledge-based and extremely competitive" (p. 13). The Qatar Foundation for Education, Science and Community Development (QF) was to become the spearhead of the implementation of the QNV. Qatar Foundation was founded in 1995 by then Emir of Qatar Hamad bin Khalifa Al-Thani and his second wife, Sheikha Moza bint Nasser, who continues to serve as chairperson. Through a variety of educational and research-oriented programs, QF promotes "an innovative and open society that aspires to develop sustainable human capacity, social and economic prosperity for a knowledge-based economy" (Qatar Foundation, 2016). Its principal project, Education City, is an innovative (and massive) educational complex comprised of eight international branch campuses of U.S. and European universities and two additional universities operated directly by QF. The constituent international branch campuses of Education City were intended to form a single entity, much like a university is comprised of a collection of schools of different disciplines. In addition to higher education, Education City also supports primary and secondary schools of a high caliber, as well as a major research hospital, several research centers in the STEM disciplines, the national research funding agency, a national library, the Qatar Science and Technology Park, and many smaller programs (Crist, 2015).

Released 13 years after the establishment of Qatar Foundation, and while Education City was still being formed, the QNV also assigns top priority to building "a modern world-class educational system ... comparable to that offered anywhere in the world" (p. 13). The QNV frames the value of education primarily in terms of human development and "unlocking human potential" (p. 16). Otherwise, there are only two references to research in the QNV. As outcomes of the development process, the document envisions for Qatar "A significant international role in cultural and intellectual activity and scientific research" and the establishment of "An effective system for funding scientific research shared by the public and private sectors and conducted in cooperation with specialized international organizations and leading international research centers" (p. 16). In addition to reducing Qatar's reliance on LNG for the future, the investment in education and research also clearly promises multiple dividends along the way – from technological innovations, patents, medical breakthroughs, and other resources necessary to promote development and address Qatari social problems.

Qatar's dependence on LNG is not the only long-term vulnerability it faces. There are multiple strategic vulnerabilities that arise from its small size and harsh climate, and the strategic choice to pursue a national research system also promises to help on these fronts. Qatar is situated between two regional hegemons – Saudi Arabia and Iran – in the middle of a dangerous neighborhood where war and invasion are distinct realities, not hypothetical possibilities. In worst case scenarios, unlikely as they may be, Qatar's capacity to defend its borders is limited because of the comparatively small size of the armed forces. To compensate for this vulnerability, Qatar has pursued cooperative relations – militarily, economically, and culturally – with its primary security guarantors, the United States and the United Kingdom (Kamrava, 2014). One can read Qatar's heavy investment in international branch campuses and R&D in part as a concerted effort in "knowledge diplomacy." By committing substantial resources to educational and research partnerships with American, British, Canadian, and French universities and institutes, Qatar signals its interest in cooperation and promotes the integration of interests among these countries beyond the realm of security. The considerably international scientific community in Qatar also provides important links to countries beyond the Gulf. These areas of investment also redound in global reputational benefits, as education and research are both highly valued commodities within the community of nations and a core part of the West's conception of its most important contributions to global culture.

Finally, there are aspirational underpinnings of the national research system policy. These involve Qatar's identity as an Arab and Islamic country, and its interest in asserting a leading role in regional politics. From the 8th to 13th centuries – thought by many to be Islam's "golden age" – Islam led the world in scientific and technological innovations, some of which were foundational developments in mathematics, astronomy, medicine, and many other disciplines. The world's oldest extant universities are each located in the Islamic (and Arab) world: the University of Al-Karouine in Morocco (founded 859 A.D.), Al-Azhar University in Cairo (founded 970 A.D.), and Al-Nizamiyya University of Baghdad (founded 1065 A.D. and now in operation in Isfahan, Iran) (collegestats.org, 2015). In addition to Quranic studies, all of these institutions specialized in the natural sciences from their inception.

In 2014, *U.S. News and World Report* identified over 800 colleges and universities operating in the Middle East and North Africa (MENA) in its sampling frame for a regional ratings scheme. Currently, however, the MENA region is among the least productive in science among the world's regions, largely due to lack of funding, the drain of scientists by European and American universities, and other deficits that create an unfavorable environment for advanced intellectual and technology development. Based on its study of science and innovation in the Islamic world, the Royal Society observed that "In 2005, 17 Arab-speaking countries together produced 13,444 scientific publications; fewer than the 15,455 achieved by Harvard University alone" (The Royal Society, 2010, p. 2). Against this backdrop, Qatar's construction of a national research system – well-funded and highly integrated within global scientific networks – is a bold move that resonates strongly with a significant element of Arab self-conception about the past. As Sheikha Moza declared in 2010, "we must build on what we have and learn how to use the past as a tool to rekindle the confidence of our ancestors, not just as a historical reference" (Qatar Foundation, 2010b, p. 28). Moreover, as Qatar continues to establish itself as a regional and global force – in politics, diplomacy, sports, global travel, or development aid, for example – Qatar asserts a leadership role in education and science within the MENA region that is out of the grasp of its regional neighbors (especially Egypt, Lebanon, Syria, and Iraq).

The regional significance of Qatar Foundation's mission has been consistently articulated by Sheikha Moza, the founding Chairperson of Qatar Foundation. In 2010, at a signing ceremony for a Memorandum of Understanding that formalized Qatar's partnership with the Royal Society of London's effort to develop "The Atlas of Islamic-World Science and Innovation," the Sheikha declared that

> I signed it myself to send a signal to the Arab world and the Islamic world about the importance of science. In order for us to enjoy a renaissance in this field, we need to send this message to leaders, particularly to academic leaders, and social leaders, about the importance of science. (Qatar Foundation, 2010a, p. 24)

ELEMENTS OF A NATIONAL RESEARCH SYSTEM IN QATAR

As the list of states pursuing a science for development strategy has grown, analysts have begun to identify common features of national research systems. There are a variety of material and human resources or capacities that are commonly thought to be essential for a national research system to succeed and without which the system is either impossible or significantly hampered (Dill & Van Vught, 2010). These include (a) research-oriented universities; (b) a pool of research personnel, including PhDs in the STEM disciplines along with doctoral students and post-doctoral researchers, technicians, research managers, and administrators; (c) independent research institutions not affiliated with universities and devoted entirely to research and development; (d) corporate research and development operations; (e) technological capacity and materials commonly in the form of laboratories, specialized research equipment, and advanced computing facilities to handle big data; and (f) a substantial research funding environment, including a national research funding agency as well as other non-government sources of research funding. There are other aspects of the environment that are vital for the productivity of a national research system, but are secondary to the capacity of the system to conduct research. Examples of such ancillary elements include a rigorous primary and secondary school system that supplies universities with students ready for post-secondary and advanced education; public media that follow and report on scientific developments and build commitment within a population for scientific endeavors and careers; and policy decision makers within the government who create a favorable regulatory environment conducive to the development and effective management of scientific capacity.

In each of these areas, but to varying extents, Qatar has launched initiatives to build capacity of its growing research system. The next section analyzes the features of these elements in Qatar. The picture is mixed: while Qatar's research infrastructure has advanced remarkably in a few short years, it confronts many of the same challenges and deficits that confound small and developing states when they build their higher education and research sectors (Crist, 2015; Powell, 2014a, 2014b).

Research-Oriented Universities

Qatar University, the first university in Qatar, was founded in 1978 with the consolidation of two teacher training colleges that opened five years earlier. Its mission was not primarily focused on research but rather on providing post-secondary education for a broad base of Qatari citizens and local residents.

Prior to this time, the only options a family had for college education were enrollment abroad or by correspondence. Despite steady effort to consolidate and strengthen the university, however, by the late 1990s prominent educational leaders in Qatar believed that "returns had been low" on the government's investments (Witte, 2010, p. 18). In 2003, the RAND-Qatar Policy Institute was commissioned to study and make recommendations for "the conditions and resources needed to turn Qatar University into a model national university" (Moini, Bikson, Neu, & DeSisto, 2009, p. xiv). This became the basis for a reform process in the following years that resulted in, among other important developments, a common core curriculum for all graduates and formal autonomy from the Ministries of Finance and of Civil Service Affairs and Housing (Moini et al., 2009, pp. 27−31). (Today, Qatar University is overseen by the Supreme Education Council, a government body that coordinates all of Qatar's educational institutions from primary school to the national university − but not the foreign university branch campuses of Education City).

For much of its history, journal article production in the STEM disciplines at Qatar University was at a stable, but modest, rate of production set between 18 and 25 articles per year. From 2003, the annual rate of production began to increase and by 2011, QU recorded its highest volume of annual production, at 110 articles, about five times the average before 2003.

Also in 2003, the main science universities in Education City − Texas A&M University-Qatar (TAMU-Q) and Weill Cornell Medical College-Qatar (WCMC-Q) − first published articles in the SCIE database. While precise figures are not available to the public, these were (and are) extraordinarily well-funded institutions composed of faculty recruited primarily from top departments in the United States, Europe, and the MENA region. Within a few years (by 2006), the annual combined number of publications from the HEIs in Education City exceeded the total of Qatar University.[2]

TAMU-Q and WCMC-Q both possess substantial facilities for research production in the natural sciences. For example, the TAMU-Q, the highest volume producer of STEM journal articles in Qatar, houses three state-of-the-art laboratories in chemical engineering (Applied Catalysis and Reaction Engineering, Fuel Characterization, Sustainable Research Engineering), and others in water and environmental engineering as well as process system and process safety engineering. The laboratories in the Education City universities were built within the past decade and with access to substantial funding for acquisition of cutting-edge equipment and new technologies. Leaders of these campuses consider the up-to-date, technical excellence of their laboratories (even compared to their parent campuses) to be among their most useful assets for attracting and retaining scientific talent to their faculties.[3]

Research Personnel

The research community in Qatar is small. Total estimates are not available. Van Servellen and Baas (2013, p. 11) put the number of "active researchers"[4] at 750 in 2011, not including laboratory technicians, support staff, and non-published researchers or PhD candidates. This number is much smaller than comparable estimates for other countries in the region – for example, Saudi Arabia (7,112), Egypt (10,401), and Turkey (42,419) (Van Servellen & Baas, 2013, p. 13).[5] The percentage of active researchers who appear to be based in Qatar exclusively is also quite small compared to native scientists in the other countries examined: 14.9% in Qatar compared to 19.7% in Saudi Arabia, 39.7% in Egypt, and 72% in Turkey. In 2013, Faisal Al-Suwaidi, president of Research and Development at Qatar Foundation, observed that "The latest statistics show that Qatar has about 600 scientists," noting also that "We need to add 1500 more by the year 2018 to meet our research targets" (Yahia, 2013, para. 3). These research scientists are based principally at the national university (Qatar University), Hamad Medical Corporation, or at one of the international branch campuses in Doha, such as TAMU-Q and WCMC-Q, that specialize in the STEM disciplines.

National Research Institutes

Qatar Foundation established three "National Research Institutes" (NRIs) to conduct research independent of the international branch campuses it sponsors. These are the Qatar Biomedical Research Institute (QBRI, founded in 2012); the Qatar Computing Research Institute (QCRI, founded in 2010); and the Qatar Energy and Environmental Research Institute (QEERI, founded in 2011). Each Institute has ambitious plans for development, including, for example, five research "centers of excellence" at QBRI devoted to research on diseases and a dozen laboratories at QEERI. The NRIs will be housed together in Qatar Foundation's Research Development Complex, currently under construction in an initial phase of 45,000 square meters with plans for 223,000 square meters when completed (Qatar Biomedical Research Institute, 2015, para. 2). The NRIs are affiliated with Hamad Bin Khalifa University (HBKU), the only university in Education City operated directly by Qatar Foundation. The National Research Institutes are "structured on the Max Planck model" (Qatar Foundation, 2014b, p. 1), and they approximate the role described by Powell and Dusdal (2017) for independent research institutes (IRIs) – sites of basic and applied research conducted by full-time professional researchers unencumbered by obligations of teaching and administration that must usually be fulfilled by those in university faculty positions. Unlike Germany's IRIs that are co-funded by Federal and state (*Land*) governments and are largely autonomous in selecting their research subjects, the NRIs of Qatar are almost entirely funded by the central government and are tapped to lead the national effort in addressing specific "Grand Challenges," priority topics set by the government to address issues of high salience for Qatar's development (Qatar Foundation, 2014b).

Corporate Research Capacity

Qatar Foundation's Research and Development division supports Qatar Science and Technology Park (QSTP), which aspires to be "a recognized international hub for applied research, innovation, and entrepreneurship" (QSTP, 2015, para. 1). QSTP is a large facility that hosts corporate business operations, technology innovation centers, and some research laboratories designed to attract global corporations to conduct business in Qatar. Because it is a part of Qatar Foundation and situated in Education City, QSTP benefits from EC's status as a kind of free enterprise zone in which the normal rules for incorporation and joint (Qatari) ownership of corporate entities do not apply. Many of the major oil companies in Qatar maintain operations in QSTP – ExxonMobil, Shell, MaerskOil, and ConocoPhillips – as do corporations from other sectors, such as Siemens, Microsoft, GE, and Rolls-Royce.[6] Currently, QSTP's primary function is to attract and host businesses (from start-ups to multi-nationals) in Qatar, with relatively limited research capacity.

Research Funding

The Qatar National Research Fund (QNRF) was established by Qatar Foundation in 2006 as a national funding agency to support research in service of the "interest of Qatar, the region, and the world" and to raise "Qatar's profile in the international research community" (Cuthbertson et al., 2012, p. xiii). It was "the first institution of its kind in the Middle East" (Cuthbertson et al., 2012, p. xiii) – a funding agency designed to create a research hub in the region, attracting global talent to the Gulf and pursuing ambitious goals to diversify an economy solely dependent upon carbon resources, and "to create a research culture in Qatar" (Cuthbertson et al., 2012, p. xv). Between 2006 and 2011, it awarded $500 million in direct grants to research institutions based in Doha and their collaborators around the world (Cuthbertson et al., 2012, p. xiii). In 2012, NPRP awarded $140 million in direct funding to projects (QNRF, 2012); in 2013, $121 million (Qatar National Research Fund, 2013); in 2014, $125 million (Gichuki, 2014); and in 2015, $90 million.[7]

Until 2015, QNRF's flagship program, the National Priorities Research Program, accounted for the majority of this funding and was configured as an open solicitation of projects selected on the basis of an international peer review process (such as the SPHERE project reported on in this volume). The program also aggressively favored projects done in collaboration with research institutions around the world, in part to improve local capacity for science production and in part to attract global attention to Qatar as an international research hub. In 2015, QNRF announced a major shift in its funding programs that substantially diminished the NPRP in favor of solicited competitions focused on specific research topics deemed of top importance for Qatar national development. These "Grand Challenges" were identified through a broadly consultative process with stakeholders in government ministries, universities, and research institutions, known as the Qatar National Research Strategy (Qatar Foundation, 2014a).

While large sums of government money have been pledged to research and development, Qatar has not been able to spend to the limit because of deficits in capacity. Faisal Al-Suwaidi, President of Research and Development at Qatar Foundation and leader of the Qatar National Research Strategy, claimed in 2013 that

> Our current spending is only a fraction of what is available. The reason is that we are still recruiting, we don't have enough manpower yet ... The budget pledged for science research will continue to increase year by year 15-20%, until they hit the 2.8% of GDP target. (Yahia, 2013, paras. 3–4)

Exact budget amounts and allocations are not publicly available. In 2014–2015, as Qatar reduced public funding across the board as a result of a depression in oil prices, the exact impact on research funding is unknown, although widely thought to be substantially negative.

PACE OF GROWTH IN JOURNAL ARTICLE PRODUCTION

With such a high level of investment in research infrastructure and development, Qatar's capacity to conduct scientific research and produce journal articles for the global scientific publication industry greatly improved. Based on the analysis of SCIE data in the SPHERE database, this section analyzes features of this growth in capacity. The first scientific journal article attributed to at least one author who listed a Qatar-based affiliation appeared in 1980. Between 1980 and 2002, well under 50 journal articles per year on average were recorded for Qatar-based authors (Fig. 1). In 2003, the number of articles broke the 50 per year watermark and began a period of steep increase, reaching 366 articles in 2011 (the last year for which we have data). While these figures are tiny in comparison with the world's larger research economies, this

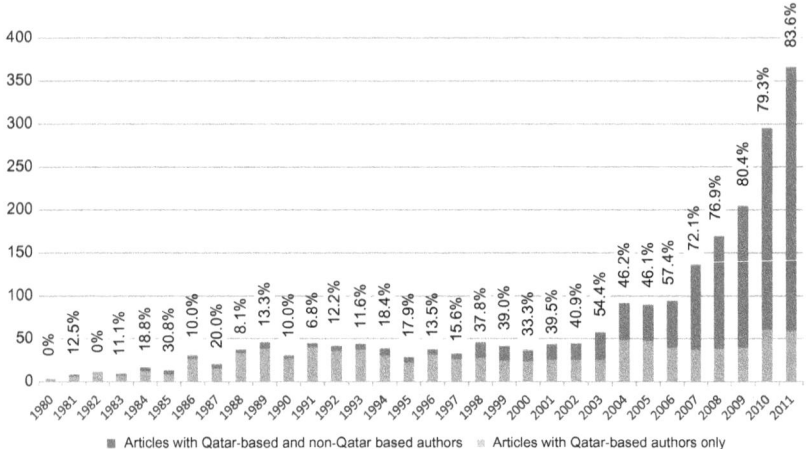

Fig. 1. Comparison of Articles Authored Only by Qatar-Based Institutions versus Those Authored in Collaboration with Non-Qatar Based Institutions, 1980−2011. *Source*: SPHERE project database of SCIE publications (Thomson Reuters' Web of Science).

is nonetheless an especially notable achievement because of the short period of time in which it occurred.

As Fig. 1 demonstrates, virtually all of the growth in published scientific work occurred in partnership with global, non-Qatar based institutions. In fact, scientific productivity exclusively published by Qatar-based research institutions (without international collaboration) remained constant between 1980 and 2011, with only marginal signs of increase in 2010 and 2011 (when the number of articles published in that sector exceeded 50 per year slightly). While the growth of scientific productivity began to accelerate in 2003, the trend toward international collaboration began as early as 1998, when the percentage of articles published in collaboration with non-Qatar-based institutions more than doubled from the previous year, from 15.6% to 37.8%. (This trend began nearly 10 years prior to QNRF's programs to promote international collaboration.) Subsequently, international collaboration accounted for over one-third of scientific productivity until 2003, when it sharply increased until its highest percentage in 2011 (83.6%, more than four-fifths). In comparison, about one-third of all articles in the global database involve international collaboration. Such international collaborations are crucial not only for Qatar, but indeed are part of a larger global trends that evidence massive increases in cross-cultural and cross-border collaboration in the STEM fields (Powell, Fernandez, Crist, Dusdal, Zhang, & Baker, 2017; Zhang, Powell, & Baker, 2015).

Productivity by Research Organization Sector in Qatar

As described in Table 1, there were 71 Qatar-based research organizations to which authors claimed affiliation in the SPHERE dataset of SCIE publications between 1980 and 2011.[8] These included 11 universities, 19 private or corporate entities, 16 government institutions, 11 hospitals or clinics, and 14 other organizations (including independent research institutions, nongovernmental, or international organizations). Together, these organizations appeared as given author affiliations in 2,292 articles.[9]

The productivity of these organizational clusters, however, varies dramatically, as seen in Fig. 2. Not surprisingly, and in keeping with the other case studies in this volume, given that universities in Qatar are home to the largest number of Ph.D. graduates, the university was by far the most productive organizational form, accounting for nearly 60% of author affiliations. Hospitals and clinics, within the medical sector known as a key producer of peer-reviewed research, contributed over 30% of author affiliations. The private corporate sector, by contrast, accounted for only 3.4% of author affiliations in Qatar's scientific journal articles. Fig. 2 depicts the relative performance of each sector over time.

Top Producers

Looking more closely at the organizational level, the four top organizational producers in the SCIE dataset are Qatar University (868), Hamad Medical Corporation (617), Texas A&M University-Qatar (324), and Weil Cornell Medical College-Qatar (131). Of the 2,292 articles in the dataset, Qatar

Table 1. Comparison of STEM Journal Article Productivity across Qatar-Based Research Organizations.

Organizational Form	Number of Organizations	Number of Articles (Including Affiliation from At least One Author)	Productivity Ratio (Column C Divided by Column B)
University	11	1,336 (58.3%)	121.5
Hospital/clinic	19	694 (30.3%)	36.5
Private/corporate	11	77 (3.4%)	7
Government/military	16	64 (2.8%)	4
Other	14	121 (5.3%)	8.6
Total	71	2,292 (100%)	32.3

Source: SPHERE project database of SCIE publications (Thomson Reuters' Web of Science).

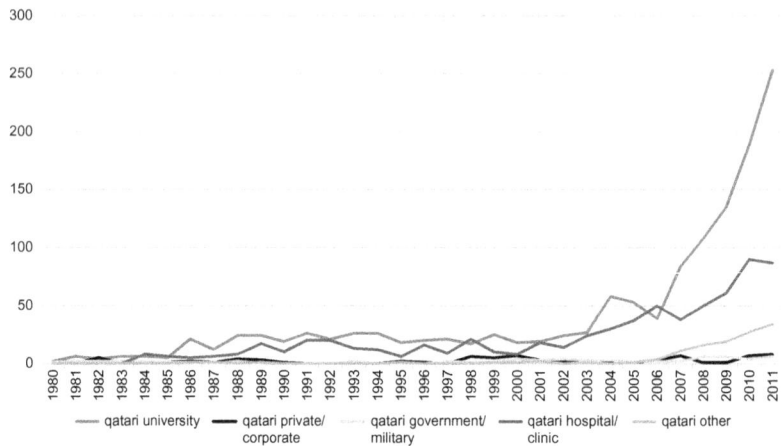

Fig. 2. Number of Publications by Research Organization Type, 1980–2011. *Note*: See the appendix for a description of the coding scheme for research organizations. *Source*: SPHERE project database of SCIE publications (Thomson Reuters' Web of Science).

University was associated with 37.4%, HMC with 26.6%, TAMU-Q with 14%, and WCMC-Q with 5.6%. One must keep in mind that these organizations are not only of varying size, but age, with Qatar University and Hamad Medical Corporation the oldest (founded in 1978 and 1979, respectively) and TAMU-Q and WCMC-Q founded in 2001 and 2002, respectively, as part of Education City. Table 2 also lists the annual rate of productivity from the date of first publication of each organization until 2011.

Because Qatar Foundation and the branch campuses of Education City are considered a single institutional complex, Fig. 3 combines amounts for all QF and EC campuses into one graph line and compares the collective scientific output to the other top producers, such as Qatar University and Hamad Medical Corporation.[10] This allows for a more meaningful comparison of the returns on investment for three major government funded research institutions.

For most years since 1980, Qatar University was the top producer of scientific journal articles, averaging between 20 and 30 per year. Hamad Medical Corporation was a close second. From 2005, the first year that a journal article with an author from an Education City branch campus appears in the dataset, it was only a few years (in 2008) before QF and Education City together surpassed QU and Hamad in the volume of papers published. Among the Education City branch campuses, TAMU-Q was the clear front-runner in the production line, with well over twice the number of publications as the next largest producer (CMU-Q). Without TAMU-Q's productivity, overall journal

Table 2. Top 20 Qatar-Based Organizations Producing STEM Research, 1980–2011.

Organization	Number of Articles	Type of Org.	Year of First Appearance in SCIE	Number of Years	Annual Average
Qatar University	868	University	1980	31	28.0
Hamad Medical Corporation	617	Hospital/Clinic	1983	28	22.0
Texas A&M University-Qatar	324	University	2003	14	40.5
Weill Cornell Medical College, Qatar	131	University	2003	8	16.4
Aspire Academy for Sports Excellence	60	Independent Research Institute	2005	6	10.0
Aspetar Orthopaedic & Sports Medicine Hospital	53	Hospital/Clinic	2008	2	26.5
Qatar Foundation	46	Other	2003	8	5.8
Qatar General Petroleum Corp.	25	Private/Corporate	1982	29	0.9
Ministry of Health, Qatar	22	Government	1980	31	0.7
Carnegie Mellon University-Qatar	20	University	2006	5	4.0
Al Wabra Wildlife Preservation	10	Private/Corporate	2006	5	2.0
Ministry of Energy and Industry, Qatar	9	Government	1988	23	0.4
Shafallah Medical Genetic Center	8	Hospital/Clinic	2008	3	2.7
College of the North Atlantic-Qatar	7	University	2009	2	3.5
Qatar Petroleum	7	Government	1982	29	0.2
Al Ahli Hospital	6	Hospital/Clinic	2009	2	3.0
Gulf Organization for Industrial Consulting	6	Private/Corporate	1982	29	0.2
Industrial Development Technical Center, Qatar	6	Private/Corporate	1985	26	0.2
Ministry of Environment, Qatar	6	Government	2010	1	6.0
Ministry of Municipality and Urban Planning, Qatar	5	Government	1998	13	0.4
Sidra Medical & Research Center	5	Hospital/Clinic	2010	1	5.0

Source: SPHERE project database of SCIE publications (Thomson Reuters' Web of Science).

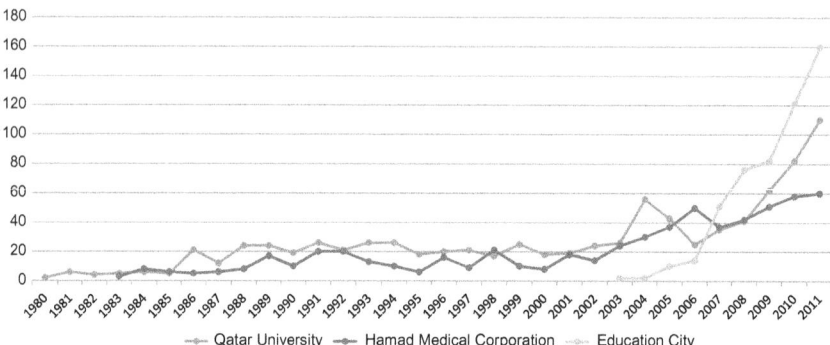

Fig. 3. Comparison of Journal Article Production among Qatar's Top 3 Producers: Qatar University, Hamad Medical Corporation, and Education City, 1980–2011. *Source*: SPHERE project database of SCIE publications (Thomson Reuters' Web of Science).

article production in Education City falls well short of that of either Qatar University or Hamad.[11]

Domestic versus International Collaboration

Science is inherently a collaborative and global activity. Based on the SPHERE project's SCIE data, this section offers an empirical profile of regional variation in the pattern of scientific collaboration in Qatar. Table 3 compares the regional partnerships associated with journal article production in Qatar. Europe accounts for the largest number of collaborations with Qatar research organizations, followed closely by North America, and only then the Middle East. Research collaborations in Qatar much less frequently rely on resources and partners in East Asia (including Southeast Asia), Africa, and India in particular, despite the considerable labor migration to Qatar from those countries. The amount of internal collaboration in Qatar is substantially higher than for each of these regions. Nevertheless, relatively few connections exist between Qatar University and the researchers in Education City, despite the fact that all campuses are located in Doha, the country's major city.

While the Middle East ranks third on the list of regions with which Qatar-based organizations collaborate, Middle Eastern universities are the most common institutional home for collaborative partners. Six out of the top ten most frequent non-Qatar based institutions identified in the dataset are Middle Eastern universities: Aim Shams University and Cairo University in Egypt,

Table 3. Regional Distribution of Global Collaborators with Qatar-Based STEM Authors, 1980–2011.

Region	Instances of Collaboration (%)
Europe	486 (28.5%)
North America	433 (25.4%)
Middle East	375 (22%)
East Asia	141 (8.3%)
Africa	81 (4.7%)
Oceania	69 (4%)
South Asia	56 (3.3%)
Southeast Asia	40 (2.3%)
South America	15 (.88%)
Central Asia	9 (.53%)
Total	1,705

Source: SPHERE project database of SCIE publications (Thomson Reuters' Web of Science).

Kuwait University, the United Arab Emirates University, and Sheikh Khalifa Medical City in the UAE, and Jordan University of Science & Technology. One American university (Texas A&M) and one British university (University of Manchester) top the list as the first and second most frequent collaborating organizations in the SPHERE dataset.

Summary of Findings and Future Dilemmas

The most important observations about journal article production in Qatar to be gleaned from the study carried out using the SPHERE dataset are as follows: (1) After a long period (1980–2002) of comparatively low production (well under 50 articles per year), Qatar scientists began to increase their rate of production dramatically between 2003 and 2011, on the order of a sevenfold increase in the annual amount of journal articles published. (2) For seven out of the nine years between 2003 and 2011, articles involving collaboration with non-Qatar based research scientists accounted for over half the total number of journal articles published, with upwards of 75% or more since 2008. (3) Scientists at Qatar-based universities account for nearly 60% of journal articles produced since 1980, and research hospitals or medical research centers account for 30%. Scientists based in corporations or the government were not significant contributors to overall journal article publications in Qatar. Between 2006 and 2011, university research increased significantly more rapidly than that of other sectors. (4) The total number of journal articles produced by each of the top three producing institutions (Education City, Qatar University, and Hamad Medical Corporation) rapidly accelerated from 2002. From 2008, scientists affiliated with Education City universities published the most journal articles annually. (5) Among those articles that resulted from international collaborations with Qatar-based scientists, those that involved collaborations with European researchers accounted for 28.5%, with North American researchers 25.4%, and with researchers based at organizations in the Middle East 22%. Except for collaborations with East Asian research organizations (8.3%), collaborations with other regions in the world contributed negligible amounts to overall journal article production.

Perhaps the most impactful reasons for Qatar's demonstrated success in boosting journal article production by local organizations are its sustained commitment of substantial resources to higher education (at least as early as 1995) and its direct funding to research activities (at least as early as 2007). These efforts also made Qatar an attractive destination for research-active scientists to conduct their work while maintaining their association with regional and global laboratories and home campuses. While plentiful resources were key in making such a strategy possible, a high level of political will or vision on the part of the cosmopolitan leadership of Qatar also fueled this growth.

Sustaining such commitment, however, is neither easy nor certain. This chapter's title captures but one part of Sheikha Moza's 2010 observation about research in Qatar. Her full statement was "There's a fever of research in Qatar, but I worry about fevers because fevers burn out" (Qatar Foundation, 2010b, p. 28). As this volume goes to press, there is more than a little prescience in this comment. With the global decline in oil prices from June 2014, the Gulf countries, including Qatar, have been forced to re-evaluate their profit forecasts and adjust domestic spending accordingly. In Qatar, this led to deep and widespread budget cuts across virtually all sectors of society (as the government subsidizes and controls, directly or indirectly, virtually the entirety of Qatar's economy). Accordingly, Qatar Foundation, Qatar National Research Strategy, Hamad Bin Khalifa University, Qatar National Research Fund, Qatar University, and each of the international branch campuses in Education City — all key contributors to research production in Qatar — suddenly faced substantial budget cuts thought to be between 20% and 45%. This resulted in the departure of a large number of high-level research administrators who had been recruited from top organizations around the world to lead the research development efforts. The eventual impact on scholarly journal article production is uncertain at this point, but with reductions in the number of researchers and the amount of funding for research, the delayed construction of new laboratories and or deferred upkeep of existing laboratories, it is hard to imagine that Qatar can sustain the high rate of growth in journal article production analyzed here for 2003−2011 into the future.

Coupled with the shifting economic situation was a transition in leadership of the country in 2013, when the Father Emir, Sheikh Hamad Bin Khalifa, handed over the reins of power to his 33-year-old son, Sheikh Tamim Bin Hamad Al Thani. With this change in power came a shift in priorities. As many have observed, the new Emir has focused his attention more fully on domestic issues and development, in contrast to the more outward looking, global agenda of his father's regime and his mother's leadership of Qatar Foundation. Even aside from the budget cuts, that shift in part accounts for the devotion of resources toward more popular nationalist projects, such as Qatar's planned hosting of the 2022 World Cup games, and to more thorough vetting of global partnerships to promote socially valuable outcomes on local development. How long global oil prices remain low is anyone's guess, but there is certainly no expectation of a rise in the near future.

NOTES

1. Actual expenditures are not available to the public.
2. At the time of writing, the student population of all universities in Education City was about 2,000. The student population of Qatar University in Spring 2014 was 14,000 (Qatar University, 2015).
3. From conversations with research directors at several campuses in Education City, October 2015.
4. "Active researchers" were defined as the number of authors who published in a scientific peer-reviewed journal included in Elsevier's collection of journal publications between 1996 and 2011 and were formally affiliated with a research organization based in Qatar.
5. The other countries included in the study were China, Brazil, India, the United States, the United Kingdom, and South Africa.
6. As of October l0, 2015, QSTP's website listed 34 corporations, mostly multinationals, as members.
7. Personal conversation with member of QNRF professional staff, May 2015.
8. This analysis is based on a subset of the SPHERE dataset that includes citation information for all peer-reviewed journal articles in the STEM disciplines with at least one author whose primary affiliation was a Qatar-based research organization. The source of the data is Thomson Reuters' Science Citation Index Expanded (SCIE).
9. This figure includes authors with multiple publications and authors from the same institution collaborating on the same article.
10. The column for Education City combines publications in the SPHERE dataset from TAMU-Q (324), WCMC-Q (131), CMU-Q (20), UCL-Q (3), NU-Q (1), VCU-Q (1), and Qatar Foundation (46). It should be noted that other branch campuses focus on other disciplines than those represented in the SCIE, such as Georgetown University School of Foreign Service at Qatar in the social sciences.
11. These figures do not account for variations in amount of research budget, facilities, or Ph.D. scientists on staff among any of the organizations considered.

ACKNOWLEDGMENTS

The research reported in this chapter was made possible by NPRP grant #5-1021-5-159 from the Qatar National Research Fund (a member of Qatar

Foundation). The findings reported here are solely the responsibility of the author. I am grateful for the expert assistance of Seungwan Nam, who prepared, checked, and cleaned the data for the figures and tables.

REFERENCES

collegestats.org. (2015). Top ten oldest universities in the world: Ancient colleges. Retrieved from http://collegestats.org/2009/12/top-10-oldest-universities-in-the-world-ancient-colleges. Accessed on September 1, 2015.

Crist, J. T. (2015). Innovation in a small state: Qatar and the IBC cluster model of higher education. *The Muslim World*, 105(1), 93–115.

Cuthbertson, S., Mattock, M. G., Nardulli, B. R., Al-Kuwari, A., Cecchine, G., Harrell, M. C., … Darilek, R. E. (2012). *Launching the Qatar National Research Fund*. Doha: RAND-Qatar Policy Institute.

Dill, D. D., & Van Vught, F. A. (Eds.). (2010). *National innovation and the academic research enterprise: Public policy in global perspective*. Baltimore, MD: The Johns Hopkins University Press.

Gichuki, C. W. (2014). QNRF awards grants to 162 proposals at 6th annual forum. *Qatar Tribune*, May 15. Retrieved from http://www.qatar-tribune.com/viewnews.aspx?n=430933C0-D1E1-4D86-84C8-ECB1E253DCD4&d=20140515. Accessed on October 20, 2015.

Kamrava, M. (2014). *Qatar: Small country, big politics*. Ithaca, NY: Cornell University Press.

Khatri, S. (2013). Qatar students rank near bottom of education index again, but gains made. *DohaNews*, December 6. Retrieved from http://dohanews.co/qatar-students-rank-near-bottom-of-education-index-again-but-gains-made/

Moini, J. S., Bikson, T. K., Neu, C. R., & DeSisto, L. (2009). *The reform of Qatar University*. Santa Monica, CA: The RAND Corporation.

National Science Foundation. (2014). International comparisons of R&D performance. In Chapter 4: National trends and international comparisons. *Science and Engineering Indicators 2014*. Arlington, VA: National Science Foundation. Retrieved from http://www.nsf.gov/statistics/seind14/index.cfm/chapter-4/c4s2.htm. Accessed on February 2, 2015.

Organization for Economic and Cooperative Development. (2014, February). PISA 2012 results: What students know and can do: Student performance in mathematics, reading, and science (Volume I, revised edition). Retrieved from https://www.oecd.org/pisa/keyfindings/pisa-2012-results-volume-i.htm

Powell, J. J. W. (2014a). University roots and branches between 'glocalization' and 'mondialisation': Qatar's (inter)national universities. *International Perspectives on Education and Society*, 24, 253–276.

Powell, J. J. W. (2014b). International national universities: Migration and mobility in Luxembourg and Qatar. In B. Streitwieser (Ed.), *Internationalisation of higher education and global mobility* (pp. 119–134). Oxford: Symposium Books.

Powell, J. J. W., & Dusdal, J. (2017). The European Center of science productivity: research universities and institutes in France, Germany, and the United Kingdom. In J. J. W. Powell, D. P. Baker, & F. Fernandez (Eds.), *The century of science: The worldwide triumph of the research university* (Vol. 33). International Perspectives on Education and Society. Bingley: Emerald Publishing Limited.

Powell, J. J. W., Fernandez, F., Crist, J. T., Dusdal, J., Zhang, L., & Baker, D. P. (2017). Introduction: The worldwide triumph of the research university and globalizing science. In J. J. W. Powell, D. P. Baker, & F. Fernandez (Eds.), *The century of science: The worldwide triumph of the research university* (Vol. 33). International Perspectives on Education and Society. Bingley: Emerald Publishing Limited.

Qatar Biomedical Research Institute. (2015). New research building. Retrieved from http://www.qbri.org.qa/facilities/new-research-building. Accessed on September 7, 2015.
Qatar Foundation. (2010a). History in the making. *Qatar Foundation Magazine*, May.
Qatar Foundation. (2010b). How Qatar is battling disease. *Qatar Foundation Magazine*, November.
Qatar Foundation. (2014a). Qatar national research strategy 2014. Retrieved from http://www.qfrd.org/Portals/2/QFQNRS2014ForumReport1.pdf. Accessed on July 4, 2017.
Qatar Foundation. (2014b). New program to give graduates first-class research opportunities. *Qatar Foundation Telegraph*, July 24, p. 116.
Qatar Foundation. (2016). About Qatar Foundation. Retrieved from https://www.qf.org.qa/about/about. Accessed on May 3, 2016.
Qatar National Research Fund. (2012). Qatar national research fund to award $140.5 million to new research projects. Retrieved from http://www.qnrf.org/en-us/Newsroom/ArtMID/672/ArticleID/300/Qatar-National-Research-Fund-to-award-1405-million-to-new-research-projects. Accessed on October 20, 2015.
Qatar National Research Fund. (2013). QNRF awards $121 million in research funding to national priority projects. *QNRF Newsletter*, August, p. 12. Retrieved from http://qnrfnewsletter.org/issue12/news3.php. Accessed on October 5, 2015.
Qatar Science and Technology Park. (2015). Vision and mission. Retrieved from http://www.qstp.org.qa/home/about-us/vision-mission. Accessed on October 5, 2015.
Qatar Statistics Authority. (2011). *Qatar in Figures*, December, p. 25. Doha: Qatar Statistics Authority.
Qatar University. (2015). Our students. Retrieved from http://www.qu.edu.qa/theuniversity/students.php. Accessed on September 7, 2015.
The Peninsula. (2010, October 29). Qatari and British research experts share experience. Retrieved from http://www.thepeninsulaqatar.com/news/qatar/130733/qatari-and-british-research-experts-share-experience. Accessed on September 15, 2015.
The Royal Society. (2010). *A new golden age? The prospects for science and innovation in the Islamic world*. Retrieved from https://royalsociety.org/~/media/Royal_Society_Content/policy/publications/2010/4294971224.pdf. Accessed on October 21, 2015.
The Royal Society. (2011). The Atlas of Islamic-World science & innovation. Retrieved from https://royalsociety.org/topics-policy/projects/atlas-islamic-world/. Accessed on January 15, 2014.
Van Servellen, A., & Baas, J. (2013). *Output growth and impact of Qatar University's scientific research*. Amsterdam: Elsevier.
Witte, S. (2010). *Inside Education City: The persistent demographic and gender imbalance in Qatar*. London: The Observatory on Borderless Higher Education.
World Bank. (2015). Research and development expenditure (% of GDP). Retrieved from http://data.worldbank.org/indicator/GB.XPD.RSDV.GD.ZS. Accessed on February 2, 2015.
Yahia, M. (2013, November 28). Qatar's peculiar research funding dilemma. Retrieved from http://blogs.nature.com/houseofwisdom/2013/11/qatars-peculiar-research-funding-dilemma.html. Accessed on October 20, 2015.
Zhang, L., Powell, J. J. W., & Baker, D. P. (2015). Exponential growth and the shifting global center of gravity of science production, 1900-2011. *Change: The Magazine of Higher Learning*, 47(4), 46–49.

APPENDIX: CODING SCHEME FOR RESEARCH ORGANIZATIONS

The code for organizational affiliation of author included the following categories: (1) university; (2) private, corporate sector; (3) government/military; (4) medical, not elsewhere classified; (5) other, not elsewhere classified; and (6) independent research institutes, not elsewhere classified (i.e., non-corporate, non-government, non-university). The general categories are self-explanatory, however, there are a few important decisions rules to keep in mind when interpreting results. The code for university included a variety of higher education institutions, including colleges, graduate universities, post-secondary technical training institutions, international branch campuses, and so forth. Institutions of higher education for the military were coded as "government/military." University hospitals were coded as "university."

In category 2, multinational corporations were coded separately by country in which the research sponsor was based. Corporate medical research institutions (such as pharmaceutical companies) were coded in this category and not in "hospital/clinic/medical research institute." The code for "medical, n.e.c." included all hospitals, medical clinics, and medical research institutions not sponsored by a university, multi-national corporation, or government body. Departments of Public Health in U.S. states and military hospitals, for example, were coded as "government/military."

The "other" category included international organizations (such as the United Nations, World Health Organization, World Bank, and global nongovernmental organizations) were also coded in this category. Qatar Foundation was included in this category because it is a hybrid organization, not fully government, corporate, or independent, but with characteristics of each of these domains. Category six was reserved for independent research institutes not elsewhere classified, that is, not sponsored by a university, corporation, government, or hospital (these were, almost entirely, organizations not based in Qatar).

Finally, among Gulf-based institutions, the high level of government support for institutions and organizations in everyday life complicated the coding. Many organizations fully funded by government in a monarchy function similarly to their counterparts in settings that are not monarchies. Effort was made to compensate for the disparity in context. For example, Hamad Medical Corporation in Qatar or King Faisal Specialist Hospital and Research Centre in Saudi Arabia – both fully funded by the government – were coded as medical institutions because that more accurately reflects the function and role of these organizations.

STEM+ PRODUCTIVITY, DEVELOPMENT, AND WEALTH, 1900−2012

Iris A. Mihai and Robert D. Reisz

ABSTRACT

Purpose − *The authors seek to better understand the relationships between science production, national wealth, inequality, and human development around the globe.*

Design − *The chapter uses econometric models, including Granger causality, to test alternate hypotheses about whether more economic wealth is related to more science or if more science leads to more wealth.*

Findings − *The immediate result of our models is that a country's wealth contributes to the conditions necessary for productive science. While large countries produce many research articles in the STEM+ fields more or less irrespective of their per capita GDP, with countries like the Soviet Union, China, or India being important contributors to world science, the most productive countries were the richer ones. GDP per capita values are important predictors for higher numbers of STEM+ research articles adjusted for population size. Nevertheless, human development and income equality also have a positive relationship with science productivity. While the effect of income equality is less strong, it has importantly and steadily increased over the last 50 years.*

Originality/Value — *This chapter is among the first to show that countries with similar levels of human development that are more equal in income distribution are more productive in science, while countries of similar wealth that are more equal in income distribution are not necessarily more productive in science.*

Keywords: Science; productivity; inequality; wealth; distribution

INTRODUCTION

Let us start with a simple observation: There must be some relationship between economic wealth and science production. Science has its costs, especially the hard sciences, medical research, and technology. Policymakers as well as scientists will also hope to find that in some way or another the production of science will increase our wealth. The cross-section time series data available to us now provide us with an opportunity: to test the nature of these relationships. We use econometric models to find out whether we may truly consider that more economic wealth is related to more science, be it that it is instrumental in creating more science or if more science leads to more wealth.

A truism, mentioned before by many, is that while large countries like the United States or China obviously contribute most to overall global scientific production in absolute terms, the most productive countries are a few smaller ones, such as Switzerland, Israel, Denmark, Finland, Norway, and Sweden. Why is this so? What makes these small countries so productive? What lessons could be learned here? Another goal of this chapter is to find correlates and hints on possible explanations for the vastly increased productivity in the hard sciences over the past century; especially the past several decades. As in the other chapters in this volume, our focus is on papers published in the hard sciences, a group of disciplines referred to as STEM+ (Science, Technology, Engineering, and Medicine).[1]

So, what determines scientific productivity? The level of investment in science and education is an obvious explanation. The most productive countries in the world of STEM+ are indeed the countries with high values of per capita GDP and high levels of investment in education and science. While this is relatively straightforward, we consider that the more important question to ask is whether they are distinguished by other factors as well. In this chapter, we investigate first and foremost the relationships between social inequality, human development, and scientific productivity. The hypothesis of a relationship emerged simply from comparing the list of countries with a high scientific production to those with high social equality. The hypothesis can be formulated as follows: *There is a positive relationship between scientific productivity and social equality.*

The social mechanisms behind such a relationship are complex and we do not wish to infer any direct causality, regardless of direction, here. Instead, let us try to offer a few possible mechanisms. There are two important additional factors that come to mind for a theoretical relationship between science and inequality. These are, on the one hand, the level of industrial productivity, and on the other hand, the overall development of the education system and of inclusion in education. One potential form of a theoretical chain of concepts might look as follows:

Science productivity ↔ Industrial productivity ↔ Economic wealth ↔ Social equality (1)

The hard sciences and especially the applied ones, technology, engineering, and medicine, are closely connected to industry. High levels of industrial productivity will be then possible where scientific results are widely applied in these industries, be they mechanical or pharmaceutical, or any other industrial area. The countries with high industrial productivity or the countries that produce cutting-edge technology are indeed among the economically wealthiest countries. Economically wealthy countries tend to have high income levels that could not be maintained without high levels of productivity. The last link in this chain might seem weaker; nevertheless, our empirical data prove a significant connection between per capita GDP and equality. For theoretical models, refer to Romer (1986), Lucas (1988), Grossman and Helpman (1991), Mankiw, Romer, and Weil (1992), Barro and Sala-i-Martin (1995), and Rangazas (2005), among others. The second hypothetical chain of concepts might look as follows:

Science productivity ↔ Education ↔ Human development ↔ Social equality (2)

In this second chain of concepts, all links are well-supported theoretically as well as by empirical findings. The Human Development Index correlates strongly with the STEM+ productivity index for the whole period for which data was available. In order to test the relationship between science productivity and social equality, we have used the Gini index of inequality, which correlates with the productivity index negatively, implying that the less inequality there is in a country, the more scientifically productive that country is. High levels of scientific productivity have to be maintained with high levels of educational inclusion and attainment and especially high levels of inclusion in higher education, one of the major producers of science and the main producer of scientists, wherever they choose to work. Education is one of the key elements of human development, and an important determinant for the other components of the concept, such as life expectancy and wealth. Finally, the last connection in this chain is the empirically well-supported relationship between human development and social equality.

Bearing in mind these considerations, we propose the following two hypothetical explanations:

> **H1.** The relationship between science productivity and inequality is determined by economic development.
>
> **H2.** The relationship between science productivity and inequality is determined by human development,[2] and especially education.

These are the two hypotheses around which the paper is built. After a short literature review, we will continue with a descriptive presentation of STEM+ development in the world, from 1900 to 2012. We will compare the top 10 countries in STEM+ production as absolute values and productivity as per capita values. Further on, we will use econometric modeling and Granger causality to test the relationship between these values and measures of inequality and human development.

LITERATURE REVIEW

Though the importance of the field has risen during the past few years, scientific productivity is still a field that we know little about. There are authors like Ben-David (1960) or Cole and Meyer (1985) who analyzed scientific productivity within an institution, others who managed to accomplish country-level analyses like de Solla Price (1963), Allison (1980), Fox (1985), Creswell (1985), Harris (1989), and Harris and Kaine (1994), yet only a few embarked on the mission to realize a cross-country study, as did Levy (1996), Gottlieb and Keith (1997), May (1997), and Cole and Phelan (1999). This is due largely to the lack of data or important differences between the various academic or political systems.

The importance of scientific productivity as a field has grown largely due to psychologists trying to analyze either creativity or motivation (Eiduson, 1962) or the organizational characteristics that maximize productivity (Pelz & Andrews, 1966; Taylor & Barron, 1963). The research carried out in this field has increased our capacity to understand how intelligence, motivation, perception, commitment to goals, and other personal traits influence productivity.

As far as individual productivity of scientists is concerned, there are basically two paradigms that provide explanations for the differences between capacity and results obtained: *The sacred spark* and *the cumulative advantage* (regarded also as *accumulation of advantage and disadvantage for scientists* or what Robert Merton (1968) called "*the Matthew Effect in science*").

The *sacred spark hypothesis* (Cole & Cole, 1973) argues that there are predetermined, substantial differences among scientists in regard to their ability, will power, and motivation for creative scientific research (Allison & Stewart, 1974). There is no doubt that people are different, have different abilities, motivations, and potential, but if we consider the scientific community as a whole, one would expect that these differences should be less pronounced, since scientists are a relatively small, rigorously selected elite who have undergone long and consistent socialization. The question that emerges is whether the unequal distribution of scientific ability is capable of explaining the unequal distribution of scientific productivity.

In 1957, Shockley proposed a mathematical model meant to shed light upon *the sacred spark* question. He argues that scientific productivity is the result of the interaction between several mental factors, such as the ability to find important problems, technical ability, and persistence (Shockley, 1957). It is important to mention that he designed the model such that the factors determine productivity multiplicatively and not additively. This accounts both for the "highly skewed distribution of productivity in science and the low correlation of productivity with any one of its determinants" (Allison & Stewart, 1974, p. 596).

The second important aspect regarding the productivity of science lies in *the accumulation of advantage and disadvantage for scientists* (Merton, 1942, 1968). This leads to social stratification in science that is basically explained by "the accumulation of differential advantages for certain segments of the population, differentials that are not necessarily bound up with demonstrated differences in capacity, in other words, the rich get richer at a rate that makes the poor become relatively poorer" (Merton, 1968, pp. 56–63). The cumulative advantage provides tools to help explain why for the rich in recognition it is much easier to find the resources that facilitate research: laboratories, grants, capable students, free time, stimulating colleagues, etc. (Allison, Long, & Krauze, 1982).

Using the cumulative advantage theory as a starting point, other authors have tried to identify whether a scientist, whose initial work gained great recognition, had better chances of becoming more productive than a fellow colleague whose first works did not receive such recognition. Cole and Cole (1967, 1973) and Lightfield (1971) confirm this hypothesis; however, Long's (1977) findings contest the effect of early recognition upon future productivity. A study by Reskin (1977) found that the difference lies in the status of the author, respectively, whether she/he is an academic scientist or a nonacademic scientist; she concludes that the early recognition has a strong impact upon the later productivity of the nonacademic scientist, while for the academic scientist, the effect is negligible.

In order to better understand the emerging inequalities in scientific productivity, the individual factors need to be addressed in relation to the context described by exogenous factors. Scientific productivity might be encouraged by the values and conditions of the organization hosting the research and by the values and conditions of the society as a whole, exemplified in policy initiatives. On the other hand, productivity may be reduced among scientists working in contexts which are not oriented toward obtaining results relevant in the field of scientific knowledge. The scientists who choose to publish in such cases may choose to do so in reaction to the existing larger scientific community mechanisms (Reskin, 1977). This means shifting the level of recognition from local to global, reinforcing the appurtenance to the global scientific community.

One of the most cited studies, which analyzes scientific productivity across nations, was conducted by Andrews (1979). He used data for six European countries, namely Sweden, Poland, Hungary, Finland, Belgium, and Austria, in his attempt to identify the main groups of factors that affect the productivity of diverse research units. He tries to explain the differences in productivity within the analyzed countries in accordance with the organizational, environmental, social, and economic factors that impact the performance of the research units.

There are great quantitative and qualitative inequalities among the world countries concerning their production of science and/or knowledge. In order to explain these inequalities, several theories of scientific progress have emerged: de Solla Price's theory concerning the relationship between the number of scientists and the rate of advance (1963), Merton's cultural theory (1970), and Ben-David's structural theory of scientific advance (1984).

de Solla Price proposed a theory based on the relationship between the rate of advance and the number of scientists, but he did not see it as a linear proportional one. He considered that the increasing number of scientists will result in a decline of the average ability to produce valuable results. According to his deduction, in order to multiply the number of prolific scientists by five, one needs to multiply the whole pool of scientists by 25. As far as the scientific capacity of a nation is concerned, he argues that it is determined almost completely by the gross national product. Cole and Phelan (1999) support this argument, explaining that wealthy countries pay scientists well and so can attract a greater number of talented people to take up scientific careers.

Merton's *cultural theory* states that a society's propensity toward science relies on the values that it associates with science, which will produce a smaller or larger number of scientists. Protestant societies, for instance, will tend to have a higher share of individuals seeking careers in science, because they consider scientific activity as being one of great value.

Ben-David's *structural theory of scientific advance* correlates the number of the potential scientists with the prospects of jobs in research. He considers that there is a linear proportional relationship between the rate of advance and the number of scientists.

In a paper published in 1980, Allison starts with a very bold conclusion: "No matter how it is measured, there is enormous inequality in scientists' research productivity" (Allison, 1980, pp. 163–179). His study, focused on disciplinary differences in the scale of productivity, emphasizes the importance of the positioning of the scientist, respectively, whether one is concerned with relative differences or with absolute differences among individuals, thus impacting the inequality measures that are chosen for the research.

May (1997) has noted important differences in productivity across countries, differences resulting from varying systems of measurement. He compared scientific productivity with the performance in the Olympic Games and debates on whether the performance should be taken as it is, or should be adjusted by the size of population, percentage of GDP spent on R&D, or the size of the economy. He finds that when analyzing scientific productivity of a country by the number of papers it publishes, or by the citations it obtains, the bigger countries, especially those belonging to G7, have the greatest results, while when analyzing scientific productivity as number of published papers or obtained citations, adjusted by the size of population or the money invested in research, instead the smaller countries dominate the world hierarchy, especially the Northern European countries and Israel. He closes his argumentation by noticing that some of the differences can be explained by the institutional settings in which the scientific research is conducted, more explicitly, arguing that universities provide a much more prolific climate for research than do research centers or institutes.

Cole and Phelan (1999) consider that there are three aspects of scientific knowledge that are generally considered important: the actual cognitive content, the foci of scientific attention or how social variables influence which problems scientists decide to investigate, and the rate of scientific advance or how social, cultural, and economic variables influence the amount of knowledge produced. They conclude that, at the end of the 20th century, the amount of research as a whole produced by a nation is influenced fundamentally by its wealth. They consider wealth a facilitator that provides talented individuals with opportunities to enter scientific careers. They find also that when controlling for population size, the production of science presents a very different perspective. Furthermore, they find that among the more developed countries, the differences in national wealth cannot explain completely the differences in scientific productivity. Another aspect highlighted by the two authors is that the countries that spend less to support research tend to produce a form of low-cost research in contrast to those who spend more money.

Teodorescu (2000) places the focus of scientific productivity in universities. In his study, comprising a 10-country sample, he identifies the similarities and differences in the patterns of publication productivity across the examined nations. He affirms that comparing the results across the countries in the sample provide insights into the factors that are relevant in shaping the scientific productivity of one nation and whether they are also relevant in shaping the productivity of the other countries. The author reaches the conclusion that a common model of publication productivity should not be assumed or implemented in different national contexts because many variables are context-specific. He highlights the importance of a cosmopolitan orientation in obtaining scientific performance, insisting on that researchers should stay connected to their respective disciplines via conferences, annual meetings, or professional associations. Faculty affiliation to prestigious international organizations can also add to the prestige and recognition of the researchers – both leading to increased productivity. He concludes that scientific productivity is influenced considerably by the national academic systems; individual achievement and ascriptive factors (age and gender) having only marginal influences. The results obtained by Teodorescu regarding age and gender as factors with potential impact upon scientific productivity are consistent with previous findings published by Clemente (1973), Allison and Stewart (1974), Bayer and Dutton (1977), Blackburn, Behymer, and Hall (1978), Cameron and Blackburn (1981), Over (1982), and Bailey (1992).

Even if the national contribution to the overall bulk of science is of uncontested importance, it is also useful to correlate the output and outcomes with the GDP, human development index (HDI), Gini index of inequality, and other relevant factors. In one of the few texts that analyzes these connections, King (2004) compares "wealth intensity" as GDP per person, with "citation intensity" as citation per unit of GDP. His analysis was carried out for the 1993–2002 time span on a group of 31 countries, including the G8 and EU15, but not limited to them. King uses, as we do, Thomson Reuters' data to find "what different countries get for their research spending," as his paper subtitle indicates. His findings show that the smaller nations that were included in the study – the Scandinavian countries, Israel, the Netherlands, and Switzerland – have very good results in citation intensity. Though his analysis includes only 31 countries out of the existing 193, it is of considerable relevance due to the fact that these are the countries that produce 97.5% of the world's most cited papers. In more in-depth analysis of the relationship between economic wealth and scientific productivity, King concentrates on the G8 countries. The subject of our research will be similar to this, but on a much longer time period and a larger number of countries, made possible by the SPHERE project database that enables a more in-depth analysis on general relationships and causality.

There are important differences between production and productivity in science, though many authors fail to distinguish these two concepts. In our view, productivity represents a ratio of outputs and the inputs needed in order to produce those outputs. The inputs can be either quantifiable such as money, infrastructure, number of scientists, time or unquantifiable such as the quality of work, cultural background, perception, state of mind. In this study, we focus our attention on the quantifiable inputs and outputs in order to build our model, but bearing in mind the unquantifiable elements when interpreting the results.

SCIENCE PRODUCTION ACROSS THE WORLD: A DESCRIPTIVE PRESENTATION

We have computed the number of papers from the Thomson Reuters' database for science, technology, engineering, medicine, and health sciences (STEM+) published by authors from all countries between 1900 and 2011.[3] The figure of the overall development of the number of papers published each year in STEM+ was introduced in the first chapter of this book. The development is highly impressive, with the overall scientific output in STEM+ having increased exponentially during the 20th century. The number of countries contributing to this development — at least those countries represented in the TR database — has also increased steadily, as the following representation manifests (Fig. 1).

According to our data, in 1900 only 26 countries were producing research papers submitted for peer review among the select journals represented in the database. In 1905, the number was 34 and it remained around that value for most of the century. As recently as 1965, only 41 countries were producing

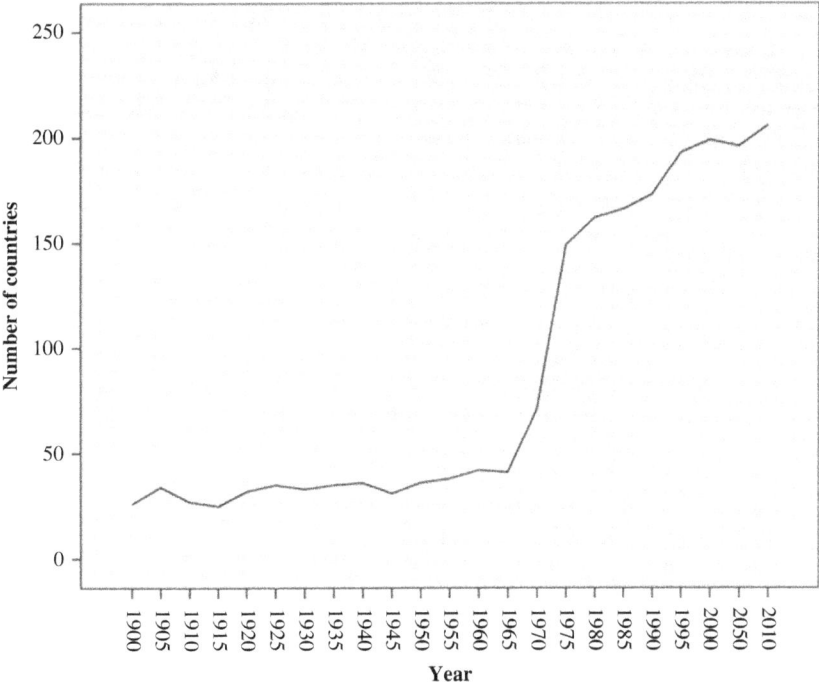

Fig. 1. The Overall Development of the Number of Countries Publishing STEM+ Research Articles. *Source*: SPHERE project database of SCIE publications (Thomson Reuters' Web of Science).

STEM+ papers. Science was a domain of the developed, rich countries. The pace of globalization was just starting to accelerate. The explosive development that made science a truly world-wide endeavor began in the 1970s. The number of countries involved in science production went from 71 in 1970 to 149 in 1975 and continued to increase for the following decades. The numbers were 162 countries in 1980, 173 in 1990, 199 in 2000, and 206 in 2010. The average number of papers produced by a country has also increased since 1900: from 416 to 1,189 in 1950, 3,779 in 2000, and 6,262 in 2010. These numbers are nevertheless misleading, as the standard deviation for the number of publications was very high and has also increased over the years. Examining the percentage of countries that participate in scientific production tells the story more accurately. While the average share of scientific production has decreased slowly, the standard deviation of the percentage shows an important decrease over the last four decades. This means that countries have gained increasingly equal shares in world science production.

If in 1900 the first 10 countries in the world published 87% of all papers, in 1950 it was 91%, in 2000, 67%, and in 2010 only 63%. So, while the increase in the number of countries and average production might not seem so important, the share of production that smaller contributors make to world science has grown considerably. The number of countries producing more than 0.1% of STEM+ papers in the world has increased from 18 in 1900, to 24 in 1950, and later to 38 in 1980, to 45 in 1990, 51 in 2000, and 55 in 2010 (Fig. 2). Adding up these results, we find that the huge increase in the number of countries involved in the production of science has occurred at the low end of the spectrum. While the number of countries producing at least 0.1% of the overall output has also increased, this was far less than the important increase in the overall numbers.

Table 1 includes the top-10 scientific producers for each selected year with their respective share of the world scientific production. There are a few remarkable issues necessary to highlight. The first one regards the United States, which is the most productive country in science of all the selected countries for the period 1900–2010. The United States has the highest share of the global scientific production for each year, except during the beginning of the period, with Germany being the most productive country in 1900. Furthermore, in 1960 the United States generated more than half of the global production of science, representing a share of 55%. Since the beginning of the analyzed period until the burst of the World War II, the United States shared the top of the ranking with Germany, which was second to the United States from 1910 to 1940; however, its share of global scientific production decreased, during the period 1950–2000, achieving the status of being either the fourth or the fifth largest science producer, whereas in 2010 it managed to occupy the third position, after the United States and China. Another major scientific producer is the United Kingdom, which occupies the third position for eight out of the 12 selected years, the second and fourth position for the remaining four

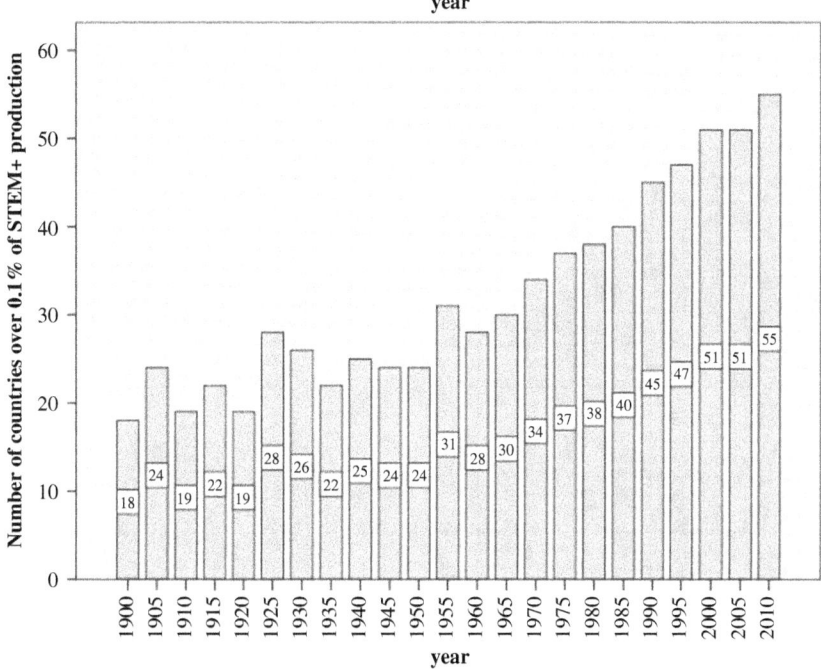

Fig. 2. The Overall Number of Countries Worldwide Publishing STEM+ Research Articles. *Source*: SPHERE project database of SCIE publications (Thomson Reuters' Web of Science).

years, two years for each. Overall, there are 22 countries that form the hierarchy during the analyzed period, interchanging the ranking among each other. As far as the distribution of the shares of scientific production between the major producers is concerned, 1960 is the year with the highest concentration on the top: the first three world science producers (United States, Japan, and United Kingdom) generating more than 80% of the overall production of science, while every other national producer generating less than 2%.

The top group of countries does not change much over the years in its composition: the same big players in science: the United States, Canada, and Australia; a number of European countries; and Japan, China and India, yet there are some important dynamics. If the century starts with the supremacy of German science, this is lost to the United States. What follows parallels political developments in the world, determined first by the competition between Germany and the United States, later including the rise and fall of the USSR, and, over the most recent decades, the rise of China. Reading the numbers is also highly instructive. The century begins with four superpowers in science, namely Germany, the United States, France, and the United Kingdom, each

Table 1. Top 10 Countries in Share of STEM+ Production, 1900–2010.

Year	\multicolumn{10}{c}{Top Country in Percentage of STEM+ Research Articles (Global)}
	1	2	3	4	5	6	7	8	9	10
1900	Germany	US	France	UK	Austria-Hungary	Switzerland	The Netherlands	Russia	Australia	Denmark
	26.56	20.62	19.33	11.99	2.79	1.87	1.34	0.58	< 0.5	< 0.5
1910	US	Germany	UK	France	Austria-Hungary	Switzerland	Italy	Canada	Russia	The Netherlands
	33.86	26.51	10.83	5.30	4.20	3.30	1.98	0.88	0.81	0.75
1920	US	Germany	UK	France	Switzerland	Canada	Austria	India	Italy	Sweden
	38.99	28.57	8.94	3.79	1.45	1.11	0.65	0.61	0.53	0.53
1930	US	Germany	UK	USSR	Austria	Canada	Japan	Switzerland	Sweden	The Netherlands
	45.97	16.94	14.24	3.69	1.93	1.60	1.25	1.16	0.93	0.85
1940	US	Germany	UK	The Netherlands	France	Austria	Hungary	Sweden	Norway	India
	43.21	20.91	15.62	4.71	1.29	1.22	1.19	1.17	0.77	0.62
1950	US	UK	France	West Germany	Australia	The Netherlands	Sweden	Canada	East Germany	Switzerland
	39.31	25.61	8.71	6.60	3.44	2.00	1.72	1.44	0.89	0.79

STEM+ Productivity, Development, and Wealth

1960	US	Japan	UK	Canada	West Germany	Denmark	Sweden	Austria	Mexico	Israel
	54.66	18.36	8.54	1.89	1.59	1.29	1.22	1.01	0.99	0.97
1970	US	USSR	UK	Canada	West Germany	Australia	Poland	Japan	India	France
	44.41	11.77	6.93	3.32	3.05	2.96	2.82	2.81	1.93	1.87
1980	US	UK	USSR	West Germany	Japan	France	Canada	India	Italy	Australia
	33.06	7.78	6.94	6.36	6.03	5.45	3.83	2.65	2.11	1.96
1990	US	Japan	UK	USSR	West Germany	France	Canada	Italy	India	The Netherlands
	32.02	7.35	7.24	6.45	6.21	5.17	4.18	2.78	2.07	1.97
2000	US	Japan	UK	Germany	France	China	Canada	Italy	Russia	Spain
	25.82	7.95	7.09	6.95	5.18	3.5	3.5	3.41	3.01	2.45
2010	US	China	Germany	UK	Japan	France	Canada	Italy	India	Spain
	20.42	9.96	5.72	5.38	5.01	4.15	3.38	3.27	3.02	2.87

Source: SPHERE project database of SCIE publications (Thomson Reuters' Web of Science).

contributing more than 10% to overall global production. For the following decades, the United States and Germany remain on top of the list, while France loses its position. The USSR appears as an important producer as early as 1930, but disappears from the list for the following decades to reappear in 1970.

While the United States remains the world's largest STEM+ producer by far, the share of papers authored in the United States has also decreased considerably since 1960, when it was 54%, to reach just 20% at the end of the period. On the other hand, the important European competitors in STEM+ production, the United Kingdom, Germany, France, and Italy have kept their positions almost entirely during the last decades. Rounding out the top-10, the same remains true for Canada, Japan, and India. The chart below presents the evolution of the scientific production realized by the top 10 producers according to the official language of the producer, not reflecting the language of publication.

As shown in Fig. 3, the English language countries (United States, United Kingdom, Canada, Australia, and India) dominate the chart during the whole analyzed period, but the percentage of their contribution changes over time. We can observe also the significant decrease in productivity of the German-speaking countries (Austria, Germany, Switzerland; not including Luxembourg or the German-speaking community in Belgium) productivity, especially during 1940−1960. French, too declines and follows the German trend from 1950

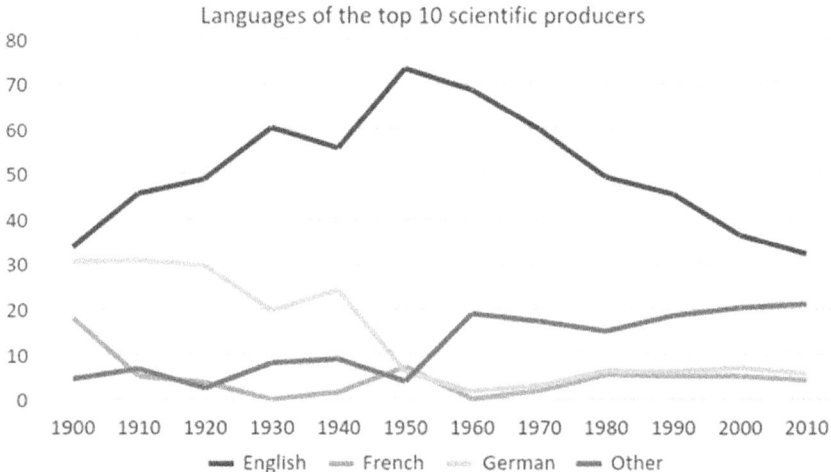

Fig. 3. The Overall Development of the Number of STEM+ Articles, by Official Language of the Countries that Host the Organizations with Which Authors are Affiliated. *Source*: SPHERE project database of SCIE publications (Thomson Reuters' Web of Science).

onward. Furthermore, we can observe an important increase in share registered by the countries speaking other languages besides those three, especially China, Japan, Russia (or former USSR), and the Northern European countries.

PRODUCTION IS NOT PRODUCTIVITY

Many larger countries have the capacity to produce many papers, whereas many smaller countries do not. Mapping science production in the world is an important and interesting endeavor, but a closer look at what makes science develop must find ways to analyze productivity rather than simply overall production. We have decided to take a look at productivity, taking as a proxy the number of research articles published per million inhabitants in each country. While taking scientists or the expenditure for science or research and development would be more logical choices to analyze scientific productivity, we have very few available and reliable data on these indicators. Population numbers are, on the other hand, widely available and reliable. First we analyze productivity by compiling the same top 10 lists we did as for production:

Such an analysis presents a very different perspective (Table 2). The United States, the former leader, shifts to fifth position in 1900 and is eliminated completely in 1910. During the rest of the period, the United States occupies mostly the second or third position, but also fourth, fifth, or even seventh. Germany manages to keep a leading position (first or second) during 1900–1940, in 1950 shifts to the ninth position and afterwards is eliminated from the top. The United Kingdom, on the other hand, manages to remain in the top for the whole period, except for 2010; until 1960 it remains in the first half of the hierarchy; however, after 1960 the United Kingdom shifts to the second half of the top list. The most productive countries prove to be the smaller ones, especially Switzerland and Israel. During 1900–1920, Switzerland shares the top of the hierarchy with Germany, while during 1980–2010 it is in leading position (second place for the first two decades and first place for the last two). Israel, on the other hand, enters the group in 1960 (being founded only in 1949) directly in first position, remaining there for four decades, until 1990, when it shifts to third place in 2000 and leaves the top 10 in 2010. Another very productive and well-represented group in this list are the Nordic countries of Sweden, Norway, Denmark, and Finland as well as the Netherlands, all of which have quite similar levels of productivity, especially most recently.

The general scientific productivity of these countries (and indeed all of the countries analyzed in this volume) has increased significantly over the 20th century. If in 1910, there wasn't any country with a productivity of at least one peer-reviewed research article per million inhabitants, by 2010 the first 10 had all productivities of more than 12 research article per million inhabitants.

Table 2. Top 10 Countries in Number of STEM+ Papers Per One Million Inhabitants, 1900–2010.[a]

YEAR	Top Country in Percentage of STEM+ Research Articles per Million Inhabitants									
	1	2	3	4	5	6	7	8	9	10
1900	Germany	Switzerland	France	UK	US	The Netherlands	Australia	Austria-Hungary	Russia	
	84.62	53.70	47.24	32.18	25.71	25.00	23.50	20.59	0.77	
1910	Switzerland	Germany	US	Austria-Hungary	UK	France	The Netherlands	Canada	Italy	Russia
	104.05	88.08	43.41	34.81	31.59	15.85	15.17	14.86	6.75	0.82
1920	Germany	Switzerland	US	UK	Canada	Austria	France	Sweden	Italy	India
	106.14	52.59	51.73	29.68	18.10	14.20	13.67	12.75	1.96	0.34
1930	Germany	US	UK	Austria	Switzerland	Canada	Sweden	The Netherlands	Hungary	Czechoslovakia
	107.69	95.68	79.63	74.05	73.28	40.24	38.88	27.88	16.17	12.96
1940	The Netherlands	Germany	US	UK	Norway	Sweden	Austria	Hungary	Czechoslovakia	France
	130.96	119.32	80.24	79.48	64.02	44.82	44.54	31.37	8.20	8.12
1950	UK	Australia	US	Sweden	France	The Netherlands	Switzerland	West Germany	Canada	Austria
	245.90	201.24	126.23	118.40	101.20	97.03	81.19	64.12	50.83	46.30

STEM+ Productivity, Development, and Wealth

Year										
1960	Israel	US	Denmark	Japan	Sweden	UK	Austria	Canada	Australia	Belgium
	318.95	210.95	196.06	138.40	113.83	113.57	100.24	73.39	63.24	62.00
1970	Israel	Australia	US	Sweden	Denmark	Canada	Hungary	UK	Czechoslovakia	Switzerland
	772.84	544.29	498.53	453.92	366.67	358.14	315.05	286.69	285.22	242.99
1980	Israel	Switzerland	Sweden	Canada	Denmark	US	UK	Australia	Norway	Finland
	907.68	852.92	685.51	593.58	581.49	554.10	526.13	509.18	486.82	469.29
1990	Israel	Switzerland	Sweden	Canada	Denmark	The Netherlands	Finland	US	UK	Australia
	1038.84	1037.59	1019.53	801.59	775.73	704.14	689.47	684.23	674.98	599.23
2000	Switzerland	Sweden	Israel	Denmark	Finland	The Netherlands	UK	Norway	Canada	Australia
	1586.94	1416.12	1238.19	1211.51	1200.29	953.43	927.14	884.44	876.57	875.94
2010	Switzerland	Denmark	Sweden	Norway	Finland	Singapore	The Netherlands	Australia	Canada	Belgium
	2352.35	1797.86	1767.83	1568.74	1557.04	1516.33	1461.89	1392.26	1289.35	1256.28

Source: SPHERE project database of SCIE publications (Thomson Reuters' Web of Science).
[a] We have included only countries that have participated more than 0.05% of the global STEM+ production.

What Correlates Better with Science Production and Productivity?

As numerous authors have found, the wealth of countries, measured by per capita GDP or other similar indicators has an essential impact on scientific production and productivity (Cole & Phelan, 1999; King, 2004). Nevertheless, others have found that wealth alone cannot completely explain the differences in scientific output (Enders & Teichler, 1997; Lacy & Sheenan, 1997; Poole, Bornholt, & Summers, 1997; Takekazu, 1998; Welch, 1997, 1998). To find other correlates and compare their impact with that of the per capita GDP we turn to the Human Development Index and the Gini indicator of inequality.

According to the UNDP (2010), the Human Development Index (HDI) is a composite index measuring average achievement in three basic dimensions of human development — a long and healthy life, knowledge, and a decent standard of living. The long and healthy life is captured by the LEI (Life Expectancy Index), knowledge is captured by EI (Education Index — obtained by aggregating the Mean Years of Schooling Index and the Expected Years of Schooling Index), while a decent standard of living is captured by II (Income Index, a function of Gross National Income at Purchasing Power Parity per capita).

GDP per capita and HDI have a high and significant correlation that has in fact changed very little over the last decades. According to our data, in 1980 the correlation was $r = 0.669$ ($p = 0.000$); in 1990, $r = 0.703$ ($p = 0.000$); in 2000, $r = 0.713$ ($p = 0.000$); and in 2010, $r = 0.682$ ($p = 0.000$). This is easily explained as the HDI contains an indicator of the standard of living. As such, we hypothesize that if general education and health have an important impact on scientific productivity, the HDI should correlate better with scientific productivity than does per capita GDP. In fact, comparing the way these two development indicators correlate with STEM+ production and productivity raised the following research question: is it money alone that determines aggregate science production and productivity or do other development indicators essentially improve the values found in these indicators? (Table 3).

STEM+ productivity correlates much better both with GDP per capita and HDI than the overall production of STEM+ research articles. There are only three significant correlations (out of 12) between STEM+ production and GDP, while there are eight significant correlations between STEM+ productivity and GDP. There are no significant correlations between STEM+ production and HDI, while all four correlations available between STEM+ productivity and HDI are significant. This might be an obvious result as bigger countries will produce more articles irrespective of their wealth or development, while this effect is controlled when numbers of inhabitants are taken into consideration by computing indexes. As the tables above show, STEM+ productivity was also more resilient after the two world wars than was per capita GDP.

Table 3. Correlations of GDP per Capita, HDI, STEM+ Production (STEM+) and STEM+ Research Articles per Million Inhabitants (STEM+p).[a]

Year	$r_{GDP, STEM+}$	$r_{HDI, STEM+}$	$r_{GDP, STEM+p}$	$r_{HDI, STEM+p}$
1900	−0.128 (0.743)		0.246 (0.523)	
1910	0.180 (0.619)		0.671 (0.034)	
1920	0.331 (0.350)		0.412 (0.237)	
1930	0.343 (0.251)		0.672 (0.012)	
1940	0.667 (0.025)		0.636 (0.035)	
1950	0.497 (0.084)		0.619 (0.024)	
1960	0.346 (0.247)		−0.050 (0.872)	
1970	0.249 (0.303)		0.270 (0.264)	
1980	0.304 (0.149)	0.177 (0.469)	0.659 (0.000)	0.603 (0.006)
1990	0.391 (0.053)	0.270 (0.249)	0.754 (0.000)	0.751 (0.000)
2000	0.379 (0.042)	0.209 (0.286)	0.793 (0.000)	0.731 (0.000)
2010	0.195 (0.279)	0.040 (0.829)	0.833 (0.000)	0.738 (0.000)

Source: SPHERE project database of SCIE publications (Thomson Reuters' Web of Science).
[a]Missing values in the table depend on the availability of data.

Table 4. Correlations for the Whole Data Pool.

		STEM+ Production	STEM*+ Productivity	HDI	GDP per Capita
STEM+ Production	Correlation	1	.267**	.172*	.466**
	Significance		.000	.051	.000
	N	408	405	130	402
STEM*+ Productivity	Correlation	.267**	1	.565**	.857**
	Significance	.000		.000	.000
	N	405	126	130	402
HDI	Correlation	.172*	.565**	1	.681**
	Significance	.051	.000		.000
	N	130	130	130	130
GDP per Capita	Correlation	.466**	.857**	.681**	1
	Significance	.000	.000	.000	
	N	402	402	130	402

Source: SPHERE project database of SCIE publications (Thomson Reuters' Web of Science).
*Significance at $p < 0.05$, ** Significance at $p < 0.01$, *** Significance at $p < 0.001$.

A surprising result is that the HDI correlates somewhat less than GDP per capita with STEM+ productivity. To test for possible selection bias, we have computed the correlations for the whole data pool. These results are consistent with those in the previous table (Table 4).

The results do not differ essentially. Production is only weakly correlated with HDI and has a medium correlation with the GDP per capita, while productivity is more strongly correlated with both indicators. The correlations with the GDP per capita are essentially stronger than those with the HDI. The weak correlation between STEM+ production and the HDI can also be explained by the effect of size. Production, as absolute values will be strongly determined by the size of the country in terms of population. As this does not correlate with the HDI, productivity, where size does not matter, will correlate with the HDI more strongly.

HOW DOES INEQUALITY MATTER?

We have used the Gini indicator for inequality. Availability of data has led us to test two Gini indicators: the one provided by the World Bank, having only 33 values and an indicator computed in the SWIID project, with a much better coverage of 234 values (of 402 overall). The two indicators cannot be pooled together as values differ for common years, and the resulting time series might have serious flaws. Thus, we have decided to compute both variants for more conclusive results. The Gini indicators show, according to our data, significant correlations with GDP per capita, respectively with HDI for the studied years. As such, considering it in the development of our model brings a certain risk of multicollinearity into the equations. A simple correlation table between the two Gini indicators and STEM+ production and productivity is shown in Table 5. Due to availability of data, we could only compute the correlations for a smaller number of countries and we have decided to pool all years, we find that the results are nevertheless a good indicator for the relationship.

There is no significant correlation between inequality and STEM+ production overall, nevertheless results are significant and negative for the relationship with STEM+ productivity. The less inequality there is in a country, the more scientifically productive that country is, or the more scientifically productive a country is, the less income inequality it has. As for the SWIID Gini indicator,

Table 5. Correlations of Gini, STEM+ Production (STEM+), and STEM+ Research Articles per 10,000 Inhabitants (STEM+p).

$r_{Gini\_WB, STEM+}$	$r_{Gini\_WB, STEM+p}$
−0.038 (0.833)	−0.581 (0.000)
$r_{Gini\_SWIID, STEM+}$	$r_{Gini\_SWIID, STEM+p}$
0.062 (0.345)	−0.183 (0.005)

Source: SPHERE project database of SCIE publications (Thomson Reuters' Web of Science).

the number of cases available is reasonably higher, thus we compute time series for years after 1960 when data is more widely available. From this point on, we use only the SWIID Gini for testing the designed models (Table 6).

As before, the table shows there is no significant relationship between STEM+ production and inequality. Nevertheless, the relationship between STEM+ productivity and inequality comes through stronger than before and a trend for a closer relationship becomes evident, as correlations increase over the last three decades from −0.369 in 1990, to −0.429 in 2000, and −0.601 in 2010.

As overall production does not correlate significantly with the other indicators, we have decided to address only productivity in the following models. We model this relationship in a regression equation using also the previous indicators for development. We will construct a series of regression models, including these data. Results below refer to the whole data pool, but include only data for the years from 1960 to 2010 (due to availability) (Table 7):

$$\text{Model 0}: \text{STEM+}_p = a + b_1 \text{ GDP}$$
$$\text{Model 1}: \text{STEM+}_p = a + b_1 \text{ GDP} + b_2 \text{ Gini}$$
$$\text{Model 2}: \text{STEM+}_p = a + b_1 \text{ GDP} + b_2 \text{ HDI}$$
$$\text{Model 3}: \text{STEM+}_p = a + b_1 \text{ HDI} + b_2 \text{ Gini}$$
$$\text{Model 4}: \text{STEM+}_p = a + b_1 \text{ GDP} + b_2 \text{ HDI} + b_3 \text{ Gini}$$

The first observation is that all regressions, including STEM+ productivity, show autocorrelation. The essential result is that the effect of GDP overshadows all other regressors in the models. Their coefficients are much smaller and most of them have weak significance values. In fact, GDP explains by itself 0.735 of the variance of STEM+ productivity, added

Table 6. Correlations of SWIID Gini, STEM+ Production (STEM+), and STEM+ Research Articles per 10,000 Inhabitants (STEM+p), 1960−2010.

Year	$r_{\text{Gini\_SWIID, STEM+}}$	$r_{\text{Gini\_SWIID, STEM+p}}$	N
1960	−0.201 (0.665)	−0.291 (0.527)	7
1970	−0.012 (0.966)	−0.504 (0.056)	15
1980	0.107 (0.634)	−0.247 (0.267)	22
1990	0.011 (0.958)	−0.369 (0.076)	24
2000	−0.098 (0.613)	−0.429 (0.020)	29
2010	0.138 (0.459)	−0.601 (0.000)	31

Source: SPHERE project database of SCIE publications (Thomson Reuters' Web of Science).

Table 7. Regression Models.

	Model0		Model1		Model2		Model3		Model4	
	Beta	Sig	Beta	Sig	Beta	Sig	Beta	Sig	Beta	Sig
GDP per capita	0.857	0.000	0.809	0.000	0.799	0.000			0.774	0.000
HDI					0.029	0.689	0.482	0.000	0.029	0.690
Gini			0.010	0.800			−0.228	0.003	−0.020	0.741
R^2		0.735		0.651		0.653		0.358		0.645
N		402		234		130		127		127
Durbin-Watson[a]		1.025		0.968		0.870		0.419		0.855

Source: SPHERE project database of SCIE publications (Thomson Reuters' Web of Science).
[a]The Durbin-Watson coefficient tests for autocorrelation. Values between 1.5 and 2.5 indicate the lack of autocorrelation, one of the Gauss-Markov preconditions for using OLS. We have computed DW because our data has a time series structure, and time series are often autocorrelated.

regressors reduce its impact even if these are significantly correlated with the target variable (as are both Gini and HDI). As the three regressors are correlated between each other, multicollinearity can be an explanation, nevertheless a more important factor is that the time series structure of the data also produces autocorrelation. To control for this, we have computed models including a time dimension. The data has in fact a cross-section time series form, with year and country characterizing each item.

Using a typical fixed effects[4] CSTS model we find the following: The models reproduce the same results as the simple regressions, but in these cases the autocorrelation issue is solved. Overall no new insight appears: GDP per capita overshadows the effect of the other two regressors, which have no significant coefficients. The power of the regression remains high. CSTS regressions generally return three different R^2 values, reflecting the impact of the regressors overall (a value equal to the simple regression value), within the development over time, and between countries. The multiple regression with all three variables (GDP, HDI, and Gini) returns the following: R^2 within $= 0.68$; R^2 between $= 0.73$; R^2 overall $= 0.64$, while using only the GDP we get higher values: R^2 within $= 0.78$; R^2 between $= 0.75$; and R^2 overall $= 0.73$. This might seem unimpressive, but the fact that the three R^2 values are so close to each other is an important result. It indicates that the time series structure has little importance here and that the prediction of STEM+ productivity by GDP has a relatively constant form over time (the within indicator) as well as in a country-by-country comparison that takes no account of the time trend (the between indicator). What we actually have is a refutation of a possible explanation of the high R^2 of the simple regression by autocorrelation, or *spurious regression*. Spurious regressions are widely discussed in literature as it often happens that time series have similar trends even if no theoretical reason for a relationship can be found. In such cases high R^2 values can be considered as false results. High autocorrelation in regression equations is an indicator that spurious regression is possible. CSTS models are used to solve such problems.

In our case, the relationship between GDP and STEM+ productivity proves genuine, and not a result of parallel unrelated time trends. In the cases of the CSTS regressions using HDI and Gini, we find that while the coefficients are significant, the three R^2 values are weak and significantly different. In both cases the between indicator is higher than the within indicator.[5] This means that both HDI and Gini contribute to the explanation of overall differences in STEM+ productivity between countries,[6] but have no explanatory power regarding changes of productivity within countries.

Summing up the results of the CSTS regressions, we find that the time series structure of the data has little impact on the explanation of the lower R^2 of the multiple regression compared to the simple regression. The explanation has to lie in the multicollinearity between regressors. The complex structure of causality between wealth, development, and income inequality leads to the surprising values in our modeling. Finally, we test the direction of the direct causal relationships using vector autoregressive models and Granger causality tests. The structure and availability of data enables us to do the tests only for the relationship between the GDP per capita and STEM+ productivity. Sufficient data on HDI and Gini coefficients to be able to develop a balanced panel of sufficient size is lacking.[7] The results are in Table 8.

First of all, we note that there are important differences between countries in the ways wealth and science productivity are related; nevertheless, we construct a typology. For the majority of countries, wealth has a direct causal effect on science productivity. This is the case for 20 of the 29 countries, but for 12 of these countries the opposite does not hold. A clear effect of the STEM+ production on the GDP (for future years) can be found for only 12 countries, including the large producers (United States, United Kingdom, West Germany, U.S.S.R., etc.) and some of the very productive smaller countries (Finland, Norway, etc.). A smaller group of countries, benefiting strongly from *brain gain* shows no relationship at all between STEM+ productivity and the GDP per capita (Israel and Switzerland, and to a lesser degree, the Netherlands and Spain). The overall picture is rather complicated and should be considered more of an indication than a proof of the directions of causal relationships. Nevertheless, a simplified summary would be the following: Scientific productivity is usually causally dependent on wealth, but mostly the large producers or the very productive ones succeed in making science productivity have a causal effect on wealth.

Table 8. Granger Causality Models after VAR.

Country	Granger sig.[a] for GDP per capita → STEM+p	Granger sig. for STEM+p → GDP per capita
Australia	0.000	0.304
Austria	0.531	0.087
Belgium	0.063	0.825
Brazil	0.028	0.135
Canada	0.001	0.818
China	0.031	0.134
Czechoslovakia	0.051	0.046
Denmark	0.793	0.002
East Germany[b]	0.000	0.560
Finland	0.427	0.000
France	0.004	0.304
Germany	0.068	0.580
Hungary	0.000	0.002
India	0.001	0.937
Israel	0.394	0.934
Italy	0.281	0.000
Japan	0.001	0.223
The Netherlands	0.191	0.429
Norway	0.000	0.000
Poland	0.000	0.000
Russia	0.004	0.505
Spain	0.407	0.501
Sweden	0.005	0.654
Switzerland	0.391	0.811
Taiwan	0.000	0.000
UK	0.000	0.016
US	0.179	0.031
USSR	0.000	0.000
West Germany	0.001	0.001

Source: SPHERE project database of SCIE publications (Thomson Reuters' Web of Science).
[a]Small significance (generally under 0.05) values indicate that non-causality can be refuted.
[b]Germany appears three times in the table as different models have been computed for East Germany, West Germany, and unified Germany (prior to 1950 and after 1990).

CONCLUSIONS AND COMMENTS

The immediate result of our models is that a country's wealth contributes to the conditions necessary for productive science. While large countries produce many research articles in the STEM+ fields more or less irrespective of their per capita GDP, with countries like the Soviet Union, China, or India being important contributors to world science, the most productive countries were the richer ones. GDP per capita values are important predictors for higher numbers of STEM+ research articles adjusted for population size. Nevertheless, human development and income equality also have a positive relationship with science productivity. While the effect of income equality is less strong, it has importantly and steadily increased over the last 50 years.

We have proposed two ways to interpret the relationship between income equality and science productivity: it is mitigated by wealth or by human development. Controlling for wealth, the relationship disappears, while controlling for the human development index it gains in strength. A synthetic reminder is that the correlation coefficient between STEM+ productivity and Gini is −0.183 (0.005), while a partial correlation coefficient controlling for GDP per capita is 0.017 (0.800) and the one controlling for the HDI is −0.259 (0.003). This means that countries with similar levels of human development that are more equal in income distribution are more productive in science, while countries of similar wealth that are more equal in income distribution are not necessarily more productive in science. A possible explanation for this configuration would be our hypothesis that the relationship between science productivity and inequality is determined by economic development. Indeed, if the relationship between STEM+ productivity and Gini is mitigated by GDP per capita or has GDP per capita as a common predecessor, we would get something close to the results above. If H_2 would hold and the relationship would be mitigated by education (and as such by human development), the second partial correlation would be lower than the first one. In fact, in econometric terms, what we find is multicollinearity that appears in the case of models, including GDP per capita and Gini; less so in the case of models including HDI and Gini.

To conclude, it is the economy that makes the relationship function rather than education or human development in general. We have proposed the following chain of concepts:

Science productivity ↔ Industrial productivity ↔ Economic wealth ↔ Social equality

We were able to test for causality only in one of the relationships above. We have found that the relationship between science productivity and economic wealth is mostly bidirectional, but showing important differences between countries. Only the largest absolute producers and the most productive countries succeed in gaining economically from their scientific production.

NOTES

1. The closer definition of STEM+ follows in "Data and Methods" section. For better reading, we have not mentioned it throughout the paper, nevertheless, all models and conclusions here are limited to those fields of knowledge.
2. Throughout the chapter we have used the concept of human development in its simplified sense, given by the Human Development Index of the UNDP.
3. A detailed presentation of methodology and dataset can be found in Chapter 1 of this volume.
4. Fixed effects models are preferred to random effects if the panel ID dimension is the country level (for a more detailed discussion of panel models see also Reisz & Stock, 2007).
5. For HDI, the values are: R^2 within $= 0.12$; R^2 between $= 0.39$; R^2 overall $= 0.31$. For Gini, the values are: R^2 within $= 0.01$; R^2 between $= 0.13$; R^2 overall $= 0.03$. For both models, the F-test significance of the regression is 0.000.
6. The R^2 between indicator is based on a single value computed for the whole time series of each country, so it does not indicate a trend difference, but a general country-by-country difference.
7. The VAR model was computed on a smaller sample including only those countries that have at least four consecutive years of over 0.05% participation to STEM+ production. This led to a number of 368 remaining observations from 29 countries. We have considered 5-year lags for both causality directions.

REFERENCES

Allison, P. D. (1980). Inequality and scientific productivity. *Social Studies of Science*, *10*(2), 163−179.
Allison, P. D., Long, J. S., & Krauze, T. K. (1982). Cumulative advantage and inequality in science. *American Sociological Review*, *47*(5), 615−625.
Allison, P. D., & Stewart, J. A. (1974). Productivity differences among scientists: Evidence for accumulative advantage. *American Sociological Review*, *39*(4), 596−606.
Andrews, F. M. (1979). *Scientific productivity: The effectiveness of research groups in six countries*. Cambridge: Cambridge University Press.
Bailey, T. G. (1992). *Faculty research productivity*. Paper presented at the ASHE Annual Meeting, Minneapolis, MN.
Barro, R., & Sala-i-Martin, X. (1995). *Economic growth*. Cambridge, MA: MIT Press.
Bayer, A., & Dutton, J. E. (1977). Career age and research professional activities of academic scientists. *Journal of Higher Education*, *48*(3), 259−282.
Ben-David, J. (1960). Scientific productivity and academic organization in nineteenth century medicine. *American Sociological Review*, *25*, 828−843.
Ben-David, J. (1984). *The scientist's role in society*. Chicago, IL: University of Chicago Press.
Blackburn, R. T., Behymer, C. E., & Hall, D. E. (1978). Research note: Correlates of faculty publications. *Sociology of Education*, *51*(2), 132−141.
Cameron, S. W., & Blackburn, R. T. (1981). Sponsorship and academic career success. *Journal of Higher Education*, *52*(4), 369−377.

Clemente, F. (1973). Early career determinants of research productivity. *American Journal of Sociology, 79*(2), 409–419.
Cole, J. R., & Cole, S. (1973). *Social stratification in science*. Chicago, IL: University of Chicago Press.
Cole, S., & Meyer, G. S. (1985). Little science, big science revisited. *Scientometrics, 7*(3–6), 443–458.
Cole, S., & Phelan, T. J. (1999). The scientific productivity of nations. *Minerva, 37*(1), 1–23.
Creswell, J. W. (1985). Faculty research performance: Lessons from the sciences and the social sciences. *ASHE-ERIC higher education report*, 4. Washington, DC: Association for the Study of Higher Education.
de Solla Price, D. (1963). *Little science, big science...and beyond*. New York, NY: Columbia University Press.
Eiduson, B. T. (1962). *Scientists: Their psychological world*. New York, NY: Basic Books.
Enders, J., & Teichler, U. (1997). A victim of their own success? Employment and working conditions of academic staff in comparative perspective. *Higher Education, 34*(3), 347–372.
Fox, M. F. (1985). Publication, performance, and reward in science and scholarship. In J. C. Smart (Ed.), *Higher education: Handbook of theory and research* (Vol. I). New York, NY: Agathon Press.
Gottlieb, E. E., & Keith, B. (1997). The academic research-teaching nexus in eight advanced industrialized countries. *Higher Education, 34*(3), 397–419.
Grossman, G. M., & Helpman, E. (1991). *Innovation and growth in the global economy*. Cambridge, MA: MIT Press.
Harris, G. T. (1989). Research and teaching: Symbiosis or conflict? *Higher Education, 18*(4), 397–409.
Harris, G. T., & Kaine, G. (1994). The determinants of research performance: A study of Australian university economists. *Higher Education, 27*(2), 191–201.
King, D. A. (2004). The scientific impact of nations. *Nature, 430*, 311–316.
Lacy, F. J., & Sheenan, B. (1997). Job satisfaction among academic staff: An international perspective. *Higher Education, 34*(3), 305–322.
Levy, D. (1996). *Building the third sector: Latin America's private research centers and nonprofit development*. Pittsburgh, PA: University of Pittsburgh.
Lightfield, E. T. (1971). Output and recognition of sociologists. *The American Sociologist, 6*(May), 128–133.
Long, J. S. (1977). *Productivity and position in the early academic career*. Ithaca, NY: Cornell University.
Lucas, R. E. Jr. (1988). On the mechanics of economic development. *Journal of Monetary Economics, 22*, 3–42.
Mankiw, N. G., Romer, D., & Weil, D. N. (1992). A contribution to the empirics of economic growth. *The Quarterly Journal of Economics, 17*(2), 407–437.
May, R. M. (1997). The scientific wealth of nations. *Science, 275*, 793–796.
Merton, R. K. (1942). The normative structure of science. *Science, 267*–278.
Merton, R. K. (1968). The Matthew Effect in science. *Science, 159*, 56–63.
Merton, R. K. (1970). *Science, technology and society in seventeenth century England*. New York, NY: Howard Fertig Press.
Over, R. (1982). Does research productivity decline with age? *Higher Education, 11*(5), 511–520.
Pelz, D. C., & Andrews, F. M. (1966). *Scientists in organizations: Productive climates for research and development*. New York, NY: Wiley.
Poole, M., Bornholt, L., & Summers, F. (1997). An international study of the gendered nature of academic work: Some cross-cultural explorations. *Higher Education, 34*(3), 376–396.
Rangazas, P. C. (2005). Human capital and growth: An alternative accounting. *Topics in Macroeconomics, 5*(1), 1–43.
Reisz, R. D., & Stock, M. (2007). Theorie der weltgesellschaft und statistische modelle im soziologischen neo-institutionalismus. *Zeitschrift für Soziologie, 36*(2), 82–99.

Reskin, B. F. (1977). Scientific productivity and the reward structure of science. *American Sociological Review*, *42*(3), 491–504.
Romer, P. (1986). Increasing returns and long run growth. *Journal of Political Economy*, *94*, 1002–1037.
Shockley, W. (1957). On the statistics of individual variations of productivity in research laboratories. *Proceedings of the Institute of Radio Engineers*, *45*(3), 279–290.
Takekazu, E. (1998). Faculty perceptions of university governance in Japan and the United States. *Comparative Education Review*, *42*(1), 61–72.
Taylor, C. W., & Barron, F. (1963). *Scientific creativity: Its recognition and development*. New York, NY: Wiley.
Teodorescu, D. (2000). Correlates of faculty publication productivity: A cross-national analysis. *Higher Education*, *39*(2), 201–222.
UNDP. (2010). Human Development Report 2010 – 20th Anniversary Edition. *The real wealth of nations: Pathways to human development*. Houndmills, Basingstoke: Palgrave Macmillan. Retrieved from http://hdr.undp.org/sites/default/files/reports/270/hdr_2010_en_complete_reprint.pdf
Welch, A. R. (1997). The peripatetic professor: The internationalism of the academic profession. *Higher Education*, *34*(3), 323–345.
Welch, A. R. (1998). The end of certainty? The academic profession and the challenge of change. *Comparative Education Review*, *42*(1), 1–14.

ABOUT THE AUTHORS

David P. Baker is Professor of Sociology, Education, and Demography at The Pennsylvania State University. He writes about the effects of education on cognition, health, and society. He is coauthor of *National Differences, Global Similarities: World Culture and the Future of Schooling* (Stanford University Press, 2005) and author of *The Schooled Society: The Educational Transformation of Global Culture* (Stanford University Press, 2014). *The Schooled Society* is the winner of the American Educational Research Association's 2015 Outstanding Book Award.

Wei Bao is Associate Professor of Higher Education in the Graduate School of Education at Peking University and served as Head of the Education Administration and Policy Program. She is also a Researcher in the Institute of Education Economy at PKU. Her research interests include economics of education; finance of higher education; college impact on student learning outcomes; and private higher education. Her latest book, *Unfinished Transformation: College Impact on Student Development* (Education Science Publishing House, 2014), received the Outstanding Publication Award for 2016 from China Association of Higher Education. She received a Ph.D. in Education from the University of Tokyo (2005), and held an appointment at Tokyo University Center of Research on University Management and Policy before joining PKU.

Junghee Choi is a doctoral candidate in Higher Education at The Pennsylvania State University. His main areas of interest are public policy and the economic and financial aspects of higher education. Further interests include socioeconomic stratification, the role of skills on labor market outcomes, and international and comparative education. He holds a BA in English Literature from Korea University and a Master of Development Policy from the KDI School of Public Policy and Management, South Korea.

John T. Crist is Dean of Academic Affairs at George Mason University, Korea. Previously, he served as a member of the senior leadership team (Director of Research) at Georgetown University's School of Foreign Service in Qatar. Prior to his career in the administration of international branch campuses, Dr. Crist spent 14 years with a prominent foreign-policy think-tank funded by the U.S. Congress, the U.S. Institute of Peace, where he was Senior

Program Officer and Associate Vice President in the Jennings Randolph Fellowship Program. His publications include journal articles, book chapters, policy reports and op-ed pieces on international education, scientific research production, social movements, and peace and conflict studies. He also has more than 25 years of experience teaching at Georgetown University (in Washington, DC, and in Doha, Qatar), Johns Hopkins University School of Advanced International Studies, Syracuse University, Colgate University, and the Catholic University of America.

Jennifer Dusdal is Postdoctoral Researcher in Sociology in the Institute of Education & Society at the University of Luxembourg. She holds a BA in Social Sciences and an MA in Science and Society from the Leibniz University of Hannover, Germany, and a doctorate in Sociology from the University of Luxembourg. Her dissertation examines scientific knowledge production and higher education development in Germany over the 20th century, charting the institutionalization of German research universities and unprecedented growth in science. In 2014, her coauthored book *Bildungschancen durch Begabtenförderung* (*Educational Opportunities Supporting Talents*) appeared, investigating the social composition, the study situation, and the societal dedication of the scholarship holders of the Hans Böckler Foundation.

Frank Fernandez is Assistant Professor at the University of Houston, Texas. He earned a Ph.D. in Higher Education from The Pennsylvania State University. He researches educational policy issues, including topics related to comparative or international studies of education and skills, access and equity for underserved students, as well as doctoral education and the future of the professoriate. His work has been published in *Educational Policy, International Migration,* and *Penn State Law Review*. He is co-editor of *Affirmative Action and Racial Equity* (Routledge, 2015).

Yuan Chih Fu received his Ph.D. degree in Higher Education from The Pennsylvania State University (2017). He serves Taiwan's Ministry of Education as a policymaker in higher education, dedicating his professional work to the construction of national data infrastructure and its application in higher education governance. Collaborating mainly with David P. Baker and Liang Zhang, his research focuses on the impact of higher education policy on scientific production and collaboration. Recent publications address the professional development of institutional research in Asia. With a dual identity of an empirical scholar and a policymaker, he translates knowledge into action, also as the founder of the Taiwan Association for Institutional Research (est. 2015).

Hyerim Kim is a doctoral candidate in Educational Theory and Policy at The Pennsylvania State University. Her main research interest is in education policy with a particular focus on the role of government in higher education. She also researches topics related to comparative and international studies. Previously, she was for 12 years a Deputy Director in the Ministry of Education in South Korea, including three years on secondment at UNESCO in Bangkok, Thailand.

Iris A. Mihai is lecturer in the Faculty of Political Sciences, Philosophy and Communication Sciences at the West University of Timisoara, Romania. She specializes in productivity at global level. Her work has been published in international journals like *Journal of International Business and Economics, Procedia – Social and Behavioral Sciences, International Journal of Advances in Management and Economics*, among others. Her academic work includes involvement in more than 15 projects financed by EU, focusing on the improvement of human capital, on extending the cooperation between higher education providers and the private sector, etc. She is a professional member of the International Society for Development and Sustainability. Two of her papers have been awarded international prizes.

Justin J. W. Powell is Professor of Sociology of Education in the Institute of Education & Society at the University of Luxembourg. His comparative institutional analyses of education systems chart persistence and change in inclusive and special education, in higher education and vocational training, and in educational governance and research policy. Having collaborated with two dozen scholars, his research results have appeared in such journals as *Comparative Education Review, Comparative Sociology, European Journal of Education, Science and Public Policy*, and *Sociology of Education*. His books include *Barriers to Inclusion* (Paradigm Publishers, 2011/Routledge, 2016) and the coauthored book *Comparing Special Education* (Stanford University Press, 2011), which received the American Educational Research Association's Outstanding Book Award, as well as edited volumes and a best-selling textbook on social inequality.

Robert D. Reisz is Professor of Statistics in the Department of Political Science at the West University of Timisoara, Romania and Dean of the Faculty of Political Science, Philosophy and Communication Sciences there. His main research interest is in the field of higher education policy, but he has also published on education policy in general, migration, and other topics. Prof. Reisz is the Head of the Sociology of Education Section of the Romanian Society of Sociologists. He has also worked as a researcher at the International Center for Higher Education and Research (INCHER) Kassel, Germany; at the Hungarian Institute for Education Research (HIER), Budapest; the Institute for Higher Education Research (HoF), Wittenberg, Germany; and was a fellow of the New Europe College (NEC), Bucharest, Romania, and the Collegium Helveticum, Zurich, Switzerland. He has published 9 books, 43 papers in peer-reviewed journals, and 28 book chapters.

Kazunori Shima is Associate Professor at Tohoku University's Graduate School of Education. His research focuses on the function and finance of Japan's national universities. In particular, he studies the effects of political, social, and economic development on Japanese higher education. His research has been published in many outlets, including *Mass Higher Education Development in East Asia: Strategy, Quality, and Challenges* (Springer, 2015); *Paying the Professoriate: A Global Comparison of Compensation and Contracts* (Routledge, 2012); and *Turkish Journal of Sociology*.

Liang Sun received her Ph.D. in Higher Education from the Department of Education Policy Studies at The Pennsylvania State University. Her research interest mainly lies in comparative and international higher education using quantitative methods. Her dissertation focuses on international student mobility and brain circulation, particularly on the role of expatriate researchers in international research collaboration. She also works with scholars of higher education and sociology on studies of education and adult competencies, education and labor market outcomes, and educational homogamy.

Mike Zapp is Postdoctoral Researcher in the Institute of Education & Society at the University of Luxembourg. His research interests include comparative institutional analyses of education systems with a particular focus on the role of international organizations and higher education. His research has appeared in such journals as *Comparative Education Review*, *International Journal of Educational Development*, *European Educational Research Journal*, and *Science and Public Policy*.

Liang Zhang is Professor of Higher Education in the Department of Administration, Leadership, and Technology at New York University. His research focuses on economics and finance of higher education, particularly on the role of governments and institutions in affecting institutional performances and student outcomes. He also does work on comparative and international education. His work has appeared in *Educational Evaluation and Policy Analysis*, *The Review of Higher Education*, *Research in Higher Education*, *Journal of Human Resources*, *Economics of Education Review*, *Education Economics*, *Journal of Higher Education*, *Journal of Labor Research*, *Industrial Relations*, and *Higher Education: Handbook of Theory and Research*.

INDEX

Academic capitalism, 9
Academic drift, 61, 74, 80, 183, 185
Academic freedom, 8, 60, 97, 147
Academic Ranking of World Universities, 43
  See also Ranking
Academy of Science, 28, 144, 145, 147, 148, 155, 157, 163–168
Access issues, 64–68
Accreditation, 43
Adams, Jonathan, 9, 20, 23, 142, 206
Aghion, Philippe, 8, 97, 109
Al-Azhar University, 232
Al-Nizamiyya University, 233
American Association for the Advancement of Science, 91
American Civil War, 88
American Mathematical Society, 95, 96
American model, 92, 175, 176, 181
American Philological Association, 91
American Society for Microbiology, 96
American University, 106, 119, 182, 243
The Anti-Rightist Movement, 148, 149
April Revolution, 210, 224n2
Arabian Gulf, 18, 20, 28
Article production, 21, 27, 29, 31, 115, 119, 123, 124, 126–129, 227–245
Asia, 2, 3, 7, 17–19, 21–23, 26, 31, 40, 41, 49, 58, 86, 109, 115, 137, 171, 200, 242–244
Assessment of Higher Education Learning Outcomes (AHELO), 43
  See also OECD

Association of American Universities (AAU), 91
Atomic energy commission (CEA), France, 68
Australia, 259–262, 264, 265, 272
Austria, 21, 254, 260–262, 264, 265, 272

Baker, David P., 1–32, 38, 40, 43, 44, 50, 56–58, 63, 69, 85–109, 138n4, 174, 176, 194, 212, 238
Bayh-Dole Act, 198
Belgium, 17, 22, 254, 262, 265, 272
Ben-David, Joseph, 58, 66, 69, 86, 88, 92, 252
Bibliometrics, 2, 9–12, 15, 30, 62, 64, 68, 114, 118, 200
Big data, 12, 233
Big science, 3, 17, 18, 31, 98, 99, 101, 107, 108
Block grants, 27, 113–138, 139n19
Blue Book of Science and Technology, The, 151
Bologna Process, 42, 61, 73
Bradford, Samuel C., 10, 73
Brain drain, 153, 182, 214
Brain Korea 21 (BK 21), 208, 216, 218–219
Brazil, 20, 170n1, 206, 245n5, 272
BRICK, 142, 170n1, 206

Canada, 5, 18, 21, 30, 259–262, 264, 265, 272
Capacity-building, 2, 7, 10, 22, 28, 31, 208, 230
Carnegie Classifications Data File, 101, 102, 104–107

Carnegie Classifications of Institutions of Higher Education, 86, 104, 106, 211–212
Carnegie Foundation, 90, 101, 102, 104–107
Catholic University of America, 106
Center of science productivity, 55–80
Center for Higher Education University Ranking, 43
Centers for Research and Higher Education (PRES), France, 65
Central Research Institute, China, 144
Centre national de la recherche scientifique (CNRS), France, 64
Chairman Mao, 146, 147
China, 3, 5, 9, 11, 17–21, 23, 25, 27, 29, 38, 44–49, 57, 58, 108, 119, 141–171, 175, 176, 201n1, 206, 245n5, 250, 258, 259, 261, 263, 272, 273
Chinese Academy of Sciences (CAS), 144, 155, 156, 163–167, 170n3, 170n4
Chinese Civil War, 143
Clarivate Analytics. *See* Thomson Reuters
Cold War, 98, 175
Collaboration, 6, 9, 15–18, 20–21, 25, 28, 30, 31, 57–59, 61, 64–66, 70–72, 77, 79, 80, 108, 142, 150, 160–163, 174, 190–199, 217, 229, 237, 238, 242–244
Collège de France, 66
Collegiate Learning Assessment, 43
Common Program of the Chinese People's Consultative Conference, 144
Communist Party of China (CPC), 145, 148
Comparative indicators, 59
Competition, 6, 17–20, 25, 27, 28, 30, 31, 50, 57–59, 70, 79, 91, 179, 182, 186–190, 207, 211, 214, 216–219, 237, 259
Competitive funds, 113–139
Cooperative Agreement of Science and Technology, 146
Cornell University, 89, 90
Corporate research capacity, 236
Cross-national comparison, 6, 15, 76
Cross-national perspective, 44–48
Cultural Revolution, China, 27, 49, 143, 149–151, 159, 164, 169
Cumulative advantage, 252, 253
  See also Matthew effect

Data Growth, 219
Decision on Expediting Progress in Science and Technology, 152
Delanty, Gerard, 9
Denmark, 219, 250, 260, 261, 263, 265, 272
Dewatripont, Mathias, 8, 97
DiMaggio, P. and Powell, Walter W., 185
Discourse, 40, 42, 43, 65, 229
Doctoral education, 71, 86, 87, 91–93
Drucker, Peter, 144
Dual pillars, 68–72
Duke University, 98, 104

East Asia, 2, 7, 17–19, 22, 23, 31, 41, 58, 115, 200, 242, 243, 244
East Germany, 16, 77, 260, 272
Ecole Normale Supérieure, France, 64
École pratique des hautes études, France, 66
Economic prosperity, 21–25, 198, 230
Economic wealth, 29, 250, 251, 256, 273
Education Act, The, 74, 209
Education City, Doha, Qatar, 46, 228, 230, 231, 234–236, 240, 242, 244, 245n3, 245n10
Education Index (EI), 266

Index

863 Program, China, 152
Elevator effect, 49
Elite higher education, 64–68, 154
Elsevier, 11–12, 30, 72, 245n4
Elzinga, Aant, 3, 50, 98, 99, 108
Emerging Global Model, 9, 99, 109
Engineering, 2, 7, 38, 57, 62, 64, 73, 86, 90, 100, 114, 117, 121, 124, 145, 167, 212, 213, 214, 217, 234, 250, 251, 257
Engineering Research Centers (ERC), 217
England, 58, 73, 76, 88, 89, 93, 98
  See also Great Britain, United Kingdom
Enrollment, 6, 25–28, 39–41, 44, 47–50, 87, 90, 94, 95, 99, 100, 108, 115, 118, 122, 145, 153, 176–179, 181, 200, 206, 210–212, 216, 224, 234
Enrollment and graduation, 48
Entrepreneurial university, 178
Erasmus Programme, 20
EU15, 256
Europe, 2, 3, 5, 7, 15, 17–20, 25, 29, 31, 43, 57–64, 69, 78, 79, 86, 92, 147, 234, 242, 243
European Commission, 20, 61, 69
European Qualifications Framework, 42
European Research Council (ERC), 20, 61
European standards, 65
European Union, 20, 22, 61
Europeanization, 25, 56, 70, 73
Excellence, 5, 59, 64, 65, 75, 130, 149, 179, 182, 187, 188, 216, 217, 234, 235
Expansion, 2, 3, 5, 6, 11, 18, 25, 28, 29, 30, 32, 37–50, 58, 61, 62, 67, 73, 74, 77, 79, 113–139, 147, 148, 177, 178, 180, 181, 183, 195, 200, 206, 207, 210–216, 219, 222, 224, 228

Expected Years of Schooling Index, The, 266

Fachhochschulen (universities of applied science), Germany, 69
  autonomy, 44, 63, 73, 96–97, 150, 178, 215, 217, 234
Finland, 21, 219, 250, 254, 263, 265, 271, 272
First World War (also World War I), 93
Framework Programme of EU Research Funding, 20
France, 3, 5, 8, 9, 11, 15–17, 19, 21–23, 25, 26, 30, 55–80, 88, 89, 96, 119, 259–262, 264, 272
Fraunhofer Society, 70
Fundamental Science and Technology Act, The, 198, 199
Further and Higher Education Act, USA, 74

G8, 256
Garfield, Eugene, 11
GDP, 21, 22, 29, 44, 45, 49, 59–61, 77, 153, 168, 206, 228, 237, 250, 251, 255, 256, 266–273
Geiger, Roger L., 5, 19, 86, 89–97, 109, 142, 192, 194
German model, 92
German Research Foundation (DFG), 69
Germany, 3, 5, 8, 9, 11, 15–17, 19, 22, 23, 25, 26, 30, 38–40, 44–49, 55–80, 86, 88, 96, 119, 121, 176, 177, 235, 258–264, 271, 272
Gibbons, Michael, 8, 63, 87, 108, 194, 199, 200
Gini index, 251, 256
Global competition (global competitiveness), 19, 28, 43, 216, 218, 219

See also Competition
Global differentiation, 18–20
Global environment of higher education, 42–43
Global partnership, 245
  See also Collaboration
Governance, 5, 6, 9, 12, 39, 73, 89, 148, 175, 176, 178
Government Administration Council of China, 163
Graduate School of Public Administration, 209
Graduate School of Public Health, 209
Grand Challenges, Qatar, 236, 237
Grandes écoles, France, 80n3
Grands établissements, France, 66
Granger causality, 252, 271, 272
Grant-in-Aid for Scientific Research program (KAKENHI), 118
Great Depression, 89
Great Leap Forward, the, China, 148–149, 169, 170
Great Recession, 5
Gross domestic expenditures on R&D (GERD), 44, 59
Gross enrollment ratio (GER), 47, 48
Growth, 3, 4, 6, 12, 17–23, 25–31, 37–50, 56–59, 61, 62, 69, 79, 80, 88, 89, 93, 109, 142, 150, 152, 156–160, 168, 169, 170, 174, 175, 177, 180, 181, 183, 188, 190, 192, 197–200, 205–225, 230, 237–245
Growth of Science, 3, 25, 37–50, 174, 180, 200, 207–209, 212, 224

Hanyang University, 221
Harvey Mudd College, 106
Health, 2, 7, 13, 62, 66, 86, 94, 105–107, 114, 144, 171, 197, 209, 241, 248, 257, 266
Helmholtz Association of German Research Centers, 70
Hierarchy, 64–68, 121, 197, 214, 255, 259, 263
Higher education (HE), 2, 3, 5–8, 10, 12, 17, 19–23, 25–31, 37–50, 56–62, 64–70, 72–76, 78, 79, 85–109, 115–118, 120–128, 138, 141–171, 174–183, 186–195, 197–200, 205–225, 229, 231, 233, 244, 248, 251
Higher Education expansion, 3, 6, 25, 37–50, 73, 178, 219
Higher education funding, 76, 114
Higher Education Funding Council (HEFC), UK, 76
Higher Education in Korea (HEIK), 208, 222
Higher education institution (HEI), 40, 46, 109, 142, 144, 145, 153, 154, 157, 160, 163–168, 170, 175, 176, 177, 179–181, 189, 190, 207, 210, 211, 212, 216, 218, 248
Higher education organization (HEO), 12, 41, 45, 102, 118
Higher education policy, 30, 87, 174, 209, 222
Higher education R&D expenditure (HERD), 44, 45
Higher Education System, 6, 17, 25, 37–50, 56, 64, 65, 69, 70, 74, 106, 107, 115, 118, 138, 143–146, 154, 164, 169, 174–178, 189, 190, 193, 200, 206–210, 224
Hong Kong, 157, 158, 170n2
Horizon 2020, 61
  See also Framework Programme of EU Research Funding
Human development, 231, 250–252, 256, 266, 273, 274n2
Human Development Index, the (HDI), 251, 256, 266, 273, 274n2
Humboldtian model, 69
  See also German model

100 talents, China, 155–156
Hungary, 21, 254, 260, 264, 265, 272

Iceland, 229
Impact, 5, 7, 11, 12, 19, 21, 22, 29, 31,
    59, 61, 62, 66, 73, 139n17, 174,
    181, 208, 224, 229, 237, 244,
    253–256, 266, 270, 271
Impact factor, 11
Income Index, 266
India, 5, 20, 30, 170n1, 206, 242,
    245n5, 259–262, 264, 272, 273
Industrial productivity, 251, 273
Industrial revolution, 147
Inequality, 250–252, 254–256,
    266–273
Institut national de la recherche
    agronomique (INRA),
    France, 68
Institut national de la santé et de la
    recherche Médicale
    (INSERM), France, 68
Institut Pasteur, France, 66
Institute of Geology of the Academy
    of Sciences, China, 148
Institutional setting, 29, 60, 62, 255
Institutionalism, 7, 30, 185
Institutionalization, 2, 6, 7, 17, 23, 25,
    26, 37–50, 57, 58, 61, 64, 76,
    77, 79, 102, 109, 185, 186
Institutionalization of education,
    39–41
Institutionalization of higher
    education, 17, 25, 37–50, 57
Institutionalization of higher
    education and research, 25
Institutionalization of science, 39, 58
International branch campus (IBC),
    18, 20, 28, 42, 73, 228, 230,
    231, 235, 244, 248
International collaboration, 6, 15, 18,
    20–21, 28, 30, 31, 58, 79, 142,
    160–162, 195, 229, 238,
    242–243
International comparison, 115,
    119–120
International Max Planck Research
    Schools (IMPRS), 70
International organization (IO), 38,
    40, 42, 231, 239, 248, 256
Internationalization, 9, 25, 42, 56, 57,
    70, 79, 152
Investment, 5, 6, 17–21, 23, 26, 27,
    30, 31, 32, 43, 47, 49. 50, 57,
    59–61, 66, 69, 70, 77, 79,
    80n2, 149, 153, 156–163, 168,
    169, 183, 192, 200, 206, 207,
    212, 216–219, 222, 224, 228,
    229, 231, 234, 237, 240, 250
Iran, 231, 232
Isomorphism, 43, 179, 185, 186, 190
Israel, 21, 229, 250, 255, 256, 261,
    263, 265, 271, 272
Italy, 5, 21, 30, 260–262, 264, 272

Japan, 3, 5, 9, 11, 17–19, 22, 23,
    25–27, 30, 38, 44–50,
    113–139, 147, 199, 259–263,
    265, 272

Kaiser-Wilhelm-Gesellschaft,
    Germany, 69
    See also Max Planck Society
Kakinuma, Sumio, 199
Karlsruhe Institute of Technology
    (KIT), 70
Karlsruhe Research Center, 70
Keio University, 121
King's College London, 73, 76
Knowledge conglomerate, 174,
    194–200
Knowledge economy, 28, 41, 43, 65,
    114, 130, 228
Knowledge production, 2, 5, 6, 8, 21,
    26, 29, 31, 59, 63, 86, 87, 91,

95, 97–99, 114, 182, 194, 199, 200, 219, 228
Knowledge triangle, 61
Korea Advanced Institute of Science (KAIS), 215
Korea Advanced Institute of Science and Technology (KAIST), 215
Korea Institute of Science and Technology, the (KIST), 214
Korea University, 224n1
Korean War, 206, 209, 212
Kuwahara, Terukata, 118, 138n1
Kyoto University, 116, 121, 132–135

Learning Science Movement, 214
Leibniz Association, Germany, 70
Liberties and Responsibilities of Universities (LRU), France, 65
Life Expectancy Index (LEI), 266
London School of Economics and Political Science (LSE), 98
Long-Term Plan of Science and Technology of China, 151
Lotka, Alfred J., 10
Luxembourg, 5, 17, 229, 262

Mass higher education, 26, 29, 85–109, 177, 178
Massachusetts Institute of Technology (MIT), 89
Mathematics, 2, 7, 38, 57, 86, 96, 100, 114, 163, 206, 232
Matthew Effect in science, the, 252
  See also Cumulative advantage
Max Planck Society for the Advancement of Science, Germany, 63, 69, 71
  See also Kaiser-Wilhelm-Gesellschaft
Mean Years of Schooling Index, the, 266

Measuring and Comparing Achievements of Learning Outcomes in Higher Education in Europe (AHELO), 43
Medicine, 57, 61, 65, 72, 76, 117, 212, 213, 232, 241, 250, 251, 257
Megascience/mega-science, 3–5, 17–18, 31, 98, 99, 108
Merton, Robert K., 62, 252–254
Mexico, 21, 261
Meyer, John W., 6. 9. 38–41, 43, 50, 56, 58, 59, 63, 185, 252
Michigan State University, 89
Middle East, 2, 7, 18, 20, 28, 232, 236, 242–244
Ministry of Education, Culture, Sports, Science and Technology / MEXT (Japan), 115, 130
Mode-1, 8
Mode-2, 8
Modernization, 143, 149–157
Multi-Rank, 43
Musselin, Christine, 64, 66

National College Entrance Examination, the, 151
National Commissions of Science, the, 151
National Committee of Science and Technology, the, 151
National innovation system, 181, 197
National Institute of Health, 197
National Priorities Research Program, the (NPRP), Qatar, 236
National research institute, 66, 68, 121, 138n5, 197, 235
National Research System, 17, 28, 30, 227–245
National Taiwan University, 189

National universities, 26, 28, 88, 114–118, 120–137, 138, 139n17, 208. 209, 220, 228, 234, 235
Nation-state building, 39–41
Neo-institutionalism / Neo-institutionalist, 39, 185
   See also Institutionalism
Neo-liberal, 44, 178
Netherlands, 256, 260, 261, 263–265, 271, 272
New Zealand, 21
985 project, China, 153–155, 160, 169
North America, 2, 3, 7, 15, 18, 31, 58, 88, 229, 230, 242–244
North Carolina State University, 98
Norway, 250, 260, 263–265, 271, 272

OECD, 21–25, 40, 42–45, 47, 57, 59–61, 65, 66, 69, 77, 80n1, 115, 174, 206, 219, 230
Organizational field, 7, 60, 62, 69, 70, 72, 106
Organizational forms, 3, 5–7, 9, 17, 26, 27, 29, 30, 41, 57, 58, 60–66, 69, 74, 76–79, 91, 108, 114–118, 120, 121, 219, 221, 239
Organization of the Islamic Conference (OIC), 229
Osaka City University, 121
Otlet, Paul, 10

Pechter, Kenneth, 199
Peer review, 3, 4, 6, 11, 12, 26, 29, 30, 32, 56, 57, 62, 68, 69, 76, 79, 100, 200, 222, 239, 245n4, 263
Peking Research Institute, 144
Peking University, 153
Pennsylvania State University, 98
Performance, 12, 157, 163–168, 182, 185–187, 239, 254–256

Performance-based funding, 5, 43
Persian Gulf. *See* Arabian Gulf
The Plan of Introducing Foreign Outstanding Talent, 155
Pohang University of Science and Technology (POSTECH), 220
Poland, 21, 254, 261, 272
Policy, 6, 7, 9, 12, 17, 20, 27–30, 40, 41, 49, 66, 69, 74, 87, 89, 108, 115, 116, 129, 130, 138n16, 142, 148–151, 159, 160, 164, 168–170, 174, 175, 181, 188, 189, 197, 207–211, 214, 216–218, 222, 224, 229, 230, 232, 233, 234, 254
Policymakers, 6, 7, 9, 12, 21, 27, 30, 40, 42, 68, 87, 94, 106, 114, 137, 198, 211, 212, 250
Post-academic science, 9
Post-baccalaureate Education, 92–93
Powell, Walter W., 1–32, 40, 42–44, 47, 50, 55–80, 86, 88, 96, 118, 121, 174, 233, 235, 238
   DiMaggio, P. and, 185
Primary education, 40, 208, 209
Private institutions, 27, 91, 94. 95, 106–108, 153, 209–211
Productivity, 2, 3, 5, 6, 8, 17, 21–31, 55–80, 86, 93, 99, 103, 105, 106, 109, 115, 118, 119–128, 137, 138n3, 139n17, 142, 152, 153, 156–163, 169, 174, 207, 219–222, 229, 233, 238, 239, 240, 249–274
Public funding, 5, 69, 178, 237

Qatar, 3, 5, 9, 11, 17, 18, 25, 28, 30–32, 38, 42, 46–49, 79, 139, 227–246, 248
Qatar Foundation for Education, Science and Community Development, the / QF, 230

Qatar National Research Fund
  (QNRF), 139, 236, 244, 245
Qatar National Research Strategy,
  237, 244
Qatar National Vision 2030 (QNV),
  230
Qatar Science and Technology Park
  (QSTP), 231, 236
Qatar University, 46, 233, 235,
  239–242, 244, 245n2
Qualification, 42, 182, 185
Quality assurance, 43
Quality control, 211–212
Quantitative analysis, 12, 64

R&D expenditures, 44, 95, 153, 228
  See also Funding, research funding
Ranking, 12, 26, 31, 43, 93, 97, 99,
  131, 137, 139n18, 179, 197,
  258, 259
Recognition, 42, 74, 253, 254, 256
Recommendation, 7, 151, 234
Recruitment Program of Global
  Experts, the, 155, 156
Reform, 58, 74, 130, 143, 150–157,
  159, 160, 168, 169, 174,
  180–182, 210, 216–218,
  224n4, 234
Regional competition, 17
  See also Competition
Research, 1–32, 38, 55–80, 85–109,
  114, 142, 174, 206, 227–246,
  248, 250
Research and development (R&D),
  21, 25, 27, 31, 44, 57, 59, 66,
  95, 142, 228, 233, 235, 236,
  237, 263
Research evaluation system, 5, 12, 23,
  31, 59, 75
Research Excellence Framework, 43,
  59, 74
Research funding, 12, 20, 59, 62, 74,
  75–76, 168, 179, 182, 186,
  187, 198, 216, 217, 228, 229,
  231, 233, 236–237
  See also R&D
Research infrastructure, 28, 39, 79,
  229, 233. 237
Research institute, 2, 6, 17, 23, 25, 26,
  29, 30, 56–60, 62–64, 66–72,
  76, 77, 79, 80, 96, 121, 138n5,
  144, 197, 198, 201n1, 215, 216,
  220, 235–236, 241, 248
Research intensity, 22, 23, 44, 45, 59,
  60, 76
  See also R&D, GDP
Research management, 12
Research organization, 16, 44, 60,
  64–66, 78, 114, 115, 120,
  138n2, 144, 165, 239, 240, 242,
  244, 245n8, 248
Research output, 18, 21, 26, 60, 76,
  114, 142, 160, 161, 168, 169,
  182, 207, 218
Research personnel, 149, 218, 233,
  235
Research policy, 6, 17, 29, 66, 69, 137
Research productivity, 27, 142, 169,
  254
Research university, 1–32, 55–80,
  85–109, 115, 130, 137, 142,
  154, 157, 168, 179, 183–189,
  192, 194, 198–200, 207, 212,
  215–221, 224, 233–234
Research workforce, 210–216
Research-based teaching, 69
Royal Society, The (UK), 5, 72, 229,
  232
Russell Group, The (UK), 74, 76
Russia/USSR, 11, 12, 15, 16, 58, 86,
  88, 159, 170, 206, 260, 261,
  263, 264, 272

S&T Workforce, 143–146
Sacred spark, the, 252, 253
Saka, Ayaka, 118, 138n1

Index

San Francisco State University, 106
Saudi Arabia, 230, 231, 235, 248
Scandinavia, 21, 256
The schooled society, 21, 50, 56
  See also Baker, David P.
SCIE. See Science Citation Index Expanded
Science, 1–32, 37–50, 55–80, 85–109, 113–139, 141–171, 173–201, 205–225, 229, 250
  See also Research
Science and technology, 21, 22, 24, 57, 60. 61. 74, 115, 117, 129, 130, 143, 144, 146–152, 163–165, 168, 198, 199, 207, 212–217, 219. 220, 222, 224, 231, 236
Science and technology policy (S&T Policy), 214
Science Citation Index (SCI), 11, 142, 222
Science Citation Index Expanded (SCIE), 2, 15, 57, 99, 118, 138n3, 174, 207, 219, 245n8
Science for development, 40, 44, 233
Science production, 3, 8–10, 17, 19, 26, 27, 30, 31, 61, 80, 85–109, 113–139, 173–201, 205–225, 237, 250, 257–263
Science productivity, 2, 5, 17, 26, 28, 55–80, 99, 103, 137, 138n3, 139n17, 207, 219–222, 251, 252, 271, 273
Science publication, 3, 6, 13, 100–101, 137, 138n3, 180, 183
Science system, 5, 7, 14, 17–20, 29, 40, 57, 59, 61, 78, 200, 229
Scientific and Technological Development Plan, the, 147
Scientific effort, 95–96
Scientific impact, 12, 19, 31
Scientific management, 12
Scientific productivity, 2, 3, 6, 8, 17, 21–31, 56–62, 64, 66, 67, 71, 75–80, 109, 115–128, 137, 142, 156–163, 229, 238, 250–256, 263, 266, 271
Scientific Progress, the Universities, and the Federal Government / Seaborg Report, 198
Scientific publication, 2, 9, 10, 26, 27, 62, 68, 86, 87, 95, 101, 103, 109, 169, 174, 180, 183, 187, 188, 198, 199, 206, 232, 237
Scientific research, 3, 5, 7–10, 26, 27, 86, 91, 94, 96, 100, 104, 108, 109, 114, 118, 131, 142–147, 149, 150, 153–157, 160, 163, 164, 166, 169, 170, 174, 188, 190, 231, 237, 253, 255
  See also Research, science
Scientometricians, 3, 17
Scopus database. See Elsevier Scopus
Scott, W. Richard, 7, 8, 44, 62, 63, 93, 97, 185
Seniority-based personnel system, 182
Seoul National University (SNU), 208, 209, 220
Shanghai University of Science and Technology, 164–165
Singapore, 229, 265
Sino-Japanese War, 143
Skilled labor, 177
Slovenia, 229
Social equality, 250–252, 273
Socialist transformation, 27, 143, 148
Sociology of science, 50
Solla Price, Derek J. de, 3, 11, 17, 98, 99, 101, 108, 200, 252, 254
South Korea, 3, 5, 9, 11, 17, 18, 19, 22, 23, 25, 27, 30, 38, 40, 44–50, 170n1, 205–225
Soviet Union, 16, 144, 146–148, 208, 273
Spain, 5, 30, 261, 271, 272
Spark Program, 152
SPHERE. See Science Productivity, Higher Education, Research

and Development, and the Knowledge Society project
Stanford University, 91, 98, 103, 104, 106, 215
Stanford-Silicon Valley Model, 106
Stein, Jeremy C., 8, 97
STEM / STEM+, 2–4, 6, 7, 11–13, 25, 31, 38, 44, 46–50, 61, 72, 76, 100, 183, 215, 231, 233, 234, 235, 238, 239, 241, 243, 245, 259, 268
Strategic partnership, 70
Stratification, 65, 74, 154, 179, 253
Structural change, 120–128, 137, 180
Structural theory of scientific advance, 254
Student mobility, 42
Suffolk University, 106
Super research university, 9, 26, 56, 85–109
  See also Research university
Sweden, 219, 250, 254, 260, 261, 263, 264, 265, 272
SWIID. *See* Standardized World Income Inequality Database
Switzerland, 21, 250, 256, 260, 262–265, 271, 272
Synergy, 26, 85–109
Syungkyunkwan University (SKKU), 221

Taiwan, 3, 9, 11, 17, 18, 22, 23, 25, 27–28, 38, 41, 45, 46, 48, 49, 119, 173–201, 272
Teaching Excellence Project, 179
Technical University of Karlsruhe, 70
Technological University, 187
Technology, 2, 38, 57, 86, 114, 143, 231, 250
Texas A&M University, 89, 95, 234, 239, 241
Third Scientific Revolution, 147

Thomson Reuters (TR), 2, 4, 11–13, 24, 26, 56, 61, 67, 68, 71, 75, 78, 79, 86, 102–105, 107, 120, 122–129, 138, 142, 158, 159, 161, 162, 163, 165, 166, 168, 174, 180, 181, 184, 188, 191, 193, 195, 196, 206, 221, 223, 238–243, 245n8, 256, 257, 259, 261, 262, 265, 267–270, 272
1,000 talents, China, 155–156
Tokyo Metropolitan University, 121
Torch Program, 152
Transformation, 5, 9, 12, 27, 28, 63, 69, 143, 148, 177, 183, 185, 186, 229
Transformation of Universities, 194–200
Transformative Regime Change, 16
Transition, 75, 101, 108, 160, 175, 177–179, 182, 186, 192, 244
Triple helix, 9
Tsinghua University, 153
20th century, 3, 17–19, 25, 26, 28, 29, 38, 41, 49, 56, 57, 63, 77, 86, 89, 90, 93–97, 101, 102, 108, 109, 142, 157, 175, 194, 206, 208, 255, 257, 263
211 project, China, 154

Undergraduate college, 72–76
Undergraduate education, 73, 91
UNDP, 266, 274n2
UNESCO, 25, 42, 43, 45, 48, 153
UNESCO World Conference, 44
United Kingdom (U.K.)/ Great Britain, 3, 5, 9, 17, 19, 21, 22–23, 25, 26, 30, 40, 43, 55–80, 119, 231, 258, 259, 262, 263, 271
United States (U.S.), 3, 5, 9, 11, 15–23, 25, 26, 29, 30, 31, 38, 39, 44, 46–50, 57, 58, 73,

85–109, 115, 119, 125, 142, 147, 151, 157–163, 169, 170, 175, 176, 198, 199, 208, 211, 212, 231, 234, 245, 250, 258, 259, 262, 263, 271
United States Naval Academy, 106
Universal education, 178–179
Université de Paris, 63, 64
University, 1–32, 38, 55–80, 85–109, 114, 142, 173–201, 207, 228, 248, 255
  See also Research university
University Act, 182
University foundings, 38
University of Alabama, 106
University of Al-Karouine, 232
University of California, 89–91, 96–98, 103, 104, 106
University of Cambridge, 72, 76
University of Edinburgh, 73
University of Heidelberg, 63, 72
University of Lyon, 68
University of Massachusetts, 106
University of Michigan, 92, 94, 103, 104
University of North Carolina, 98, 104
University of Oxford, 63, 72, 76
University of Science and Technology of China, 149, 164
University of Tokyo, 116, 120, 121, 125–127, 131, 133–136
University Reform Policy, 216–218
University Research Model, 91–99
University-based scientist, 2, 87, 101, 102, 228

Visible hand, 43

Wartime Associated University, 209
Waseda University, 121
Wealth, 22, 29, 31, 77, 249–274
Web of Knowledge, 2
  See also Thomson Reuters

Web of Science (WoS), 2, 4, 11–14, 24, 32n3, 61, 62, 67, 68, 71, 75, 78, 79, 102–105, 107, 118, 120, 122–129, 138n3, 158, 159, 161–163, 165, 166, 168, 180, 181, 184, 188, 191, 193, 195, 196, 221, 223, 238–243, 257, 259, 261, 262, 265, 267–270, 272
  See also Thomson Reuters
Weill Cornell Medical College in Qatar, 106, 234, 241
The Well-Known Overseas Scholars Program, 155
West Germany, 16, 260, 261, 264, 271, 272
  See also Germany
World Bank, 153, 197, 228, 229, 248, 268
World Class University Project, The (WCUP), 179, 186–189, 192, 200
World Higher Education Database (WHED), 25, 41, 46, 47
World-class research, 115, 130, 132
World-class research university, 97, 137, 154, 207, 216–219, 224
World-class university, 74, 115, 130–136, 138n16, 169, 170, 179, 187, 222
World Trade Organization (WTO), 42
WWII / Second World War, 40, 49, 174, 175, 177, 181

Xiaoping, Deng, 150

Yale University, 95, 103, 104
Yangtze River Scholar Scheme, 155
Yonsei University, 221, 224

Zipf, George K., 10

www.ingramcontent.com/pod-product-compliance
Lightning Source LLC
Chambersburg PA
CBHW050529300426
44113CB00012B/2008